CORPORATE FORMS AND ORGANIZATIONAL CHOICE IN INTERNATIONAL INSURANCE

Corporate Forms and Organizational Choice in International Insurance

Edited by

ROBIN PEARSON AND TAKAU YONEYAMA

OXFORD

UNIVERSITY PRESS

OXFORD

UNIVERSITY PRESS

Great Clarendon Street, Oxford, OX2 6DP,
United Kingdom

Oxford University Press is a department of the University of Oxford.
It furthers the University's objective of excellence in research, scholarship,
and education by publishing worldwide. Oxford is a registered trade mark of
Oxford University Press in the UK and in certain other countries

Published in the United States of America by Oxford University Press
198 Madison Avenue, New York, NY 10016, United States of America

British Library Cataloguing in Publication Data
Data available

Library of Congress Control Number: 2015938193

ISBN 978-0-19-873900-5

Printed and bound by
CPI Group (UK) Ltd, Croydon, CR0 4YY

Acknowledgements

The editors wish to thank the Dai-ichi Life Insurance Corporation for its generous support for the research project upon which this book is based. We offer our sincere thanks to Ms Yukie Owada and Ms Yuki Fukui, assistants at Hitotsubashi University, who handled the administrative side of the project with great skill and efficiency. We are also most grateful to those colleagues who do not appear as chapter authors in this volume but who nevertheless made invaluable contributions during the course of the project, namely Christopher Kopper, Tim Guinnane, Heather Nelson, André Straus, and Jochen Streb. We thank the anonymous readers for Oxford University Press for their insightful comments on an early draft and last, but not least, we wish to thank the team at OUP, in particular Clare Kennedy and David Musson, for their patience and support in helping us bring this book to publication.

Robin Pearson and Takau Yoneyama

Contents

Contents

List of Figures

List of Tables

Notes on Contributors

Lars Fredrik Andersson is Associate Professor at the Department of Geography and Economic History, Umeå University, Sweden. His research encompasses financial, business, and economic history. His main publications in the insurance field include 'Competing Models of Organizational Form: Risk Management Strategies and Underwriting Profitability in the Swedish Fire Insurance Market between 1903 and 1939', *Journal of Economic History* 72 (2012); 'Mutuality as a Control for Information Asymmetry: A Historical Analysis of the Claims Experience of Mutual and Stock Fire Insurance Companies in Sweden—1889 to 1939', *Business History* 53 (2011); and 'Life Insurance and Income Growth: the Case of Sweden 1830–1950', *Scandinavian Economic History Review* 58 (2010). His current research interests include life, health, and sickness insurance.

Leonardo Caruana de las Cagigas is Lecturer in economic history, Faculty of Economics, University of Granada, Spain. His main publications are: 'From Mutual Fund to Multinational. MAPFRE 1933–2008', co-authored with Gabriel Tortella and José Luis García Ruiz; 'Private Insurance in Spain, 1934–2004', in Leonard Caruana de las Cagigas and José Luis García Ruiz (eds), *Encuentro Internacional sobre la Historia del Seguro* (Madrid: Fundación Mapfre, 2010); and 'La Internacionalización del seguro español en el siglo XX', *Revista de Historia Industria*. His current research is on Spanish insurance history in the twentieth century.

Helen Doe is Fellow of the Centre for Maritime Historical Studies at the University of Exeter. She gained her MA and PhD in maritime history at Exeter. Her research interests are in the field of maritime business history. Her articles have appeared in the *Economic History Review, International Journal of Maritime History, Mariner's Mirror*, and the *Journal of Transport History*. Her books include 'Enterprising Women in Shipping in the Nineteenth Century' and 'From Coastal Sail to Global Shipping', both published in 2009. She co-edited with Professor Richard Harding, 'Naval Leadership and Management, 1650–1950' (Boydell and Brewer, 2012). She is Trustee of the British Commission for Maritime History and the SS Great Britain and a fellow of the Royal Historical Society. She is currently editing (with Philip Payton and Alston Kennerly) 'A Maritime History of Cornwall', to be published by University of Exeter Press.

YingYing Jiang is Lecturer in Meiji Gakuin University, Japan. She was formerly Adjunct Assistant Professor of Graduate School of Commerce and

Management, Hitotsubashi University (2011–12). Her research focuses on corporate forms in the Japanese life insurance industry. She received her PhD degree in commerce from Hitotsubashi University in 2011 with the dissertation 'Corporate Forms in the Japanese Life Insurance Business: An Application of Corporate Ownership Theory'.

Hisaaki Kamiya is Research Fellow of the Mitsubishi Economic Research Institute. His principle publication is 'The Emergence of Competition in Japanese Marine Insurance Business and the Premium Cartel', *Japan Business History Review* 44 (2010) (in Japanese) and 'The Marine Insurance Business in 1920s Japan: Background of the Establishment of the Hull Insurers' Union', *Songai Hoken Kenkyu* 74 (2012) (in Japanese). His current research interests are the history of marine insurance business and the development process of risk management methods.

Monica Keneley is Professor of Finance at Deakin University, Victoria, Australia. She has published in the area of business and insurance history. The focus of her research has been on the impacts of financial deregulation, the nature of institutional change, and adaptive and innovative responses to change. Recent publications include 'The Path to Project Darwin: The Evolution of the AMP's Organizational Structure', *Business History* 54 (2012) and 'The Development of the Institutional Investor: The Case of Australian Life Insurers', *Australian Economic History Review* 52 (2012).

Natsuki Kinoshita is Lecturer in the Department of Liberal Arts, Hokkaido Musashi Women's Junior College. Her main publications are: 'The Post-War Issei: A History of Japanese Chamber of Commerce of Southern California, 1949–1990s', *Economic Journal of Hokkaido University* 39 (2010); 'Kokujin Seimei Hoken Gaisha No Hanbai Soshiki: Golden State Mutual No Jirei, 1925–1940', *Keieishigaku* 45 (2010); and 'Minami California Ni Okeru Kokujin, Nikkei, Hispanic-Kei Kigyou Keiei No Shiteki Kohsatsu: Business to Jinsyu, Ethnicity, Nation, Local Community', PhD dissertation, Hokkaido University, 2010. Her current research interests are the multinational business strategies of US life insurance companies in the nineteenth century.

Mats Larsson is Professor at the University of Uppsala, Department of Economic History, and Head of the Uppsala Centre for Business History. His most recent publications are 'Bank Mergers in Sweden: the Interplay between Bank Owners, Bank Management, and the State 1910–2010' (with Sven Jungerhem) in Helén Andersson, Virpi Havila, and Fredrik Nilsson (eds), *Mergers and Acquisitions: The Critical Role of Stakeholders* (Routledge, 2013) and as an author and editor of *Det svenska näringslivets historia 1864–1914* [The History of Swedish Industry and Trade 1864–2014] (Dialogos, 2014). His current research interest concerns big business in Sweden, insurance and banking history, the Stockholm Stock Exchange, and the Swedish film industry.

Magnus Lindmark is Professor in the Department of Geography and Economic History at Umeå University, Sweden. His research interests include insurance history and environmental history. His publications in insurance history include articles in the *Journal of Economic History, Business History, Journal of Financial History*, and the *Scandinavian Economic History Review*. A main theme of these articles is to combine historical narratives with contemporary theories in insurance economics and cliometric techniques.

Mikael Lönnborg is Associate Professor at Södertörn University, Department of Social Sciences, School of Business Studies, Stockholm, Sweden and at the BI Norwegian Business School, Department of Innovation and Economic Organisation, Centre for Business History, Oslo, Norway. His most recent publications are 'SCOR Sweden Re. 100 Years of Swedish (Re)Insurance History' (co-authored with Mats Larsson); 'Banks and Swedish Financial Crises in the 1920s and 1930s' (co-authored with Michael Rafferty and Anders Ögren) in Christopher Kobrak and Mira Wilkins (eds), *History and Financial Crises: Lessons from the 20th century* (Routledge, 2013); and 'Entreprenörskap och varumärken' [Entrepreneurship and Corporate Brands] (Gidlunds, 2013), co-edited with Mats Larsson and Karin Winroth. His current research interests concern insurance and corporate forms, financial markets in transition countries, institutional ownership strategies, financial crises, and financial entrepreneurs.

Robin Pearson is Professor of Economic History at the University of Hull, UK. He has published widely on British and international economic and business history, with a particular focus on the insurance industry. His article 'Moral Hazard and Insurance in Eighteenth-Century London' won the 2002 Harvard-Newcomen Best Article Prize. His book, *Insuring the Industrial Revolution: Fire Insurance and the British Economy, 1700–1850*, won the 2004 Wadsworth Prize for Business History. Recent edited books include *History of the Company*, eight volumes (2006–7) and *The Development of International Insurance* (2010). His latest book, *Shareholder Democracies? Corporate Governance in Britain and Ireland before 1850* (University of Chicago Press, 2012), co-authored with Mark Freeman and James Taylor, was awarded the 2013 Ralph Gomory Prize for Business History by the US Business History Conference.

Jerònia Pons Pons is Senior Lecturer in economic history at the University of Seville, Spain. Her research focuses on the economic history of insurance in Spain. She has edited with M. Angeles Pons, *Investigaciones Históricas sobre el Seguro Español* (Fundación Mapfre, 2009). Her work on insurance history has been published in P. Borscheid and R. Pearson (eds), *Internationalisation and Globalisation of the Insurance Industry in the Nineteenth and Twentieth Centuries* (Philipps-University, Marburg, 2007); R. Pearson (ed.),

The Development of International Insurance (Pickering and Chatto, 2010); and in P. Borscheid and N. V. Haueter (eds), *World Insurance* (Oxford University Press, 2012). She has published on social insurance in Geoffrey Clark (ed.), *The Appeal of Insurance* (Toronto University Press, 2010) and in Bernard Harris (ed.), *Welfare and Old Age in Europe and North America* (Pickering and Chatto, 2012). Currently she is working on a Spanish insurance history project sponsored by Fundación Mapfre.

Grietjie Verhoef is Professor in accounting, economic, and business history in the Department of Accountancy at the University of Johannesburg and Director of the South African Accounting History Centre. She has published widely on insurance and banking history as well as the history of South African conglomerates, with special reference to the rise of Afrikaner business in South Africa. She is engaged in research on the accountancy profession in South Africa in comparative perspective with other Commonwealth countries, with research into the reconstruction of gross domestic product for South African colonies in the second half of the nineteenth century; as well as research into big business groups and family businesses in South Africa. She has published chapters in eleven books, fifty-four peer-reviewed articles, and delivered sixty international and national conference papers. She is the current president of the International Economic History Association.

Takau Yoneyama is Professor of Risk Management and Insurance in the Graduate School of Commerce and Management, Hitotsubashi University, Tokyo. He has also held executive positions in the Japanese Business History Society and the Asia-Pacific Risk and Insurance Association. His research interests include insurance history and insurance regulation. Recent publications include 'The Role of Insurance in the Rapid Modernization of Japan' in P. Borscheid and N. V. Haueter (eds), *World Insurance* (Oxford University Press, 2012).

1

Corporate Forms and Organizational Choice in International Insurance

An Overview of the History and Theory

Robin Pearson and Takau Yoneyama

The association of individuals to prevent or mitigate risks, or to compensate for losses caused by risk events, is an ancient impulse. Such associational or cooperative activity includes the burial clubs of the Roman Empire, medieval Europe, and Tokugawa Japan; the mutual aid associations of the Philippines, which rebuild barrio houses and dams after typhoons and floods; or the sea-rescue clubs of Senegalese fishermen.[1] Most mutual, non-profit, and non-probabilistic efforts at risk mitigation were private, voluntary, and informal. Sometimes, however, such efforts were organized, managed, or sanctioned by state-governing bodies. Examples include the public grain reserves of Chosun Korea and Imperial China, or the armed convoys protecting merchant caravans in medieval Europe.[2]

Given the infinite variety of risks and their contingent circumstances throughout history, it is perhaps unsurprising that insurance, from its infancy, also developed an extraordinary range of vehicles through which it was delivered. Yet we know little about how and why different insurance vehicles were chosen in the past, or why they survived or disappeared. Although there has been extensive research on the coexistence of contemporary mutual and stock company forms, the few historical studies in this area sometimes point to conclusions that confound economic theories or modern empirical results.[3]

---

[1] Platteau 1997; Pearson 2003a; Bankoff 2008.

[2] Sun et al. 2007, 598; Pearson 2010a, 2; Kim and Lee 2012.

[3] One example is the uncertainty raised by the history of mutual life insurers in the US about the influence of regulatory factors on the development of company forms. See Zanjani 2007. This and other examples of insurance history supporting or contradicting modern organizational theory are discussed in the following sections.

This book represents the first attempt to explore the foundation, survival, and performance of multiple organizational forms in the history of insurance, to situate these forms in an international comparative context, and to relate the results of historical analysis to modern organizational theory. The following section provides an overview of the development of organizations in insurance from the origins of the industry to the present day. The second section summarizes the theoretical and empirical literature on this topic. The final section describes the research project that underpins this book, outlines the contributing chapters, and points to some conclusions that have a wider relevance for modern theory.

THE HISTORY OF ORGANIZATIONAL FORMS IN INSURANCE

Modern insurance first developed in the Mediterranean trade of the late middle ages, although it had antecedents in the ancient world.[4] Individual merchants with surplus cash acted as underwriters for other merchants, while notaries were employed to draw up the contracts. By the early fifteenth century there were hundreds of notaries working in this field in Genoa, Pisa, Florence, Marseille, Milan, and Barcelona. Over time they helped to standardize underwriting practices in marine insurance, practices which were also adopted in northern European ports. By the early eighteenth century there were 150 specialist marine underwriters in London, fifty underwriters and several hundred brokers (not all broking insurance) in Amsterdam, and up to a dozen underwriters and brokers each in other Dutch towns.[5] Insurance underwriting and broking also came to be regulated and taxed by state and municipal authorities in Spain, Italy, Flanders, England, and the United Provinces.

This organizational form—with a merchant seeking insurance, a broker acting as intermediary, and a merchant or banker as underwriter—was in part dependent upon the nature of the risk. In the maritime trades each risk was relatively large, discrete, and short term—weeks for coastal tramping and for sea routes around Europe, up to eighteen months for transatlantic and African voyages. Few individuals had the financial capacity, or were willing, to undertake such liabilities entirely on their own account. Thus, the coinsurance of one risk by several merchants, each underwriting part of a ship and its cargo,

---

[4] Pearson 2003a.
[5] Spooner 1983, 27, 55–9; Cockerell and Green 1994, 5; Go 2009, 89, 130–1.

became the predominant form of marine insurance in the major European and American trading centres.[6]

The character of the risk, however, cannot have been the sole factor determining the form of early marine insurance, for there was already plenty of organizational variance. In England between 1720 and 1824 two joint-stock corporations had a monopoly of corporate marine insurance, but competed with the brokers and underwriters working out of Lloyd's and the Royal Exchange. In the coal, timber, and fishing trades of northeast and southwest England, numerous small mutual clubs for hull insurance were established by shipowners. These clubs did not breach the legal monopoly of the London corporations because each member underwrote a share in the risk for which he was individually liable.[7]

Similarly, in the Netherlands private joint-stock corporations were founded in Rotterdam in 1720 and Amsterdam in 1772, while in Groningen the guilds of skippers of peat-carrying smacks operated mutual hull insurance boxes. Box members' contributions were fixed according to the destination or the value of their ships and payments were made both to cover ship damage and loss, as well as illness and pensions to skippers and their families. The boxes remained competitive for over 150 years until the first private underwriters and brokers appeared in the Groningen region during the later eighteenth century.[8] Elsewhere, private joint-stock marine insurance companies emerged. At least eight were established in Trieste between 1766 and 1803, and thirty-seven in Hamburg between 1765 and 1807.[9] They coexisted with individual brokers and underwriters, with mutual organizations, with small insurance partnerships—as formed, for example, by British merchants in China—and with public monopoly corporations, such as those established, often for fiscal or mercantilist reasons, in Copenhagen (1726), Genoa (1742), and Naples (1751).[10] Some of the private companies combined marine with fire insurance and also wrote inland transport insurance on Europe's waterways. In Philadelphia, the first marine insurance company in the United States, incorporated in 1794, emerged out of a failed life insurance tontine.[11] The ease of state incorporation in the American republic led to thousands of such stock companies being formed in insurance and other sectors after 1790.[12]

---

[6] Ruwell 1989, 42–5.

[7] Raynes 1948, 186–7. On organizational forms in UK marine insurance, see Chapter 3 by Pearson and Doe.

[8] Go 2009, 54–8.   [9] Hamburger Feuerkasse 1976, 16; Rohrbach 1988, 172–9.

[10] Spooner 1983, 43–6; Rohrbach 1988, 234–9. On the first marine insurance companies in China, commencing in 1805, see Le Pichon 2006.

[11] James 1942.

[12] Between 1790 and 1860, 22,419 business corporations, including 2,121 insurance companies, were chartered by state legislatures in the US. Sylla and Wright 2013, 654–5.

This early variety of organizational forms was also found in other branches of insurance. From the late seventeenth century fire insurance developed via three basic types of organization—public, proprietary, and mutual. The Great Fire of London, which destroyed 13,000 houses in 1666, gave rise to all three forms. There were also many local cooperative or collective schemes, such as 'briefs', official letters authorizing *post-hoc* collections, sometimes compulsory, for the relief of victims of fires. Collections were organized at a county level in Denmark, for instance, and at a parish level in Germany and England. In England the collections died out with the rise of private fire insurance companies. In Europe they came to be regarded with antipathy, not least because they could be a means of fraud.[13] Rural mutual insurance unions also became widespread across northern and central Europe, in which villagers helped their neighbours with materials, labour, and money to rebuild houses and farm buildings in the aftermath of fires. On some landed estates, membership was compulsory for all tenants, with contribution rates graded according to the size of their holdings. In Austria, at their peak in the late 1880s, there were around 300 farmers' insurance unions with 320,000 members.[14]

In some early modern towns residents voluntarily combined to draw up 'fire contracts', written agreements between groups of property owners. Members, whose property fell victim to fire, received compensation from a mutual fund accumulated from *post-hoc* flat rate calls on members for losses incurred, calls that were not proportionate to the sum insured by each.[15] The difficulty of spreading risk in a confined area led Hamburg's senate in 1676 to combine all the private agreements in that town into one new insurance fund, the *Feuercasse*, to be administered by council officials. This was the world's first public association for the insurance of buildings. The new fund was accumulated from *ex ante* payments at fixed rates, but if this proved insufficient to cover payments for losses, members were liable for further calls at rates proportionate to the sums they had insured.[16]

During the following century similar public insurance societies, some with compulsory membership, were formed across northern and central Europe. They were essentially extensions of state bureaucracy and revenue, managed by civil servants. They had no corporate identity, the business often being administered from a desk in a government office as one of several public funds. No actuarial calculation or profit seeking was involved. The societies mostly charged flat fees regardless of the type of property or its location.[17] They usually excluded large and hazardous risks and restricted their business

---

[13] Briefs were banned, for instance, in Saxony in 1729, in Mainz in 1780, and in Bavaria in 1845. Arps 1965, 24–30.

[14] Rohrbach 1988, 145–52, 221.   [15] Zwierlein 2011, 226–8.

[16] On the Hamburg Feuercasse, see Chapter 6 by Pearson.

[17] A primitive risk classification was introduced by the *Hamburger Feuercasse* in 1753 and later by other associations.

to buildings, leaving owners and occupiers to insure goods and contents with private companies. Accumulated funds were used to pay for the rebuilding of property and to supplement other welfare expenditure. As towns expanded and the value of urban property increased, however, the public societies increasingly suffered from a lack of funds. As mandatory buildings insurance in the public societies began to be abolished by many states during the nineteenth century, private mutual and stock companies attracted an increasing share of this business.

In the market to insure household contents and commercial stock against fire, and buildings where this business was open to entry, mutual non-profit associations were often successful early movers. These had no share capital and all policyholders were voting members who participated in a periodic division of surpluses. Funds were accumulated from initial deposits by members upon entry, together with *post-hoc* levies or calls on members to meet losses. Operating costs were low and agency commission payments few or none. Three mutual offices together accounted for over half of all fire insurance premiums earned in London during the first two thirds of the eighteenth century.[18] As losses from fires increased towards the end of the century, however, the burden of calls became more onerous and enforcement more difficult. The London mutuals suffered liquidity problems and lost ground to the stock companies. One of them, the Union Fire Office, responded by demutualizing in 1805, possibly the first corporate demutualization in history.[19] By the early 1820s the fifteen largest fire insurers in the UK were all stock companies.[20]

In the US the earliest fire insurance companies, beginning in Charleston and Philadelphia in 1731 and 1752 respectively, were also mutually owned.[21] They generally insured only select residential properties within their home towns. During the early nineteenth century, town mutuals became supplanted by stock companies as the dominant form of property insurance provider in the US. By 1810 over seventy stock companies had received state charters to write marine or fire insurance or both. As demand rose, mutuals were found to be too selective and too restrictive in the amounts they would insure on single risks. One advantage of US stock companies lay in their links to banks and their ability to lend to policyholders and shareholders. The capital resources of the mutuals, it has been claimed, proved too limited for such purposes.[22] By 1900, the seven mutual fire insurers based in New York state

---

[18] Pearson 2004, table 2.1.   [19] Pearson 2002.

[20] Pearson 2004, table 5.1. The UK's biggest mutual fire insurer of the time, the Norwich Union, converted to a stock company in 1821.

[21] Baranoff 2003, 34–40. The Charleston office was wound up following a large fire there in 1741. Cf. Hart 2012, 244.

[22] Baranoff 2003, 41–6.

wrote less than $37m, compared to the $6.5bn insured by the fifty-five stock fire insurance companies there.[23]

Large private stock companies, however, never dominated most insurance markets everywhere and at all times. The one exception was reinsurance, a major innovation of the nineteenth century. The specialist reinsurance companies that first appeared in Germany from the late 1840s were all stock companies. As Kopper has pointed out, this was almost certainly due to the nature of their business. As organizations that underwrote the surplus risks ceded to them from other insurers, reinsurers could not have been formed as mutuals owned by their policyholders, for the latter were competing companies who would have gained access to confidential information about the business of their rivals.[24]

Even in the US, the foremost land of the joint-stock corporation, mutuals remained important in some markets. Beginning in New England, factory owners who had been refused insurance by the stock companies, or who disliked their high rates, joined together to form 'factory mutuals'. These pioneered safety inspection and fire prevention technologies and focused on the best large manufacturing risks. Consequently, they were able to offer low rates to members who complied with their rigorous safety standards.[25] Factory mutuals also appeared in Europe, for example the Kiev Union for the Insurance of Sugar Refineries that operated in Russia before the First World War. Towards the end of the century, to save on the cost of commercial insurance, large enterprises such as Standard Oil began to establish their own internal organizations to insure their property and employees. These captive insurers have rarely been studied before, so Chapter 4 on Mitsubishi by Hisaaki Kamiya in this volume is pioneering in its subject. Self-insurance by big business became commonplace during the twentieth century. It was the trend, for instance, in corporate group insurance in the US during the 1970s, helping large employers to reduce costs while also providing an investment income from their self-insurance reserves.[26]

In many countries mutual societies competed successfully with public insurance institutions and private stock companies. In Russia, Sweden, Finland, and Germany large regional or national mutuals and numerous small local mutual associations together held between 35 and 60 per cent of their respective national markets before the First World War.[27] Econometric analysis has shown that Swedish mutual fire insurers enjoyed on average lower loss ratios (claims paid as a proportion of premiums earned) than their

---

[23] Baranoff 2003, 201. On mutual and stock insurers in the US, see Chapter 6 by Pearson.
[24] Kopper 2012.   [25] Wermiel 2000, 104–37.   [26] Graham and Xie 2007, 37.
[27] Estimated market shares calculated for Russia, *Assecuranz Jahrbuch* 14, 1893, 404; for Finland, *Assecuranz Jahrbuch* 16, 1895, 368; for Sweden, Hägg 1998, table 14; for Germany, *Assecuranz Jahrbuch* 10, 1889, 278; Gesellschaft fuer Feuerversicherungs-geschichtliche Forschung 1913, vol. 2, table XIII, 590.

joint-stock rivals throughout the period 1889 to 1939. It has been suggested that mutuals attracted low-risk customers, who, as owners entitled to a share in their company's surpluses, had a self-interest to act responsibly, thereby reducing moral hazard, although this relationship was qualified by other variables such as firm size, age, and leverage.[28]

In some places mutual organizations were more trusted by governing authorities and supported accordingly. They were particularly successful in British settler colonies.[29] By 1900, for instance, there were more than 150 farmers' mutuals in Canadian fire insurance, competing effectively with the stock companies there.[30] In North Africa mutual societies were established to insure French settlers against drought, hail, locusts, and fire. In Algeria and Tunisia, the colonial authorities made it compulsory for the Muslim peasant population to join provident societies.[31] From the 1860s through to the inter-war years mutual and cooperative organizations were established among citrus producers in Palestine, farmers in Mexico and Spain, and ethnic immigrant groups in Argentina to provide a range of cover against hail and fire damage to crops and buildings, funeral expenses, pensions, workplace accidents, and automobile damage.[32] Some governments, for economic, political, or ideological reasons, introduced differential regulation of stock and mutual companies that favoured the latter.[33] Following Spain's Workplace Accidents Act of 1900, for instance, tax exemptions for mutual insurance encouraged employers to set up their own mutual schemes. By 1935 there were 155 Spanish employers' mutuals and seventy-eight farm mutuals competing alongside thirty stock companies.[34]

Mutual organizations remained powerful players in many non-life insurance markets throughout the second half of the twentieth century. In Canada 20 per cent of property and casualty insurance was accounted for by mutual companies in 2003. In the same year mutuals held about one third of the business in France and the USA, a higher level than had been attained in 1850 when the markets were much smaller.[35] In the early 2000s about half the Japanese population were members of not-for-profit agricultural and consumer cooperatives called 'Kyosai' and the volume of their business was increasing, not least because they generally charged lower premium rates than the stock companies. In 2004 Kyosai accounted for 11 per cent of the total assets of all Japanese insurers (life and non-life).[36]

---

[28] Adams et al. 2011.
[29] See the Chapters 7 and 8 by Verhoef and Keneley, respectively.
[30] Macpherson 1977.   [31] Saul 2012.
[32] Martel and Rabetino 2012; Del Angel 2012; Borscheid 2012a, 357; Pons Pons 2012.
[33] See Chapter 9 by Pons on Spanish mutual insurers under Franco.
[34] Pons Pons 2010, 160.   [35] Bernier and Nathan 2007, 411–12.
[36] Yamori and Okada 2007, 189–90.

In other non-life markets mutuals have declined. In Spain, for example, following a law in 1941 that eliminated some of their privileges, many mutual insurers became for-profit companies, though a large number continued to operate through the Franco years, especially in occupational accident and automobile insurance. In 1950 there were 256 mutuals with a market share of 21 per cent. By 1970 numbers had fallen to 150, accounting for 11 per cent of premiums. By 2003, after demutualization, mergers, and concentration, just forty-six remained.[37]

Various forms of mutual organization were also common from the outset in life, health, accident, and other forms of non-property insurance. In the later Roman Empire, and among the guilds and fraternities of medieval Europe and Tokugawa Japan, burial societies provided compensation from a mutual fund to the relatives of deceased members. In medieval Germany and Austria *Knappschaften* were formed to provide miners with sickness, accident, and death benefits. By 1850 they had become compulsory in the German mining industry and survived well into the twentieth century.[38] Across Europe mutual societies were established to provide a widow and her children with a perpetual annuity upon the death of her husband. Some were confined to particular groups such as physicians, lawyers, or military officers. Some states—such as France from 1671, England from 1692, and Austria from 1727—also directly provided pensions and disability allowances for key groups of state employees.[39]

By contrast, early private for-profit life insurance often took the form of gambling on the lives of famous people such as kings and popes without a legal insurable interest and was regarded by many authorities as morally offensive. From the fifteenth to the eighteenth century it became prohibited in many European states. Where a profit could be made for the public purse, however, governments willingly endorsed life insurance in the form of the tontine, a contribution scheme in which annual payments were shared out among surviving members. The first, abortive, public tontine was devised by Lorenzo Tonti in 1652 to raise revenue for the French royal treasury. It was followed by other state and municipal tontines in France, England, Germany, and the Netherlands. In London a wave of private tontines, reversionary annuity and mutual contribution schemes was launched in the early eighteenth century. These coexisted alongside the outright speculative wagers that were later banned in England.[40] Most of the early London societies were short lived, but the tontine remained a popular, if controversial, product which was later

---

[37] Pons Pons 2012, 204, 210; Rubio-Misas 2007.

[38] Guinnane and Streb 2011; Rohrbach 1988, 65–7.

[39] The dates refer to the foundation, respectively, of Les Invalides in Paris, Greenwich Hospital in London, and the first of the military hospitals in the Austrian Empire.

[40] Clark 1999, 73–85. Wager policies demonstrating no insurable interest were banned in England by the Gambling Act of 1774.

sold by companies alongside other forms of life insurance. Between the 1870s and the First World War, the biggest American life insurance corporations wrote a large quantity of tontine policies across the UK and Europe, in the face of fierce hostility from competitors and regulators.

From 1721 life insurance was also sold on a premium basis by the two English marine insurance corporations, who acquired the right to sell fire and life insurance under additional charters.[41] These offered fixed-fee and fixed-benefit plans by which company profits were dependent on correctly predicting the future mortality of policyholders. This was a more risky business for underwriters than the older redistributive schemes, where price was determined a posteriori. Not until the mutual Society for Equitable Insurances on Lives and Survivorships was formed in 1762 were age-specific premiums introduced. The success of the Equitable encouraged a number of new premium-based life assurance companies to appear. Some were funded mutually, but the majority raised a joint-stock. In part this might be explained by the rapid growth in the UK gilt, share, and bond markets. The equity raised from investors by stock companies gave them a purchasing power in these markets that mutuals did not enjoy. When the stock market slowed down, however, as in the late 1820s and early 1830s, more mutual offices were formed.[42] By the late nineteenth century mutual life insurers in the UK were significantly more efficient than their joint-stock rivals, both in terms of costs and management. They distributed higher bonuses on with-profits policies, earned better returns on their investments, and enjoyed greater longevity.[43]

In the US, as in Britain, research suggests that there was a correlation between periods of economic depression and the attraction of mutual forms of life insurance. The latter became more popular during the early 1930s as consumer distrust of stock companies increased. Zanjani has found that when capital was expensive insurance entrepreneurs preferred those organizational forms that required less capital.[44] Furthermore, it has been argued that in times of economic uncertainty, mutual companies, being owned by their policyholders, prove more able than stock companies to deal with the growing problems of moral hazard and asymmetric information.[45] This may also have held for the nineteenth century. According to Murphy, the initial rise of mutual life insurance in the US was the result of the tight capital markets and lack of investor confidence that followed the bank panic of 1837. Whereas

[41] Drew 1949; Supple 1970.
[42] Alborn also explains the preponderance of stock companies by the continued inadequacy of mortality tables in nineteenth-century England. The latter, however, was a problem for both stock and mutual offices and, in any case, mutual insurers tended to follow the age-specific rates of their stock counterparts. Alborn 2009, 46.
[43] Johnson 2010, 175–6; O'Brien and Fenn 2012.
[44] Zanjani 2007, table 5.   [45] Smith and Stutzer 1995.

the first life insurance companies had been mostly joint-stocks, by 1850 the ten largest were all mutuals.[46]

After the Civil War there was a boom in new life insurance company promotions. Competition increased, margins became tighter, claims more contested, and bankruptcies increased, resulting in a massive loss of consumer confidence. Some of the vacuum was filled by not-for-profit fraternal, benefit, and cooperative societies that developed a huge market in health, accident, and death insurance for the urban working class. By 1920 one in three adult male workers in the US was a member of such societies. Cooperative insurance was successful because there was little alternative state or employer provision at the time and because it was low cost and charged non-actuarial prices.[47] After the First World War, however, the fraternals rapidly lost market share. Some have attributed this decline to competition from industrial assurance sold by large private insurers and to the introduction of social insurance and consequent crowding-out effects.[48] Some have pointed to the imposition of burdensome solvency regulations that had previously applied only to commercial insurers.[49] The slowdown of immigration after the war, and the assimilation of the ethnic communities that had been the main recruiting ground of cooperative insurers, may also have been a contributory factor.

In sum, the growth of life insurance was accomplished through a great variety of organizational forms. Alongside the emergence of large premium-based stock companies, both premium-based and assessment-based mutual societies held their own or even expanded in markets such as Sweden, Japan, and the Netherlands. In the US the share of mutuals fell to 50 per cent of life insurance in force in the 1890s, before recovering to 75 per cent in the 1910s with the mutualization of the three leading stock companies. This high level was sustained until the 1950s when decline began. By 1975 market share was again at 50 per cent. Thereafter decline was precipitous, driven by a collapse in the number of new mutual company formations and waves of demutualizations. By 2000 mutuals accounted for less than 10 per cent of life insurance in the US, their lowest share for nearly 200 years.[50]

Life insurance became the first branch to be widely subjected to regulation and state intervention during the nineteenth and early twentieth centuries, amidst concerns about protecting the public from fraudulent joint-stock promotions, from mutual offices with a weak financial base, or from industrial assurance companies with exorbitantly high administrative expenses and a high drop-out rate of policyholders. Regulation could seriously affect the organizational structure of the industry. In France the restrictions on share

---

[46] Murphy 2010, 168–72, 207–37. US life insurance before 1914 is further discussed in Chapter 6 by Pearson.
[47] Gottlieb 2007.   [48] Kantor and Fishback 1996.
[49] Zanjani 2007.   [50] Zanjani 2007, figure 2.

transfers, imposed on stock companies by a law of 1867, gave mutuals an advantage that they enjoyed well into the following century.[51] By contrast, deposit requirements introduced by many US states suppressed the formation of mutual companies.[52] In his study of US life insurance between 1900 and 1949, Zanjani found that the regulatory impact on organizational forms differed according to the nature of the regulation. Mutuals were formed most frequently in states with low capital requirements and with differentially higher ones for stock companies. As regulation increased capital requirements over time, and as the differential between the requirements for stock and mutual companies decreased, the mutuals' inferior access to capital markets became a handicap for start-ups.[53]

Direct state participation in the market has also affected the organizational structure of the industry in major ways. We noted above the abundant examples of this in early modern Europe. From the late nineteenth century many governments either set up mandatory schemes for unemployment, accident, health, and pensions insurance, invested in joint ventures with private companies, or established fully state-owned corporations with a partial or complete monopoly. Compulsory contribution employment-based social insurance first emerged in Germany in the 1880s with national health insurance, accident insurance, and state disability and old age insurance and this provided a model for many countries, although programmes varied greatly in terms of their coverage, organization, finance, and method of delivery. Some countries, such as Denmark (1892), Sweden (1891), and Belgium (1894), began with voluntary rather than compulsory schemes. In some places private health insurance providers who submitted themselves to state regulation received government subsidies.[54] Some state insurance schemes, such as the statutory pensions in Denmark (1891), New Zealand (1898), and the UK (1908), were initially non-contributory, means-tested, and funded through tax revenue. By contrast, statutory workmen's compensation insurance was generally sold by private companies, or, as in the case of the German scheme, by newly created, state-supervised mutual associations to which firms paid their premium contributions.[55] As the work of Guinnane and Streb has shown, in these types of state-mandated and supervised, but privately delivered, schemes, the nature of regulation could directly affect performance. The German miners' insurance associations before World War One found

---

[51] Straus 2012.   [52] Murphy 2010, 117–20.

[53] Zanjani 2007. Others have also pointed to the costs of raising capital as a determinant of organizational choice in insurance; see, for instance, Harrington and Niehaus 2003.

[54] Winegarden and Murray 1998.

[55] Guinnane and Streb 2012. Similarly, in 1894 South African mine owners established the Rand Mutual, in response to legislation introducing compulsory compensation for mine workers. The Rand Mutual supplied the insurance while the state collected the funds from a levy on employers. Vivian 2007.

that their incentive structure was distorted by administrative processes and the rigid requirements of the Imperial German Insurance Bureau.[56]

During the twentieth century many public-private joint ventures appeared with widely varying levels of state investment. In Mexico, for instance, a life insurance company, *Seguros de Mexico*, was founded in 1935 with 60 per cent state ownership.[57] Fully state-owned enterprises also competed directly with the private sector. Uruguay established a state accident insurance company in 1911, the *Banco de Seguros del Estado*, which enjoyed a virtual monopoly in the country from 1926.[58] In Japan from 1916, and in colonial Korea from 1929, the government introduced a compulsory state-run industrial life assurance for workers, known as *Kampo*, delivered via the post office on a non-profit basis. It became hugely popular. In 2004 *Kampo* accounted for nearly one third of the total assets of all Japanese insurers.[59]

Reinsurance also became an object of mandatory state participation or control in numerous countries between the 1920s and the 1970s, often driven by the autarchic policies of military or nationalist regimes, and by monetary and exchange concerns and a desire to limit the flow of premiums abroad to foreign-domiciled companies. The usual procedure was to establish a national reinsurance corporation, either in whole or partial public ownership, and to pass legislation requiring private insurers to cede a certain percentage of their surplus risks to that corporation. Such a scheme was discussed in Russia as early as 1890.[60] The first state reinsurance vehicle appears to have been launched in Chile in 1927. Others followed in Turkey (1929), Iran (1935), Brazil (1939), France (1946), and Argentina (1948), and from the 1950s in many countries across North Africa and Asia. Most commenced with a partial monopoly, though this was often subsequently extended.

Full nationalization of other branches of insurance was debated in several countries during the nineteenth century, but it only occurred extensively during the twentieth century, particularly in communist and nationalist states, in dictatorships, and in countries newly liberated from colonial rule. Life insurance was nationalized in Italy in 1912, India (1956), Ceylon (1963), and Pakistan (1972). State monopolies for all lines of insurance were introduced in Russia (1918), Costa Rica (1924), China (1949), Syria and Burma (1963), Iraq and Cambodia (1964), Algeria (1966), Libya (1969), Yemen (1970), Afghanistan and Bangladesh (1972), and Laos (1975)—this list is not exhaustive.[61] The reasons given for outright nationalization derived usually from a mixture of autarchic economic policies and public welfare concerns.

---

[56] Guinnane and Streb 2011. See also Guinnane and Streb 2012.

[57] Borscheid 2012c. The Irish Life Assurance Company was formed in 1939 with the state taking an 18 per cent stake that increased to 90 per cent by 1947. Greenford et al. 2007, 573–4.

[58] Borscheid 2012c.   [59] Borscheid 2012b, 526.

[60] *Insurance Times* 23, 1890, 20.

[61] Dates of insurance nationalization are from Kwon 2010.

Deregulation and liberalization since the 1980s have reduced the dominance of state insurance institutions, even under communist governments, but this can be a slow process. As late as 1996, after ten years of liberalization, the People's Insurance Company (founded in 1949) still accounted for nearly three quarters of the insurance market in China.[62] Nevertheless, more liberal insurance markets have seen important changes in their organizational structures with, for example, waves of demutualization, the growth of corporate captives, the formation of mutual holding companies, and the rise of bancassurance.

The late twentieth-century trend of converting mutuals into stocks has provoked a large volume of research. The demand for capital features prominently in economic explanations of this phenomenon.[63] Mutuals, having no tradable capital, are protected from predatory takeovers and from the volatility of share values that stock companies are subject to. When supernormal growth needed to be financed, however, access to the buoyant capital markets of the 1980s and 1990s became more attractive and demutualization more tempting.

Changes in regulatory capital requirements and the search to improve managerial incentives and business efficiency have also been proposed as factors explaining demutualization.[64] None of these are fully satisfactory nor explain why many mutuals did not convert.[65] The modern evidence for the greater efficiency of former mutuals after conversion is inconclusive or contradictory.[66] Historical evidence, as we have seen, also does not point to mutual insurers being less efficient than their joint-stock competitors.

Legal reform, the search for structural flexibility, and the desire of some mutuals to build links with non-insurance financials such as banks have also been suggested as catalysts for recent mutual-stock conversions.[67] The deregulation of financial services in many countries during in the 1980s and

---

[62] Sun et al. 2007, 600–1; Faure and Köll 2012.

[63] For example, the study of the demutualization of forty US property and liability insurers 1968–87 in Fitzgerald 1990.

[64] Mayers and Smith 1986, 2004; Viswanathan and Cummins 2003; Zanjani 2007. Better remuneration for company managers was found to be an important incentive to demutualize from a survey of the executives of over 340 US mutual insurers conducted in 1999, Butler et al. 2000.

[65] MacMinn and Ren 2011, 108.

[66] Erhemjamts and Leverty 2010 found that US life mutuals achieved significant improvements in efficiency after demutualization. Cummins et al. 2004 and Jeng and Lai 2005, however, report similar efficiencies of mutual and stock insurers in the US, Spain, and Japan. McNamara and Rhee 1992 examined the demutualization of thirty-three US life insurers between 1902 and 1986 and found a significant increase in capital and surplus, but also an increase in management turnover following conversion. Cagle et al. 1996 found no great change in the profitability of twenty-seven US property and liability insurers following demutualization between 1972 and 1988 and describe these conversions as 'neutral mutations' driven by changes in marketing strategy. Jeng et al. 2007 found only ambiguous evidence of efficiency improvements among US life insurers after demutualization in the 1980s and 1990s.

[67] Butler et al. 2000.

1990s had important structural consequences for insurance markets.[68] In Canada, for instance, following legislative changes in 1997, the four largest mutual insurers opted to convert to joint-stocks. This was followed by global expansion, greater access to capital markets, and their participation in cross-border mergers and acquisitions. By 2003 only 6 per cent of the Canadian life and health insurance market was accounted for by mutuals.[69]

Demutualization carried the serious risk of exposing a converted mutual to a hostile takeover. The Mutual Holding Company (MHC) was developed, in part, as a solution to this problem. The first conversion of US mutuals into mutual holding companies took place in 1996, but the corporate form has been also adopted in other countries, as Chapter 13 by Caruana de las Cagigas shows. An MHC was 100 per cent policyholder owned. It could own other financial companies but, as a legal mutual, it could not be owned by anyone other than its policyholders. It functioned as the parent company holding the capital of a newly formed joint-stock enterprise that inherited the assets and liabilities from the original converting mutual. MHCs allowed the managers of mutual insurers to claim that they were preserving policyholder value and the mutual ethos of their company, while at the same time acquiring the benefits of the stock company form, including access to capital for acquisitions and expansion. In the US a total of fifty-three MHCs were created in the life and health insurance industry between 1996 and 2003, including four of the ten largest demutualizations.[70]

Some stock conversions were used to bring mutual companies into larger financial groups, whilst also increasing managerial compensation through payment in stock options. Deregulation allowed other institutions, especially banks, to enter the insurance market. The phenomenon of 'bancassurance' took off in some countries. In the US large financial services holding companies emerged, especially in life and health insurance. In the Netherlands insurance came to be dominated by 'all-finance' groups such as ING and Fortis. In France bancassurers had acquired 62 per cent of the life insurance market by 2003. In Spain eight of the ten largest life insurers became affiliated with banks and used bank branches to sell their products.[71]

In sum, the private insurance industry has continued to expand through different organizational vehicles during the twentieth century, notwithstanding the growth of social insurance and widespread nationalization. In addition, the modern state has played an important role in risk mitigation in ways that have helped the private insurer, for instance by interventions to protect the

---

[68] See Chapter 13 by Caruana de las Cagigas and the papers presented to this project on demutualization in South African and Australian life insurance that have been published elsewhere: Keneley 2010, 2012; Verhoef 2012.

[69] Bernier and Nathan 2007, 411–12.   [70] Graham and Xie 2007, 75.

[71] Graham and Xie 2007, 39–43; Venard 2007, 296; Oosenbrug 2007, 489–90; Rubio-Misas 2007, 534–5.

public from insurer insolvency, or by disaster relief schemes that effectively subsidize areas that insurance coverage cannot fully reach. Among the former are the state guaranty funds in the US, first established in New York in the 1940s.[72] An example of the latter is the US Federal Emergency Management Agency, established in 1978, but with antecedents in federal, state, and municipal relief organizations earlier in the century.

The above survey has demonstrated that multiple organizational forms coexisted at an early stage in the history of insurance and, although some older forms declined or disappeared, others survived or revived and were joined by new forms of organization, or by adaptations of older forms such as captives, pools, holding companies, and fully nationalized or partially state-owned monopoly corporations. Two key questions about this phenomenon immediately arise, which several of the essays in this book address. First, why did this multiplicity of forms occur? What were the factors determining organizational choice in different places and at different times in history? Second, what was the impact on the insurance market, on its structure and performance, and on risk mitigation more generally, of diverse and competing forms of organization? The following section outlines the approaches taken and answers suggested to these questions by the modern economic and business literature.

THE ECONOMICS OF ORGANIZATIONAL FORMS IN INSURANCE

In the 1970s two main tracks, sociological and economic, emerged in the theoretical literature on organizations. The first proved largely to be a cul-de-sac. The second opened up diverse routes towards explaining the coevolution of different forms of business organization, especially in insurance. From the mid-1970s what appeared to be a paradigm shift in the sociology of industries occurred with the rise of so-called 'population ecology'.[73] Advocates of this approach aggregated companies into 'organizational species' and measured their distribution frequencies and density. They argued that the organizational population of an industry was the product of three Darwinian-type processes, namely variation, selection, and retention. The basic idea was that some forms of company were selected for survival or extinction according to their compatibility with the social environment that they operated in. Later, non-environmental predictors of survival or failure were added, such as the age

---

[72] Graham and Xie 2007, 34.

[73] Notable contributions include Hannan and Freeman 1977; Carroll 1984. The following draws on the useful summary provided in Budros 1989, 16–29.

and size of an organization. This ecological approach to organizations, however, eventually came under criticism for examining too narrow a range of variables and too few industries, and for the weakness of its empirical research. Indeed, one scholar writing in 1988 argued that population ecology theory had failed to contribute to a better understanding of organizations and should be abandoned.[74]

Despite such criticism, the population ecology approach has persisted in the form of 'community ecology' with a new focus on the relations between organizations and other social institutions within a particular place, sometimes with interesting results.[75] One recent work adopting this approach is by Greve and Rao on mutual business institutions in Norway.[76] They find that those communities that were the earliest to establish mutual fire insurance societies and mutual savings banks were the ones most likely (much) later to establish cooperative stores. They come to the interesting conclusion that an 'institutional legacy . . . amplifies variations in the civic capacity of communities', although the question is left open as to why certain communities and not others established particular types of institutions in the first place.

Economists writing about organizational forms have largely focused on a range of issues around the choice between mutual and stock forms of insurance.[77] These issues include the relative efficiency, performance, and ability of each form to resolve agency problems between owners, managers, and customers; second, the ability of each form to resolve adverse selection and asymmetric problems; third, the incentives to demutualize; and fourth, the impact of regulation on different corporate forms. The literature embraces several, often contradictory, models offering agency, uncertainty, and efficiency explanations for the coexistence of mutual organizations alongside joint-stocks, together with explanations of the reasons for conversion between the two forms.[78] The focus has usually been on insurance companies, but it has also been extended to banks and other financial institutions. Most attention has been paid to the agency problems that appear under conditions of asymmetric information, in particular moral hazards arising between customers, owners, and managers because of diverging interests.[79] According to agency theorists, mutual insurance arises in order to eliminate conflicts between owners and policyholders by doing away with the division between the two groups.[80] Intuitively, mutuals are free of the moral hazard to be found

---

[74] Young 1988.   [75] Cf. Ruef 2000; Freeman and Audia 2006.
[76] Greve and Rao 2012.
[77] One notable exception is Hansmann 1996, who examined a range of ownership forms across all sectors, including manufacturing, banking, and insurance. The elements of Hansmann's model relevant to insurance are examined below.
[78] For a recent survey, see MacMinn and Ren 2011.
[79] The seminal article is by Fama and Jensen 1983.
[80] Fitzgerald 1986; Mayers and Smith 1988.

in stock companies, namely the incentive for shareholders to expropriate wealth from policyholders.[81] Some modern US studies support this idea by showing that stock companies use less reinsurance and select riskier investments in an effort to earn higher returns for their shareholders, although historical evidence from property insurance in inter-war Sweden contradicts this.[82]

It has been widely argued, however, that mutual organizations give rise to other agency problems, notably those between policyholders and managers. The stock company is said to provide more effective mechanisms to control managerial behaviour, such as share options, proxy fights, share price, and the threat of a predatory takeover. Thus, the cost of managerial opportunism is said to be higher in mutuals than in stock companies. Mutual companies, especially the largest, are allegedly characterized by unaccountable managers, whose compensation is less responsive to performance than that of their stock counterparts.[83] As a result, mutuals compete best in lines requiring less 'managerial discretion' in risk selection, where the need for individualized underwriting is low, or where long-time horizons are involved and long-term commitment is important.[84] Such types of insurance include some forms of liability cover and standardized personal lines such as automobile insurance. By contrast, stock companies are said to concentrate in higher-risk commercial, international, and short-tail property and casualty lines, while paying their executives higher compensation for having to exercise greater discretion in underwriting.[85]

This 'managerial discretion' hypothesis, therefore, predicts that where the opportunity for managerial intervention is limited, the elimination of the owner-policyholder conflict will give mutuals an edge over stock companies. Analysis of over 400 US insurance companies, 1981–90, supports the contention that mutuals have cost and technical advantages in underwriting long-tail personal lines.[86] Thus, it is argued that market segmentation occurs via the comparative advantage of company form, with mutuals prospering in insurance lines with a longer time horizon. The coexistence of both types of organization is viewed as the result of a trade-off between the respective costs

---

[81] Smith and Stutzer 1995. It has been claimed that the introduction of the conflicting claims of shareholders into a mutual company would reduce the investment returns to its policyholders by around 10 per cent. *Financial Times* 22 July 2000. Cf. Clayton and Osborn 1965, 56.

[82] Lamm-Tennant and Starks 1993. Kader et al. 2010 found a degree of substitution between investment earnings and reinsurance demand, and that in this period Swedish joint-stock insurers used more reinsurance than their mutual counterparts.

[83] Greene and Johnson 1980; Mayers and Smith 1992; Knights and Willmott 1993; Cummins et al. 1999b.

[84] Mayers and Smith 1986.

[85] Mayers and Smith 1981, 1986, 1992; McNamara and Rhee 1992; Lamm-Tennant and Starks 1993; Pottier and Sommer 1997.

[86] Cummins et al. 1999b.

and benefits of each. Some authors, however, have pointed out that this hypothesis fails to explain the popularity of mutual insurers in high-risk areas like medical malpractice, fishing, and agriculture, while others have found that modern mutuals have lower operating costs than stock companies in both life and non-life lines of insurance, a finding supported by the historical research, discussed above, on Swedish fire insurance before 1939 and US and UK life insurance before 1914.[87] Principal-agent problems between owners and managers, therefore, cannot be the sole factor explaining organizational forms in insurance in the present or the past.[88]

Adverse selection under conditions of uncertainty has been offered as another explanation. Customers, it is said, adversely select stock companies for insurance when the aggregate risk is high, because the risk is transferred to shareholders, but they choose to insure in mutuals when the aggregate risk is low. Investors, by contrast, avoid investing in lines with high risk and therefore the mutual becomes the only form available for customers in those lines. Informational asymmetries explain the kind of contracts offered by mutuals, such as participating or 'with-profits' insurance policies, because these help mutuals control the free riding on the insurance pool that may arise with high-risk policyholders.[89] This may help explain why mutuals exist in both low-risk and high-risk lines of business. In sum, the coexistence of mutuals and stocks is the result of adverse selection by investors and customers pulling in opposite directions.

The historical evidence surveyed above tends to support this adverse selection under uncertainty model. We have seen that mutual and other non-stock forms of insurance were most likely to originate in states of high uncertainty about loss probabilities and when risks were non-diversifiable, for example, where catastrophic events occurred, or where frequent but unpredictable hazards led to high losses (for example, piracy and war in early marine insurance); where reliable data on which to base probability calculations were absent (for example, accurate mortality tables or systematic data on fire events); and where unpredictable legal decisions suddenly changed liability levels (for example, in late twentieth-century commercial liability judgements). In such circumstances, mutual organizations were established primarily because their participating policies

---

[87] Doherty and Dionne 1993; Pottier and Sommer 1997. A study by Swiss Re calculated that mutual property-casualty insurers in France, Germany, and the US, 1995–7, had higher operating efficiencies than those of their stock rivals, while mutual life insurers were as efficient as stock life companies, *Sigma* 4, 1999. Hansmann 1985 also disputes the claim that mutuals are 'significantly inferior' to stock companies in their ability to minimize costs, a point reiterated in Hansmann 1996, 274.

[88] Hansmann 1996, 287–97.

[89] Mayers and Smith 1988, 1994; Smith and Stutzer 1990, 1995; Lamm-Tennant and Starks 1993; Laux and Muermann 2010. Hansmann 1996 makes a similar point in a slightly different way, namely that the benefits of mutual ownership outweigh the costs in circumstances where market contracting cannot eliminate problems of asymmetric information.

and common ownership provided the most effective means of reducing moral hazard and asymmetric information problems, which are usually perceived as increasing in times of high losses and economic uncertainty.

In situations of high uncertainty regarding tightening credit and capital markets, it has also probably been easier to form mutuals. As we have seen, the history of life insurance in the early nineteenth century and again in the 1930s revealed that new mutual company formation remained buoyant and the market share of mutuals grew, in periods when asset values were falling and when it became difficult for stock company promoters to attract investors. When capital markets were buoyant and credit expanding, for example in the mid-1980s and later 1990s, conversion to a joint-stock became irresistible for many mutuals. By contrast, in the most recent economic downturn mutual insurers have performed well relative to their stock counterparts and increased their global market share. According to Best's report of 2010, mutuals benefited from the lack of pressure to return capital to shareholders and 'from their tendency to retain a loyal customer base'.[90] Yet capital costs clearly do not explain everything about the organizational structure of the insurance industry. As Hansmann has noted, while stock companies have an advantage in being able to raise capital quickly in the short run, over the long term there is no evidence of great differences in capital costs between different ownership forms.[91]

Beyond the mutual versus joint-stock debate, much less attention has been paid by economists to other vehicles for insurance, for example, not-for-profit organizations, individual underwriters, and public insurance bodies. Wright has usefully summarized the arguments for and against the latter.[92] Governments have powers that private insurers do not have, for instance the power to limit adverse selection through compulsory insurance. Governments are better equipped to prevent or mitigate hazards, including road and workplace accidents and natural disasters. Public insurers may have longer time horizons and, being underpinned by state revenues, they may be better able to withstand economic downturns than private providers. State insurance, however, can also be inefficient. The guaranty funds against insurer insolvency operated by most US states may have increased risk taking by insurers. The existence of federal deposit insurance may have induced US banks to take on unwarranted levels of risk in the savings and loans crisis of the 1980s. State insurance, subsidies, and relief programmes may crowd out private insurance alternatives and affect the risk-taking behaviour of the public, generating major asymmetric

---

[90] Best 2010. The report also noted that as mutuals could not access the capital markets to raise money, they tended to retain accumulated capital. Moreover, their investments tended to be in bonds and fixed-income products rather than riskier products such as collateralized debt obligations. Consequently, during the crash of 2008 mutual asset values fell only marginally.
[91] Hansmann 1996, 274, 291–2.   [92] Wright 2010.

information and adverse selection problems. Federal flood insurance, for instance, has allegedly induced construction and weakened natural defences against floods and hurricanes in southern Louisiana. In sum, while public insurance is often mooted as an answer to the failure of the market, it can create problems as costly as those it solves. Our historical survey above, however, also suggests that the net effect of public insurance schemes was contingent on their precise nature. In the case of late nineteenth-century Germany, for example, government social insurance schemes grew a market rapidly and provided a boon for private insurers.

In sum, many factors—agency problems in governance, adverse selection, and asymmetric information in assessing different types of risk, the impact of regulation, the business cycle, and access to capital—have been cited as explanations of organizational form in insurance. A single theory that successfully embraces all these factors, however, does not exist.[93] Moreover, other factors, such as entrepreneurship, and political, cultural, and ideological influences, have either been ignored, or dismissed.[94] Several chapters in this volume explore these neglected explanatory factors in different historical contexts.

ABOUT THE PROJECT AND THIS BOOK

The project that gave rise to this book commenced in 2010 and was generously sponsored by the Dai-ichi Life Insurance Company of Japan and the Dai-ichi Life Research Institute. It sought to explain why different corporate forms emerged and coexisted in insurance in different countries during the modern era, and what the costs, benefits, and relative performance of these forms were under different political, regulatory, and economic systems. The project initially posed a number of hypotheses derived from the theoretical and empirical literature surveyed above, namely that mutual insurance arose to resolve asymmetric information and risk assessment problems, and to eliminate conflicts of interest between owners and policyholders; that, other things being equal, the annual claims experience of mutuals was lower than that for stock insurers; that in economic downturns the market share of mutuals increased at the expense of stock companies; that mutuals were commonly preferred by states pursuing policies of autarky and economic intervention;

---

[93] MacMinn and Ren 2011, 109.
[94] Hansmann 1996 dismisses the role of entrepreneurship in organizational choice on the grounds that stock-mutual conversion has gone in both directions, but history shows that this has not always been easy, for example, the restrictions in many early modern states on private stock company formation.

that mutual and cooperative insurance was preferred by frontier and settler economies. It was left open to the contributors, however, to pursue other questions outside this framework, provided they were relevant to the overall theme of organizational forms. During 2011–12 two workshops were held in Japan and a session was convened at the World Economic History Congress in Stellenbosch, South Africa, which brought together seventeen scholars from ten countries (Japan, USA, Germany, UK, Sweden, Spain, South Africa, Australia, France, and Canada), who between them contributed twenty-four research papers. This book presents a selection of these papers grouped under the four headings noted below.

The distribution of papers was not random, of course, as it reflected the clusters of insurance historians currently working in particular countries. Nevertheless, as a result of this process of selection and self-selection we have chapters that cover eight major insurance markets, which together accounted for 58 per cent of world insurance in 2010 (measured by premium volume in US$).[95] All eight are in the top quartile of countries by this measure. They include the three largest markets in the world in 2010 (USA, Japan, and UK), plus Germany (ranked 5), Spain (13), Australia (14), South Africa (17), and Sweden (21). Furthermore, companies from the US, UK, Germany, and Sweden have been major exporters of insurance since the nineteenth century, while those from Japan, Australia, South Africa, and Spain became important in export markets towards the end of the twentieth century, and in some cases earlier. In other words, the countries covered by this book are representative of major markets in world insurance, and we believe that the chapter contributions are diverse enough to enable general conclusions to be drawn.

Part I brings together five chapters on the variety, choice, governance, and regulation of organizational forms. Takau Yoneyama discusses the career of Tsuneta Yano, who founded Dai-ichi Life Insurance as Japan's first mutual insurance company in 1902. Yoneyama concludes that, for all his life-long advocacy of mutualism, Yano's decision to opt for the mutual form was ultimately a pragmatic one, based on his view that mutuals could reduce contracting and governance costs more effectively than stock companies. Robin Pearson and Helen Doe examine the changing organizational forms in UK marine insurance. Technological, political, and financial factors played a part, alongside market information problems and business networks, in shaping the variegated structure of UK marine insurance from the Lloyds system of individual underwriting of hull and cargo risks, to the protection and indemnity clubs that emerged to cover other types of shipowners' liability. In what may be the first historical study of a captive insurer, Hisaaki Kamiya provides a unique glimpse into the risk management business of one of Japan's

---

[95] Calculated from *Sigma* 2, 2011, table III.

most famous zaibatsu, Mitsubishi Gōshi Kaisha. In 1919 Mitsubishi established its own insurance company, partly to pool its risks across the industrial
group with the aim of reducing costs and partly in response to new legal
restrictions on holding companies insuring the risks of subsidiaries. In 1933 it
sold its captive after conditions in the external market had changed. The
persistent strength of the mutual sector in Swedish insurance is the focus of
the chapter by Mats Larsson and Mikael Lönnborg. They argue that this was
the result, first, of the regulatory changes of the 1940s and the role of the social
democratic state in creating a congenial market environment for mutual
insurers. Second, the internal organizational capabilities of Swedish mutuals
helped them to adapt to market and regulatory change. Robin Pearson
compares the history of organizational forms in German and US insurance
before 1914. His chapter reveals the great variety of organizational structures
in both countries. While access to capital, governance issues, and risk types
affected organizational choice in insurance, he also highlights the importance
of regulation, public trust, and cultural preference in favouring particular
forms of organization at different times.

The second section of the book presents three chapters on mutual insurance
in uncertain environments. Grietjie Verhoef examines insurance companies in
colonial South Africa. From the 1840s, once settler identities began to take
shape, mutual life assurance companies began to mobilize settler support.
Verhoef identifies factors that made the mutual form particularly successful
in life insurance, including an element of trust and growing feelings of a shared
destiny in the settler economies. Her chapter suggests that the ethos of
mutualism may have been particularly conducive to colonial or settler societies
like those at the Cape. Mutualism also had deep roots in Australian life
insurance since the nineteenth century. In her chapter Monica Keneley discusses a grid of economic, social, market, and environmental factors that
provided the context and opportunity for the development of Australian
mutuals. She stresses the entrepreneurship of the first mutual life companies
and their innovations in product development and marketing. Market failure,
she argues, provides only part of the explanation for their emergence and
success. In her study of Spanish mutuals under the Franco regime, Jerònia
Pons Pons finds that they enjoyed important fiscal and regulatory advantages
over stock companies. Yet the regime's support was not unequivocal. From
1944 mutuals were banned from writing reinsurance and in the 1960s there
were fears that they might also be excluded from providing social insurance.
Mutuals responded to the uncertainty of the 1960s by acquiring shares in stock
companies and by creating groups out of the companies that they controlled.

Part III contains two chapters on the performance of different organizational forms. YingYing Jiang analyses Japanese life insurance from the turn of
the century to the 1930s. During this period the large Japanese mutuals
enjoyed much lower expense ratios than their stock counterparts and this,

together with innovations in marketing and product development, gave them a persistently high market share. Mutuals also benefited from good governance, often deriving from the leadership of their founder figures, while for their part the stability of stock companies was ensured by an increasing concentration of their capital in the hands of large shareholders. Magnus Lindmark and Lars Fredrik Andersson ask why mutual life insurers grew so rapidly in Sweden from the 1890s to the late 1940s. Contrary to much organizational theory, they find little evidence to support the idea that mutuals had comparative advantages in dealing with information asymmetries. Instead, timing and business strategy were the key factors. The success of mutuals is explained by their greater ability to adapt to the growth of real wages and the mass demand for industrial life assurance that required extensive sales networks and higher levels of trust between vendor and policyholder. By contrast, Swedish stock companies were locked into the market for larger middle-class policies, a more slowly growing sector and one that benefited less from the decline in mortality rates.

The final section presents two studies of demutualization. Natsuki Kinoshita provides the first history of African-American life insurance in the US and examines the case of the abortive demutualization in 1968 of the black-owned Golden State Mutual Life Insurance Company (GSM) of Los Angeles. Conversion of the GSM was sought because of the company's deteriorating business performance due to rising black unemployment and increasing competition from white life insurance companies. At the same time changes in the political context led black insurers to reach out to national rather than local and racially circumscribed markets. GSM's demutualization, however, was scuppered by its lack of organizational capabilities and the high costs of the conversion process, as well as by concerns about the loss of community ownership. Kinoshita demonstrates how, in certain circumstances, social and political factors can influence the choice of corporate form. Leonardo Caruana de las Cagigas examines the demutualization of the Spanish insurer Mapfre. In the 1960s Mapfre, which had commenced as an agricultural mutual accident insurer in the 1930s, began to diversify into other lines of insurance by establishing subsidiary stock companies. In 1965 its statutes were altered so as to vest the assets of the mutual holding company in a new social organization, the Mapfre Foundation. Upon demutualization in 2007, the Foundation became the majority shareholder in the new Mapfre stock company, thus providing the group with a degree of protection from a hostile takeover while attempting to retain the mutual ethos of the original company.

What conclusions can be drawn from the chapters in this book, and from the other contributions to the project, which advance our understanding of the history and theory of corporate forms? First, regulatory or legislative intervention played an important, sometimes decisive, role in determining the prevalence or survival of specific organizational forms in insurance across several countries and at different times. Historical examples of state intervention were numerous and could shape the organizational structure of insurance markets over the long term.

Second, this project, and in particular the chapter by Jerònia Pons Pons on mutual insurers under Franco, has uncovered evidence to support the hypothesis that certain political systems and their regulatory regimes favoured some forms of business organization over others. It is unlikely, however, that political regimes sharing similar ideological tendencies approached the question of corporate form in similar or consistent ways. The Nazis during the 1930s, for instance, seem to have had an ambivalent attitude—views differed widely within the regime—towards the competition between public and private and mutual and stock organizations in insurance, notwithstanding the fact that the brother of the Reich's propaganda minister was a director of one of Germany's largest public insurance companies.[96] How legislators in different countries over time viewed the relative advantages and disadvantages of different corporate forms is surely worth further investigation.

Third, a culture of mutualism and a self-help ethos, as well as information and agency problems associated with an uncertain market environment, helped drive the promotion of early insurance mutuals in settler or frontier societies such as Australia and South Africa. As noted above, the role of culture has been ignored or treated with scepticism by many organizational theorists, yet the historical evidence for its importance appears strong.

Fourth, the importance of entrepreneurship in establishing or driving forward particular organizational forms has also been documented in several contributions to this project. The chapters by Pearson and Doe and Yoneyama point to the roles, respectively, of Sydney Crowe, the force behind the expansion of the Steamship Mutual Underwriting Association in the 1930s and 1940s, and Tsuneta Yano, the founder of the Dai-ichi Life Insurance, in the success of their mutual companies.[97] Entrepreneurial dynamism is not regularly associated in the historical or economic literature with mutual forms of organization. For that reason it may be surprising to see mutual insurance companies and their executives cast in the role of innovators in product development and marketing, for example in the chapters by Verhoef and Keneley. Entrepreneurship has also been largely ignored by organizational theory, but the historical evidence suggests that for some of the most dynamic business people in developing economies the selection of a form of

---

[96] Feldman 2001.

[97] An unpublished paper on the Wawanesa Mutual Insurance Company, presented to the project by Heather Nelson, also provides support for the significance of entrepreneurship. The company was founded in 1896 as a local farmer's mutual in Manitoba, but it became one of the largest property and casualty insurers in Canada thanks to several initiatives in organizational restructuring, marketing, and lobbying. Nelson 2012.

organization for new insurance ventures was not always an obvious or un-complicated choice.

A fifth conclusion is that organizational choice has always been contingent on historical circumstances. There is little convincing evidence from insurance history to suggest that some process of 'natural selection' has ever operated in the evolution of corporate forms. In particular, there is little to suggest that any advantages of joint-stock over mutual organization were persistent over time. In several papers written for this project demutualization appears as either an enticing option, a threat to be avoided, or an abortive choice. Much of the literature on the most recent waves of demutualization offer standard explan-ations that highlight the need for mutuals to enhance their capital resources when faced with the challenge of competing in a global economy. These standard explanations, however, do not always take into account firm and local market-specific factors, as Verhoef has demonstrated in her recent study of the demutualization of South Africa's two leading life insurance companies in 1998.[98]

This project has also contributed to the expanding literature on the relative performance of different corporate forms. The evidence presented in the chapters by Jiang for Japan and by Lindmark and Andersson for Sweden indicates the relative efficiency of mutual insurers, which supports the findings of most other recent research in this area. It seems, therefore, that expectations of costs and future performance, and the ability to resolve agency problems between owners and managers, were not the only reasons for the choice of organizational form in insurance throughout history. Settlers in colonial Australia and South Africa, landowners in Franco's Spain, or African-Americans in twentieth-century America provided new markets for mutual as well as joint-stock insurers, in part because of the cultural, legal, and political environments in which they found themselves.

Finally, one of the most interesting results to emerge from the project, reflected in the contributions to this book, is the evidence that the variety of organizational forms in insurance history was far greater than previously suspected. In his chapter Caruana de las Cagigas presents examples of mutual insurers controlling stock companies via the holding company device, the first historical study of this form. Pearson and Doe examine the rarely studied mutual partnerships in marine insurance known as protection and indemnity clubs, and Kamiya's chapter is the first to explore the creation of a captive insurer by a major business corporation. The Mitsubishi case highlights a wider phenomenon in insurance history, the learning process that invariably took place among founders and managers as different organizational forms were experimented with. In this instance, costs, regulation, underwriting

---

[98] Verhoef 2012. This paper was presented to the Tokyo workshop of the project.

results, and access to technical skills determined Mitsubishi's choice or rejection of different forms of insurance.[99] To a significant extent, therefore, the choice of organizational form may be regarded as a risk management decision in the face of market and other uncertainties. This suggests the inadequacy of agency theory, which is based on the binary opposition of just two corporate forms, mutual versus joint-stock, to explain the complexity of history and the great variety of organizational forms coexisting in different political, legal, and economic contexts.

[99] In a paper presented to this project but published elsewhere, Keneley describes the 'knowledge pathway' that Australia's leading life insurer, the Australian Mutual Provident, had to follow in order to transform itself into an international financial services group between the 1960s and the 1990s. Keneley 2012.

Part I

The Variety, Choice, Governance, and Regulation of Organizational Forms

2

Tsuneta Yano, Founder of the First Mutual Company in Japan

Was He an Obstinate Mutualist?

Takau Yoneyama

Tsuneta Yano was a founder in 1902 of the Dai-ichi Life Mutual Insurance Company, the first mutual company in Japan.[1] He was not only one of the most prominent top managers in the Japanese life insurance business, but also a well-known mutualist in the history of business thought in Japan. In an early marketing publication, Yano emphasized the merits of mutual life insurance and insisted that the Dai-ichi should not aim to be the biggest company in Japan, but rather the best company for its policyholders. After comparatively slow growth in its early stage, the Dai-ichi Life Mutual ranked among the big five in Japanese life insurance by the 1920s. It is not too much to say that the history of the Dai-ichi Life is the history of the mutual insurance company in Japan.

In April 2010, the Dai-ichi Life Mutual converted its corporate form into that of a stock company. The public reacted with surprise to the news, because the company was the original mutual company in Japan and a conversion did not seem inevitable. Did the company make a decision to convert that was contrary to the intentions of its founder, or did the company manage to select a path that did not contradict his principles and ideas? In this chapter we examine these questions by reconsidering the life and thought of Tsuneta Yano, using documents available in the company's archives.[2]

[1] The company was the forerunner of the Dai-ichi Life Insurance Company, Ltd which was the sponsor of the project from which this book derived. I wish to offer my sincere thanks to the company for giving such generous support to us.

[2] I wish to thank the company's staff for their assistance in helping me to use the materials in the archive in the Oi-Matsuda branch.

This chapter consists of five parts. The first explains corporate forms in Japanese insurance before the passing of the Insurance Business Act in 1900. Part two describes Yano's early life and career in the insurance industry. Third, the passing of the Insurance Business Act in 1900 and Yano's involvement in this process are explained. Part four provides a short history of the early business of the Dai-ichi Life Mutual. The final part discusses Yano's ideas about the mutual form of company organization and draws a conclusion.

CORPORATE FORMS BEFORE THE INSURANCE BUSINESS ACT OF 1900

At the time the modern insurance business was introduced from the West, there were no general company laws at all in Japan. In 1879, the Tokio Marine, the first insurance company in Japan, applied to the Governor of Tokyo to be established on a joint-stock principle.[3] A second enterprise, the Meiji Life, also applied to the governor in 1880 and it too was founded as a joint-stock company.[4]

Before the Meiji Life, there were two projects to establish a life assurance business. One was known as the Kyosai 500 Members and the other was the Nitto Life. The former was only a trial venture with the aim of writing mutual insurance on an assessment basis.[5] The Nitto Life was the first, but abortive, modern life assurance company in Japan. Its promoter, Yoshikazu Wakayama, had experienced Western cultures when he accompanied the Iwakura Mission in 1871.[6] He aimed to promote a life assurance enterprise along the lines of an American life insurance company.[7] At first he tried to found a stock company, but facing financial difficulties he tried the project again in the form of a

---

[3] Japan Business History Institute 1979.   [4] Meiji Life Assurance Company 2004.
[5] Yoneyama 2010, 104–6.
[6] The Iwakura Mission was a Japanese diplomatic journey to the Western countries, initiated in 1871 by the early Meiji Government. It was one of the most important events for the modernization of Japan after a long period of isolation from the West. The mission was headed by Iwakura Tomomi, Minister of Foreign Affairs, in the role of ambassador extraordinary and plenipotentiary, assisted by four vice-ambassadors, three of whom (Ōkubo Toshimichi, Kido Takayoshi, and Itō Hirobumi) became political leaders in Meiji Japan. Also included were a number of administrators and scholars, totalling forty-nine people, including a historian, Kume Kunitake, who was the official diarist, keeping a detailed log of all events and impressions. In addition to the mission staff, about sixty students accompanied the mission. Several of them were left behind to complete their education in Western countries, including five young women who stayed in the United States to study.
[7] Although he modelled his project on the Prudential Company of the US, Wakayama's insurance company was actually modified for Japanese culture. Mizushima 1992, 4–7.

mutual, and this was approved by the governor of Tokyo. The company, however, failed to open for business because of a lack of powerful supporters.[8]

When the first Japanese Company Act was passed in 1893, most nascent life assurance ventures took the joint-stock form, while some became limited partnerships. The act thus gave a general legal basis to business firms. It did not, however, stipulate any rules for the formation of mutual companies. While mutual companies were not legally prohibited, it was the case that no one tried to launch a mutual company notwithstanding the absence of any regulations in the new Company Act. Despite this legal vacuum, many small quasi insurance companies were in fact established in local areas before the passing of the Insurance Business Act in 1900. Most of these companies were so-called assessment insurance organizations. While they operated upon the mutual principle, they were quite different from the mutual companies with corporate status provided for under the Insurance Business Act.

With Chandler's model of industrial organization in mind, we can identify the first movers in early Japanese life assurance as the Meiji Life, the Teikoku Life, and the Nippon Life.[9] The Meiji Life mainly wrote life assurance for the professional and middle classes, the Teikoku Life created a life assurance market for soldiers and public officials, and the Nippon Life developed provincial markets making use of local bankers as agents. Lots of life assurers followed these first movers.[10] Some companies survived for a comparatively long time, but they did not become strong competitors to these three.[11]

The above three were founded as stock companies, but they did not emphasize the return of profits to their stockholders. Instead, they highlighted their contribution to the improvement promised by insurance to the living standards of their policyholders. This may be simply explained as part of their sales strategy. Nevertheless, it is also certain that almost all the top managers in contemporary Japanese life assurance companies regarded business success in the same light as national or social prosperity. These companies, therefore, did not hesitate to add some ostensibly mutual factors to their life assurance business. The Meiji Life, for example, restricted directors' expenses and only its executive directors were paid full remuneration.[12] When the statistician, Dr. Rikitaro Fujisawa, agreed to construct the first premium table based on Japanese mortality for the Nippon Life, the latter in return promised Fujisawa that it would pay future surpluses to its policyholders.[13]

---

[8] Association of Life Insurance Companies 1934, vol. 1, sec. 2, no. 2: 148ff.
[9] Chandler 1994.
[10] See in detail Yoneyama 2010, 110–13.
[11] As we shall see, the serious challenge to the big three came from two important mutual insurers, the Dai-ichi Mutual and the Chiyoda Mutual. These became strong rivals of the big three stock companies in the 1920s.
[12] Meiji Life Assurance Company 2004.
[13] Nippon Life Insurance Company 1992a, 27.

Thus, while mutual insurance companies in Japan were first legally recognized by the Insurance Business Act of 1900, some stock companies had already added some mutual elements to their life assurance products, such as the payment of dividends to policyholders.[14] In sum, the major companies in Japanese life assurance had already transformed into a 'mixed' organizational form before the passing of the Insurance Business Law.

TSUNETA YANO: EARLY LIFE AND CAREER THROUGH TO HIS RESIGNATION FROM THE KYOSAI LIFE

Tsuneta Yano had already made a deep personal commitment to the new business of life assurance even before he founded the Dai-ichi Life in 1902. In order to understand his thought, it is instructive to have a look at his early life. He was born as the first and only son of Saneki Yano and his wife, Ise, in Okayama prefecture on 18 January 1866. His father was a medical practitioner in a small village and his mother died when Yano was just thirteen years old. In order to succeed to his father's clinical practice, he entered the Okayama medical class in 1878. He left to go to Tokyo in May 1880, however, without completing his school curriculum. The details and reasons for his flight to Tokyo are not known. In any case, he returned home again in 1882, and in January 1883 he re-entered the Medical Department of the Third High School, later renamed the Okayama Medical School. He completed his medical studies in 1889.

Having graduated, Yano thought it was better for him first to work in the city before returning home as a medical practitioner. He asked a former medical teacher for help with his search for a suitable post. In 1890, following this teacher's recommendation, Yano got a job as the examining physician of Nippon Life. At the time, life assurance salesmen in Japan used to make their sales trips accompanied by an examining physician. This was also the main sales procedure of the Nippon Life. Remarkably, Yano was able to complete nearly 500 examinations in his first year. The following year he moved to the Tokyo branch of the company. In 1892 Yano participated in the company's celebration of reaching 5 million yen of policies in force, and he made a successful speech on behalf of all the medical physicians of Nippon Life. After the celebration, Yano appealed directly to the vice president, Naoharu Kataoka, to improve the company's treatment of and dealings with its medical practitioners. This was a bold step and Yano fully expected to be fired.

---

[14] There were several different ways of paying policyholder dividends. See Jiang's Chapter 10 in this book.

Although in advance of this appeal Yano had already decided to resign from his post, the company promptly sent him a dismissal notice with effect from 31 December 1892 and a retirement lump sum of 150 yen. This drew an angry response from Yano, who was upset that the notice amounted to a one-sided dismissal, rather than being a retirement at his own request. In reaction, Yano inserted a public notice in a newspaper that he had resigned from his post in the Nippon Life at his own request.

This experience with the Nippon Life was the reason that he became absorbed in studying life assurance even after leaving the company's employment. Yano abandoned his plan that he would work for a living as a medical practitioner. In a sense, he had become spiritually awakened that his personal mission was the improvement of the life assurance business. Just after his resignation, he published a pamphlet on *The New Idea of Life Assurance Rules*, in which was concentrated his business experience in the life assurance business and the knowledge that he had gleaned from Western books.[15] Yano had been reading Western insurance literature extensively in the Imperial Library and he published many articles in journals and newspapers, in total sixteen titles between February and October 1893.[16] In particular, it seems that discovering more about the mutual company form in various Western books was something of a revelation for him. At his own expense he published a pamphlet titled *In Expectation of the Establishment of a Non-Profit Based Life Assurance Company*, by which he was referring to a mutual life assurance company. It is interesting that Yano did not directly advocate the merits of the mutual company, but he did clearly explain for policyholders the functional differences between stock and mutual forms. He also concluded in this pamphlet that it was useful for nations to establish mutual life assurance companies.

As noted above, a mutual organization called the Kyosai 500 Members was already in operation. This was privately run by Zenjiro Yasuda, a founder of Yasuda Zaibatsu (a family-based business group of banking and industrial enterprises). The Kyosai 500 Members was a mutual aid cooperative run for the benefit of its original 500 members. Its business system was simple. When a member passed away, every surviving member made a contribution of 2 yen and paid 1,000 yen for the bereaved family. All managerial expenses were covered by the Yasuda Bank. It was inevitable that this type of mutual mortuary tontine would encounter financial problems as its members got older. As the liquidity problems became serious by 1893, Zenjiro sought a way out. He approached

---

[15] The pamphlet of sixty pages was published by himself and sold at 5 sen, namely 0.15 yen. It was reviewed by Goro Takahashi in a journal, *Kokumin no Tomo (Nation's Friend)* 186, April 1993.
[16] There is not space to discuss all of Yano's early papers here. They appeared in a variety of economics and medical journals.

Tsuneta Yano and asked him to reorganize the Kyosai 500 Members into a new life assurance company. Yano commenced this task in December 1893 and by April 1894 he had successfully established the Kyosai Life Insurance, into which was transferred all the insurance liability for the existing Kyosai 500 Members. During the process, Yano constructed a life table from his own calculations and wrote contract rules for each new life assurance product. He hoped initially that the new company would take a mutual form, but he had to reconcile himself to selecting the limited partnership form of business organization because there was no legal basis for mutual companies in Japan at that time. Zenjiro agreed with Yano's aim of converting the new company to a mutual in the future.[17] As a sign of this intention, he stipulated in the company rules that the proportion of profits to be paid as stock dividends was never to be more than 6 per cent. At the commencement of the new company, Yano became a manager in charge of business at a salary of 50 yen a month. There were two other managers alongside him, one in charge of accounting and another in public relations.[18]

In May 1895, supported by Zenjiro's financial assistance, Yano visited several European countries in order to study the insurance business further. In September that year he participated in the First International Congress of Actuaries in Brussels. He spent his time, however, mainly in Germany, where he worked on a temporary basis for more than a year at the venerable *Gothaer Lebens-versicherungsbank*, founded in 1829.[19] After returning to Japan in March 1897, he was appointed as General Manager of the Kyosai Life. The company increased his salary to 100 yen a month, which was the highest among the employees of the Yasuda Zaibatsu. Yano improved the company's management by employing some of the advanced systems he had seen in Germany, and he introduced a card and loose-leaf process in the company's book recording system. He abolished the Osaka branch and integrated its office operations into the Tokyo head office in order to enhance efficiency. He also abolished the system of local travelling agents and replaced this with local sales offices containing resident agents in major towns.[20]

In June 1898 Yano decided to resign from his post in the Kyosai Life and to enter government service in the Ministry of Agriculture and Commerce. It is not clear exactly why he moved to government employment, although there may have been an important difference of opinion about business strategy between Yasuda and Yano.[21] Whether or not this is true, the most important factor appears to have been an invitation from Keijiro Okano to join the team charged with drafting a new legislative bill on the insurance business. This invitation seemed a golden opportunity for Yano, who hoped to use it to

---

[17] Yano 1957, 54.   [18] Yasuda Mutual Life Insurance Company 1961, 26–8.
[19] Yoneyama 2012.   [20] Yasuda Mutual Life Insurance Company 1961, 34.
[21] Yano proposed to recruit a large number of medical doctors to support the sales offices, but Zenjiro did not agree. This is a reason, it seems, why Yano decided to quit the company.

achieve legal recognition for the mutual form of corporate organization.[22] In short, in spite of having received warm and generous treatment by Zenjiro Yasuda, Yano appears to have felt some responsibility as the author of *In Expectation of the Establishment of a Non-Profit-Based Life Assurance Company* to put his ideas into practice.

TSUNETA YANO AND THE INSURANCE BUSINESS ACT

After taking the job of an examining physician for the Nippon Life, studying the life insurance business and its actuaries, undertaking a substantial study of insurance in European countries, and running the Kyosai Life as General Manager, Yano then took part in designing the legal framework of the Japanese insurance business.

In October 1898 Yano joined the committee for drafting an insurance bill as an assistant member helping Professor Okano. As a result of their labours, the Insurance Business Act was successfully enacted in March 1900. Following the passing of the act, Yano was appointed as head of the section of insurance, which had just been established in the Bureau of Commerce and Industry of the Ministry of Agriculture and Commerce. In other words, he was the first person in charge of official insurance supervision in Japan.

One interesting episode occurred while Yano was section head that reveals the personal relationships that characterized the relatively small community of insurance experts and managers in the early Japanese insurance industry, and how these relationships could intersect, sometimes in a problematic way, with the new state regulatory regime introduced in 1900. The Insurance Business Act provided strict rules for a company's insurance reserve. These rules had a serious impact on those non-life insurance companies that had incurred large losses from their recent and novel incursions into overseas underwriting. The Tokio Marine was the first Japanese insurance company to develop its business abroad, but it was fortunate that an able manager dispatched to London soon realized the potential losses from foreign business and he reduced the company's financial exposure as far as possible.[23] Another large non-life insurance company like the Nihon Kairiku Insurance, a subsidiary of the Nippon Life, developed its foreign business in the wake of the Tokio Marine, but ran into serious financial difficulties from overseas losses. Although Naoharu Kataoka, president of both companies, tried to recover the possible loss, the Nihon Kairiku Insurance eventually became insolvent after the state

---

[22] He was guaranteed his salary of 100 yen a month by Okano. Yano 1957, 50.
[23] Inagaki 1951; Japan Business History Institute 1979.

insurance supervision was established in 1900. When Yano inspected the Nihon Kairiku in Osaka as head of the insurance section, he met Kataoka, who had been responsible for Yano's dismissal from the Nippon Life ten years previously. Newspapers at the time reported that Yano took the opportunity to avenge himself on Kataoka for that dismissal. The Nihon Kairiku was indeed liquidated after making due settlement abroad.[24]

As this episode showed, the new supervisory system under the Insurance Business Act not only imposed a heavier burden on companies, it also affected business practices in insurance. One of the most important changes was to provide some regulatory advantage to the mutual form of company. The act not only formally recognized the mutual company, it also stipulated how stock companies should convert themselves into mutuals. It is indeed curious that the act did not stipulate how mutual companies could be legally converted into stock companies.[25]

Although there is no direct evidence to clinch the point, one might reasonably suggest that these legal advantages provided to the mutual company form were the result of Yano's powerful influence in this direction. His earlier experience in the Gothaer Lebensversicherungsbank and his articles and pamphlets on mutualism and the mutual company both support this suggestion. It must also be pointed out, however, that Keijiro Okano was also a positive force for introducing the mutual company clauses into the act. Indeed, it may be the case that Yano revealed his intentions as an advocate of the mutual form under Okano's influence.

TSUNETA YANO AND INSURANCE MANAGEMENT

Yano resigned from his post in the Ministry of Agriculture and Commerce in December 1901. The reason was that he wished to promote a mutual life insurance company by himself, for he felt that hitherto he had seen no similar promotions on a sound basis. He expressed his views in a newspaper article entitled *A Word about the Primary Avocation to Promote a Mutual Insurance Company*.[26]

In fact, there were already some mutual insurance projects being promoted elsewhere in 1901, including the Aishin Mutual in Fukuoka, the Chugai Mutual in Kyoto, and another mutual in Yokohama. Yano recognized, however, that all these projects had fragile management bases and weak financial standings, so

---

[24] Nippon Life Insurance Company 1963, 41–3.

[25] This omission was not rectified until the newly revised Insurance Business Act of 1995.

[26] Yano contributed the article to *Chugai Shogyo Shinpo (Chugai Commerce News)* 29 December 1901.

that the supervisory authority adopted a cautious approach in approving them. In fact, by the end of 1901 no new projects had been approved. Taking this situation into account, Yano decided to establish a mutual life company by himself, and left the government service to do so.[27] His mutual company was launched in 1903. The word 'Dai-ichi' means 'first' in English, so the Dai-ichi Life Mutual became by title the first mutual life insurance company in Japan.

The early business of Yano's Dai-ichi Life was extremely careful and prudent. For example, Yano never accepted the need to pay agency fees. He insisted that Dai-ichi's policyholders should recommend their friends to the company if the mutual life insurance product proved profitable for them. Such a passive sales strategy depended not only on Yano's firm conviction about the merits of mutual life insurance, but it also derived from his sense of responsibility to the policyholders and the insurance authorities.

In Yano's mind the need was to aim not for the biggest but for the best insurance company possible. This goal, however, was not to be automatically achieved by establishing a mutual company. The best company for policyholders, in Yano's view, was the product of both good management and adequate corporate governance from the start of the business. According to Henry Hansmann, the most advantageous corporate form for an industry is the one that can realize the lowest aggregate costs of market contracting and the lowest costs of distributing ownership.[28] Yano would have agreed. He understood that the most important thing was not the selection of the mutual form per se, but the costs of distributing ownership. Under certain historical conditions, the mutual insurance form could indeed minimize aggregate costs because of its method of 'payment first and settling up later'. However, if the costs of management and governance began to grow excessively in mutual firms, the effect of saving market contracting costs could be offset. This is the primary reason why the Dai-ichi Life did not follow the strategy pursued by its near contemporary the Chiyoda Life Mutual. As Table 2.1 shows, the latter grew much faster than the Dai-ichi Life through the 1910s, principally by its extensive use of a sales agency system, the expense of which Yano resolved to avoid.

THE EARLY BUSINESS OF THE DAI-ICHI LIFE AND THE CHIYODA LIFE

The Dai-ichi Life Mutual Company opened its business on 1 October 1902. The Chiyoda Life was established in 1904 as Japan's second mutual life

---

[27] He recollected the process in a lecture at Meiji University on 28 November 1935. The record of the lecture was included in Yano 1936, 294.
[28] Hansmann 1996, 35–49.

Table 2.1. New business of two major mutual Japanese life insurance companies, 1903–32

Year	Dai-ichi Life		Chiyoda Life		%	%
	D1 policies	D2 ¥ insured	C1 policies	C2 ¥ insured	D1/(D1+C1)	D2/(D2+C2)
1903	904	1,118,500				
1904	1,106	1,323,500	3,055	2,643,500	26.6	33.4
1905	966	1,559,700	5,025	4,189,500	16.1	27.1
1906	967	1,860,100	5,530	5,329,400	14.9	25.9
1907	1,149	1,969,200	6,572	6,227,300	14.9	24.0
1908	1,279	2,195,000	7,550	7,379,600	14.5	22.9
1909	1,227	2,333,300	8,098	8,417,400	13.2	21.7
1910	1,546	3,050,200	7,831	8,806,900	16.5	25.7
1911	2,915	5,573,500	8,602	10,750,100	25.3	34.1
1912	3,594	6,353,400	9,300	12,609,300	27.9	33.5
1913	5,280	6,772,600	9,186	12,540,200	36.5	35.1
1914	3,749	5,537,300	7,388	9,457,500	33.7	36.9
1915	2,873	4,028,500	5,752	7,492,700	33.3	35.0
1916	3,471	5,182,400	7,378	11,231,400	32.0	31.6
1917	4,856	7,528,500	12,905	18,733,700	27.3	28.7
1918	6,801	11,911,300	20,818	28,020,800	24.6	29.8
1919	12,144	21,277,600	25,107	36,479,300	32.6	36.8
1920	14,494	30,661,200	23,325	35,819,000	38.3	46.1
1921	17,470	35,745,300	22,445	38,108,300	43.8	48.4
1922	18,591	41,999,300	24,881	49,028,800	42.8	46.1
1923	20,814	46,876,400	23,661	49,325,800	46.8	48.7
1924	22,978	56,230,000	26,101	57,992,900	46.8	49.2
1925	30,841	78,815,100	36,465	88,200,500	45.8	47.2
1926	34,990	91,431,500	42,274	105,458,700	45.3	46.4
1927	41,941	111,269,500	42,302	111,321,500	49.8	50.0
1928	48,735	129,317,200	54,256	145,952,000	47.3	47.0
1929	55,267	151,257,200	60,259	155,758,800	47.8	49.3
1930	63,982	166,404,100	54,173	132,821,700	54.2	55.6
1931	78,371	191,346,400	77,331	196,317,900	50.3	49.4
1932	79,851	184,706,400	85,128	194,109,000	48.4	48.8

assurance company. Several small mutual life companies, the Kokko, the Horai, the Chuo, and the Tokai, followed the Dai-ichi Life and the Chiyoda Life between 1908 and 1913. In 1919, a large number of medical doctors established the Japan Doctors Kyosai Life, which was the last mutual life company before World War Two. Besides these small mutual life companies, a conscription insurance company was established as a mutual in 1923. In sum, the total number of mutual companies set up before World War Two was eight.

Except for conscription insurance, the Dai-ichi Life and the Chiyoda Life were the only successful mutual enterprises. The strategies of the two companies, however, were clearly different. The Chiyoda Life was established by alumni of the Keio School, whose founder was Yukichi Fukuzawa, a famous educator. The first president was Ikunoshin Kadono, a school master of the Keio. The Meiji Life had also been founded by pupils of Yukichi Fukuzawa. Since the Meiji Life established itself as a first mover in Japanese life assurance business, the Chiyoda found an opportunity to enter the market as a mutual by using the Keio network as well. As noted above, its sales strategy was more aggressive than that of the Dai-ichi Life. From the start, the Chiyoda increased its agencies rapidly and its business quickly grew. Consequently, the Chiyoda outstripped the Dai-ichi within just a few years of its foundation.

The Dai-ichi Life hesitated to create agency outlets because of the expense. Yano hoped that policyholders who were aware of their responsibility as members of the company would invite new recruits because they recognized the benefits of the company's life insurance products. Under the contemporary conditions of the Japanese market where it was difficult for consumers to compare and distinguish between insurance products on the basis of price, the mutual form was more advantageous in minimizing market contracting costs than the stock form of company. If this hypothesis is reasonable, however, the costs of a rapid growth of business could offset the benefit of market contracting costs; in other words, the benefit of selecting the mutual form.

Yano did not follow the aggressive sales strategy of the Chiyoda Life. He retained his prudent and cautious approach to the life assurance business, not because of his strong faith in the benefits of mutualism, but because of having an insight into the potential costs involved in selecting different corporate forms, in addition to his continued sense of responsibility with regard to insurance regulation. The experience of a small mutual company like the Kokko Life reveals the sagacity of Yano's approach. As Table 2.2 shows, after early years of rapid growth, the Kokko Life began to falter towards the end of the First World War and by the 1920s it was suffering a severe loss of market share. The heavy governance expenses associated with rapid growth meant that the company failed to take full advantage of its mutual form of organization. From the evidence of a manager of the Kokko Life, who wrote a memorandum on the troubles of the company at this time, it is clear that most of the company's difficulties arose from the costs of its governance.

In contrast, by the 1920s the success of the Dai-ichi Life had become clear. The pursuit of a strategy of being the best company rather than the biggest one gave it a good reputation in large cities. Its life products on the mutual principle were increasingly accepted by middle-class families. Urbanization in the 1920s also proved a favourable wind for the Dai-ichi Life. In the end, the Dai-ichi Life caught up the first movers and became one of the big five life insurers in Japan.

Table 2.2. Insurance in force of all mutual life assurance companies in Japan, 1903–27 (end-of-year results)

Year	Dai-ichi Life Policies	Dai-ichi Life ¥ insured	Chiyoda Life Policies	Chiyoda Life ¥ insured	Kokko Life Policies	Kokko Life ¥ insured	Tokai Life Policies	Tokai Life ¥ insured	Horai Life Policies	Horai Life ¥ insured
1903	886	1,105,000								
1904	1,850	2,311,300	3,013	2,611,300						
1905	2,691	3,710,000	7,710	6,589,700						
1906	3,385	5,230,600	12,470	11,343,200						
1907	4,344	6,903,100	17,973	16,669,000						
1908	5,377	8,680,433	23,789	22,449,650	1,612	1,319,500				
1909	6,221	10,369,372	29,379	28,527,770	5,294	3,855,700				
1910	7,367	12,760,021	34,504	34,828,330	9,596	6,706,900	4,510	3,728,000		
1911	9,849	17,561,450	40,363	42,728,920	15,226	10,105,100	18,456	12,636,700	1,532	1,621,500
1912	12,765	22,768,515	46,879	52,333,555	22,530	14,187,339	33,699	22,765,500	6,552	5,500,800
1913	16,991	27,785,877	52,261	60,583,983	33,226	20,070,356	48,997	33,679,056	13,823	10,453,400
1914	19,312	31,013,782	55,136	64,260,200	44,641	26,434,911	58,132	40,428,924	14,316	10,508,900
1915	20,355	32,132,994	55,054	64,579,422	48,031	28,209,069	52,935	37,085,403	12,331	9,089,000
1916	22,455	35,276,041	57,933	70,595,954	48,451	28,612,933	44,508	31,015,869	12,008	8,648,800
1917	26,310	41,347,041	67,887	85,941,078	51,748	30,617,955	48,955	31,351,101	12,927	9,133,914
1918	31,958	51,622,373	85,645	110,018,053	58,074	34,178,053	53,348	17,114,203	18,496	12,906,963
1919	42,661	70,595,890	104,854	138,669,605	72,426	42,243,665	58,093	41,176,096	25,378	18,074,798
1920	54,925	97,243,169	121,595	165,645,190	91,301	55,922,972	63,818	47,512,366	32,757	25,201,417
1921	68,879	125,609,803	136,173	192,854,731	102,964	65,352,623	69,604	54,003,236	35,645	27,314,190
1922	83,484	159,892,399	153,226	230,304,887	111,667	74,090,847	73,819	59,119,070	34,015	25,559,550
1923	98,905	195,137,039	167,334	264,718,631	108,664	74,632,816	75,482	61,554,131	34,421	26,592,230
1924	113,726	234,541,122	181,671	304,119,246	106,746	75,972,799	77,984	65,572,320	34,525	27,764,900
1925	137,496	297,551,941	208,182	372,268,773	119,050	92,023,524	81,079	69,693,911	38,010	31,832,695
1926	163,493	367,709,296	237,364	452,463,632	127,104	101,882,837	81,320	70,438,628	42,546	37,850,380
1927	194,716	452,071,503	263,933	534,006,865	127,430	103,209,023	78,810	68,132,082	41,942	38,334,148

Year	Chuo Life		Nihon Ishi Kyosai		Totals	
	Policies	¥ insured	Policies	¥ insured	Policies	¥ insured
1903					886	1,105,000
1904					4,863	4,922,600
1905					10,401	10,299,700
1906					15,855	16,573,800
1907					22,317	23,572,100
1908					30,778	32,449,583
1909					40,894	42,752,842
1910					55,977	58,023,251
1911					85,426	84,653,870
1912					122,425	117,555,709
1913	278	307,200			165,576	152,879,872
1914	2,089	1,806,700			193,626	174,451,417
1915	2,107	1,807,900			190,813	172,903,788
1916	6,272	5,038,000			191,627	179,187,597
1917	10,688	8,185,360			218,515	206,576,449
1918	15,736	12,248,953			263,257	238,088,598
1919	20,167	15,823,212	708	1,031,300	324,287	327,614,566
1920	24,937	20,022,792	4,527	6,685,500	393,860	418,233,406
1921	27,305	22,136,807	12,826	18,344,700	453,396	505,616,090
1922	32,180	26,770,270	20,603	29,625,100	508,994	605,362,123
1923	34,758	29,403,833	25,603	37,441,400	545,167	689,480,080
1924	36,638	31,505,180	31,434	45,507,800	582,724	784,983,367
1925	39,170	34,364,310	37,772	54,993,076	660,759	952,728,230
1926	40,722	35,930,639	44,875	68,870,443	737,424	1,133,145,855
1927	39,451	35,702,948	48,887	74,023,806	795,169	1,305,480,376

(*Continued*)

Table 2.2. Company shares of mutual totals (%) (Continued)

Year	Dai-ichi Life Policies	Dai-ichi Life ¥ insured	Chiyoda Life Policies	Chiyoda Life ¥ insured	Kokko Life Policies	Kokko Life ¥ insured	Tokai Life Policies	Tokai Life ¥ insured	Horai Life Policies	Horai Life ¥ insured	Chuo Life Policies	Chuo Life ¥ insured	Nihon Ishi Kyosai Policies	Nihon Ishi Kyosai ¥ insured
1903	100.0	100.0												
1904	38.0	47.0	62.0	53.0										
1905	25.9	36.0	74.1	64.0										
1906	21.3	31.6	78.7	68.4										
1907	19.5	29.3	80.5	70.7										
1908	17.5	26.8	77.3	69.2	5.2	4.1								
1909	15.2	24.3	71.8	66.7	12.9	9.0								
1910	13.2	22.0	61.6	60.0	17.1	11.6	8.1	6.4						
1911	11.5	20.7	47.2	50.5	17.8	11.9	21.6	14.9	1.8	1.9				
1912	10.4	19.4	38.3	44.5	18.4	12.1	27.5	19.4	5.4	4.7				
1913	10.3	18.2	31.6	39.6	20.1	13.1	29.6	22.0	8.3	6.8	0.2	0.2		
1914	10.0	17.8	28.5	36.8	23.1	15.2	30.0	23.2	7.4	6.0	1.1	1.0		
1915	10.7	18.6	28.9	37.3	25.2	16.3	27.7	21.4	6.5	5.3	1.1	1.0		
1916	11.7	19.7	30.2	39.4	25.3	16.0	23.2	17.3	6.3	4.8	3.3	2.8		
1917	12.0	20.0	31.1	41.6	23.7	14.8	22.4	15.2	5.9	4.4	4.9	4.0		
1918	12.1	21.7	32.5	46.2	22.1	14.4	20.3	7.2	7.0	5.4	6.0	5.1		
1919	13.2	21.5	32.3	42.3	22.3	12.9	17.9	12.6	7.8	5.5	6.2	4.8	0.2	0.3
1920	13.9	23.3	30.9	39.6	23.2	13.4	16.2	11.4	8.3	6.0	6.3	4.8	1.1	1.6
1921	15.2	24.8	30.0	38.1	22.7	12.9	15.4	10.7	7.9	5.4	6.0	4.4	2.8	3.6
1922	16.4	26.4	30.1	38.0	21.9	12.2	14.5	9.8	6.7	4.2	6.3	4.4	4.0	4.9
1923	18.1	28.3	30.7	38.4	19.9	10.8	13.8	8.9	6.3	3.9	6.4	4.3	4.7	5.4
1924	19.5	29.9	31.2	38.7	18.3	9.7	13.4	8.4	5.9	3.5	6.3	4.0	5.4	5.8
1925	20.8	31.2	31.5	39.1	18.0	9.7	12.3	7.3	5.8	3.3	5.9	3.6	5.7	5.8
1926	22.2	32.5	32.2	39.9	17.2	9.0	11.0	6.2	5.8	3.3	5.5	3.2	6.1	5.9
1927	24.5	34.6	33.2	40.9	16.0	7.9	9.9	5.2	5.3	2.9	5.0	2.7	6.1	5.7

CONCLUSIONS

Tsuneta Yano was in many respects quite unique as a top manager in Japanese business circles before the Second World War. His uniqueness was threefold. First, he engaged consistently in the life assurance business. From working as a medical practitioner for the Nippon Life, he went on to acquire expertise in almost every conceivable aspect of life assurance. Arguably, no one has accumulated more all-round experience than Yano in the history of life insurance in Japan. He was an insurance regulator, a medical practitioner, a founder and director of a major life insurance company, and a leading researcher of insurance statistics and actuarial science. Second, he was a versatile man. Besides his insurance jobs, he was a critic who wrote on Japanese society and culture and a bestselling author who penned an introductory book on the Analects of Confucius. His interests were very wide and he published many books and articles on subjects from the natural sciences to the humanities. Third, Yano was the only person at the time who advocated mutualism and also put it into practice in Japan. In addition to life assurance, he intended to introduce mutualism into the fire insurance, banking, and newspaper industries, although he failed in this regard, partly for legal reasons. He did, however, found the Dai-ichi Mutual Savings Bank, which paid dividends to depositors following the accrual of a surplus over a certain period. Indeed, Yano believed that this bank had built into its structure an important principle of mutualism.

Why was Yano eager to introduce mutual companies into Japanese business? Some Japanese intellectuals in this period had mixed feelings with regard to the emergence of Western socialism. Yano himself thought that the goal of social improvement was important, though he did not sympathize with socialism. With this goal in mind, the mutual form was attractive to him as a possible alternative to socialism. He was not, however, a mutualist on any kind of sentimental level, not least because he had learned the potential rationality of the mutual business form from his early career experience in Germany with the Gotha Life.

From his writings in the 1930s, it is clear that Yano was a supporter of the free market economy. In his essay on the French Revolution, for instance, he concluded that social equality was not the most important thing for the revolutionaries of that time, rather it was freedom that was their final goal.[29] Yano's rationalism was rooted in Confucianism. He never believed a superstition and was keen to dismantle the remnants of traditional ideas that had survived the Meiji Restoration. He learned the Analects of Confucius in his childhood, as many young students did in those times. Confucian thought has

---

[29] 'Equality and Freedom' (in Japanese), in Yano 1936, 17.

a character of pragmatism and it proved beneficial to the early stages of industrialization in Japan. Many business leaders were influenced by Confucian thought, the most famous being Ei-ichi Shibusawa.[30]

The key, therefore, to an understanding of Yano's thought is that he was not only a supporter of the free market economy, but also a Confucian pragmatist. He was eager to introduce the mutual form into business, because he believed that it might be efficient for all stakeholders. Ultimately he abandoned his attempt to establish a mutual fire insurance enterprise because he came to believe that it was not an efficient form of organization for the fire insurance business.[31]

What did Yano understand by the mutual form of business? As Yano was one of the key actors who introduced the mutual clauses into the Insurance Business Act of 1900, it was natural for the contemporary public to conclude that he was an advocate of mutualism in Japan. But this was not true. From the start of the Dai-ichi Mutual Life, Yano clearly explained what he considered to be the differences between mutual and stock companies in the sales pamphlets that he composed.[32] He did not conceal the demerits of the mutual company, for example, the possibility of the reduction of the value of a member's policy by *post-hoc* assessments to meet losses. In 1935 Yano gave a lecture at Meiji University. The text of the lecture provides a real insight into his understanding of the mutual company form. Although it is somewhat long, the following excerpt contains the key remarks.

> I am an old man behind the times, so I don't have to adhere to any very decisive views about the mutual company. I don't say that we mustn't do business corporations and that the mutual form is the best one for every type of business. Before everything else, I should say that I would have definitely selected the stock company form, if no stock company had been in existence in life assurance when I set out to promote a life assurance company. I would not like to publicize my doubts about the mutual company form, but I do hope that you are clear about the merits and demerits of both the mutual company and the stock company. I used to have a question about the superiority or inferiority of different corporate forms. Someone asked me once, do you think it is better to buy a life insurance product from a mutual company or a stock company? This is almost same question as asking which house is better to live in, the wooden house or the stone house? There are good and bad houses built of wood and the same is true for stone. The most important question is, is it a good house or not?[33]

---

[30] Shibusawa 1985.

[31] There is no definitive evidence to confirm this interpretation, but we can presume it from the surviving records of the Dai-ichi Mutual Fire project.

[32] There are still many sales pamphlets of the early Dai-ichi Mutual Life still in existence. Yano wrote every word in all the sales pamphlets from the early years of the company's business.

[33] 'Mutualism' (in Japanese), in Yano 1936, 299–300.

We can recognize Yano's pragmatic rationalism in this quotation. He consistently sought explanations of the differences between corporate forms and he was a consistent supporter of the free market economy. He concluded his lecture in the following way: 'Imagine the perfect ideal condition: I believe that commercially-based organizations are better than mutual companies and the member-based industrial unions . . . If traders and businessmen would make fair profits and deliver goods properly, I believe it is not necessary for us purposely to create such complicated organizations like mutual companies and voluntary unions.'[34] If Yano is regarded as a pure mutualist, these statements amount to a contradiction. His statements, however, make more sense if we see him both as a Confucian pragmatist and a supporter of the free market economy. It is certain that Yano was a Confucian rationalist by the 1900s. As for his faith in the free market, however, it is not clear whether or not he believed in this in his youth. This is something that might be resolved by further research.

Given the importance of Confucian rationalism to Yano's approach to the question of corporate forms, it is worth commenting on it a little further. Confucian rationalism was differed from Western rationalist thought, so it did indeed sometimes prove contradictory to the principles of modern business. Yano, like Shibusawa, was a typical Confucian rationalist. Shibusawa considered Confucian ethics important, yet kept mistresses. Yano supported monogamous marriage, but he understood the calling of geishas as part of Japanese traditional culture. In his business operations, Yano generally acted as a rational leading manager. For example, he preferred practical investments, with a focus on returns, to 'policy-oriented' or strategic investments that were aimed at promoting the company. Thus, arguably, he was more in tune with modern management practice. He was, however, often troubled when selecting full-time employees and in this one can also see aspects of his Confucianism pushing through. Although Yano thought that the hiring of workers through personal connections was not a rational way of proceeding, he sometimes reluctantly accepted such employment practices. His distress over this issue was revealed in an essay:

> I used to be troubled inwardly when selecting new employees every year, because I was placed in a dilemma between a sense of duty and my loyalty to the company. If a benefactor asked me to employ his relative, I would wish to repay his kindness as my moral responsibility. However, if I acted in this way, I would also throw away my responsibility as a public official. Loyalty and filial compliance are not compatible for me. How difficult my public life in the mutual company is![35]

---

[34] 'Mutualism' (in Japanese), in Yano 1936, 300.
[35] 'A Scream' (in Japanese), in Yano 1936, 348.

Although he often faced such dilemmas, his thinking on corporate form did not change throughout his business life. As noted above, in 2010 the Dai-ichi Mutual Life was converted into a joint-stock company under the stipulations of the Japanese Insurance Business Act. Did Yano really believe that 'commercially-based organizations are better than mutual companies'? What we can say is that he would not have rejected the conversion, because he recognized that the free market is predominant in the global economy.

3

Organizational Choice in UK Marine Insurance

Robin Pearson and Helen Doe

During the eighteenth and early nineteenth centuries there were three principal forms of organization in British marine insurance: individual underwriters working at Lloyd's or the outports, two large chartered corporations in London, and small mutual associations of shipowners in London and provincial ports. The two corporations, the Royal Exchange Assurance and the London Assurance, enjoyed monopoly privileges granted by the famous Bubble Act of 1720, by which no other stock companies or partnerships were permitted to write marine insurance. Other organizational vehicles were added when the Bubble Act was finally repealed in 1824, including new unincorporated joint-stock and mutual companies and new 'protection and indemnity' (P&I) clubs that evolved from the older shipowners' associations. The growth and internationalization of one of the P&I clubs, the Steamship Mutual Underwriting Association of 1909, is examined in the fourth section below.

At times the issue of what was the best organizational vehicle to deliver marine insurance became a hotly debated topic both within the industry and in parliament. The questions that this chapter addresses are: why did these different organizational forms emerge; what were the relative advantages and disadvantages that might explain their subsequent performance; and what conclusions can be drawn from this history that have relevance for organizational theory?

EARLY MARINE INSURANCE: FINDING SOLUTIONS TO THE PROBLEM OF ADVERSE SELECTION?

By 1700 maritime insurance had diffused from the Mediterranean to the Atlantic, Baltic, and North Sea routes and specialist communities of underwriters had emerged in northern Europe. Edward Lloyd's coffee house in London became the most important of several places where underwriters, brokers, and shippers exchanged the latest commercial news and did business. Lloyd's was the first coffee house systematically to collect intelligence on shipping movements and political developments affecting trading routes. Some information came from customers, some from runners employed by Lloyd's on the docks, some from correspondents paid to collect shipping news from English and foreign ports. Lloyd's also had an arrangement with the Post Office by which, in return for an annual fee, letters were delivered free of postage and sorted for collection by a Lloyd's messenger. From 1692 a weekly newspaper that collated the latest information relevant to brokers and merchants was issued by the coffee house, the forerunner to *Lloyd's List* (published from 1734).[1] These features of the early market indicate that good information was critical for the success of durable and large-scale marine underwriting. Maritime risks were extraordinarily heterogeneous, differing by type of ship, crew, route, sea currents, weather, and by political factors affecting the routes. The market was especially volatile during the Anglo-French wars of the 1690s and 1700s, when ships were vulnerable to attack by enemy navies, privateers, and pirates and when marine underwriting was subject to 'many frauds and deceits . . . to the great discouragement of the fair traders and navigation'.[2]

Notwithstanding such uncertainties, the market grew. In 1720 about 150 marine underwriters in London were joined by the two new stock corporations noted above.[3] In the months before their incorporation, the petitions of the two groups of promoters were met with counter-petitions from hundreds of merchants and underwriters in London and Bristol. The arguments reveal what contemporaries considered to be the advantages and disadvantages of different ways of organizing marine insurance at this time.[4] A corporation, the promoters claimed, offered three advantages over private underwriters: first, its large capital fund would provide greater security for merchants; second, it could offer lower premium rates; third, a corporation would make it easier for merchants to make claims, in so far as a law suit could be brought against one body in its corporate name, in contrast to the trouble and expense of suing each individual who might underwrite the policy at Lloyd's.

The counter petitioners argued, first, that the existing market arrangements provided marine insurance more efficiently and more cheaply than anywhere else, and that this attracted many foreign merchants to buy their insurance in

---

[1] McCusker 1991.

[2] Citing a merchants' petition to the English parliament in 1700 for a bill 'to prevent fraudulent insurance'. *Journal of the House of Commons* 13, 19 February 1700 – 4 April 1700. No details of the bill have been traced. The bill passed through three readings in the House of Commons but failed to win the final vote. On the impact of war on marine insurers in the 1690s, see Raynes 1948, 98–9.

[3] Estimate from Cockerell and Green 1994, 5.   [4] Raynes 1948, 102–3.

London. Second, a corporation would discourage brokers from seeking out persons of 'good substance' to underwrite policies. This would inevitably lead to a monopoly. As to the supposed superiority of a capital fund, the counter petitioners pointed out that a corporation 'has no sense of shame'. In other words, because it was answerable to its shareholders, it would not operate on the same basis of reputation and trust that underpinned the business of the private underwriters. Furthermore, the counter petitioners claimed that the real motives of the investor syndicates behind the petitions was to job stocks for their own personal gain, part of the wave of speculative promotions in 1719–20 that became the infamous South Sea Bubble.

In the end, charters were sold to the two insurance groups as part of Robert Walpole's plan to reduce Crown debt and a bill was passed to this effect. All other partnerships and stock companies were henceforth banned from doing marine insurance.[5] Thus the 'Bubble Act' gave the two London corporations a legal monopoly on corporate marine insurance until it was repealed in 1824. Shortly after the act was passed, the bubble burst. As their shares lost value, both corporations sought additional charters to permit them to write fire and life insurance, without monopoly rights. Table 3.1 indicates that marine insurance, although much more volatile than other lines (see the coefficients of variation), remained the staple business of both corporations through the rest of the century. Yet they probably never captured more than 10 per cent of British marine insurance at any time. In 1809 together they insured 3.8 per cent of the £162.5m insured. A further 14 per cent of marine insurance was written outside London, in English and Scottish ports. Lloyd's transacted most of the rest.[6]

Why did corporate competition not drive out the private underwriters as the latter had initially feared? Different and to some extent competing explanations have recently been offered. Kingston has argued that information asymmetries and agency problems inherent to contemporary overseas trade hold the answer.[7] Marine risks remained highly discrete, particular to one ship on one voyage with a specified route and cargo and often subject to deviations from the standard terms. The accurate evaluation of risk required reliable information about the reputation of the merchant applying for insurance, the condition and size of the vessel, the nature of the cargo, the expertise and character of the captain, the number and quality of the crew and armaments, sea and weather conditions en route, political conditions and the likelihood of war, the danger of capture by enemy ships, privateers, or pirates, and risk of

---

[5] Supple 1970, 30.

[6] Calculated from *Select Committee on Marine Insurance* 1810, report 6. Kingston has estimated that the average market share of the two corporations between 1800 and 1823 was just 6 per cent. Kingston 2007, 384.

[7] The following is based on Kingston 2007 and 2011.

Table 3.1. Marine and fire insurance premiums of the two London corporations, 1720–1819

Royal Exchange Assurance			London Assurance		
Gross premiums £ (annual averages rounded)			Premiums net of returns £ (annual averages rounded)		
	Marine	Fire		Marine	Fire
1761–5	36,000	10,700	1720–9	26,500	3,331
1766–70	18,400	14,700	1730–9	20,191	5,477
1771–5	23,000	19,200	1740–9	55,837	5,554
1776–80	76,500	20,300	1750–9	54,690	6,233
1781–5	116,500	29,100	1760–9	33,719	6,984
1786–90	73,900	28,800	1770–9	18,838	7,583
1791–5	155,200	45,800	1780–9	32,320	6,316
1796–1800	275,100	64,000	1790–9	52,241	6,901
1801–5	165,000	79,800	1800–9	56,420	8,251
1806–10	220,200	72,900	1810–19	128,454	8,878
SD	86,933	25,425	SD	31,979	1,576
CV	75.0	66.0	CV	66.7	24.1

Note: SD = standard deviation (£); CV = coefficient of variation (%). Gross marine premiums include returns. Supple 1970, table 3.1 states that the Royal Exchange's returns averaged just over 25 per cent of gross marine premiums in 1796–1815. Life assurance income was much smaller than fire or marine for both corporations until after 1800.

Sources: Supple 1970, 62, table 3.1, 61 n.2: London Metropolitan Archive, Ms 8735, London Assurance, Board of Directors' Minutes, 1721–1820; London Metropolitan Archive, Ms 8746A, London Assurance, Fire Assurance Annual Account, 1721–1854.

seizure while in a foreign port. Such discrete risks to be underwritten profitably required a good flow of information between merchant and insurer to minimize the problems of adverse selection and moral hazard. The latter could range from excessive risk taking by the insured to outright fraud, such as the deliberate wrecking of an insured ship, misrepresenting the value of cargoes, insuring the same goods or hulls more than once, or seeking to insure a ship already known to be lost.

Individual underwriters, who were often merchants themselves, were in a good position to evaluate information flows. Coffee houses and the brokers' offices in and around the Royal Exchange provided hubs for merchants and underwriters to exchange information about shipping movements, the supply of goods, issues with masters and crews, or political developments overseas. Regular flows of shipping intelligence from around the world were gathered in *Lloyd's List*, and later in *Lloyd's Register of Shipping* (established in 1760). Within Lloyd's, underwriters' specialization in particular routes enhanced the quality of information and risk assessment. As the link between merchants and underwriters, brokers had an important monitoring function that could enhance levels of trust. Reputable brokers could get policies written more quickly and cheaply than others, so merchants valued their relationship with them. The credit mechanism provided another metric by which trust could be measured. Underwriters often gave brokers a year or more to collect the premiums from their clients, while in turn brokers granted credit to merchants. Brokers received percentage shares of premium income and net underwriting profits as their customary fee, so they had an interest in this credit system. It was also in the underwriter's interest to maintain a credit balance with the broker, for if a loss should occur a proportion of it would fall on the broker. Thus, all market players had incentives to avoid acting opportunistically and to maintain a reputation for prudence and honesty. In sum, underwriters developed formal and informal institutions that helped to mitigate the problems of asymmetric information, agency, and transaction costs that accompanied overseas trade.

The capital funds of the stock corporations were no substitute for good information. According to Kingston, asymmetric information problems outweighed the greater security provided by large capital resources. The best risks insured with the private underwriters who charged lower premiums than the corporations because they were better placed to recognize risk quality. This left the corporations with poorer risks, forcing them to raise their premium rates, which in turn induced more of the better risks to go to Lloyd's. The market, therefore, was characterized by multiple equilibria, where the better risks were insured by private underwriters at lower rates, while corporations charged higher rates for worse risks. The corporations were also less informed. They were not allowed to write lines on Lloyd's policies, so they had to issue their own policies with their own terms and conditions. Moreover, their underwriters did not interact on a daily basis with those at Lloyd's and did not benefit from their social and business networks.

Leonard has challenged this view.[8] He claims that 'opportunities for knowledge shortfalls' were 'limited' in the small and well-informed London marine insurance market of the eighteenth century, where 'information was as complete as perhaps is possible'. At least one of the London corporations subscribed to the Lloyd's publications—a point that Kingston also makes—and regular interaction between the corporations and brokers operating in Lloyd's would have minimized any information disadvantages that the former may have laboured under.[9] According to Leonard, the principal reason for the corporations failing to capture a larger share of the marine insurance market was their cautious risk selection and high pricing policy, reflecting their 'limited appetite for marine risk'.[10]

---

[8] Leonard 2013, 52-3.   [9] Kingston 2007, n.71.

[10] Leonard has subsequently conceded that there may have been a 'lemons' problem in marine insurance, but insists that the corporation's pricing policy was the more important factor in shaping the market. Personal communication, Adrian Leonard to Robin Pearson, 21 January 2014.

We cannot be absolutely sure of the reasoning behind the corporations' approach to marine insurance—the records of both corporations were extensively destroyed by fires in 1748 and 1838. Nevertheless, it seems that the corporations did become more conservative in their marine underwriting over time. Their premiums were 20 to 30 per cent higher than Lloyd's by the end of the eighteenth century. Following several frauds, they became reluctant to insure cross risks—ships sailing between two foreign ports—and they refused to cover the risk of seizure in a foreign port. They placed low ceilings on the amount they would insure on a single risk, restricted the deviations permitted from the planned routes of ships they insured, and made a greater fuss about establishing the identity of claimants after a loss. Such lack of flexibility appears to have pushed merchants to insure at Lloyd's. Because Lloyd's captured a large part of the market, this further discouraged the corporations from raising their acceptance limits. Evidence of cautious underwriting and a high pricing policy, however, does not necessarily undermine the argument that the corporations suffered under asymmetric information problems of the type that Kingston identifies. If information flows in the London market were as perfect as Leonard claims, and eighteenth-century shipping as predictable, presumably there would have been little need for Lloyd's to invest in the *List* and the *Register* and an expanding network of agents in overseas ports. Presumably also the corporations would have been able to charge lower— not higher—premiums for their carefully selected risks. As Table 3.1 indicates, however, the corporations' appetite for marine insurance risks was not so 'limited' that it precluded these from becoming by far the largest part of their business. While some merchants may have purposefully chosen to pay higher rates for insuring their quality risks with the corporations because of the perceived security of their capital, it is not improbable that the corporations also, inadvertently, picked up some lower-quality risks that could not find cheaper insurance in Lloyd's. At the same time, some of the poorer risks also appear to have been accepted at Lloyd's if they were bundled up by brokers with better quality insurances. A witness to the Select Committee on Marine Insurance of 1810 argued that the greater opportunity to insure inferior risks at Lloyd's also attracted most of the better risks to Lloyd's, as brokers knew that the former would only be accepted by underwriters in conjunction with the latter.[11]

Legal developments also likely played a role in shaping the organizational structure of marine insurance by reducing the risks and costs of insuring with the private underwriters. First, the principle of insurable interest was enshrined in statute in 1746 after mounting concern about marine insurance

---

[11] Cited by Supple 1970, 189.

frauds.[12] Second, Lord Mansfield, Chief Justice of King's Bench 1754–88, developed the principle of 'utmost good faith' as the basis of all insurance contracts. In a series of judgements Mansfield tried to remove the dangers of concealment and misrepresentation and to eliminate the legal requirement for the insured to bring an action against each individual underwriter separately in the event of a disputed claim.[13] Lloyd's also benefited from the exclusive privileges of the corporations, which prevented other stock companies from entering the market. The ban on marine reinsurance imposed by the 1746 statute drove the market towards coinsurance, the basis of underwriting at Lloyd's. The lack of a reinsurance facility restricted the capacity of the corporations to accept the larger risks. For shipowners who wanted as much cover as they could get, the high transaction costs of taking out one policy with one of the corporations, and then searching for the remaining cover elsewhere, seems to have been a disincentive for many, if they could get all their insurance needs more easily and more cheaply through a broker at Lloyd's.

During the American and French wars in the final quarter of the century demand for marine insurance rose. The number of subscribers at Lloyd's rose from 179 in 1775 to over 2,000 by 1801.[14] This expansion accelerated the development of formal institutions at Lloyd's. A standard policy form was introduced in 1779 and a method of claims settlement was developed to ensure that losses were promptly paid by brokers. The previously ad-hoc Lloyd's committee began to produce annual reports from 1796. New corresponding agents were appointed, 269 of them by 1820. A deed of association was drawn up in 1811 to formalize the committee's powers and responsibilities, which included the right to elect subscribers and to represent the underwriters as a group. These institutional changes helped secure Lloyd's as a world centre for marine insurance.

SHIPOWNERS' MUTUAL ASSOCIATIONS: THE PRIMACY OF RISK SELECTION

During the late eighteenth century a number of mutual shipping insurance associations, or 'hull clubs', were organized by shipowners among collier and fishing fleets of the northeast and southwest and in the London timber and coal trades.[15] Having no capital and no transferrable shares ensured that they

---

[12] *Journal of the House of Commons* 19 Geo. II, 1746, *c.* 37; and see the debate on marine insurance in the *Journal of the House of Commons* 14 Geo. II, 1740, 180–200.

[13] Raynes 1948, 163–4; Oldham 2004, 174.   [14] Kingston 2007, 389.

[15] See, for example, the advertisement in 1785 for a new mutual shipping insurance society in North Shields, *Newcastle Courant* 11 June 1785.

did not fall foul of the corporations' monopoly. Raynes suggests that there were about twenty such associations around 1800, including several in Sunderland, Whitby, Shields, and Newcastle. They averaged about eighty to 100 members, all owners or part-owners of one or more ships.[16] It is probable, therefore, that these mutual associations evolved from, or were directly influenced by, the customary fractional shareholding form of shipownership that was later regulated by maritime law. Under this system each ship was held to be a separate enterprise divided into a number of transferable shares.[17] Each share owner was regarded as a joint-adventurer or 'tenant-in-common'. Thus, they had a closer and more direct relationship with their asset than was generally the case with shareholders in ordinary stock companies. The majority of owners were actively involved in the trades that their ships undertook, often appointing a manager, or 'ship's husband', from among their own ranks.[18] Forming an insurance club together with other local owners to cover their risks and handle claims may have been a natural extension of the business of shipownership for many.

Some associations had rules stating that if membership fell below twenty, they would automatically dissolve.[19] Some fixed a term for their business, for example twenty-one years in the case of the associations in North and South Shields. They usually elected a committee each year to manage their affairs, insured only hulls, and issued twelve-month policies, balances being settled at the annual meeting of members.[20] The system was therefore geared to coastal and short-sea trades, where multiple voyages could be made within a year, rather than to long-distance ocean shipping. Indeed, the associations in Shields excluded the winter months between November and February from their cover because of the icing up of the Baltic Sea.[21]

---

[16] The Unanimous Association of South Shields, established in 1786, had ninety-one members by 1794. The London Union Society of 1803, also in the coal trade, had around eighty members in 1810, insuring about 100 ships. The Unanimous Association for the Mutual Insurance of their Ships, *Articles of Agreement, 3 January 1791* (South Shields, 1794); Raynes 1948, 186–7.

[17] A maximum of sixty-four shares and thirty-two owners per ship was fixed by the Registry Act, 4 Geo. IV, 1823, *c.* 41, but before this, and even after the legislation, a remarkable range of different fractions were used. See Jarvis 1959. For the relationship between this form of ownership and the earliest joint-stock companies in UK shipping, see Freeman et al. 2007. Boyce 1992 shows how the 64th system and private capital, raised through local networks, continued to characterize the finance of shipping companies into the early twentieth century.

[18] Freeman, Pearson and Taylor 2007, 577–8; Doe 2013.

[19] The Union Association for the Mutual Insurance of their Ships, *Articles of Agreement, 12 January 1786* (North Shields, 1790).

[20] Some mutual associations for cargo insurance, however, were also established. Cf. *Copy of Articles of the Tyne Cargo Insurance, established in North Shields, May 28th 1799* (North Shields: W. Kelley, 1799).

[21] Echoes of this practice can be found in today's P&I clubs—discussed below in the fourth section—where the underwriting year and club membership begins on 20 February, the traditional date for the opening of the Baltic Sea.

The constitutions of most associations contained provisions for monitoring the quality of risks insured. Members were admitted by election and had to 'enter an interest . . . nowhere else insured' in ships or parts of ships to a given value, for example £800 in the case of the Union Association of North Shields, £1,400 in the Unanimous Association of South Shields. All ships proposed for insurance had to be of a minimum value—£1,000 in North Shields, £1,800 in South Shields. In the latter association ships had also to be 'British built . . . and not trading from Sunderland'. Inferior and badly built vessels were not accepted and an annual inspection of insured ships was carried out. Any repair and maintenance work required had to be carried out within a given period, or members faced expulsion and a loss of cover. Details of the vessels insured—size, value, master's name—were entered into a register and attested by the member concerned and the managing committee. Ships engaging in 'unlawful' or contraband trades were excluded, as were ships in the Greenland trade, or ships 'when carrying stones, rock, salt, or iron ore, or when lying on the main shore'. Vessels going to the East and West Indies were required to be 'sheathed' (against worms), or their insurance was void. In wartime there were further stipulations about the number of cannon to be carried and sailing in convoys.[22]

There were also limits to the cover provided—£700 in North Shields, £1,200 in South Shields. Thus, members had to carry a significant amount of self-insurance, 30 and 33 per cent respectively. Later the general rule was to confine insurance to three quarters of the value of a hull. Expenses and losses were met from a central fund accumulated from the annual subscriptions of members, which were proportionate to the sum insured. Not all associations were clear about the liability of individual members, but in North Shields they were liable to pay for losses in proportion to the number or parts of ships they had insured, and members failing to meet their share of calls to cover losses were expelled. Measures were also taken to offset the dangers of multiple losses within a short period, which was a device to reduce any moral hazard in the case of a member insuring more than one ship. In both the Shields associations, when two or more ships were lost within a forty-eight-hour period, the victims were required to contribute to each other's losses in proportion with the other members. Other regulations to contain moral hazard and minimize adverse selection include proscriptions against deliberate overinsurance and attempts to parcel up different levels of risk within the association and to ring-fence the most risky members.[23]

The main concern of these mutuals, therefore, was not market competition, but to maximize the effectiveness of risk selection and monitoring of moral

---

[22] Unanimous Association, *Articles of Agreement, 3 January 1791*, appendix: bye-law 18 February 1793.
[23] Union Association, *Articles of Agreement*, bye-law 8 January 1789.

hazard for the benefit of the membership as a whole. Their system of underwriting presented few organizational problems. Administrative costs were low—no agents were employed or commission paid. It was fairly easy for committee members personally involved in shipping to identify bad risks and false claims and this, together with low overheads, allowed the associations to provide cheaper cover than could be obtained at Lloyd's. In 1809 the secretary of the London Union estimated that, once all losses had been paid, the cost of insurance to their members was about 5 guineas per cent, compared to the usual Lloyd's rate of 9 guineas per cent for similar ships in the coal trade.[24] Despite their exclusions, the insurances offered by the associations were also more comprehensive than those issued at Lloyd's. Collision at sea, for instance, was normally covered, but not by Lloyd's. This was a prime benefit for those in the coastal trades, where the risk of collision was much higher than in ocean shipping.

It is uncertain how many shipowners in the provincial coal and fishing trades sought out Lloyd's or the stock corporations to obtain insurance. The London Assurance Corporation had agents in Newcastle between 1769 and 1784 and Whitby from 1780 to 1789, but they mostly insured property against fire, including ships in dock.[25] It was said that one of the London mutuals, the Friendly Insurance, established in 1804, 'arose from several gentlemen thinking it better to insure as is the practice in the north of England in clubs than go to the Coffee house', which implies that some comparison took place between the different systems of underwriting to hand.[26] With their small specialist field of insurance and localized area of operations, however, the mutual associations probably did not represent much of a threat to Lloyd's or the corporations. Although they were cheaper than these alternative suppliers of insurance, their survival depended above all on careful selection based on local knowledge and small pools of risk, so that the limits to their growth remained narrow. Their tight quality controls over members and ships were less practical in larger organizations.

THE NEW MARKET STRUCTURE AFTER 1824

After 1800 Lloyd's and the chartered corporations came under sustained attack, the former for the alleged inadequacy of their capital reserves, the latter for their monopoly privileges. The promoters of two new joint-stock projects led the attack. They claimed that the supply of marine insurance in the UK had failed to keep pace with the expansion of trade and that business

---

[24] Raynes 1948, 187.   [25] Pearson 2004, 105.   [26] Cited by Raynes 1948, 187.

was moving away from London to new companies being formed abroad. Large new corporations and repeal of the monopoly were needed to attract insurance back to Britain.[27] In response, representatives of Lloyd's claimed that the promoters were merely seeking to set up a new monopoly and lacked the expertise to write marine insurance. Echoing Adam Smith, they also argued that marine insurance could not be reduced to a routine, like fire or life insurance, and therefore was not generally suitable for joint-stock companies.[28]

The House of Commons appointed a committee to consider the arguments. It reported that the monopoly had worked to the benefit of both Lloyd's and the corporations, and unfairly had prevented the merchants of outports from associating legally. The committee concluded that the best mode of insurance was that which delivered the best security at the lowest price, and that free trade was most likely to deliver this. It recommended that the monopoly be repealed and the business thrown open to a range of suppliers: partnerships, companies, private underwriters, and mutual associations. A bill to this effect, however, provoked a hostile response from the corporations, underwriters, brokers, shipowners, and City merchants, and was defeated in the Commons, narrowly, in 1811.[29]

Nevertheless, with the abolition of other monopolies such as the East India Company in 1813 and the Bank of Ireland in 1821, political opinion was swinging decisively towards free trade. In 1824, during the next wave of company promotions, the founders of the Alliance British and Foreign Fire and Life Assurance Company petitioned for repeal in order to be allowed to write marine insurance. Counter-petitions were lodged by the two corporations, by Lloyd's, and by underwriters at Hull and Newcastle. Despite this support for vested rights, the repeal bill was passed. Following the abolition of the corporations' monopolies, several new marine insurance companies were formed, but they entered a depressed market and some of the smaller ventures did not survive for long.[30]

It was not, therefore, obvious that the joint-stock company, operating in a market free of monopoly restrictions, was the natural successor to the private underwriter or the mutual association. The debate about the optimal organizational form for marine insurance continued beyond repeal.[31] Underwriters at Lloyd's, for instance, claimed that the low proportion of capital actually paid

[27] Raynes 1948, 191–2.

[28] Anon 1813; Anon 1811. For the opposition of Lloyd's members, see the account of their general meeting, *Caledonian Mercury* 30 June 1810.

[29] Raynes 1948, 193–8.

[30] E. S. Roscoe, 'The Progress of Marine Insurance in England', *Fraser's Magazine* 1877, 707–19.

[31] Cf. Anon, 'On the Most Preferable Plan of Ship Insurance', *Newcastle Magazine* 10, January 1831, 14–18.

up in stock companies meant that the latter provided little security to the insured. By contrast the underwriters staked the whole of their property and were fully liable for losses. They were particularly keen to ensure that shareholders in the new companies did not benefit from limited liability, so that competition would be on a level playing field.[32]

Some thought that a hybrid form of organization combining features of the stock and mutual systems would be optimal for marine insurance. The Indemnity Marine, for example, was originally planned as a mutual company in 1824 but its promoters had second thoughts.[33] A revised prospectus noted that a lack of capital could lead to 'inconvenience and delay' before losses could be covered through a levy on members, and that a stock company could overcome this problem. The company plan, therefore, was restructured to comprise the 'mutual insurance of merchandise as well as ships', but with a capital of £5m in 50,000 shares, with compulsory insurance for shareholders, and profits to be distributed on the basis of number of shares held and premiums paid. This hybrid form of mutual membership with a capital stock, however, did not work out well. The take up of shares was poor, managers found it difficult to vet applicants for shares, and bad debts, bankrupt shareholders, and rising losses at sea forced the company to make further demands on the unpaid proportion of members' shares. In 1827 a new chairman identified the mutual element as the chief cause of the problems. Shareholders' obligation to insure was ended, the office was fully opened to the public and recovery followed. By 1832 the Indemnity Marine was insuring more on ships and cargoes than the venerable London Assurance Corporation.

The shipowners' mutuals survived the emergence of new mutual and joint-stock companies after 1824 but they often found themselves overloaded with older ships, while newer vessels were insured at Lloyd's and the new companies. Some went out of business. Others began to cover excess collision and other types of liability that were excluded by Lloyd's policies, giving rise to a new marine liability insurance sector that became big business in the twentieth century.[34] The development of mutual 'protection and indemnity' insurance clubs is examined in the following section.

The private underwriting system also survived, and even expanded in outports such as Liverpool, Bristol, Hull, and Glasgow. Growing numbers of brokers and marine insurance companies could also be found in overseas ports in Europe, North America, India, China, South-East Asia, and the West Indies. Underwriters in the major outports often took slices of larger or more difficult marine risks not fully covered by their counterparts at Lloyd's or by the London corporations. By 1860 the Liverpool Underwriters' Association

---

[32] *Morning Chronicle* 19 May 1824.   [33] The following is based on Palmer 1984.
[34] Morris 1956.

consisted of eleven Lloyd's-type syndicates with nearly 300 private under-writers. Beginning that year, private underwriting partnerships began to join forces to launch stock companies that gradually replaced the syndicates in Liverpool.[35] The first of these companies, the Thames and Mersey, was launched in 1860 with a nominal capital of £2m, 20 per cent paid up. Its 100,000 shares were distributed in a fixed ratio to investors in London, Liverpool, and Manchester, although within a few decades the majority of shares found their way back to the northwest. The company operated local management boards in the three cities and appointed overseas agents in India, the Far East, Australia, and the US. By 1877 the Thames and Mersey was Britain's largest marine insurance company with a premium income of £310,000.[36] Other new stock companies followed, mainly in Liverpool and London, profiting from the huge transfer of US marine insurance to the UK during the American Civil War. By the 1870s there were several dozen companies underwriting marine insurance, together accounting for perhaps 40 per cent of the UK market.[37]

The economic conditions of the 1870s and 1880s, with the slowdown in international trade, the lower premium rates required for steamships, and the competition from the new companies that pooled information and standard-ized practice in trade associations—notably the Institute of London Under-writers founded in 1884—made life tougher for the private underwriters. Lloyd's responded by embracing regulatory and organizational change. It was incorporated by an act of parliament in 1871, though this did not remove the personal liability of its members for losses. Deposits and guarantees became compulsory for members to help safeguard against underwriting failures. The number of members and the average size of syndicates increased. Broking firms became larger, managing a growing volume of business through agencies in Britain and abroad. Lloyd's also diversified into new lines, such as loss of profits, burglary, trade credit, earthquake, hurricane, motor, and aviation insurance.[38] At the same time the newer stock companies and the two old London corporations experienced falling profits and dividends.[39] Between 1900 and 1920 across the industry there was a wave of mergers and acquisi-tions that left a smaller number of large composite companies writing multiple lines. These composites came to dominate the UK corporate market for insurance for the next fifty years. The result was that few specialist marine insurance companies remained in Britain by the second quarter of the twen-tieth century.

---

[35] The final private marine underwriting firm in Liverpool ceased business in 1908. Anon 1960, 27–8.
[36] Anon 1960, 40.   [37] Raynes 1948, 316–23.   [38] Pearson 2006; Brown 1980.
[39] The average annual net marine insurance premiums of the Royal Exchange Assurance, for instance, fell from £528,533 in 1856–60 to £114,058 by 1886–90. Supple 1970, 205, 258–9.

THE P&I CLUBS: NETWORKS AND INNOVATION

As noted above, from the 1850s mutual 'protection and indemnity' (P&I) clubs emerged to cover other risks in UK marine insurance. While the existing mutual associations generally only insured hulls, and the stock companies only hulls and cargoes, the new P&Is offered cover for a different range of shipowners' liabilities. Several factors appear to have been behind this development.[40] First, there was the growing public debate in Britain about accidents, injuries, and loss of life on railways and emigrant ships. This was accompanied by a raft of legislation. The Passenger Acts of 1842 and 1847 and the Steam Navigation Act of 1846 stipulated the liability of shipowners, charterers, and masters for the construction and seaworthiness of their vessels, the provision of lifeboats, fire hoses, ship lights, fog horns, the condition of machinery (in the case of steamships), the lighting and ventilation of passenger decks, the quality of food on board, and the storage of gunpowder. Fines of up to £100 for owners and £50 for masters were specified for breach of these regulations through 'wilful neglect or negligence', or three months in prison if fines were not paid. Shipowners were required to return ticket money and pay compensation to their passengers for any avoidable delay or cancellation of voyages, while passengers maintained the right to take out private lawsuits against masters and owners for injury or loss of life or property.[41] An amendment act of 1852 stipulated that passengers' insurance of their passage money was not invalidated by any liabilities imposed on owners and masters by this legislation.[42] Furthermore, the Fatal Accidents Act of 1846, which was aimed at, but did not exclusively specify, railway companies, declared that a right of action at common law should not be entirely lost by the death of the person injured by the 'wrongful act, neglect or default' of the defendant, as had previously been the case.[43] Henceforth, the close relatives of a deceased plaintiff, or executors on their behalf, could sue to recover compensation to the extent of their financial loss.

Further legislation and judicial rulings increased the range of liabilities to which shipowners were subjected. For instance, the Harbours, Docks and Piers Clauses Act of 1847 gave harbour authorities the power to recover for damage done to port infrastructure by shipping, and for the cost of wreck removal.[44] Before 1870 liability for lost cargoes could be avoided by writing an appropriate exemption clause in the bill of lading, but a court ruling of that year, involving a ship lost off the Cape, held the shipowner liable, because the

---

[40] Ledwith et al. 1957, 4–5.
[41] 5 and 6 Vict. 1842, *c.* 107; 9 and 10 Vict. 1846, *c.* 100; 10 and 11 Vict. 1847, *c.* 103. For contemporary concerns outside parliament about safety at sea, see Jennings 1843, 1844.
[42] 15 and 16 Vict. 1852, *c.* 44, clause 51.　　　[43] 9 and 10 Vict. 1846, *c.* 93.
[44] 10 and 11 Vict. 1847, *c.* 27, clauses 74–5.

cargo had been carried beyond its destination and the exemption clauses in the bill of lading did not cover that eventuality.[45]

Various merchant shipping acts from 1894 also increased the statutory responsibilities of shipowners with regard to the illness and repatriation costs of their seamen. The Workmen's Compensation Act of 1906 extended this to groups of seamen and stevedores previously omitted. During the twentieth century such pressures increased with further crew liabilities, cargo claims, and the complications of new forms of transport. After the Second World War international law also paid greater attention to ship-owners' liability issues, most notably in relation to the environmental risks resulting from oil tanker wreckages and the carriage of nuclear materials and other dangerous cargoes.

Some factors alleviated shipowners' liability for these various risks. During the nineteenth century any damages awarded by a court following a suit at common law were, apparently, subject to a deduction by the value of any other relief that the victim had received, including any sums paid out from insurance policies.[46] This deduction was finally abolished by the Fatal Accidents (Damages) Act of 1908, which stipulated that 'any sum payable on death under any contract of insurance should not be taken into account in assessing damages'.[47] The Merchant Shipping Act of 1854 also limited the risk exposure of shipowners in various ways, for instance, by stipulating that no owner was liable to make good any loss or damage to goods on board by fire or theft 'that may occur without his actual fault or privity of', and by restricting liability for damages, injury and loss of life to the value of the ship and freight.[48]

Nevertheless, the Victorian debate about safety at sea, and the legislation that accompanied it, instigated a fundamental change to the liability environment for mariners and shipowners and had a long-term impact on the UK insurance industry. First, it led to the formation of several new personal accident insurance companies by the early 1850s, including in marine insurance.[49] Second, shipowners' liability for third-party risks became a promising new field to develop. Managers of the mutual hull associations were aware that

---

[45] Ledwith et al. 1957, 5.

[46] Although there were exceptions, such as insurance against the loss of money paid for passenger tickets. See note 42 above.

[47] 8 Edw. VII 1908, *c.* 7, cited by Raynes 1948, 285. It should be noted that the 1849 incorporating act of the most important of the early accident insurance companies, the Railway Passengers Assurance Company, placed it in a privileged position, because it provided that in no circumstances should any sum payable under its policies be applied in relief of damages awarded against a negligent party. The fact that this was a special clause in an act suggests that the common law default was for such insurance sums to be deducted from court-awarded compensation. Dinsdale 1954, 63.

[48] 17 and 18 Vict. 1854, *c.* 104, part IX.

[49] Some of these companies also offered luggage insurance to ship passengers. Dinsdale 1954, 274 n. 3.

in their traditional field they were getting the older and more hazardous risks and thus were in danger of going out of business from competition by Lloyd's and the stock companies. From the 1850s several of them formed new mutual clubs offering protection and indemnity insurance to their members on a familiar not-for-profit basis.[50] Some clubs covered hulls as well, a class of insurance that they inherited from the older associations. P&I clubs, like many of the mutual associations, did not issue individual policies.[51] Members joined for the year, supplied details of the risk they wished to insure, paid a contribution, known as an 'advanced call' calculated at the beginning of each insurance year, and agreed to abide by the club's rules and be liable for supplementary calls to meet any future losses.[52] Faced with an increasing range of liabilities, and driven in part by the new type of consumer protection legislation, shipowners turned to the P&I clubs for their insurance cover. Generally the new P&I clubs did not compete with Lloyd's underwriters or the stock companies. Some catered for the needs of liner and tramp owners and some covered particular trades, such as trawler owners operating out of Fleetwood.

By the end of the nineteenth century P&I was a well-established sector of the marine insurance industry. Liabilities, however, were getting larger, driven by the growth in the size of ships and the increase in new risks such as bulk oil tankers. In 1899 the first pooling agreement was drawn up between six British clubs, whereby large claims on one club in excess of a certain sum were shared, proportionate to their size, among all the member clubs.[53] The pool, later known as the London Group, also set up reinsurance facilities with other UK and foreign clubs that were not members of the pool. In this way the P&I clubs were able to offer unlimited cover on most risks, via coinsurance and excess loss reinsurance contracts. The same principle of mutuality underpinned the pool as it did the individual clubs. It only worked if smaller losses were retained by the insuring member, and if the risks shared across the pool were similar. Member clubs also agreed not to bring to the pool losses from new risks, hitherto excluded, that had occurred by a change of club rules. Indeed, the pooling system ensured that changes to clubs' liabilities resulting

---

[50] The first such club was the Shipowners' Mutual Protection Society, founded in 1855 and still operating today as the Britannia.

[51] Some mutuals appeared to have just kept lists of ships. Sometimes these were entered directly in the association rule book. Cf. 'A List of Ships entered in the Exeter Shipping Insurance Association' (1844), reproduced in Craig et al. 1994, 100. However, some association rule books also referred to the issue of policies. Cf. *Rules of the Gloucester & Severn Estuary Mutual Marine Insurance Society Limited*, Gloucester, 1904. The extent of either practice in the mutual marine insurance sector remains unclear.

[52] The amount of the 'advanced call' was based on an estimate made by the club's managers of the total income required for the next insurance year and the proportion of that income that each member should pay for his/her vessels, expressed as a rate per tonne.

[53] Young 1995, 20–5.

from their insurance of new risks such as containerized cargoes, the use of helicopters for pilotage, or the pollution prevention costs of salvage operators, had to be agreed by all pool members, or else the risks would not be covered by the pool.[54]

The history of the last British P&I club to be established, the Steamship Mutual (SSM) of 1909, helps reveal the factors that led to the growth and internationalization of this little studied organizational form in marine insurance.[55] Typically, the SSM originated with a small hull club in the West of England, the Gloucester and Severn Estuary Mutual Marine Insurance Society. In 1906 the leaders of the latter incorporated the Sailing Ship Mutual Insurance Association, through which the SSM later reinsured. The Sailing Ship Mutual insured mostly small wooden sailing vessels in the UK coastal trade and was established in response to liabilities arising from the Workmen's Compensation Act.[56] In the early years both clubs were jointly managed. The prime movers were two shipowners from Gloucester, together with a shipbroker, Lionel Sage, and a marine lawyer, Alfred Stocken. The managers were part time and the club advertised the club committee's expertise in coastal shipping as a means of attracting subscribers.[57] As in other small clubs, the committee, or later 'board', members personally examined ships subject to claims, rather than appointing a permanent surveyor.[58]

Part of Sage's early tactics in expanding the SSM was to target small mutual clubs and point out the advantages of belonging to a larger organization, which included greater capital resources, a broader pooling of risks, and quicker loss adjustment for members. Although the business acquired in this way was not all P&I insurance, the targeting of the smaller sailing ship clubs, as well as members of other mutual steamship P&I clubs, helped expand the new organization.[59]

By 1919 the club's business remained firmly focused on British coastal ships and estuarine barges carrying coal, bricks, and other low-value cargoes.[60] Sage gave up his management role, apparently to concentrate on brokerage, and Stocken appointed another shipbroker, John Plincke, to fill his place. Managerial sclerosis, however, gradually became a problem. As the SSM and other clubs became larger, their management functions grew and became more complex, requiring full-time employees with specialist experience. Managers became organized into separate organizations, usually taking the form of partnerships, contracted to provide a range of services to the club. In the

[54] Ledwith et al. 1957, 28–40.   [55] Doe 2009.
[56] Under the act, those seamen previously excluded from employee protection legislation could henceforth sue sailing shipowners for injuries received at work.
[57] Steamship Mutual Archives, Steamship Insurance Management Services Ltd, London, Sailing Ship Mutual booklet *c.* 1906; Doe 2009, 17 .
[58] SSM, Sailing ship committee meeting minutes, June 1912.   [59] Doe 2009, 19.
[60] SSM, Steamship minutes, June 1925.

case of the SSM, this was Alfred Stocken and Co (Managers) Ltd. Furthermore, there had always been a regular rotation of chairmen at the SSM, but this changed in 1923 when Abbie Anderson became chairman of the club. Anderson had joined the SSM in 1912, when it had acquired his own mutual club in the Whitstable coal trade. He commenced a reign as chairman that only ended with his death in 1950. Anderson's impact was to slow down innovation and to preserve an amateur approach to business. He was also determined to cling to power. As late as 1949 a special resolution allowed him to stay on in his post beyond the age of seventy-two. He died six months later, however, and the management committee then unanimously agreed to rotate the chairmanship every three years.[61]

It was a conservative environment, therefore, which Sydney Crowe entered when he joined Alfred Stocken and Co as a clerk in 1931. Crowe eventually became a partner and he transformed the club into a major international P&I insurer. Crowe's first gambit was in 1936, when, thanks to his friendship with a young fleet owner, Jack Billmeir, the SSM captured the business of large vessels carrying cargoes to and from Republican Spain. It was a risky step into the ocean maritime insurance market with a new and untried shipowner, but it paid off. After the Second World War, Crowe returned from naval service to become the senior full-time manager and by 1950 Anderson was no longer there to block his initiatives. The market had also changed. Britain no longer had the largest merchant fleet, but those of the US, Australia, Canada, and India had expanded while European countries had begun to rebuild their fleets.[62] This presented opportunities that Crowe and managers at the other UK clubs seized vigorously.[63] In 1948–49 Crowe gained personal introductions to German shipowners and managed to insure five vessels belonging to the DG Neptun Line of Bremen. Other British clubs were also successful in acquiring German business that before the war had been insured by the Norwegian P&I club Skuld. The SSM also wrote the P&I insurance of surplus American Liberty ships that had found their way into foreign merchant fleets after the war and, following the appointment of an agent in India, the club insured a major part of the expanding Indian fleet.

By 1960 the SSM was an established international club with assets of over £1m. Seven of its eleven board members were non-UK-based shipowners. It also gained admission to the London Group, which eventually expanded into the current International Group of P&I clubs. This was a direct result of the intensive lobbying of the managers, who were well rewarded since they were paid on performance. The growth of the SSM and other clubs was also good for shipowners, as joining a large well-managed pool led to a better sharing of risks.[64]

---

[61] SSM, Steamship minutes, May 1950.   [62] Sturmey 1962.
[63] Young 1995, 44–5.   [64] Young 1995, 46.

In sum, key managers of the SSM actively pursued an expansionist strategy at critical periods in its history. Initially this involved the acquisition of other small local clubs. In a world of escalating liability, mutuality remained a favoured choice with shipowners, not just in the UK. P&I clubs, for example, were established in Sweden in 1909, in the US in 1917, and in Japan in 1950. Until the Second World War most of the British-based clubs had some foreign shipping on their books, but foreign shipowners rarely appeared on their managing committees. This changed after the war, when the managers of the British clubs began to travel the world seeking business that had previously gravitated to them.[65] The influence of entrepreneurship, the active seeking out of new risks and business opportunities, therefore, was significant in expanding and internationalizing the P&I form of organization. While Lionel Sage had worked hard to expand the SSM in its early days, this momentum faltered in the 1920s and early 1930s. Given a different set of circumstances and personalities, the SSM might have simply faded away. Without Sydney Crowe, the club would have continued quietly to insure the diminishing number of vessels in the coastal and estuarine trades. The arrival of an ambitious new type of manager, and the adventurous underwriting of ships owned by entrepreneurs such as Billmeir, set the SSM on a new path. This movement away from its traditional base placed it in a good position to seize the opportunities presented after 1945. The expansion of the global P&I market after the war provided the SSM with the final step change in its position. Important personal connections were nurtured, constant travel was undertaken by managers in Europe and India, and the club's business was internationalized. The SSM is indicative of the success and longevity of the British P&I industry. In 2012 eight of the thirteen members of the International P&I Group had UK origins, all founded between 1855 and 1909. Between them the British clubs have the greatest proportion of tonnage covered by the International Group. All are London based, even if they are now registered offshore and carry out their transactions in US dollars.

CONCLUSIONS

This chapter has sought answers to some questions about organizational forms in British marine insurance. Why did the marine insurance corporations emerge in the early eighteenth century? Why did they not compete more successfully with Lloyd's? Why did the mutual hull associations emerge and how did they survive? Why did the market structure change after 1824 in

---

[65] Young 1995, 45–6.

the way it did? What drove the success of the P&I clubs after 1850 and through the twentieth century?

The two chartered corporations of 1720 were the product of specific financial and political circumstances—the speculative bubble of 1719–20, the willingness of the Crown to trade charters for cash—and more generally the culture of innovation that accompanied the financial revolution of the period. The corporations were certainly not the result of any prior experience of joint-stock forms of organization in marine insurance. There were none. In that sense they were an experiment that happened to work.

Yet the corporations did not drive out private underwriters as some had feared they would. On the contrary, the latter benefited from the exclusive privileges of the corporations, which prevented other groups of capitalists from entering the market. Underwriters, especially those operating out of Lloyd's, developed institutions that helped to mitigate the problems of asymmetric information, agency, and transaction costs that accompanied shipping and overseas trade in the period. These problems appear to have outweighed the greater security provided by the larger capital resources of the corporations. Cautious underwriting and pricing policies on the part of the corporations further drove business towards Lloyd's. The best risks insured with the private underwriters because they charged lower premiums than the corporations and offered more flexible policy terms. The underwriters were able to do this, at least in part, because they were better placed to recognize risk quality and because their overheads were low. In the later eighteenth century the development of formal governance structures at Lloyd's drove out the gamblers and provided greater security for the insured. These and later institutional changes helped secure Lloyd's as a world market for marine insurance for the next two centuries.

The mutual associations of shipowners that appeared from the late eighteenth century were the product of specialization in the marine insurance market, the growth of regional ports, and the traditional fractional form of shipownership. They offered a system of insurance that was geared to coastal and short-sea trades, where multiple voyages could be made within a year. They had the advantage of local knowledge and carefully monitored the quality of the risks that they insured. They suffered few agency problems, as they employed no agents or brokers and maintained simple flat managerial structures. They had lower transaction costs, charged lower premiums than Lloyd's or the corporations, provided more comprehensive cover, and aimed to offer good customer service, with rapid and non-litigious claims settlements. The close quality controls, however, placed narrow limits on their growth. They remained specialist niche operators tied to local trades.

One compelling reason for the structural changes after 1824 was the political swing towards free trade and the British parliament's removal of the corporate monopoly restrictions in marine insurance. However, the debate surrounding repeal suggests that it was not obvious that the stock company operating in a free market was the natural successor to the private underwriter or the mutual association. Supporters of Lloyd's argued that the low proportion of stock companies' capital paid up meant that the companies provided little security to the insured, whereas Lloyd's underwriters staked the whole of their property. The unlimited liability of Lloyd's members was held up as a badge of strength for much of the nineteenth century and beyond. Others argued that mutual schemes were optimal because they ensured lower costs, cheaper insurance, more liberal claims settlements, and bolstered the relationship between insurers and the merchant community. Proponents of joint-stock insurance claimed that the lack of capital in mutual organizations, and their need to call on their members to contribute towards each loss, led to delays in payment for the insured. Premium insurance, operated by all stock companies, as opposed to a posteriori calls operated by most mutuals, related the price to the risk run and thus attracted better quality risks. It also allowed the insured to know in advance the cost of insurance, which helped owners estimate their expenditure on their ships. Generally, the latter arguments appear to have gained the upper hand as the nineteenth century progressed. The global scale of business conducted by the new Liverpool and London companies entering marine insurance from the 1860s, and their close ties to local broking and shipping interests, gave them an edge in the competition with Lloyd's and forced the latter to diversify out of marine insurance.

Mutuality survived, however, and some of the mutual associations morphed into the successful P&I clubs still working in the London market today. Technological change and the transformation of the liability environment for shipowners and mariners from the middle of the nineteenth century, which was the result of growing public concern about safety at sea and subsequent legislative intervention, helped drive the growth of the P&I sector. These factors alone, however, do not explain why P&I insurance was largely delivered by not-for-profit mutuals rather than by stock companies or private underwriters. The case of the SSM indicates that the entrepreneurial qualities, risk taking, and innovation of individual managers could play an important role in the growth of clubs out of small or declining markets. Moreover, the fact that most P&I clubs have firmly resisted the trend to demutualize suggests that the attraction of mutuality remains strong in a sector where specialist knowledge, high-trust business relations, and extensive pooling and inter-club cooperation are more critical to success than the resolution of capital needs or agency conflicts in governance.

4

Risk Management by Mitsubishi

From Self-Insurance to Captive Insurance

Hisaaki Kamiya

Mitsubishi Gōshi Kaisha (Mitsubishi Limited Partnership ('Mitsubishi') was established in 1893. Mitsubishi recognized the significance of insurance in its early days and its risk management business was one of the most advanced in Japan. Indeed, Hisaya Iwasaki, president of Mitsubishi, was a major shareholder of the Tokio Marine Insurance Company. However, the relationship between Mitsubishi and the Tokio Marine was complex. Mitsubishi commenced with self-insurance and set its original tariffs for this. Why did Mitsubishi start using self-insurance? Was it a success or failure? This chapter seeks to answer these questions, among others. Its objective is to investigate Mitsubishi's risk management strategies from 1898 to 1933 and, for the first time, to present an historical study of self-insurance and captive insurance by a large business corporation. From 1898 to 1919 Mitsubishi flexibly combined self-insurance with the external purchase of non-life insurance. In 1919, confronted with new regulatory conditions, Mitsubishi changed its strategy and established a captive insurer, the Mitsubishi Marine and Fire Insurance Company (hereafter Mitsubishi Marine). Fourteen years later, under very different market conditions, this captive was sold and Mitsubishi reverted back to the external sourcing of its insurance requirements. This case study helps illustrate that the choice of organizational form for the supply of insurance can be an important means of corporate risk management.

Insurance is an important element of large enterprises. At the beginning of the twentieth century, for instance, the United States Steel Corporation established fire and accident insurance departments to carry its own insurance.[1] The Standard Oil Company also carried its own tank insurance.[2] In

---

[1] Spectator 18 April 1901, vol. LXVI, 225.
[2] Spectator 22 August 1901, vol. LXVII, 90.

Japan, the former Mitsui Bussan Kaisha (now Mitsui Co. Ltd) adopted self-insurance, although the details of its self-insurance and its tariffs are unclear due to a lack of surviving documentation.[3]

According to Harrington and Niehaus, risk management methods can be broadly classified as (1) loss control, (2) loss financing, and (3) internal risk reduction.[4] This chapter focuses on loss financing. Loss financing methods include retention, insurance, hedging, and other contractual risk transfers.[5] Retention is often called self-insurance. We define self-insurance as 'the payment of losses as they become due by an individual, partnership or corporation that retains all or part of its own risks'.[6] Mitsubishi provides an early example of corporate risk management through a form of loss financing.

Corporate self-insurance involves setting up a reserve fund out of which an enterprise adjusts and pays the claims for its own losses—in the case of Mitsubishi these largely related to marine and fire losses. This has the advantage, first, that the enterprise can utilize any surpluses arising from the self-insurance fund; second, that the enterprise can benefit in the event of a decline in risk. Conversely, self-insurance has the disadvantage, first, that it may not spread risks sufficiently widely; second, that it may be unable to deal with a catastrophic loss.

This chapter also examines why Mitsubishi established a captive insurance company, defined as a limited-purpose, wholly owned insurance subsidiary of an organization not in the insurance business, which has as its primary function the insuring of some of the exposures and risks of its parent or the parent's affiliates.[7] Paul Bawcutt points out the benefits of captive formation—such as meeting insurance needs, providing a funding mechanism, and reducing the price cycle.[8] He also discusses the advantages and disadvantages of captive insurance. The advantages are the ability to gain access to the reinsurance market, which is not possible through self-insurance, and to select the risks that are retained within the insurance company.[9] The disadvantages of captive insurance are the internal and external pressures on the company in relation to premium rating and claims settlements, and that the captive is affected if the parent company's control over its losses deteriorates.[10] In time Mitsubishi was to experience both the advantages and the disadvantages of having a captive insurance company.

Few studies have investigated this theme. The company history of the Tokio Marine refers to the terms and conditions of self-insurance, but does not analyse the loss ratio and the mechanism of self-insurance.[11] It refers to the

---

[3] Asajima 2007.   [4] Harrington and Niehaus 2003, 9–12.
[5] Harrington and Niehaus 2003, 11–12.   [6] Bennett 2004, 278.
[7] Bawcutt 1997, 1.   [8] Bawcutt 1997, 17–28.   [9] Bawcutt 1997, 28.
[10] Bawcutt 1997, 32–3.   [11] Japan Business History Institute 1979, 279–96.

business results of the Mitsubishi Marine, but does not clearly explain why Mitsubishi ended its captive insurance venture.[12]

The rest of this chapter is structured as follows: in the first section we discuss why Mitsubishi initially adopted self-insurance and examine Mitsubishi's first period of using self-insurance. In the second section we focus on the scale of Mitsubishi's self-insurance and discuss why the Mitsubishi Marine was established as a captive. Next, we analyse the business of the latter. Finally, we conclude that the self-insurance and captive insurance ventures of Mitsubishi were largely successful.

SELF-INSURANCE: THE FIRST PERIOD

The roots of Mitsubishi's self-insurance date back to 1877. Yuubin Kisen Mitsubishi Kaisha (Mitsubishi Mail Steamship Company, hereafter Mitsubishi Kaisha), the predecessor of Mitsubishi, established a clear set of bookkeeping regulations as a condition of receiving support from the Japanese Government.[13]

Initially, Mitsubishi Kaisha reserved a sum equivalent to 12 per cent of the value of their ships every year as a form of security to cover the potential costs of future claims in accordance with its bookkeeping regulations. However, this represented a form of depreciation allowance rather than self-insurance.[14] This system continued for five years. In 1882 Mitsubishi Kaisha abolished this form of reserve fund because it was not needed as a provision against maritime accidents. Indeed, the fund had not been used to cover losses from maritime accidents at all. A few years later, in 1885, Mitsubishi Kaisha sold all its ships to Nippon Yusen Kaisha, a company that was established as a result of competition between Mitsubishi Kaisha and Kyodo Unyu Kaisha. Subsequently, Mitsubishi Kaisha focused on mining and shipbuilding.

After the establishment of Mitsubishi, the relationship between Mitsubishi and the Tokio Marine deepened. In 1894 Mitsubishi entered into a contract with the Tokio Marine that gave the former a discount on its cargo insurance premiums.[15] In 1897 the Tokio Marine gave notice that it was rescinding the contract due to the risks incurred on certain legs of some voyages.[16] Mitsubishi, in response, tried to renegotiate the risk-rating conditions with the Tokio Marine. The latter demanded strict conditions, however, almost doubling the risk rating.[17] Mitsubishi considered starting its own self-insurance

---

[12] Japan Business History Institute 1979, 434–6, 476–9.   [13] Kuno 1970, 93.
[14] Takatera 1975, 121–2.   [15] Mitsubishi Syashi 1981, 7.
[16] Japan Business History Institute 1979, 279.
[17] Mitsubishi archives, *Kohon (The Original Draft History of Mitsubishi)* 12 February 1897.
Note: except where stated otherwise, all documents cited from the Mitsubishi archives are in

scheme, but these plans were dropped after the Tokio Marine withdrew its demands.[18]

In 1898 the Tokio Marine, the Nippon Sea and Land Insurance Company, the Imperial Marine Insurance Company, and the Nippon Marine Insurance Company entered into a tariff agreement.[19] Based on this agreement, the Tokio Marine gave notice that it was to withdraw the premium discount allowed to Mitsubishi.[20] This time, Mitsubishi went ahead and established its own self-insurance business. The Tokio Marine, however, continued to insure Mitsubishi's ships and cargoes, so that the range of self-insurance undertaken was limited. Mitsubishi self-insured 30 per cent of the amount insured on the hulls of Japanese-style ships and cargoes of coals loaded on such ships.[21]

Two years later Mitsubishi contacted the Tokio Marine with a revised special agreement, the terms of which were as follows.[22] First, the range of non-life insurance coverage provided by the Tokio Marine was revised. The Tokio Marine was to insure coals, cokes, ores, and mining timbers transported by steamship; Japanese-style ships were excluded. Second, the structure of insurance was revised. The Tokio Marine was to issue an open policy for Mitsubishi's cargo insurance and to fix the insured goods, legs of voyage, and terms of insurance in advance. As a result, Mitsubishi did not need to negotiate the conditions for every shipment. Third, the range of self-insurance of coals, cokes, ores, and mining timbers was to be expanded.

As a result of this agreement, therefore, the extent of risks covered by the Tokio Marine contracted, while Mitsubishi expanded the proportion of its self-insurance. In August 1900 Mitsubishi laid down the terms and conditions of self-insurance, in which the company set the tariffs for different goods and legs of voyages.[23] The objective of the terms and conditions was to prevent the underinsurance of the company's ships and goods. Thus, at this stage, the expansion of self-insurance was based on a passive rather than an active response to risk. Mitsubishi, above all, feared underinsurance.

In a very important development for Mitsubishi's self-insurance business, the terms and conditions were revised in December 1900. This revision

Japanese. In these notes the Japanese transliteration and an English translation (in brackets) of the document title are both given.

[18] Mitsubishi archives, *Kohon* 29 January 1897.
[19] Japan Business History Institute 1979, 164.
[20] Mitsubishi archives, *Kohon* 20 May 1898.
[21] Mitsubishi archives, *Kohon* 22 July 1898.
[22] Mitsubishi archives, *Tokyo Kaijyo Hoken Kabushikikaisha To Mitsubishi Gōshi Kaisha Tono Hoken Yakuzyousyo Meiji 33 Nen 8 Gatsu (The Insurance Contract between Tokio Marine and Mitsubishi)* 1 August 1900.
[23] Mitsubishi archives, *Honsha-Nissi 4 (The Diary of the Headquarters of Mitsubishi)* 31 July 1900.

Table 4.1. Volume of Mitsubishi's marine self-insurance on hulls

	1902	1903	1904	1905
Steamships	£43,050	£43,050	£48,750	£69,600
	¥352,303	¥618,053	¥695,482	¥1,202,200
Japanese-style ships	¥111,050	¥108,700	¥91,669	¥79,850

Note: Two different currency amounts are shown because some steamship hulls were insured in £ and others in ¥.
Source: Mitsubishi archives, *Kaijyo-Jihoken Houkokusho (Business Review of Marine Self-Insurance)*. Annual publication.

Table 4.2. Mitsubishi's premiums from marine self-insurance on hulls and cargoes (¥)

	1902	1903	1904	1905
Hulls (steamships)	26,870	26,954	34,847	41,623
Hulls (Japanese-style ships)	6,963	6,015	6,307	6,468
Cargoes (steamships)	1,157	1,154	1,237	924
Cargoes (Japanese-style ships)	19,229	21,314	23,715	25,396
Total	54,219	55,437	66,106	74,411

Source: Mitsubishi archives, *Kaijyo-Jihoken Houkokusho (Business Review of Marine Self-Insurance)*. Annual publication.

contained four key points.[24] First, the range of self-insurance was further expanded. Mitsubishi was to self-insure cargo loaded on other companies' ships at an additional 10 per cent of the regular rate. Second, Mitsubishi set an extra rate for dangerous cargoes. The rate for gunpowder, explosives, acid goods, and oils was an additional 50 per cent of the regular rate. Third, Mitsubishi was to self-insure 30 per cent of the hull risk of steamships and cargo loaded on steamships. Fourth, Mitsubishi was to self-insure all cargo valued at less than 3,000 yen.

Table 4.1 shows the amounts of Mitsubishi's hull self-insurance from 1902 to 1905. It reveals an increasing trend towards steamship insurance and a downsizing of hull insurance for Japanese-style ships. Some data are presented in pounds sterling because the company operated on the London insurance market via Willis Faber, a Lloyd's broker and acting agent for the Tokio Marine.[25]

Table 4.2 shows the changes in the sources of marine self-insurance premiums from 1902 to 1905. It can be seen that the increase in premiums for steamship hulls drove the increase in the total premiums for marine self-insurance.

[24] Mitsubishi archives, *Reiki-Taizen 1 (The Reform of Marine Self-Insurance Rules)* 27 December 1900.
[25] Mitsubishi archives, *Meiji 35 Nen Takou-Raikan (Letter from Tokio Marine to Mitsubishi)* 17 March 1902.

Table 4.3. Loss ratios on Mitsubishi's marine self-insurance (claims paid as a % of premiums)

	Premiums (¥)	Claims paid	Loss ratio (%)
1901	48,471	12,053	24.9
1902	54,219	34,426	63.5
1903	55,437	4,937	8.9
1904	66,106	58,459	88.4
1905	74,411	7,331	9.9

Source: Mitsubishi archives, *Kaijyo-Jihoken Houkokusho (Business Review of Marine Self-Insurance)*. Annual publication.

Table 4.3 shows the loss experience of Mitsubishi's marine self-insurance business from 1901 to 1905. The loss ratios were high in 1902 and 1904. In 1902 a large loss occurred with the sinking of the steamship Hatsune Maru. In 1904, Mitsubishi self-insured 50 per cent of the risk on two steamships, one of which—the Akunoura Maru—sank at a cost of 46,602 yen. This clearly indicates one problem of self-insurance. While the increasing value of assets covered by self-insurance enables an enterprise to reduce its insurance costs, in the event of a major accident it may become liable for a heavy financial loss.

Mitsubishi discontinued its self-insurance scheme in August 1908. According to the memoirs of the person in charge, the reasons were complex, especially in relation to the setting of tariffs.[26] At the time the advantages of self-insurance appeared limited. Premium rates were on a downward trend in 1908. The Tokio Marine's average rate fell by 20 per cent from 1905 to 1908.[27] In addition, the market premium rates for fire insurance declined due to increasing competition among fire insurance companies.[28] It seems, therefore, that for these reasons in 1908 Mitsubishi again opted to buy in its non-life insurance rather than continue with self-insurance.

SELF-INSURANCE: THE SECOND PERIOD

According to the memoirs of the person in charge, a few years later Mitsubishi tried to negotiate its rating with the Tokio Marine, but the latter declined Mitsubishi's request.[29] In 1913, therefore, Mitsubishi re-established its self-

[26] Mitsubishi archives, *Mitsubishi-Hoken 25 Nen-shi Zadankai Sokki (A Round-Table Record of Mitsubishi Marine's Twenty-Five Years)* 1943, 8–9.
[27] Statistics Section of the Cabinet, *The Annual Statistics of the Empire of Japan* 1906, 1909.
[28] Yoneyama 2009, 19.
[29] Mitsubishi archives, *Mitsubishi-Hoken 25 Nen-shi Zadankai Sokki (A Round-Table Record of Mitsubishi Marine's Twenty-Five Years)* 1943, 12.

insurance business. Before doing so, Mitsubishi studied carefully the products of each of its departments that required insurance. The objects of the investigation included ratings, insured amounts, and premium payments.[30] Based on the results of this research, the new terms and conditions of self-insurance were framed in December 1912.

The main features of the second period of self-insurance were as follows.[31] First, Mitsubishi set up an insurance section in its General Affairs department. Second, it self-insured all cargoes and ships as a principle. Third, the operative clauses of marine self-insurance were copied from the contracts with the Tokio Marine, and those of fire self-insurance were adopted from the contracts with the Meiji Fire Insurance Company, so that Mitsubishi's self-insurance terms emulated the operations of both those companies.

Furthermore, Mitsubishi issued a notice on the same day that the terms and conditions were adopted, clearly stating its position on self-insurance. Mitsubishi emphasized that each section of the corporation was to be responsible for its own self-insurance and loss reduction.[32] Mitsubishi also paid attention to the issue of internal moral hazard. If an accident occurred, the General Affairs Department paid expenses to the department affected, such as shipbuilding, mining, etc. If accidents occurred too frequently, however, there could be a shortfall in the self-insurance fund, so that monitoring moral hazard was a concern for the managers of the scheme.

In February 1914 Mitsubishi fixed the tariff for its cargoes and ships.[33] The tariff differentiated between steamships and Japanese-style ships, and a higher rate was set for dangerous goods. Premiums fluctuated according to the loss experience and the situation during World War One.

Mitsubishi intended that the re-establishment of self-insurance would make it independent of the Tokio Marine, as it had become dissatisfied with the rates charged by the latter.[34] In 1913 Kusuyata Kimura, the manager of the General Affairs department, informed staff that the self-insurance business was to be developed and an insurance company would be established in due course.[35] With this in mind, Mitsubishi personnel were sent to the Lloyd's broker, Henry Head and Co., to be trained in underwriting.[36]

---

[30] Mitsubishi archives, *Mitsubishi Gōshi Kaisha Arakawa Kouzan Honsha Tokugou (About the Tariff Rates)* 24 October 1912.

[31] Mitsubishi archives, *Reiki-Taizen 2 (About the Establishment of an Insurance Section)* 20 December 1912.

[32] Mitsubishi archives, *Reiki-Taizen 2 (About the Handling of Self-Insurance)* 20 December 1912.

[33] Mitsubishi archives, *Reiki-Taizen 2 (About the Establishment of an Insurance Section)*.

[34] Mitsubishi archives, *Mitsubishi-Hoken 25 Nen-shi Zadankai Sokki (A Round-Table Record of Mitsubishi Marine's Twenty-Five Years)* 1943, 48–52.

[35] Mitsubishi archives, *Mitsubishi-Hoken 25 Nen-shi Zadankai Sokki (A Round-Table Record of Mitsubishi Marine's Twenty-Five Years)* 1943, 36–7.

[36] Mitsubishi archives, *Mitsubishi-Hoken 25 Nen-shi Zadankai Sokki (A Round-Table Record of Mitsubishi Marine's Twenty-Five Years)* 1943, 46–7.

At the beginning of its second period of self-insurance, Mitsubishi rescinded its contract with the Tokio Marine.[37] The ideal of independence, however, was not immediately realized. Two months later, Mitsubishi contracted with the Tokio Marine for some insurance cover. According to this contract, the Tokio Marine was to insure 70 per cent of Mitsubishi's goods and ships with effect from 1 April 1913.[38]

In April 1916, there was a step change in the relationship between Mitsubishi and the Tokio Marine. Mitsubishi gave notice that it would henceforth self-insure all cargo imported by its London branch, and that the agreement with Tokio Marine would in future be confined to Japanese risks.[39] Furthermore, Mitsubishi entered into a special non-life insurance agreement with Henry Head and Co.[40] Since the outbreak of World War One, Mitsubishi had been purchasing its war insurance from Lloyd's broker Willis Faber, the agent of the Tokio Marine. The details of Mitsubishi's choice of broker were discussed in a letter from Kenkichi Kagami to Kantaro Kikuchi, a manager of the London branch of Mitsubishi. Kikuchi asked Willis Faber to reduce the rates to match those of Lloyd's, which offered the lowest rates for marine insurance. However, this was refused by Willis Faber, leading Mitsubishi to contract with Henry Head and Co.[41]

As with Mitsubishi's first period of self-insurance, the Mitsubishi archives contain the results from 1913 to 1919. These have been used to explore the changes in the amounts self-insured, the premium income, rates, and loss ratios. As Table 4.4 shows, the volume of Mitsubishi's self-insurance was comparable to that of a middle-ranked non-life insurance company. The table also shows the rapid growth of premium income. The premium rate of Mitsubishi's self-insurance was lower than the average for non-life insurance companies from 1913 to 1915, although this relationship was later reversed, and Mitsubishi's rate became much higher by 1918. This change reflected the lack of an integrated self-insurance strategy among Mitsubishi and its subsidiaries, which is discussed further below.

Table 4.5 shows the amounts insured externally and self-insured, and the respective premiums, from 1913 to 1919. The total insured on both fire and marine risks increased from 55.9 million yen in 1913 to 272.4 million yen in 1918. Over 80 per cent of these totals related to marine insurance in 1913–14 and 1917–18 (data are missing for 1916). As the table shows, the proportion of self-insurance tended to decrease from 1916, so that Mitsubishi was increasingly relying on the external purchase of insurance towards the end of World

---

[37] Mitsubishi Syashi Publishing Group 1980, 1605.
[38] Mitsubishi Syashi Publishing Group 1980, 1726–7.
[39] Mitsubishi archives, *Reiki-Taizen 3 (About Self-Insurance)* 26 April 1916.
[40] Japan Business History Institute 1979, 287.
[41] Mitsubishi archives, *Tokio Offices, Including Reports from No.80, Letter from Kenkichi Kagami to Kantaro Kikuchi* 11 August 1916. These reports were written in English.

Table 4.4. The performance of major marine insurance companies and Mitsubishi, 1913–18

A. Premium income (¥ '000)

	1913	1914	1915	1916	1917	1918
Tokio Marine	5,810	6,736	10,849	23,555	58,178	70,049
Imperial Marine	1,117	1,311	1,637	2,403	5,661	7,552
Nippon Marine	989	1,146	1,211	1,468	2,542	4,454
Kobe Marine	926	1,050	1,385	2,626	5,529	10,936
Toyo Marine	593	646	674	724	1,954	2,514
Tomei Marine	183	179	158	962	1,879	4,578
Yokohama Marine	130	152	220	518	1,336	3,544
Osaka Marine	23	16	20	776	7,825	22,204
Nissin Fire	81	88	132	238	607	835
Tokyo Fire	75	72	136	235	415	862
Fuso Marine					6	6,972
Total of non-life companies	10,067	11,573	16,569	33,757	87,112	137,820
Mitsubishi	283	252	267	410	954	1,439

B. Total sum insured (¥ thousand)

	1913	1914	1915	1916	1917	1918
Tokio Marine	1,323,459	1,416,375	2,172,880	3,450,164	6,660,266	8,104,165
Imperial Marine	199,134	229,049	319,878	427,920	680,337	774,093
Nippon Marine	325,523	359,858	360,734	445,938	679,402	1,142,378
Kobe Marine	169,645	175,719	217,670	333,712	489,161	672,400
Toyo Marine	103,725	117,499	121,878	120,959	294,613	386,381
Tomei Marine	39,165	42,364	38,619	116,397	280,387	369,391
Yokohama Marine	50,060	58,522	83,987	184,840	329,677	764,208
Osaka Marine	7,388	7,744	9,441	151,529	836,028	1,965,712
Nissin Fire	12,655	16,164	27,508	60,619	142,472	202,838
Tokyo Fire	19,309	18,855	35,631	50,048	90,005	149,799
Fuso Marine					305	430,248

	1913	1914	1915	1916	1917	1918
Total	2,286,083	2,490,681	3,426,590	5,394,359	10,701,814	15,489,096
Mitsubishi	46,310	52,336	48,985	n/a	126,202	228,761

C. Premium rate (¥ per ¥100 insured)

	1913	1914	1915	1916	1917	1918
Tokio Marine	0.23	0.21	0.20	0.15	0.11	0.12
Imperial Marine	0.18	0.17	0.20	0.18	0.12	0.10
Nippon Marine	0.33	0.31	0.30	0.30	0.27	0.26
Kobe Marine	0.18	0.17	0.16	0.13	0.09	0.06
Toyo Marine	0.17	0.18	0.18	0.17	0.15	0.15
Tomei Marine	0.21	0.24	0.24	0.12	0.15	0.08
Yokohama Marine	0.39	0.39	0.38	0.36	0.25	0.22
Osaka Marine	0.32	0.48	0.48	0.20	0.11	0.09
Nissin Fire	0.16	0.18	0.21	0.26	0.23	0.24
Tokyo Fire	0.26	0.26	0.26	0.21	0.22	0.17
Fuso Marine					0.05	0.06
Average of non-life companies	0.23	0.22	0.21	0.16	0.12	0.11
Mitsubishi	0.16	0.21	0.18	n/a	0.13	0.16

D. Loss ratio (losses paid as % of premium income)

	1913	1914	1915	1916	1917	1918
Tokio Marine	52.9	36.1	32.4	32.4	46.9	43.1
Imperial Marine	67.6	50.9	53.0	53.0	64.7	153.6
Nippon Marine	104.5	62.6	73.2	73.2	71.8	65.3
Kobe Marine	54.2	59.8	51.2	51.2	61.0	52.5
Toyo Marine	55.1	55.1	71.5	71.5	61.3	67.7
Tomei Marine	63.2	52.8	52.8	52.8	35.1	20.4
Yokohama Marine	111.9	85.3	54.2	54.2	68.7	68.9
Osaka Marine	79.7	76.7	79.7	79.7	12.5	22.2
Nissin Fire	70.8	65.9	67.2	67.2	52.1	111.9

(continued)

Table 4.4. Continued

A. Premium income (¥ '000)

	1913	1914	1915	1916	1917	1918
Tokyo Fire	96.7	54.3	91.0	91.0	66.1	119.6
Fuso Marine					0.0	1.4
Average of non-life companies	59.3	45.1	42.8	60.2	47.1	46.4
Mitsubishi	n/a	n/a	n/a	15.1	11.9	4.6

Notes: (1) All premium income and sums insured are based on new contracts; (2) all data for non-life companies are gross of reinsurance; (3) Mitsubishi's data are for self-insurance; (4) the loss ratios of Mitsubishi are not available for 1913–15; (5) Mitsubishi's amount of self-insurance for 1916 is not available, therefore its premium rate cannot be calculated.

Sources: Ministry of Agriculture and Commerce (Japan), *The Insurance Yearbook* (in Japanese). Annual publication 1915–35; Mitsubishi archives, *Nenpō Mitsubishi Gōshi Kaisha* (*Yearbook of Mitsubishi*). Annual publication.

Table 4.5. Insured amounts and premiums, Mitsubishi, 1913–19 (¥ '000)

1913

Type of insurance	Insured amounts					Premiums				
	Insured	Self-insured (A)	Total (B)	Type as % of total	A as % of B	Insured	Self-insured (A)	Total (B)	Type as % of total	A as % of B
Fire	5,437	4,173	9,610	17.2	43.4	18	16	34	10.7	46.3
Marine	19,554	26,755	46,310	82.8	57.8	159	124	283	89.3	43.9
Total	24,991	30,928	55,919	100.0	55.3	177	140	317	100.0	44.2

1914

Type of insurance	Insured amounts					Premiums				
	Insured	Self-insured (A)	Total (B)	Type as % of total	A as % of B	Insured	Self-insured (A)	Total (B)	Type as % of total	A as % of B
Fire	6,229	4,663	10,892	17.2	42.8	18	13	31	11.0	41.1
Marine	14,190	38,145	52,336	82.8	72.9	109	143	252	89.0	56.7
Total	20,420	42,808	62,338	100.0	67.7	128	156	284	100.0	55.0

1915

Type of insurance	Insured amounts					Premiums				
	Insured	Self-insured (A)	Total (B)	Type as % of total	A as % of B	Insured	Self-insured (A)	Total (B)	Type as % of total	A as % of B
Fire	7,133	5,981	13,114	21.1	45.6	15	17	33	11.0	53.1
Marine	8,884	38,145	48,985	78.9	77.9	109	157	267	89.0	58.9
Total	16,017	44,127	62,100	100.0	71.1	125	175	300	100.0	58.3

(continued)

Table 4.5. Continued

1916

Type of insurance	Insured amounts					Premiums				
	Insured	Self-insured (A)	Total (B)	Type as % of total	A as % of B	Insured	Self-insured (A)	Total (B)	Type as % of total	A as % of B
Fire	7,301	6,818	14,120	n/a	48.3	22	20	42	9.3	48.3
Marine	n/a	n/a	n/a	n/a	n/a	167	243	410	90.4	59.3
Transport	0	516	516	n/a	100.0	0	1	1	0.3	100.0
Total	n/a	n/a	n/a	n/a	n/a	189	265	453	100.0	58.4

1917

Type of insurance	Insured amounts					Premiums				
	Insured	Self-insured (A)	Total (B)	Type as % of total	A as % of B	Insured	Self-insured (A)	Total (B)	Type as % of total	A as % of B
Fire	17,308	8,227	25,535	16.6	32.2	47	10	57	5.6	17.0
Marine	40,061	86,141	126,202	81.8	68.3	427	527	954	94.0	55.3
Transport	43	2,493	2,536	1.6	98.3	0	4	4	0.4	98.9
Total	57,412	96,861	154,273	100.0	62.8	474	541	1,014	100.0	53.3

1918

Type of insurance	Insured amounts					Premiums				
	Insured	Self-insured (A)	Total (B)	Type as % of total	A as % of B	Insured	Self-insured (A)	Total (B)	Type as % of total	A as % of B
Fire	25,670	15,503	41,173	15.1	37.7	164	202	366	20.2	55.2
Marine	96,261	132,500	228,761	84.0	57.9	785	654	1,439	79.5	45.5
Transport	0	2,510	2,510	0.9	100.0	0	5	5	0.3	100.0
Total	121,931	150,514	272,445	100.0	55.2	949	861	1,810	100.0	47.6

1919

Type of insurance	Insured amounts					Premiums				
	Insured	Self-insured (A)	Total (B)	Type as % of total	A as % of B	Insured	Self-insured (A)	Total (B)	Type as % of total	A as % of B
Fire	25,962	9,492	35,453	26.1	26.8	161	39	200	25.1	19.6
Marine	35,131	62,592	97,722	72.0	64.1	297	294	592	74.2	49.7
Transport	180	2,323	2,503	1.9	92.8	0	5	5	0.7	95.1
Total	61,273	74,406	135,678	100.0	54.8	458	339	797	100.0	42.5

Notes: (1) Insured amounts and premiums are based on new contracts; (2) insured amount of marine insurance is not available for 1916; (3) data in 1919 are for January to May.
Source: Mitsubishi archives, *Nenpō Mitsubishi Gōshi Kaisha* (*Yearbook of Mitsubishi*). Annual publication.

War One. Premium payments increased enormously after 1916. The evidence suggests that Mitsubishi was using non-life insurance flexibly in this period, purchasing it on the open market as the need arose.

In terms of the loss ratio, the results for marine self-insurance were good except in 1919 (see Table 4.6). As Table 4.4 shows, Mitsubishi's loss ratio was relatively low compared with the average for non-life insurance companies. As a result, Mitsubishi's self-insured goods and ships were considered good risks. The underwriters at Mitsubishi recognized the advantage of self-insurance, and Mitsubishi therefore continued to self-insure risks across the group.[42]

In 1917 Mitsubishi introduced some changes to its self-insurance business. Each department of the corporation was reorganized as a separate, independent joint-stock company.[43] Among the subsidiaries were Mitsubishi Shipbuilding and Engineering Co., Ltd, Mitsubishi Trading Co., Ltd, and Mitsubishi Iron and Steel Co., Ltd. The Insurance Business Act of 1900, however, meant that Mitsubishi could not continue to insure the risks of these companies.[44] The problem was that under the act Mitsubishi's insurance underwriting of its subsidiaries would require a license and be subject to the scrutiny of the regulatory authorities. Moreover, insurance companies were prohibited by Article 3 of the act from doing other business. The solution was that the subsidiaries became self-insurers in their own right.

Table 4.7 shows the differing transformations in self-insurance among Mitsubishi's subsidiaries. Mitsubishi retained almost 80 per cent of the insured amounts and still insured the steamboats, buildings, and storehouses of the company. On the other hand, for instance, Mitsubishi iron and Mitsubishi shipbuilding retained only 30 per cent of its insured amounts. One reason for such differences in the level of self-insurance may have been the high rates for steamship cargo insurance during World War One that increased the premium payments of the subsidiary companies. Another reason may have been the differing proportions of fire insurance in each company's insurance portfolio. These portfolios consisted of cargo, hull, and fire insurance. As competition drove down the rates for fire insurance, some companies may have opted to buy more fire insurance in the external market, thus reducing their level of self-insurance. The differences in the self-insurance strategies among its subsidiaries hindered overall risk management within Mitsubishi. Such conditions soon induced Mitsubishi to establish a captive insurer.

In September 1918, Mitsubishi applied to the Ministry of Agriculture and Commerce to establish the Mitsubishi Marine. At first, the Tokio Marine

---

[42] Mitsubishi archives, *Mitsubishi-Hoken 25 Nen-shi Zadankai Sokki (A Round-Table Record of Mitsubishi Marine's Twenty-Five Years)* 1943, 39–41.

[43] Mishima 1989, 187–90.

[44] The Insurance Business Act was enacted in 1900 to regulate bubble companies within the life insurance sector. Article 1 of the act prohibited entry to the insurance sector without the approval of the competent authorities.

Table 4.6. Claims paid and loss ratios, Mitsubishi, 1916–19 (¥ '000)

1916

Type of insurance	Premiums			Claims paid			Loss ratio % (D/B)	Loss ratio % of self-insurance (C/A)
	Insured	Self-insured (A)	Total (B)	Insured	Self-insured (C)	Total (D)		
Fire	22	20	42	93	54	147	347.1	264.4
Marine	167	243	410	41	21	62	15.1	8.7
Transport	0	1	1	0	0	0	0.0	0.0
Total	189	265	453	133	75	209	46.0	28.4

1917

Type of insurance	Premiums			Claims paid			Loss ratio % (D/B)	Loss ratio % of self-insurance (C/A)
	Insured	Self-insured (A)	Total (B)	Insured	Self-insured (C)	Total (D)		
Fire	47	10	57	0	0	0	0.0	0.0
Marine	427	527	954	47	66	113	11.9	12.5
Transport	0	4	4	0	0	0	0.0	0.0
Total	474	541	1,014	47	66	113	11.2	12.2

(continued)

Table 4.6. Continued

1918

Type of insurance	Premiums			Claims paid			Loss ratio % (D/B)	Loss ratio % of self-insurance (C/A)
	Insured	Self-insured (A)	Total (B)	Insured	Self-insured (C)	Total (D)		
Fire	164	202	366	7	27	34	9.4	13.3
Marine	785	654	1,439	3	64	67	4.6	9.7
Transport	0	5	5	0	0	0	0.0	0.0
Total	949	861	1,810	11	91	101	5.6	10.5

1919

Type of insurance	Premiums			Claims paid			Loss ratio % (D/B)	Loss ratio % of self-insurance (C/A)
	Insured	Self-insured (A)	Total (B)	Insured	Self-insured (C)	Total (D)		
Fire	161	39	200	417	68	485	242.7	173.5
Marine	297	294	592	0	864	865	146.2	293.8
Transport	0	5	5	0	0	0	0.0	0.0
Total	458	339	797	418	933	1,350	169.4	275.4

Notes: (1) All data are based on new contracts; (2) data in 1919 are for January to May; (3) differences in totals are due to rounding.
Source: Mitsubishi archives, *Nenpō Mitsubishi Gōshi Kaisha* (*Yearbook of Mitsubishi*). Annual publication.

Table 4.7. Self-insurance of Mitsubishi's subsidiary companies, 1918–19 (¥ '000)

Cargo (steamship) insurance

Company name	1918					1919				
	Insured amount	Self-insured amount (A)	Total (B)	Company as % of total insured	A as % of B	Insured amount	Self-insured amount (A)	Total (B)	Company as % of total insured	A as % of B
Mitsubishi	2,481	10,017	12,498	13.4	80.1	0	1,018	1,018	3.8	100.0
Mitsubishi Mining	367	1,084	1,452	1.6	74.7	262	892	1,154	4.4	77.3
Mitsubishi Trading	8,490	20,578	29,068	31.1	70.8	2,542	8,314	10,856	41.0	76.6
Mitsubishi paper mill	0	22	22	0.0	100.0	0	0	0	0.0	0.0
Tokyo stockhouse	1,716	298	2,014	2.2	14.8	767	172	938	3.5	18.3
Mitsubishi shipping	18,756	5,274	24,030	25.7	21.9	3,341	2,520	5,861	22.1	43.0
Mitsubishi iron	16,709	7,534	24,243	26.0	31.1	3,428	3,159	6,586	24.9	48.0
Total	48,520	44,836	93,356	100.0	48.0	10,340	16,140	26,479	100.0	61.0

Total insurance

Company name	1918					1919				
	Insured amount	Self-insured amount (A)	Total (B)	Company as % of total insured	A as % of B	Insured amount	Self-insured amount (A)	Total (B)	Company as % of total insured	A as % of B
Mitsubishi	9,633	28,290	37,924	13.9	74.6	3,671	2,795	6,466	6.3	43.2
Mitsubishi Mining	3,511	5,374	8,885	3.3	60.5	1,345	3,119	4,464	4.3	69.9

(continued)

Table 4.7. Continued

Total insurance

Company name	1918					1919				
	Insured amount	Self-insured amount (A)	Total (B)	Company as % of total insured	A as % of B	Insured amount	Self-insured amount (A)	Total (B)	Company as % of total insured	A as % of B
Mitsubishi Trading	18,332	65,918	84,250	30.9	78.2	4,074	34,237	38,311	37.2	89.4
Mitsubishi paper mill	4,313	4,912	9,224	3.4	53.2	267	103	370	0.4	27.8
Tokyo stockhouse	1,911	2,631	4,543	1.7	57.9	1,767	548	2,315	2.2	23.7
Mitsubishi shipping	62,234	28,776	91,010	33.4	31.6	25,093	13,370	38,822	37.7	35.4
Mitsubishi iron	20,230	10,607	30,837	11.3	34.4	5,904	4,073	9,977	9.7	40.8
Total	122,171	150,352	272,523	100.0	55.2	42,759	60,329	103,088	100.0	58.5

Notes: (1) All data are based on new contracts; (2) data for 1918 are not equal to those in Table 4.6; (3) data for 1919 are for January to April.
Source: Mitsubishi archives, *Nenpō Mitsubishi Gōshi Kaisha* (*Yearbook of Mitsubishi*). Annual publication.

opposed this plan, arguing that Mitsubishi was its major shareholder and should therefore cease this hostile plan.[45] Mitsubishi rejected this, but the Tokio Marine did not relent. Following intense negotiations, Mitsubishi and the Tokio Marine agreed the terms of a compromise, as follows. First, the Tokio Marine would acquire 25 per cent of the Mitsubishi Marine's stock. Second, the Mitsubishi Marine's business would be limited to the risks of Mitsubishi and its subsidiary companies, which would be reinsured by the Tokio Marine. Third, Kenkichi Kagami, who was then an executive managing director of the Tokio Marine, would serve concurrently as a managing director of the Mitsubishi Marine.[46] The Ministry of Agriculture and Commerce approved the establishment of the Mitsubishi Marine in March 1919 and the new company commenced business three months later. The risks of Mitsubishi and its subsidiary companies were transferred to the Mitsubishi Marine. Subsequently, Mitsubishi's self-insurance scheme was abolished.

CAPTIVE INSURANCE: THE MITSUBISHI MARINE

In contrast to the Mitsubishi Marine, which only underwrote the risks of Mitsubishi and its subsidiaries, another captive insurer, the Taisho Marine and Fire Insurance Company that was established by Mitsui Bussan, jointly insured the goods and ships of Mitsui Bussan with the Tokio Marine.[47] During the process of establishing the Mitsubishi Marine, the Tokio Marine proposed that Mitsubishi coinsure the goods and ships of Mitsubishi and its subsidiaries. However, Mitsubishi turned down this plan, for it wished to continue to hold the initiative with regard to underwriting.[48] The Mitsubishi Marine, therefore, approached its familiar London broker Henry Head for the terms of a marine reinsurance treaty.

Table 4.8 shows the marine insurance results of the Mitsubishi Marine for 1919–33. Two trends emerge. First, the data illustrate the rapid growth in gross premium income, from 0.71 million yen in 1919 to 6.25 million yen in 1929. Second, the Mitsubishi Marine's combined ratio was very low compared with that of other non-life insurers.[49] This positive performance was attributed to the low risks of items insured by Mitsubishi and its subsidiaries. From 1926 the Mitsubishi Marine also issued hull insurance for Nippon Yusen Kaisha.[50]

---

[45] Hirao 2011, vol. 3, 33–4. At that time, Hirao was an executive managing director of the Tokio Marine.

[46] Japan Business History Institute 1979, 355.

[47] Japan Business History Institute 1996, 74–6.

[48] Mitsubishi archives, *Mitsubishi-Hoken 25 Nen-shi Zadankai Sokki (A Round-Table Record of Mitsubishi Marine's Twenty-Five Years)* 1943, 53, 90.

[49] The combined ratio is the sum of the net loss ratio and the expense ratio.

[50] Kamiya 2012, 44.

Table 4.8. The marine insurance results of Mitsubishi Marine, 1919–33 (¥ '000)

Year	Gross premium (A)	Ceded premium	Net premium (B)	Expenses (C)	Claims paid (D)	Reinsurance claims	Net claims paid (E)	Balance B-(C+E)	Expense ratio % (C/B)	Loss ratio % (D/A)	Net loss ratio % (E/B)	Combined ratio % (D+E)/B	% of non-life insurance company's combined ratio
1919	709	208	499	40	14	5	10	449	8.0	2.0	2.0	10.0	77.5
1920	2,646	1,375	1,239	206	602	180	422	611	16.6	22.8	34.1	50.7	67.6
1921	2,633	1,253	1,281	186	842	285	558	537	14.5	32.0	43.6	58.1	94.9
1922	3,274	1,988	1,174	256	1,269	719	550	368	21.8	38.8	46.8	68.6	123.8
1923	3,125	1,794	1,272	252	1,873	1,457	416	604	19.8	59.9	32.7	52.5	102.8
1924	3,765	2,507	1,197	312	4,052	3,150	903	–18	26.1	107.6	75.4	101.5	100.1
1925	4,022	2,748	1,253	360	5,211	4,619	592	301	28.7	129.6	47.2	75.9	112.5
1926	4,519	2,963	1,518	336	2,791	2,008	783	399	22.1	61.8	51.6	73.7	98.3
1927	5,116	3,465	1,546	384	4,520	3,620	90	1,072	24.8	88.4	5.8	30.6	92.0
1928	5,752	4,206	1,448	436	4,518	3,678	840	172	30.1	78.5	58.0	88.1	101.5
1929	6,254	4,492	1,700	410	4,362	3,672	690	600	24.1	69.7	40.6	64.7	95.0
1930	5,885	4,265	1,620	424	3,647	2,714	933	687	26.2	62.0	57.6	83.8	102.9
1931	5,071	3,709	1,362	359	2,265	1,585	680	682	26.4	44.7	49.9	76.3	102.4
1932	5,216	3,750	1,466	432	2,715	2,141	575	891	29.5	52.1	39.2	68.7	96.7
1933	5,717	3,237	2,480	554	2,777	1,856	922	1,558	22.3	48.6	37.2	59.5	90.0

Source: Mitsubishi archives, *Nenpō Mitsubishi Gōshi Kaisha* (*Yearbook of Mitsubishi*). Annual publication.

Table 4.9. The cargo insurance premiums from Mitsubishi and its subsidiaries, 1919–28 (¥ '000)

Year	Gross premium (A)	Premium from head offices of Mitsubishi and its subsidiaries	Premium from branch offices of Mitsubishi Trading and Mining companies	Total premium of Mitsubishi and its subsidiaries (B)	B as % of A
1919	335	54	133	186	55.6
1920	1,025	154	443	597	58.2
1921	1,021	161	465	626	61.3
1922	1,379	268	645	913	66.2
1923	1,358	167	643	810	59.6
1924	2,155	301	775	1,075	49.9
1925	2,292	347	849	1,196	52.2
1926	2,365	364	884	1,248	52.8
1927	2,671	369	909	1,278	47.9
1928	2,908	402	877	1,279	44.0
Total	17,509	2,587	6,622	9,209	52.6

Note: The decline of gross premium in 1923 was caused by the Great Kanto Earthquake.

Source: Mitsubishi archives, *Mitsubishi Kaijyou Kasai Hoken Kabushikikashia 25 nenshi (Twenty-Five Years History of Mitsubishi Marine)*.

Nippon Yusen was at that time the largest Japanese maritime transport company and the insurance rates for its ships were lower than the average rate. The exceptionally poor result of 1924 was caused by claims related to the Great Kanto Earthquake.

Table 4.9 shows that the business base of the Mitsubishi Marine was strongly supported by Mitsubishi and its subsidiaries, representing an average of 53 per cent of Mitsubishi Marine's gross cargo insurance premiums between 1919 and 1928.

In 1925, there was a change in the relationship between the Tokio Marine and the Mitsubishi Marine. Kenkichi Kagami, who was president of the former and managing director of the latter, became simultaneously the president of both; and Rinjiro Kimura, who was Managing Director of the Mitsubishi Marine, began to serve concurrently as Managing Director of the Tokio Marine. This exchange of senior executive personnel was triggered by the resignation of Hachisaburo Hirao from the position of Executive Director of the Tokio Marine to devote himself to the management of Konan Gakuen, which he had established. Moreover, Hirao disliked Mitsubishi's attitude toward insurance, believing that, as the major shareholder of the Tokio Marine, Mitsubishi should support its business.[51]

Hirao had long wished to resign as Executive Director, but had been dissuaded by Kagami. Hirao had managed the Kansai region since 1900 and

[51] Hirao 2012, vol. 5, 359–61, entry for 13 July 1923.

was trusted by the enterprises in the region. He would be difficult to replace, and Kagami initially did not permit him to leave.[52] A few years later, while travelling in the USA and Europe, Hirao again proposed his resignation to Kagami.[53] The latter negotiated a personnel exchange with Mitsubishi to address Hirao's departure. Consequently, Kagami accepted Hirao's request and changed course to cooperate with Mitsubishi. In 1926, the Mitsubishi Marine contracted for fire reinsurance with Willis Faber and Partners, the fire insurance division of Willis Faber, now known as the Willis Group. The Tokio Marine had already contracted with Willis Faber and Partners three years previously, but this was a change of direction for the Mitsubishi Marine.

As a result of this negotiation, the proportion of the Tokio Marine's ceded premiums that went to the Mitsubishi Marine increased from 0.8 per cent in 1924 to 6.8 per cent in 1929.[54] This growth in the reinsurance business was caused directly by the personnel changes of 1925. The Tokio Marine's results were relatively good, indicating that few payouts were made on the amounts it reinsured.[55] This business generated large profits for the Mitsubishi Marine.

In April 1933, the Tokio Marine decided to increase its stockholdings from 30 million yen to 35 million yen. The aim was to acquire all the shares of the Mitsubishi Marine from Mitsubishi. Mitsubishi had invested in 5 million yen of the stock and this was increasing in value at that time.[56] The proportion of Tokio Marine stock held by Mitsubishi had already increased from zero in 1926 to 13.3 per cent in 1933.[57] The Mitsubishi Bank, which was a subsidiary of Mitsubishi and the leading shareholder of the Tokio Marine, took over 14.7 per cent of the latter's stock in 1933.[58] Concurrently with a capital increase by Tokio Marine, Mitsubishi sold all of its Mitsubishi Marine stock to the Tokio Marine, so that the Mitsubishi Marine became a subsidiary of the latter and Mitsubishi's captive insurance venture was abolished. This decision was beneficial for both Mitsubishi and the Tokio Marine. It is true that the Mitsubishi Marine's results had been good. However, the Mitsubishi Marine had competed with the Tokio Marine for contracts beyond those of Mitsubishi and its subsidiaries. As a result of competition among non-life insurance companies during the 1920s, premium rates for marine insurance became seriously depreciated. The potential advantage of captive insurance, therefore,

---

[52] Hirao 2011, vol. 4, 363–4, entry for 22 September 1921.

[53] Hirao 2012, vol. 6, 480–2, entry for 8 January 1925.

[54] Mitsubishi archives, *Dai-65-ki Jigyou Houkokusho (The Business Report of Tokio Marine)* 1924, 97; *Dai-70-ki Jigyou Houkokusho (The Business Report of Tokio Marine)* 1929, 140.

[55] Despite the bad results of non-life insurance companies overall in this period, the loss ratio of the Tokio Marine never exceeded 100 per cent.

[56] Japan Business History Institute 1979, 476.

[57] Japan Business History Institute 1979, 488.

[58] Japan Business History Institute 1979.

was reduced. In addition, the Tokio Marine accounted for the majority of non-life insurance sold in Japan. Changing price trends and market power, therefore, help explain why Mitsubishi altered its hostile attitude toward the Tokio Marine and abolished its captive insurance venture. For the Tokio Marine, the purchase of the Mitsubishi Marine enabled it to remove a competitor and acquire some good quality business. Acquiring the Mitsubishi Marine business generated profits for the Tokio Marine, while the funds from Mitsubishi strengthened its financial position.

CONCLUSION

To summarize Mitsubishi's complex and fluctuating risk management story is not easy. The corporation commenced self-insurance in 1898 because of the withdrawal of the special rate previously offered by the Tokio Marine. Mitsubishi's primary aim was to prevent any underinsurance of the company's ships and goods. At first, the range of self-insured items was limited. However, as a result of a consistently low loss ratio, Mitsubishi gradually increased the proportion of risk retention in order to reduce its premium payments to external insurers. Mitsubishi set tariffs according to the types of goods and ships that it needed to cover.

The value of the amounts self-insured by Mitsubishi expanded significantly during World War One. In the context of the marine insurance business, the amount self-insured by Mitsubishi was equivalent to that insured by a middle-ranked non-life insurance company. Mitsubishi's marine loss ratio was very low compared with the average among non-life insurance companies, and therefore the risks self-insured were considered good.

Subsequent to a restructuring of the corporation, the Insurance Business Act prevented Mitsubishi from continuing to insure the risks of its subsidiary companies. Article 1 of the Act prohibited entry to the insurance sector without the approval of the competent authorities. Thus, Mitsubishi's subsidiaries had to become self-insurers in their own right. However, this system proved not to be effective. Self-insurance strategies differed greatly between each subsidiary and premium payments tended to increase over time. In response, therefore, Mitsubishi established the Mitsubishi Marine as a captive insurer in order to pool these companies' risks.

The underwriting results of the Mitsubishi Marine were relatively good. At first, the relationship between the Tokio Marine and the Mitsubishi Marine was hostile. An exchange of top executives between the two companies, however, changed the relationship and brought them closer together. Furthermore, as a result of growing competition among non-life insurance companies during the 1920s, the premiums for marine insurance became seriously depreciated. The advantages of captive insurance, therefore, were diminished, which led Mitsubishi eventually to abolish its captive insurance venture.

In sum, the Mitsubishi story provides an interesting example of a firm managing risk through changes in the organizational vehicle by which its insurance cover was supplied. These changes took place in response to changing conditions in the external market and the internal governance environment. These included the short- to medium-term trends in internal loss ratios on retained risk, the trends in market prices for marine insurance, new legislative constraints, and personal relations between the top executives of Mitsubishi and its principal external insurance provider, the Tokio Marine. It remains to be revealed by further research on the captive insurance and self-insurance phenomena whether the factors that determined organizational choice in Mitsubishi during the early twentieth century were part of a more general historical pattern among large business corporations.

5

The Survival and Success of Swedish Mutual Insurers

Mats Larsson and Mikael Lönnborg

Mutual insurance has a long history and still plays an important role in the Swedish insurance market. The first insurance measures were built on the fact that people cooperated and developed common principles in order to minimize various risks. When the first stock companies were established in the 1850s, they were assumed to improve efficiency. These represented economies of scale compared to small and often local mutual insurance companies. However, the view that insurance should not be driven by an anticipated profit, and that all surpluses should be returned to policyholders, was also an important notion in contemporary Sweden. According to advocates of this notion, insurance was a form of social policy that should not be confused with anticipated profit. Since policyholders were also the owners of mutual companies, their control was—at least in principle—guaranteed.

Demutualization among insurers has often been seen as a strong indicator that the joint-stock ownership structure is a superior organizational form. From a theoretical standpoint, joint-stock companies have several advantages, for instance more active owners, more channels for financing their business, and better opportunities for exploiting economies of scale and scope compared to mutual companies.[1] Mutual insurance companies have to some extent been regarded as an organizational form that suited underdeveloped financial markets and, as economies progressed, such firms, where the customers were also the owners, made less economic sense. However, in the case of Sweden, demutualization has only occurred a couple of times and the results have not reinforced the belief that the joint-stock is a superior organizational structure.

---

[1] Cummins et al. 1999b.

This chapter analyses the Swedish insurance market from a long-term perspective to explain how mutual insurance companies have developed through fierce competition with joint-stock insurers, how they have benefited from institutional changes and survived major disinvestment, and how they still prevail as the most important agents in Swedish life and non-life insurance today. The competitive situation between mutual and stock insurance companies in Sweden is elaborated in Chapter 11 by Magnus Lindmark and Lars Fredrik Andersson in this volume. This chapter will instead focus on the impact of legislation, institutional, and market changes that made it possible for mutuals to survive and even dominate the insurance market. We also examine two case studies in order to illustrate the success of the mutual organizational form in Sweden.

THE EMERGENCE OF THE MODERN INSURANCE MARKET

The earliest Swedish insurance form was fire insurance organized as a mutual and semi-official institution, the so-called *Brandstuth* (Fire Aid), similar to the British fire briefs. This existed in most of the medieval landscape laws and in King Magnus Eriksson's National Law Codes from the mid-fourteenth century and was not abolished until the mid-nineteenth century. The Fire Aid, in principle, meant that all inhabitants within an administrative county district had to mutually support each other in case of damage by fire.[2]

The Fire Aid was successful in distributing the risks in a pre-industrial agrarian society, but the system could not be changed at the same rate as the restructuring of society. A major problem was that larger insurance objects, such as manor houses, churches, and factories, could not get proper protection. Local parish associations were created in order to insure these, but they proved insufficient for larger buildings. A national company, the Allmänna Brandförsäkringsverket, was established as a government initiative in 1782 in order to insure buildings both in the countryside and in cities.[3]

In the early 1840s, the Fire Aid was gradually replaced by parish and county companies that insured both real estate and personal property. Membership of these companies was voluntary and the business was financed by fees charged on a yearly basis in arrears, depending on the extent of the damages. The biggest problem, however, was the absence of institutions that could satisfy the need for insurance protection of personal property and lives as well as

---

[2] Söderberg 1935; Ohlmarks 1976; Adams et al. 2011.
[3] Lille 1882; Åmark 1932; Bucht 1936.

industrial works. A solution began to develop when the first joint-stock insurance company, the Skandia, was established in 1855. The Skandia was a so-called mixed company that wrote both life and property insurance. Altogether, three mixed companies were established, namely the Skandia in Stockholm, the Svea in Gothenburg in 1866, and the Skåne in Malmö in 1884.[4]

From the 1870s, several additional companies appeared that wrote only life insurance. Particularly important was the Thule, which, though a stock company, introduced several new principles, for example limiting the dividends to shareholders and returning some of the profit to customers. In addition, policyholders were also given the opportunity of appointing an auditor in order to safeguard their interests. These measures attracted new customers, but they also proved of great importance for the design of new life insurance companies.[5]

In nineteenth-century Sweden there was, in principle, freedom of establishment in the insurance market, which led to a swift increase in the number of companies. Those life insurance companies that were established at the end of the nineteenth century were either mutuals or joint-stocks with limited capital stocks and with profit rights and mutual decision rights for their policyholders.[6] The smaller mutual companies contributed to the renewal of the market for life insurances by introducing so-called industrial insurance, with low weekly premium payments aimed at the working population.[7]

As a consequence, at the beginning of the twentieth century there were two different groups of mutual firms. The first generation consisted of county, administrative county district, and parish companies that mainly issued property insurance, and which had emerged in the first part of the nineteenth century in response to the shortcomings of the Fire Aid. The second generation of mutual companies, appearing from 1887, issued life insurance and were a response to the fact that stock companies earned money from people's savings for old age and illness. The critics of the stock companies came mainly from the business press associated with the mutual insurance industry and the labour movement, which at the time lacked political influence. Mutual companies considered it natural that the insurance business should be run on a non-profit basis and that surpluses should be returned to policyholders.

The formation of mutual companies towards the end of the nineteenth century contributed to give the Swedish insurance business a fragmented structure. In numbers, the market was entirely dominated by regional and local mutual companies, but there also existed a relatively large number of nation-wide companies. There was no overall structural change in the market during the first half of the twentieth century, except for the rise and fall of foreign companies during the early decades (see Table 5.1 and Chapter 11 by Lindmark and Andersson in this volume).

---

[4] Englund 1982; Adams et al. 2011.   [5] Grenholm 1955.
[6] Larsson 1991.   [7] Larsson et al. 2005.

Table 5.1. The number of Swedish and foreign insurance companies, 1889–1950, by company type

Company type	1889	1900	1910	1920	1930	1940	1950
Stock	22	35	34	55	45	47	49
Mutuals:							
Nationwide	18	30	66	99	93	94	75
County	123	127	108	85	214	177	135
Parish	398	550	1,012	1,005	1,050	993	1,124
Total mutuals	539	707	1,186	1,189	1,357	1,264	1,334
Foreign	44	77	113	66	41	42	38

Sources: Statistics of Sweden (hereafter SOS), *Försäkringsväsendet i riket* (1889, 1900); SOS, *Försäkringsinspektionens underdåniga berättelse till Kungl. Maj:t beträffande försäkringsväsendet i riket* (1910); SOS, *Enskilda försäkringsanstalter* (1920–50).

MUTUALITY AND LEGISLATION

The regulation of insurance was vital for the creation of legitimacy both for the market and its actors, especially given the stiff competition between stock and mutual companies from the late nineteenth century. Mutuals were accused by stock companies of having too small capital reserves, while stock companies were criticized for prioritizing dividends to shareholders instead of lower insurance premiums. The special insurance legislation of 1903 helped create the necessary stability in the insurance market, while, as discussed below, the legislation of 1948 represented an adjustment of regulation to the new economic and political situation in Sweden.

Given the absence of legislation, during the nineteenth century the insurance industry created its own rules of the game through agreements or trade organizations. Initially, these were substitutes for non-existent laws, but in due course they became instruments for interpreting new legislation as it was put into practice. Market traditions in Sweden have often supported the formal regulatory framework and vice versa. With the insurance law of 1903, the legislation for mutual and stock insurance companies was homogenized. The differences between company forms no longer appeared to be critical and the previous controversies that had been observed between stock and mutual companies were played down. From a legal perspective, after the law of 1903 stock and mutual companies were considered as equal organizational forms before the courts.[8]

The principles framed in the legislation of 1903 remained the basis for the Swedish insurance business over the next forty-five years, with some minor supplements. In 1948, however, a new law was adopted, which introduced a number of new principles that came to govern the Swedish insurance market

[8] Enskilt Försäkringsväsen 1954; Larsson et al. 2005.

for the following forty years.[9] Underlying these regulatory changes, there was both a recognition that the law required adapting to the transformation of society and the economy, as well as a desire to reinforce government control of the insurance market. The latter was closely connected to the growing interest of the state in influencing social development. The insurance industry was of great importance, not only because the companies accounted for an important part of the credits in the Swedish financial market, but also because private pension insurance could fulfil a significant role as a supplement to the compulsory social insurance system.

The Principles of Need and Equity

The aim of several of the new legislative principles that were introduced in 1948 was to make the private insurance business more rational and improve the position of customers, both with regard to costs and their influence on the operations of the companies. The aim of making the industry more efficient was closely connected to the criticism of the private insurance industry for being too decentralized and inefficient, points that had been already made in the 1930s. This criticism, in particular, came from the political left (now in government) and, among other things, resulted in several government bills for the nationalization of the private insurance business.[10]

Through the introduction of a special 'principle of need' in the legislation of 1948, insurance companies became subject to stricter regulation. For a new company to be allowed to start selling insurance, it had to demonstrate that there was a shortage of supply in the market.[11] Those companies that were already registered for a certain type of business, however, were automatically allowed to continue their business. Larger companies that wanted to expand their business into new areas of insurance could get permission, but it was difficult for smaller companies to enter new markets. Thus, the smaller mutual companies in local and regional markets had problems in defending their market position and in the long run they were forced either to wind up or merge with other companies.[12]

---

[9] Since the last decades of the nineteenth century Swedish life insurance was based on the so-called 'solidity' principle, whose purpose was to guarantee the economic basis of the industry. Besides the principles of need and equity, a principle of separation was also adhered to, which meant that companies kept their life and non-life operations and funds separate from each other. This principle was integrated into the legislation of 1948, which stipulated that life and property insurance could not be sold by the same company. Shortly after this the three mixed companies, Svea, Skandia, and Skåne, formally created new 'independent' companies for life insurance, but, as noted, this was little more than a codification of their existing practice.

[10] Grip 1987; Larsson et al. 2005.   [11] Statens Offentliga Utredningar 1946.
[12] Larsson et al. 2005.

Another of the principles in the legislation of 1948 worked in the same direction—the principle of equity. This meant that no policyholder was supposed to pay a higher premium than what could be considered reasonable in relation to the insurance provided by the corporations.[13] Behind this principle was a desire to make the private insurance business more efficient and reduce premium costs.[14] The government authorities considered that the industry was too fragmented and could endanger economic stability. The smaller companies were regarded as unstable, since they accumulated inadequate reserves, while, due to poor economies of scale, they also had difficulties in keeping up with the efficiency improvements of the large companies. The latter became increasingly obvious towards the end of the 1950s and in the 1960s after the insurance business had begun to be computerized.[15]

For companies dealing in property insurance, the principle of equity provided an incentive to develop more object-oriented insurance products. In the 1950s, there was a breakthrough for different kinds of combined insurances, where an object was insured against several different risks in the same policy. In combination with the principle of need, the principle of equity thus helped to limit the possibilities for the expansion of small and medium-size firms.

For many of the smaller mutual companies, however, expansion was not always desirable. These companies had been established by private persons with a common view of risk and a common need to protect themselves against certain risks. The companies were often focused on local marine insurance as well as protection against fire or hail damage and they had no interest in entering new areas of insurance or expanding geographically. They seldom had large management expenses as they were run on a more or less voluntary basis.

For such companies, a bigger problem was that the legislation strengthened the powers of the Insurance Inspection Board. Before the law of 1948, the smaller companies had been exempt from the control of the supervisory service. The new legislation, however, brought the county district companies under the board's control. This not only subjected them to similar controls as the large companies, it also meant that they were required to apply regularly for permission to continue their business.[16] After a few years this legislation was extended to cover the smallest associations—the parish companies—that

---

[13] The legislation was very unclear about how this regulation should be interpreted. It was left to the Insurance Inspection Board to determine what reasonable costs were. Companies were obliged to report their costs to the inspectorate, but an analysis of this information has failed to detect any reaction or penalty issued by the board.

[14] Statens Offentliga Utredningar 1946.   [15] Gunnarson et al. 1996.

[16] This meant that a large number of smaller companies were continuously required to report the technical foundations for insurance and their business ratios to the Insurance Inspection Board. The board also appointed an auditor for each company who made an annual report to the board. See *Lag om försäkringsrörelse (Insurance Business Law)* 1948.

mainly sold fire and marine insurance.[17] This meant that 184 parish companies were brought under the control of the board, while 775 parish companies dealing in the insurance of cattle remained outside public control. Altogether, 424 insurance companies were subject to the Insurance Inspection Board by 1955 and most of these were smaller companies.[18]

Prohibition against Distribution of Dividends

A special 'principle for mutuality' was also introduced for life insurance companies shortly after the 1948 legislation, which aimed to prohibit the distribution of profits to owners (dividends). At the end of the nineteenth century the policy of distributing profits in life insurance companies had already been the subject of a lively debate, since some companies began to give policyholders a share of profits. This formed part of the competition between stock and mutual companies, but gradually the former adjusted to this mutual principle. With the government investigations into the industry during the late 1940s, the preference against distributing dividends to the owners of life insurance companies became a norm, but not yet a legislative requirement. By the 1950s and 1960s, dividends were only paid to shareholders in a few companies, and these mainly took the form of capital transfers between subsidiaries and parent companies.[19]

Despite the fact that since 1969 no life insurance companies had distributed dividends to shareholders, an amendment of the law was introduced in 1982 that completely prohibited such dividends. This created a company structure that was more or less unique for Sweden, and is an example of the important influence of regulatory authorities that characterized relations between the state and the insurance market in Sweden from World War Two to the mid-1980s. It is somewhat surprising that this measure was introduced in a period of financial market deregulation. Nevertheless, the prohibition against the distribution of dividends confirms the strong formation of norms in the life insurance market and the relationship that existed between companies and policyholders in this area. Finally, in 2000 the prohibition against the distribution of dividends by life insurance companies was withdrawn, long after the general deregulation of the insurance market in the 1980s. There was no similar tradition of restricting the distribution of dividends in property insurance, even if there were routines for the distribution of profits, particularly in the mutual companies, which benefited the policyholders.[20] The confirmation of norms, for example the basic rules for premium calculation, reserves, or

---

[17] Statens Offentliga Utredningar 1946.   [18] Larsson 1991; Hägg 1998.
[19] Brundin 1950; Larsson et al. 2005.
[20] Bohlin and Sjöblom 2005; Larsson and Lönnborg 2010.

measuring solvency, had been important in the creation of the first insurance law in 1903, but was not that important in 1948.

The law of 1948 put the Insurance Inspection Board in a stronger position. The Inspectorate was supposed to interpret the new regulations and control how the new principles were followed. This was not that simple. The principle of equity, in particular, became only an indirect means of pressure on companies since it was difficult to specify what expenses were reasonable for different types of insurance firms. The inspectorate, however, did acquire a considerably more important role in the insurance market for the simple reason that an increasing number of companies were subject to its work.

The design of the regulatory framework, the intervention of the supervisory authority, and the cooperation between different companies contributed to the fact that the insurance market came to be characterized by a low degree of competition. The government authorities had a clear responsibility for this trend. As a result of the state's lack of faith in the self-regulatory ability of the market and too much confidence in the efficacy of government regulation, premiums and insurance policy terms were equalized between companies in the 1950s, 1960s, and 1970s. This, in turn, reinforced the position of the large companies at the cost of small and medium-size players, which was, however, in line with the aims of the government.[21]

THE INFLUENCE OF INSURANCE CUSTOMERS/OWNERS

The principal aim of the insurance law of 1948 was to safeguard the interests of policyholders. This permeated both the basic idea of the legislation—to make the industry more efficient—and a number of individual rules and principles. The protection of policyholders was also reflected in the attempts to reinforce the influence of insurance customers. In practice, these changes favoured mutual corporations at the expense of joint-stock insurers. In particular, Folksam—the trade-union insurers with close connections to the Social Democratic Party—was regarded by the Social Democratic Government as the ultimate blueprint for how an insurance company should be organized.

Differences between Joint-Stock and Mutual Companies

In the investigations carried out prior to the law of 1948 it had already been discussed how the position of policyholders was to be reinforced. The

---

[21] Larsson et al. 2005.

influence of customers constituted one of the cornerstones of the mutual companies, since these were to be run on their behalf. How this actually worked in practice, however, varied a great deal between companies. Indeed, because mutuals differed so widely, it was impossible to find one solution to governance that suited all. As long as a company was run under uncomplicated and uniform conditions, with a small number of policyholders and a limited area of business—both by geography and by product—the influence of policyholders was protected. The larger a company became, the more difficult it was to realize the basic idea of mutuality, although there was a large variation between companies in how the decision-making process was organized. In those companies where strategic decisions were transferred to the board or the management, the influence of policyholders was extremely limited.[22]

In some of the larger companies, the influence of customers worked both formally and in practice, while the influence of the policyholders in other companies was only a chimera. The committee that prepared the 1948 legislation thought that in the larger companies it was desirable to create an agency—an assembly of delegates—to be appointed in such a way that they could make decisions that were in the owners' interest. The formation of an assembly of delegates (which was normally called for annual general meetings but could also be called for additional meetings) differed among the mutual insurers. It could be achieved through direct elections among policyholders, but also by special organizations, for example county councils, chambers of commerce, and the congress of the Swedish Cooperative Wholesale Society, appointing delegates. According to the 1948 committee, other guiding principles were also possible, but the most important point was that the electoral system should be adapted to the business and organization of the company. Among the smaller county and administrative county district companies, the influence of customers might be guaranteed by voting at the annual general meeting.[23] In short, mutual insurers were supposed to have annual general meetings where every policyholder had the opportunity to attend, but with poor attendance and with the system of delegates appointed by different associations, owner participation in the governance of mutual insurance companies was not always assured or effective.

Since the question of the representation of policyholders formed part of a mutual company's application for a concession, it was possible to have several views about how this was to be organized. The situation was different for stock companies since this was already a legally established organizational form. However, this did not prevent the committee from recommending that the influence of the policyholders be strengthened in these companies too.[24] In the

---

[22] Statens Offentliga Utredningar 1946.
[23] Statens Offentliga Utredningar 1946.
[24] Statens Offentliga Utredningar 1946.

end, the variety of methods for achieving owner participation—direct or indirect—in the governance of mutual insurers defeated the committee's search for one model for all. Its chief proposal, for an assembly of delegates, was left couched in vague terms and not adopted in the new legislation.

In parallel with revising the Insurance Business Law of 1948, another special committee—comprising parliamentarians—had been examining since 1945 the question of the nationalization of the insurance industry, among other things. Nationalization was rejected in the final report of the committee, however, with the justification that state control had already been reinforced by the new business legislation. The Social Democratic majority in the committee not only advocated a democratization of both mutual and stock companies; they also had a generally positive attitude to mutual companies as an organizational form.[25] This largely reflects the spirit of the time at the end of the 1940s and in the 1950s, when the so-called 'Swedish model'—the concord between the Social Democratic Government, the labour movement, and private business that shaped state economic and social policies for decades—got its final design. Cooperation between different parties—as in this case between company representatives and policyholders—was considered the foundation for creating as efficient a system as possible. Mutuality as an organizational form fitted well into the general political priorities. At the same time, the Swedish Cooperative movement was expanding rapidly, building facilities for the production of consumer items and competing fiercely with private industry. In short, mutual companies producing goods and services increased their market shares greatly during this period.

The insurance committee of 1945, to an extent, took other aspects of the influence of policyholders than the traditional ones as the starting point for its legislative proposals. In particular, there was an emphasis on the complexity of the insurance business and the difficulties that a policyholder would face if she wanted to acquire an understanding of how various kinds of insurance worked. The insight into and the understanding of different kinds of insurances were closely related to the representation problem, according to the committee. In order to solve these problems, the committee suggested a reform programme that, among other things, meant that mutual companies would be given priority before stock companies when applying for permission to establish a new insurance venture or line of business.

The representation of policyholders on the boards of the nation-wide companies, in particular, was to be ensured by the election of delegates to shareholders' general meetings, where the elections could be made either directly by the policyholders or indirectly via collective organizations. If the interests of the policyholders could not be safeguarded in any other way, it

---

[25] Statens Offentliga Utredningar 1949.

should, however, be possible for the government to appoint representatives to the company boards.[26] Representation on the board by customers ensured their insight into the business, but in particular at the local level it was important that the contacts between companies and policyholders were more direct. County, administrative county district, and parish companies could in this case, the 1945 committee suggested, serve as a role model for the companies at the national level.

The Responsibility of the Companies

When the question of representation was evaluated by insurance experts from the cooperative insurance company Folksam in 1958, it was found that in the large insurance companies it had been difficult to create functioning electoral systems where the policyholders themselves elected delegates to the general meeting. The lack of commitment of policyholders was attributed to their lack of affinity with large companies, but also to the fact that the Swedish insurance industry was economically stable and that the companies did not put enough effort into motivating their customers to become involved.[27] This argument clearly illustrates the problem of combining large-scale business while providing for the real influence of customers.

The system of letting organizations or interest groups appoint delegates to company general meetings and to the boards of national companies had worked better than direct elections at general meetings, at least at the formal level. The Folksam experts of 1958, however, emphasized that it was important that these organizations really did represent the policyholders. Most large companies had such a spread in their clientele that a number of different organizations needed to be represented. The experts, at the same time, emphasized the need for strong local connections, even in companies operating on a national level, since this guaranteed that customers would gain insight into the business.[28]

The Folksam experts made no suggestions for changes to the legislation concerning policyholder representation. On the contrary, they emphasized that companies themselves must take responsibility for the design of their customer representation. The most important thing was not precisely how this was to be organized, but rather that it was desirable that policyholders could influence the business of companies at local and national levels. As noted above, different systems were developed in the next few decades in order to ensure this influence.

---

[26] Statens Offentliga Utredningar 1949.
[27] *Folksams försäkringsutrednings betänkande* 1962.
[28] *Folksams försäkringsutrednings betänkande* 1962.

THE RESTRUCTURING OF THE SWEDISH
INSURANCE SYSTEM AFTER 1980

The beginning of the 1980s commenced a period of change for the Swedish insurance industry. A thorough transformation took place in the following decade when Swedish private insurance underwent a decisive adjustment to the market, having previously largely been governed by government priorities. The deregulation of the international financial market, which also began to have an impact on Swedish policy from 1980, underpinned this transformation. In particular this had consequences for bank lending, but it also affected the insurance companies, for example through the abolishment of the interest regulation of unsecured bonds (1980) as well as the control of issues (1983) and the investment obligation for insurance companies (1986).[29]

An important part of the changes in the insurance market was also based on a gradual adjustment to the European Community (later European Union, EU). The Swedish adjustment to the basic regulations of the EU started in the mid-1980s when the principle of need was abolished, i.e. several years before Sweden's formal application for membership was made in 1991. The principle of need was hardly compatible with the freedom of establishment that would in the longer run re-emerge in the EU—since a concession would be sufficient for running a business in all EU member countries. The principle of reasonableness and the prohibition of the distribution of profits were maintained for a few more years and not abolished until 2000. Other changes were also made to Swedish insurance regulations against the background of adjustment to Europe. The most strategically important change occurred in 1991, when the possibility of insurance companies being able to operate businesses outside insurance was opened up. Market orientation became even more pronounced when the investment possibilities for companies were liberalized and gradually adapted to other EU members (in 1991, 1995, and 2000). Specialized insurance brokers were allowed in 1990 and in the following year funded pension plans were introduced (unit linked).[30] Deregulation also meant that it became possible to convert stock companies that did not distribute their profits into companies that could. This was the case, for example, with the life insurance companies owned by the banks Nordea and Svenska Handelsbanken.

Today, there is a high degree of concentration in Swedish insurance, where a small number of groups of companies dominate the market. Concentration

[29] The control of issues meant that, from 1952, the Riksbank controlled and approved all new issues on the bond market. In practice, this constituted an end to the issue of industry bonds. An early control of the investments of the insurance companies had been introduced after negotiations between the insurance industry and the Riksbank in 1948. This control was then gradually reinforced in the 1950s. Grip 1991; Jonung 1999; Larsson et al. 2005.

[30] Osterman 1989; Statens Offentliga Utredningar 1991; Rees and Kessner 1999; Symreng 2000.

began to increase at the beginning of the 1960s, when the majority of joint-stock companies merged into the Skandia group.[31] At the same time, there was a structural change among the nation-wide mutual companies that resulted in the establishment of the Trygg-Hansa group of companies in 1971. Among the county and parish companies, there was also a clear tendency towards mergers (see Table 5.2).

After deregulation, there was a crucial change in the structure of the insurance market both as regards the number of companies and their organizational form. The most important was a dramatic change in the number of groups of companies, which has several different explanations. First, the introduction of funded pension plans in 1991 led to the establishment of several new stock companies solely for such business. Second, after 1985, a large number of captive insurers, slightly more than thirty, were established that were also solely run as stock companies. Another explanation is that several mutual companies were restructured as stock companies, while new stock companies were established after the abolishment of the principle of need in 1985. On the other hand, there was a dramatic decrease in the number of mutual companies, both nation-wide and smaller local companies (previously defined as parish companies). A large part of this restructuring can be explained by a consolidation of local business into larger regional or nation-wide companies.

Another important structural change in the Swedish insurance market during the last fifteen years—not reflected in Table 5.2—is the possibility since 1990 of operating independent brokerages. This business grew swiftly in importance and in 2005 there were 333 registered insurance brokers. Due to these brokers and the expansion of information technology, it has become possible to enter new national markets without being established in that country in the physical sense. This might explain why the number of foreign insurance companies remained relatively limited in 2005 (see Table 5.2).

Table 5.2. The number of Swedish and foreign insurance companies, 1960–2005, by company type

Company type	1960	1965	1970	1975	1980	1985	1995	2005
Joint-stock	50	33	26	26	29	34	79	113
Mutuals: Nationwide	53	46	39	27	26	27	19	13
County	126	115	102	98	89	36	45	36
Parish	856	754	627	497	434	440	132	81
Total mutuals	1035	915	768	622	549	503	196	130
Foreign	33	32	26	17	15	14	16	25

Sources: SOS, *Enskilda försäkringsanstalter* (1960–85); *Swedish Insurance Yearbook* 1996, 2006.

[31] Englund 1982.

MUTUALITY AND THE MARKET:
TWO CASE STUDIES

The large changes in insurance regulation and in the insurance market have led to the dismantling of the 'Swedish insurance model', with its strict regulation of private insurers, which was developed after World War Two. Instead, Swedish private insurance has grown increasingly similar to the Western European insurance market. However, the mutual companies have succeeded in maintaining a strong market position. Using the following case studies, we examine two of the most important mutuals, to identify the factors that have helped them to survive.

Länsförsäkringar: From a Fire Aid Company to a Federation of Financial Department Stores

One of the most important mutual agents in Sweden is Länsförsäkringar which, in practice, consists of twenty-four independent regional companies, who jointly own a common central organization in Stockholm. Länsförsäkringar is built on the regional county companies that were established in order to supplement the Fire Aid. The first regional mutual insurance company at county level was established in 1801 and from the end of the 1830s a large number of administrative county district- or county-wide Fire Aid companies were established. However, not until 1917 did the various county companies begin to cooperate, when Landsbygdens Ömsesidiga Brandförsäkringsbolags Förening was established, mainly to run the reinsurance of the regional companies. In 1944 the name was changed to Landsbygdens Insurance and the company started to sell direct insurance for the entire group.[32] Thus, it became possible to sell insurances for which the regional companies did not hold a concession, combining a locally anchored business with scale economies in a mutual organization. Adams et al. also emphasize the importance of the strong local and regional tradition in mutual insurance. Even though centralization and rationalization might lead to economies of scale, it could also result in the loss of local knowledge that is important to reduce risks.[33]

While the regional companies were firmly anchored among the rural population, that market was shrinking with increasing urbanization. As a consequence of migration to urban areas, but also due to the increasing concentration in the insurance industry from the 1960s, several internal committees were appointed by the mutuals of the Länsförsäkringar organization in order to explore new strategies and ensure the survival of the county

---

[32] Hjärtström 2005.   [33] Adams et al. 2011.

companies. One of the most important conclusions was that a widening of the market was essential, since the declining population in the countryside was insufficient to ensure a steady growth. This strengthened the cooperation between the county companies. A new organization was introduced in 1968 and in the following year, most companies started to use the common brand Länsförsäkringar (hereafter LF) in their company names. In the following year, the brand name was extended since housing and home insurance were supplemented with automobile insurance as a core area of the group's activities. In the 1970s and the 1980s, there was a further extension of the business into company insurance. One explanation for the swift expansion in the cities was that, at the beginning of the 1970s, LF chose not to follow other property insurers that had to raise their premiums due to heavy losses.[34]

In order to create an overarching concept for all their customers' needs, it was important to extend the business to other lines of insurance. In 1971, LF started to cooperate with a mutual insurance company in order to sell life insurance. Due to the 1948 legislation and the so-called principle of need, it was not possible to get a concession for a new subsidiary. Not until the legislation was changed in 1985 was LF able to obtain a concession to establish its own life insurance company. Slightly more than a decade later, in 1996, LF also obtained permission to run a banking business and thus become a financial department store. Both the life insurance company and the banking business were formed as stock companies, while the regional companies kept their mutuality.

In 1973, an international reinsurance venture was initiated with the company Stockholm Re, but, in contrast to the Swedish stock companies and the cooperative insurer Folksam (discussed below), the liquidation of LF's international business began as early as 1993. Thus, LF succeeded in limiting those reinsurance losses that came to hit other companies so hard during the 1990s. Henceforth, LF concentrated on the Swedish market.

In the mid-1970s, the companies in the LF group had grown into an important player, accounting for nearly 20 per cent of total premiums in Swedish insurance. The group of companies continued to grow further in the following decades, as their business became more extensive. Another reason why LF succeeded in achieving such a strong position was the merger in 1998 with the banking and insurance group Wasa. In the 1980s, four mutual companies, Vegete, Allmänna Brand, Skånska Brand, and Valand, merged and formed Wasa with a market share of about 12 per cent. When Trygg-Hansa was restructured into a stock company at the end of the 1980s, Wasa also had similar plans. According to the company, there were several reasons for this reconstruction. The most important was to access capital for an international

---

[34] Svenberg 1997.

expansion and to form strategic alliances with European partners. Another reason was that Swedish tax regulations were more favourable for stock than for mutual companies. Wasa's aim was to demutualize both the life and non-life insurance companies in the group, but things did not go entirely to plan. The non-life company was demutualized first, and bought by its sister life insurance company that remained mutual, with the non-life policyholders receiving compensation for the loss of their mutual ownership stakes. With the onset of the financial crisis in Sweden and the collapse of stock prices, however, Wasa's management did not dare to risk listing its life insurance company on the stock exchange, and so demutualization remained incomplete, though the intention was to complete the process later. In fact, subsequently, after one failed attempt at a merger with LF, a successful merger finally happened in 1998. Thus, in the end, by joining the LF group, Wasa's mutual company form was maintained.[35]

In short, the strategy initiated in the 1960s, to integrate independent regional corporations, to establish companies to sell under a common brand, and to seek new geographical markets, was very successful. LF succeeded in the difficult balance of establishing a federation of regional companies with strong local connections, together with a central organization that ran the business for the entire group. The strategy of concentrating on the Swedish market, avoiding risky markets, emphasizing the mutual organizational form, and promoting the same corporate brand for all regional markets was successful. While several other Swedish insurance companies were taken over by foreign interests, the mutual form helped LF survive as an independent insurance group.

Folksam: a Mutual Cooperative Trade Union Insurance Business

Folksam has been another important mutual player in the Swedish insurance market. Folksam was established by the Swedish Cooperative Movement and closely cooperated with the trade union movement (Landsorganisationen, LO). In 1908, the company Samarbete (Co-operation) was established to write property insurance, and in 1914 the life insurance company Folket was established (by taking over the company Praktiska Liv) in order to sell so-called *folkförsäkring* (pension insurance), which mainly targeted the working class. In 1925 Samarbete started to write collective personal accident insurance, and in 1947 the group of companies also began to sell group life insurance to members of various trade unions. Through its cooperation with the trade union movement, Folksam created a strong position as a supplier of

---

[35] Larsson et al. 2005.

group insurance, in particular in connection with the emergence of labour market insurance in the 1960s.[36] In the 1980s, it also started to offer group property insurance, which attracted considerable criticism from other companies. In particular, LF opposed Folksam since group insurance was not considered compatible with a 'sound' development in the insurance market as it limited the choice for individual policyholders. Several group insurance schemes have subsequently been amended to allow policyholders to choose between different companies and types of insurance.[37]

The Folksam group succeeded in creating a strong financial base and this was used in 1946 in order to reduce its premium rates and strengthen its competitive position against both stock and other mutual companies. The low-price policy turned out to be a successful strategy and partly due to this, but also due to its links to the labour movement, Folksam developed rapidly. In many cases, Folksam was a driving force for new solutions in the insurance market, which has contributed to an increase in the rate of innovation within the industry. Folksam's success also greatly helped the development of private insurance, for example by increasing competition over premiums and by introducing new products. Due to the fact that Folksam avoided joining tariff and trade associations, it also counteracted various kinds of cartels.[38]

Folksam is a politically independent organization, but due to its deep roots within the trade union movement and the Swedish Cooperative Union, there has been a strong connection to the labour movement and the Social Democratic Party. This was underlined by the membership of individual company managers in the Social Democratic Party. This probably contributed to the fact that during the 1950s and 1960s, Folksam was held up as a model of how an insurance company should be run and managed.[39]

International reinsurance was a venture that turned out to be costly for Folksam. This business began in 1949 when a special stock company was formed to carry it out. It was initially run entirely from Stockholm and the first foreign subsidiary was not formed until 1977. In Britain, the business was developed in conjunction with the Finnish company Kansa and the

---

[36] 'Labour market insurance' provided supplementary pension insurance to members of trade unions connected to the labour movement. In addition, trade union members could sign up for group home insurance contracts offered by Folksam that were much cheaper than individual home insurance policies. This was regarded by Folksam's rivals, especially LF, as an attempt to tie all trade union members to Folksam, and therefore unfair competition.

[37] Jüring 1978, 1983; Blomberg 1964; Grip 1994; Grip 2009; Larsson 2011.

[38] Larsson et al. 2005. Research, however, has shown that despite its official critical view of cartels, Folksam did indirectly support a large number of these types of agreements. Boksjö and Lönnborg-Andersson 1994.

[39] Larsson 1991. It should also be noted that Folksam played an important role in undermining the proposals for a partial or complete nationalization of the individual insurance business after World War Two. The last government bill on this subject was presented in Swedish Parliament in 1971. Larsson et al. 2005.

Norwegian company Samvirke. In 1979, a New York subsidiary was added—also in association with other cooperative companies. In 1990, a branch was established in Singapore. At the beginning of the 1990s, profitability in international reinsurance was low and several Swedish companies left the market. Folksam, however, continued its international business, but was hit by considerable losses and was forced to sell up (the business in Britain went bankrupt). At the beginning of the 2000s, Folksam once again only operated in the domestic market, but still enjoyed a considerable market share.[40] Like LF, Folksam managed to retain its independence in the turbulent Swedish market during the 1980s and 1990s thanks to its mutual organizational form. Folksam developed very rapidly during the interwar period and early post-war years, primarily as a result of its connections with the trade union movement but also as a consequence of its low-price policy. However, in a market that is now much more competitive than it was in the 1960s and 1970s, Folksam no longer stands out as a low-price company.

In spite of their different mutual traditions—Folksam with its roots in the cooperative movement and LF in Swedish rural history—both companies managed to develop into two of the dominant companies in Swedish insurance. Today they both operate a large variety of financial services while their connections to their traditional policyholders have gradually diminished.

CONCLUSION

Swedish mutual insurance companies have often been connected to various popular movements, for example the labour movement and the farmers' movement, and have, therefore, in practice obtained quasi-monopoly rights for writing certain kinds of insurance. This has been important as a means of obtaining economies of scale and creating efficient organizations, which in turn has contributed to these companies being able to compete with their joint-stock rivals. The mutuals have also succeeded in remaining important players in the insurance market by keeping policyholders' interests in focus through creative adjustments in strategy, such as LF's expansion of its customer base in the big cities during the 1970s, or Folksam's efforts to attract customers from outside the labour movement.

We think, however, that it is not possible to draw any strong conclusions from Swedish insurance history about which company form—stock or mutual—has been most suitable for the business. Instead, changing competitive situations have forced both mutual and stock companies to rationalize and

---

[40] Kennedy 1999; Larsson et al. 2005.

become more efficient. Competition between the different forms of organization has been an important driving force for making the Swedish insurance market more efficient and supplying the customer with quality products for which there has been demand. Moreover, competition between mutual companies, in particular between LF and Folksam, has helped to promote the search for new insurance products and to increase the rate of innovation.

The development of the Swedish market in the last few decades, with a larger share of foreign ownership, has probably increased the opportunities for mutuals to reinforce their market position. In particular, LF has extended its business and now offers a very wide range of financial services adapted to customers' needs. However, Folksam has also demonstrated that it is a viable mutual insurer and the fact that Skandia (the first stock company in Sweden founded in 1855) now has re-entered as a mutual company will further strengthen the position of mutual insurers in the market.[41]

Over a longer period of time, there have been large changes in attitudes towards mutual insurance. After the legislation of 1948, the political view was that mutual companies were to be encouraged since they were considered better suited to the 'Swedish model', that compromise between the state, the labour movement, and private business that was emerging in the financial market and in society as a whole. However, it is doubtful whether most policyholders understood the differences between stock and mutual companies. Various committees pointed to the lack of interest of policyholders in participating in company decision making, so the opportunity to influence their companies' business can hardly have been decisive for most customers. As a result, the differences between mutual and stock forms emphasized by principal agent theory were in practice minimized. In the 1950s, 1960s, and 1970s, cartel agreements within the insurance industry also helped to eradicate the differences between company forms.

An important change in the relationship between the market and the state further contributed to the convergence between joint-stock and mutual insurers in Sweden. The Swedish insurance model that dominated the market until the mid-1980s meant an extensive state governance, with the insurance inspectorate supervising the activities of companies in detail. Thus, individual companies were, through their capital management, required to take responsibility for implementing the economic policy of the government. An advantage

---

[41] In a hostile takeover in 2006 the entire Skandia group was acquired by the South African insurance group Old Mutual. The daughter company Skandia Life, however, although formally a joint-stock company, was obliged by the 1948 legislation described in this chapter to act as a mutual-type organization and return all profits to its policyholders. Subsequently, it proved impossible for the Old Mutual to change the organizational form of Skandia Life and so, in 2013, the Old Mutual sold the Skandia group (with the exception of Skandia UK) to Skandia Life, a case of the daughter buying back the mother company. From 2014 Skandia is a fully fledged mutual company with business only in Sweden.

for some mutual companies, for example LF, was, however, that they were not obliged to follow certain regulations, for example the investment obligation. From the 1980s deregulation and membership of the EU meant that the Swedish model was dismantled and replaced by a more liberal approach to the relationship between the market and the state. During this phase, the joint-stock corporation was considered the most efficient ownership structure and given institutional benefits. Nevertheless, the mutual companies succeeded in adjusting their business to these changes.

After deregulation in the 1980s, there was an upturn for stock companies, in particular because they found it easier to mobilize capital and implement rationalization. Internationally a large number of conversions of mutuals into stock companies were carried out. In Sweden this demutualization wave only affected one group of insurance companies, i.e. Trygg-Hansa (and partly Wasa). In the long run, this did not turn out to be a successful strategy either. Today, after the sale of joint-stock companies to foreign competitors, the mutual insurers have a strong position in the market. Despite this, one can hardly claim that organizational form has been a major issue in Swedish insurance, particularly since the large mutual groups also contain commercial businesses operating as stock companies.

It is not easy to identify the key historical characteristics of mutual insurance in Sweden. The changes since the interwar period, however, do reveal some of the most important trends. Concentration and rationalization have led to a general transformation that has affected mutual companies in particular. Above all, they have successfully managed to attract policyholders from outside their traditional customer base. From the end of the 1940s this led to a tendency for larger mutual insurers to focus on safeguarding the interests of their policyholders through governance systems that today enjoy a relatively high degree of legitimacy among customers.

Another trend in Swedish mutual insurance has been for companies to develop into nation-wide enterprises open to all citizens, despite the fact that they have had an historical connection to certain special interests. There have existed, and still do exist, insurance companies that have targeted certain professions, but these have never played an important role in the market as a whole. Although most mutuals were founded with, and fostered through, strong connections to specific interest groups, history has shown that in order to develop and compete successfully in the growing national market they needed to attract customers beyond their core constituency. Specialized or niche companies, therefore, proved scarcely compatible with the 'Swedish model'. Within the framework of this model, priority was instead given to insurance provision that was homogenous for all citizens. This focus in the Swedish insurance system was supported by central agreements between the parties in the labour market that concerned salaries and working hours as well as insurance protection.

In short, to explain the survival and successful development of Swedish mutual insurers one might point to the fact that at an early date they were regarded as insurance providers with a high solvency, cheap premiums, and a focus on protecting their customers. During the heyday of the regulated financial market they were treated favourably by the Swedish Government and managed to grow and take advantages of economies of scale. In turn, this gave them a chance to compete with joint-stock corporations when insurance legislation became more market-friendly. Institutional and regulatory change in the 1980s and 1990s was, indeed, intended to make it easier for stock companies to develop. However, Swedish mutuals were aided by the fact that most of the larger stock companies invested heavily in expanding abroad, a strategy that eventually resulted in extensive losses and a greater vulnerability to hostile takeovers by foreign corporations. The ownership structure of the mutual insurers made them invulnerable to foreign takeovers, which is probably the most important reason why they dominate the Swedish insurance industry today. There is nothing to suggest that the mutual companies will lose their strong market position in Sweden during the next few decades.

6

Organizational Forms in Insurance

A Comparison of the USA and Germany during Industrialization

Robin Pearson

In his introduction to a recent history of reinsurance, the banking historian Harold James asserted that 'the history of insurance is also . . . the history of the joint-stock company'.[1] As the chapters in this book demonstrate, James's statement is quite misleading. Insurance has always been characterized by a multiplicity of organizational forms, not all of which easily, or indeed ever, succumbed to the purported superiority of the joint-stock corporation. The answer to the question why multiple forms co-existed in insurance was not always obvious to contemporaries, and it remains a subject of debate among economists and historians. With this in mind, this chapter offers the first historical comparison of organizational choice in two leading insurance markets, the United States and Germany, before 1914. The following section provides an overview of the context in which insurance developed in both countries. Section II describes this development and outlines the organizational trends in the industry to the extent that existing data allow. Section III explores the possible factors behind these trends. Section IV concludes.

I

Before the First World War insurance in Germany and the US expanded with large and complex populations of different organizational types. There are grounds for the comparison. In 1914 both countries were federations of states,

---

[1] James 2013, 8.

united or reunited after civil wars, and both were far into a process of rapid industrial and urban growth. Their citizens were, on average, becoming wealthier and more productive. Real per capita GDP more than doubled in Germany and the US between 1870 and 1913.[2] Despite very different migration histories, both countries underwent similar demographic transitions. By 1910 birth and death rates were much lower than forty years before and had reached about the same level.[3] Despite this positive trend and the associated improvements in medicine and public health, the spectres of unexpected illness, disability, and death remained sufficiently chilling to help underpin the growth of life, health, industrial, and accident insurance in the decades before the First World War.

In each country, economic growth was accompanied by new technologies and new challenges to the way that risks to life and property—disease, natural hazards, workplace accidents—were perceived and managed. The widespread response to such challenges involved greater regulatory control, technical improvements in risk prevention and management, and a huge expansion of insurance provision. Building construction became more closely regulated. Greater attention was paid to fireproofing, firefighting, and water systems, to the storage of hazardous materials and the control of dangerous manufacturing processes in urban areas. Communication innovations such as the telegram and telephone, the development of surveying, mapping, and geological science, the systematic collection of data on railway, road, and workplace accidents, on shipping losses, births, and deaths, fires, and burglaries together helped, in Daston's words, to 'domesticate risk'.[4] Such innovations also made the task of insurance underwriting more certain, by improving the flow and quality of information about risks, by facilitating greater precision in the pricing of risks, and by speeding up the processes of rating and loss adjustment.

The insurance industry and its collective organizations were active in pressing for safety reforms. The US National Board of Fire Underwriters (founded in 1866 by over 100 fire insurance companies) advocated improved construction methods and water systems, lobbied for relevant legislation, and introduced a national inspection of cities with the aim of standardizing fire protection and improving the urban infrastructure.[5] Public insurance societies in Germany in the 1880s introduced inspection systems for firefighting facilities and lobbied for the installation of lightning conductors and the replacement of thatch and timber with brick.[6]

The safety advances in the built environment, however, never reduced risk to the extent that the need for insurance was removed. On the contrary,

---

[2] Tipton 2003, table 4.5, 133.
[3] Namely average birth and death rates of around 29 and 15 per 1,000 respectively (US figures applying to whites only). Mitchell 2003b, table A6, fn5, and 2003a, table A6.
[4] Daston 1987.   [5] Tebeau 2003, 171–80, 199.   [6] Borscheid 1997, 100–1.

persistently high property losses at land and sea had the effect of increasing demand for insurance cover. Moreover, the insurance industry fell short on many fronts in its attempt to make business practices more risk-preventative. By 1900, for instance, across American and German towns there remained no uniform building or firefighting codes and no systematic approach to either.[7] Fireproof buildings continued to account for only a small proportion of all new structures, even in centres of fireproofing such as New York City. Automatic sprinklers were common in mills, but they remained rare in most non-industrial buildings, not least due to the cost and the reluctance of insurers to discount premiums for property owners that deployed them.[8] Fires continued to destroy entire districts of cities, small towns, and villages. Larger and more diversified insurance industries helped Germans and Americans manage the costs associated with continued levels of risk and uncertainty.

II

The insurance markets in the German states and the young American republic entered the nineteenth century with a range of different organizational forms. Most of these forms continued to coexist, compete, and sometimes cooperate throughout the century and into the next.

Marine and Transport Insurance

In Germany and America, as elsewhere, marine insurance originated with merchants underwriting each other's ships and cargoes, sometimes in an individual capacity, more often in small partnerships or syndicates. This remained the staple method of organizing marine insurance in Germany from the sixteenth to the nineteenth century. It was not until 1765 that the first stock company was successfully launched by a group of Hamburg merchants. This was quickly followed by a similar enterprise in Berlin. Between 1765 and 1807 a total of thirty-seven private marine insurance companies, some also writing fire insurance, were formed in Hamburg alone. Most did not survive the Napoleonic Wars. River transport insurance adopted the corporate form in the same period, with stock companies launched in Berlin and Hamburg in 1765 and 1792, respectively.

We cannot be certain about developments in German transport insurance during the nineteenth century for there has been no modern scholarly study of

---

[7] Rosen 1986; Sawislak 1995, 153–9; Tebeau 2003, 201.
[8] Wermiel 2000, 103, 132.

the industry. An examination of partial data, however, provides some clues about trends. The primary organizational development was the rise of the joint-stock company in ocean marine insurance, but this was also accompanied by the survival of some 'private' underwriting by individuals and partnerships in the north German ports, by the formation of several large companies modelled on the London Lloyd's scheme of subscription underwriting, and by the emergence of mutual companies, especially in inland and river transport insurance. Ten Hamburg companies accounted for over a quarter of the 65.4m RM transport insurance premiums earned by the forty-seven joint-stock and Lloyd's-type companies operating in Germany in 1891.[9] Marine underwriting in Germany was also becoming more international. In 1877 27 per cent of marine insurance in Bremen was written by ten foreign companies.[10] The industry's first collective organization was the International Transport Insurance Association, established in 1874 by thirty-six companies from Germany, Austria, Sweden, and Russia. Administered from Berlin, it promoted tariffs and other collective interests of the stock companies across European borders, giving them an advantage, albeit of uncertain extent, over private underwriters and other competitors.[11]

Mutual companies were more prominent in river transport insurance, but their aggregate business was small. In 1891 eleven German mutuals together earned just 0.27m RM in premiums from river insurance, compared with the 65.4m RM earned by joint-stock and Lloyd's companies from all forms of transport insurance.[12] One further point can be suggested. Twenty-seven of the forty-six transport insurance companies operating in 1893 had been established before German unification in 1871. This indicates that the growth of the corporate sector in German transport insurance, and the decisive displacement of the private underwriters, may have been a phenomenon of the early and middle decades of the nineteenth century, before the onset of major industrialization.

In the United States marine insurance took a similar organizational trajectory. Before the American Revolution corporate marine insurance in British North America was subject to the English legal prohibition in favour of the monopoly rights of the two London stock corporations of 1720, even though the latter sold no insurance there. Agents for Lloyd's of London, however, operated in some of the Atlantic ports and several American merchants also opened insurance offices. The latter's underwriting was modelled on the Lloyd's plan, whereby they drew up policies for shippers, then invited

---

[9] *Assecuranz Jahrbuch* 16, 1895, 194–7, 270–9.
[10] Calculated from data in *Rundschau der Versicherungen* 27, 1877, 1–11.
[11] Ehler 2009, 7; *Rundschau der Versicherungen* 26, 1876, 467–73. By 1877 there were forty-seven member companies. *Rundschau der Versicherungen* 27, 1877, 1–11.
[12] *Assecuranz Jahrbuch* 16, 1895, 194–7, 270–9.

individuals to subscribe for whatever portion of the policy they wished to insure. It has been estimated that twenty-two insurance brokers and some 164 underwriters operated in Philadelphia during the period 1721–1805. Smaller numbers appeared in the southern colonies, and a mutual marine insurance association was launched in Charleston in 1739.[13] American insurers, however, never replaced the supply of marine insurance from London at any time before the Revolution.

After independence the United States broke with the British legislative tradition of restricting corporate privileges and introduced liberal incorporation laws. From the 1790s, commencing with the Insurance Company of North America, established in Philadelphia in 1792, new corporations began pushing private underwriters out of the field. By 1810 they dominated the market. That year Boston had fourteen, Philadelphia had eight, New York had six, and others operated in Maryland, Connecticut, South Carolina, Maine, and Rhode Island.[14] The volume of American marine insurance purchased in London fell away. Thereafter, and until the Civil War, the business remained in the hands of American corporations, both mutual and joint-stock, many of which combined maritime with inland marine and fire insurance. Mutual companies grew particularly rapidly in the 1840s and 1850s. Marine insurance premiums earned by mutuals based in New York City, for example, rose from $0.4m in 1839 to a peak of $13.7m by 1856.[15]

The Civil War witnessed a sharp decline in American shipping, followed by the re-entry into American insurance markets of Lloyd's agents and foreign companies. In 1859, 70 per cent of US trade by value was carried in US ships. By 1887 this had fallen to just 14 per cent.[16] This collapse, together with the growing competition from overseas insurers and the ease by which the telegraph allowed American risks to be placed at lower rates in London, crushed many native marine insurers, both stock and mutual.[17] In 1859 there were four American stock and ten mutual marine insurance companies operating in New York. By 1883 there were just two and four respectively.[18] Native marine underwriting became concentrated in two enterprises, the Atlantic Mutual Marine of New York and the joint-stock Insurance Company of North America. These accounted for nearly half of the premiums earned by American companies in 1904. At this point there were as many foreigners as native companies writing marine insurance in the US. By 1910 foreign companies had captured nearly 60 per cent of the US market.[19]

---

[13] Crothers 2004, 611–12.   [14] Crothers 2004, 615, 632; Kingston 2007, 396.
[15] *United States Insurance Gazette* 10, 1859–60, 34.   [16] *Insurance Times* 21, 1888, 70.
[17] *Insurance Times* 20, 1887, 440; *Insurance Times* 21, 1888, 385.
[18] *Insurance Times* 17, 1884, 106, 117.   [19] *Spectator* 21 August 1919.

Fire Insurance

The first American fire insurance organizations, beginning in Charleston in 1731 and Philadelphia in 1752, were mutual contribution schemes. With the rise of state incorporation following American independence, the number of joint-stocks increased rapidly until they became the dominant form of fire insurance organization by the 1830s. During the following two decades, however, as in US marine insurance, there was a sharp upswing in new mutual ventures. Table 6.1 shows the distribution of company numbers by organizational form during the 1850s in three of America's largest markets and reveals the prominence of mutuals. Towards the end of the 1850s, however, their numbers began to fall. In New York, mutual companies fell from fifty-nine in 1852 to twenty-eight by 1859, though they still accounted for nearly one quarter of all fire insurance premiums earned in the state.[20]

From the Civil War to the First World War, the number of mutual organizations in American fire insurance generally declined, yielding ground to native and overseas stock companies. The decline, however, was not linear, and it did not occur everywhere. In New York mutuals shrank to insignificance. By 1870 mutual companies accounted for less than 2 per cent of the amount insured against fire in the state.[21] Mutuals also had a tiny share of the market, 3 per cent or less, in Illinois, Wisconsin, and California. At the other end of the spectrum, mutual companies accounted for over three quarters of fire insurance in Rhode Island in 1886.[22] In other states too, as

Table 6.1. Distribution of fire and fire and marine insurance companies by organizational form in three American states

	Total	State mutual	State joint-stock	Out-of-state mutual	Out-of-state stock	Foreign stock
New York 1854	145	45	67	2	28	2
New York 1859	187	28	97		45	3
Massachusetts 1856	126	70	36		17	3
Massachusetts 1860	166	80	35		47	4
Pennsylvania 1855	69	33	28			8

Sources: New York: *New York Insurance Reports*, Condensed Edition, vol. 1, 2, vol. 2, 1014; *Insurance Times* 17 (February 1884) 106. Massachusetts: Massachusetts Insurance Commission, *Annual Report* 1867. Pennsylvania: *United States Insurance Gazette*, 7 (1858), 33.

[20] *Insurance Times* 17, 1884, 106.
[21] *12th Annual Report of the New York Insurance Superintendent for 1870*, pt. 1.
[22] Figures for Rhode Island, Illinois, Wisconsin, and California are calculated from data respectively in *Insurance Times* 13, 1880, 212; *Insurance and Commercial Magazine* 1 May

Table 6.2. Distribution of fire and marine insurance companies and market shares in three American states (market share percentages in brackets)

Massachusetts (fire and marine)	Total	State mutual	State joint-stock	Out-of-state stock	Foreign joint-stock
1870	207	77	33	92	5
1874		(21.6)	(18.1)	(45.8)	(14.5)
1880	194	51	21	98	24
1881		(20.7)	(14.5)	(40.0)	(24.8)
1887		(25.1)	(10.0)	(40.3)	(24.6)
1890	220	81	15	99	25

Maine (fire and marine)	Total	State mutual	State joint-stock	Out-of-state mutual	Out-of-state stock	Foreign stock
1880	124	35 (2.6)	3 (n/k)	3 (1.7)	62 (72.4)	21 (23.4)
1900	151	28 (3.8)	2 (n/k)	4 (1.4)	66 (63.8)	33 (30.9)
1910	152	46 (7.5)	2 (n/k)	7 (3.3)	64 (67.3)	23 (21.8)
1915	182	53 (5.0)	2 (n/k)	39 (21.5)	61 (55.1)	27 (18.4)

Connecticut (fire only)	Total	State mutual	State joint-stock	Out-of-state mutual	Out-of-state and foreign stock
1890	118	17 (13.3)	9 (22.9)	4 (0.8)	88 (63.0)
1910	160	14 (6.7)	8 (19.1)	17 (1.9)	121 (72.3)
1915	166	14 (5.8)	10 (18.8)	19 (2.2)	123 (73.2)

Note: Company numbers for Massachusetts and Maine comprise companies writing fire and both fire and marine. All market shares are percentages of gross sums insured by these companies against fire only. Market share calculations for Maine exclude the very small, but unknown, business of the local stock companies.

Sources: Massachusetts: *20th Annual Report of the Insurance Commissioner of the Commonwealth of Massachusetts for 1874*, pt. 1; *31st Annual Report of the Insurance Commissioner of the Commonwealth of Massachusetts for 1885*, pt. 1; *33rd Annual Report of the Insurance Commissioner of the Commonwealth of Massachusetts for 1887*, pt. 1; *Indicator* 10 (1891): 112. Maine: *13th Annual Report of the Insurance Commissioner of the State of Maine for 1880*, pt. 1, table 7; *33rd Annual Report of the Insurance Commissioner of the State of Maine for 1900*, tables 8, 9; *43rd Annual Report of the Insurance Commissioner of the State of Maine for 1910*, tables 8, 9; *48th Annual Report of the Insurance Commissioner of the State of Maine for 1915*, table 1. Connecticut: *26th Annual Report of the Insurance Commissioner of the State of Connecticut for 1890*, table 11; *40th Annual Report of the Insurance Commissioner of the State of Connecticut for 1910*, table 11; *51st Annual Report of the Insurance Commissioner of the State of Connecticut for 1915*, table 10.

Table 6.2 demonstrates, mutuals remained populous and even increased in numbers. By the late 1880s in Massachusetts they far outnumbered local stock companies and had captured over one quarter of the market.

Large or increasing numbers did not always translate into market power. In Maine thirty-five of the thirty-eight local companies in 1880 were mutual, but they accounted for less than 3 per cent of sums insured against fire. Most business in Maine was written by stock companies from other US states and

1876, 75; *Indicator* 3, 1884–85, 169; *33rd Annual Report of the Insurance Commissioner of the State of California for 1900*, table 3.

overseas. After a drop in numbers during the 1880s and 1890s, mutual organizations grew rapidly through to the First World War. By 1915 fifty-three of the fifty-five Maine fire and marine insurance companies were mutual, as were thirty-nine of the 100 out-of-state companies operating in the state. These two groups of mutual companies together accounted for over a quarter of the market, having greatly eroded the position of their joint-stock rivals.[23] In Connecticut mutual companies accounted for 15 per cent of fire insurance in 1885. Their numbers declined through to 1900, though not precipitously. Thereafter, Connecticut also experienced a revival of local mutuals, coupled with an invasion by mutuals from other states. By 1915, however, together they still only accounted for 8 per cent of sums insured against fire, barely more than half the share they had enjoyed twenty-five years earlier. This kind of state-level data on US market trends, together with an examination of the factors behind such trends, remains very incomplete. Much more primary data is available than has been processed to date. It is anticipated that future research will be able to provide a far more comprehensive analysis of the American property insurance market than can be given here.[24]

The total sum insured by fire and marine insurers in the United States rose nearly ninefold (in current prices) from an annual average of $6.4bn in 1877–80 to $56.0bn by 1914.[25] Between 1850 and 1910 fire insurance grew eleven times faster than the US population and over three times faster than the economy as a whole.[26] In Germany, too, fire insurance grew rapidly. Premiums increased nearly four times as fast as the population between 1852 and 1910. The organizational structure of German fire insurance, however, was much more complex than its American counterpart. In 1890, for instance, there were twenty-five public buildings insurance societies with monopoly privileges, including six in Prussia with compulsory insurance rights. Another thirty-one similar societies operated without monopolies. There were nineteen private mutual companies writing on a nationwide basis, and 235 smaller local mutual associations in Prussia—seventy-nine insuring only buildings, 156 insuring contents—plus an unknown number of such associations based outside Prussia. Stock companies totalled only thirty, a figure that had remained almost unchanged for three decades. Although some German stock companies were among the largest fire insurers in Europe, as Table 6.3 shows

---

[23] Calculated from the *48th Annual Report of the Insurance Commissioner of the State of Maine for 1915*, table 1, 12; *13th Annual Report of the Insurance Commissioner of the State of Maine for 1880*, pt. 1, table VII.

[24] This work is the subject of my ongoing project: *Insuring America: Multinational Insurance Enterprise in the US 1850–1920*. The general history of the industry has been recounted skillfully by Baranoff 2003.

[25] *Statistical Abstract of the United States 1929*, table 311.

[26] Pearson 2010a, tables 1.1, 1.2.

Table 6.3. Distribution of total net fire insurance premiums in Germany by organizational type (%)

	Total premiums (mRM)	Joint-stock	Public mutual	Private mutual	Foreign
1882	104.1	48.8	38.7	12.5	n/k
1900	179.9	50.2	35.3	14.5	n/k
1905	235.4	44.0	32.6	13.6	9.9
1910	265.2	44.6	31.4	13.7	10.3

Sources: 1882: *Assecuranz Jahrbuch* 6 (1885) 327; 1900–10: Gesellschaft fuer Feuerversicherungsgeschichtliche Forschung 1913, vol. 2, 590, table XIII.

they usually accounted for less than half of the German domestic market before the First World War.[27]

This fragmented market had its origins in the early modern period. The oldest form of fire insurance were the fire guilds (*Brandgilden*) widely found across northern Germany from the fifteenth century. These were local fraternal societies in which residents of villages and small towns agreed to assist each other with labour, materials, and funds in the event of a fire. In central and southern Germany the fire guilds had less formal counterparts in the mutual clubs of peasant farmers (*Bauernassecuranz*). Another early form of mutual insurance, found widely across northern Europe, the county- and parish-based contributions, derived directly from the medieval tradition of compulsory collections for victim relief in the wake of fires.[28]

In late sixteenth-century Hamburg a new type of private insurance emerged, the 'fire contract', which was a written agreement between owners of property within the town walls, known as 'consorts'. In return for a fixed subscription, consorts who became victims of a fire received a payment from the joint fund, which had to be used for the repairing or rebuilding of the damaged property—contents were not insured. The fire contracts were entered into the town's central registry of documents and had to be confirmed by the senate, thus lending them a degree of official status.[29]

By the 1670s there were some forty-six 'fire contracts' operating in Hamburg. However, their small scale and the difficulty of spreading risk in a confined area led the senate in 1676 to merge all inner-city contracts into one new fund, the *Feuerkasse*, to be administered by municipal officers. A maximum of 15,000 marks, and no more than three quarters of the rateable value of a property, could be insured by each member, for an *ex-ante* premium rate of 4 shillings per 1,000m insured. There was no compulsion on existing householders to join the

---

[27] Boenigk 1895: 7.
[28] On fire guilds, see Helmer 1925–6. On *Bauernassecuranz*, see Rohrbach 1988. On compulsory contribution schemes, see Feldbæk et al. 2007.
[29] The earliest recorded fire contract in Hamburg was dated 1591, but this may have had predecessors. Büchner 1976, 4–13.

fund—full compulsion was not introduced until 1817—but whoever built a new house or bought or inherited a house was required to join. If the fund proved insufficient, members were liable for further calls at rates proportionate to the amounts they had insured. The fund was also to be used to pay the medical bills of citizens injured fighting fires, annuities to those rendered permanently disabled, and the burial costs of the victims of fires. Thus the Hamburg *Feuerkasse*, probably the world's first 'modern' fire insurance organization, combined elements of private mutual and public service functions.[30]

The *Feuerkasse* quickly provided a model for others to follow. Zwierlein counted ninety-six public societies to insure buildings in German states between 1676 and 1817, sixty-five of them founded before 1780.[31] Some of the territorial fire insurance schemes achieved impressive coverage, insuring between 50 and 75 per cent of all property in their regions.[32] Some were based on *ex-ante* payments made proportionate to the value of the property insured (though not apparently to the risk involved). Others operated with the older system of *post-hoc* levies on members to meet losses.[33] Regardless of the payment system adopted, insurance in these societies was usually made compulsory, except for a few privileged groups. They operated essentially as extensions of state revenue systems, managed by civil servants on a not-for-profit basis, with surpluses put towards the rebuilding of property damaged by fire and to supplement other forms of welfare expenditure.[34]

Public buildings insurance multiplied in *ancien regime* Germany partly because of cameralist suspicions of private for-profit insurance, but there were limits to state involvement. Private companies selling contents insurance were tolerated because their customers were mostly wealthier property owners who were regarded by authorities as literate and numerate enough to understand what they were buying. The fluctuating values and heterogeneity of household contents also made that category of underwriting more complex, and the public institutions were generally content to leave it to the private companies. Property owners increasingly turned to private insurers to cover that proportion of the value of their buildings, usually 25 per cent, which the public institutions would not insure, so that in both contents and buildings insurance the scope grew for a private market. One of the earliest insurance companies to insure contents was a mutual office founded in Hamburg in 1795. Other private stock and mutual fire insurance companies followed in the early nineteenth century in Berlin, Leipzig, Elberfeld, Gotha, and Aachen. This took place against a background of increasing criticism of the

[30] The regulations of 1676, *Die Punkta der General Feur-Ordnungs Cassa*, are reproduced in Büchner 1976, 116–24. Zwierlein 2011, 223–42, describes the *Feuerkasse* as a hybrid of the older mutual aid contract and modern premium insurance.

[31] Zwierlein 2011, appendix II. For an account of the first public fire insurance schemes in Brandenburg-Prussia, in 1705 and 1718, see Dorwart 1958.

[32] Zwierlein 2011, 297–8.   [33] Zwierlein 2011, 301.   [34] Borscheid 1997, 42–4.

costs, inefficiency, and compulsion associated with the public societies, views influenced by the growth of the liberal reform movement in the German states.

As private companies began to carve out a market for the insurance of moveable goods, various states responded by removing the monopoly of buildings insurance enjoyed by their public societies.[35] Henceforth the latter had to compete with the private stock and mutual companies in more open markets. Germans, however, never abandoned the idea of public fire insurance. Considerable efforts were made during the 1820s and 1830s to combine the small municipal and local societies into larger units to improve their competitiveness and risk distribution. Nevertheless, in places such as Westphalia the new provincial societies were hampered by adverse selection problems caused by legislation requiring them to insure all property offered to them.[36]

From the 1860s the public societies conducted a fightback, as they formed new national associations to represent their interests and lobbied hard for the nationalization of the insurance industry.[37] Among German bureaucracies traditional suspicions of private insurance lingered long after the national economy commenced its industrial transformation. Compulsory buildings insurance continued to be extensive. In 1877, 65 per cent of the 23bn RM written on buildings by the seventy-seven public fire insurance institutions in Germany was insured under compulsion, a proportion that had little changed in over twenty years. Indeed, through to the end of the century some German states continued to legislate for compulsory insurance in public societies.[38] Thus in German fire insurance some of the oldest and most traditional organizational forms survived, albeit somewhat transformed, and even thrived to the end of the nineteenth century and beyond.

Life, Health, and Accident Insurance

Of the three founding branches of modern insurance, life insurance was the last to develop in Germany and America. Between the fifteenth and eighteenth centuries in Germany, as in many European states, governments placed restrictions on life insurance or prohibited it altogether as a morally iniquitous form of betting on lives.[39] Where there was the prospect of adding to state revenue, however, governments were prepared to endorse tontines, a

---

[35] From 1840 private insurers were allowed to compete freely with the public institutions in three Prussian provinces, Rhineland, Westphalia, and Poznan. Borscheid 2010, 49.

[36] Borscheid 1997, 82–6.   [37] Arps 1965, 81–98.

[38] Oldenburg, for example, passed a law requiring compulsory contents insurance in 1879. The data cited are calculated from *Rundschau der Versicherungen* 29, 1879, 255–6.

[39] For example, the ordinances of 1730, part of the Brandenburg-Prussian maritime laws, banned 'insurance on men's lives'. Walford 1878, 288.

contribution scheme in which annual payments were shared out among surviving members. These were used, along with lotteries, to finance the military spending of many smaller German states. Other forms of mutual aid were usually confined to particular groups. The Knappschaften, for example, a medieval fraternal institution, provided miners with sickness, accident, and death benefits. They expanded and became compulsory during the nineteenth century.[40] Numerous benefit societies also appeared that provided a widow with a perpetual annuity against the payment of regular contributions during her husband's lifetime. Most involved a few dozen members and were confined to particular groups such as physicians, lawyers, and military officers. A few had much larger risk pools, such as the 5,000-strong Calenbergische Witwen-Verpflegungsgesellschaft, founded in Hannover in 1766.[41] A few private and state-owned manufacturing enterprises also operated sickness, accident, and burial funds for their employees.[42] Some states not only authorized such ventures, but also participated directly by providing pensions, sickness, and disability allowances for key groups of public employees.[43] From the 1840s many states encouraged the growth of voluntary mutual aid funds in which membership was often made compulsory. By 1876 there were nearly 7,600 such funds in Germany with more than 1.8m members.[44] None of these schemes relied on a priori actuarial pricing or risk classification. Many remained poorly managed and financially precarious, problems that by the 1870s drove commentators and politicians to consider statutory national social insurance.

The earliest private life insurance companies in Germany appear to have been the mutual and joint-stock ventures founded in Hamburg in 1778 and 1806, respectively, and the mutual institution for clergy, teachers, and widows founded in Brunswick in 1806.[45] All these confined their business to the residents of their cities and were short-lived. The first durable institution that utilized a sales agency network was founded in the duchy of Gotha in 1827. The mutual Gotha Life Insurance Bank quickly became one of Europe's largest life insurers. A small number of other mutuals and stocks followed. By 1850 there were ten life insurance companies in Germany, equally divided between joint-stocks and mutuals. These ten, plus two companies in Austria, together insured £7.4m in 38,000 policies. The Gotha Insurance Bank alone accounted for 16,000 of these policies and £3.6m (49 per cent) of the total insured.[46] At this point, life insurance remained expensive and confined to the wealthier middle classes. Industrial workers and small farmers continued to

---

[40] Guinnane and Streb 2011.   [41] Rosenhaft 2004.   [42] Borscheid 1984, 59.

[43] The Austrian pension scheme for state employees of 1763 provided the model for similar German schemes during the nineteenth century. Rohrbach 1988, 75–83.

[44] Borscheid 1984, 61, n. 11.

[45] Borscheid 1984, 61–2. On the Hamburg mutual venture, see Borscheid 1989, 13–15.

[46] Walford 1878, 288–94.

resort to savings banks and mutual benefit societies. As yet few life insurance companies marketed their products, few utilized the latest actuarial techniques to determine premium rates or the distribution of profits, and few maintained technical reserves to meet outstanding liabilities. In some states a private company was granted a limited term monopoly, which further hindered improvements in efficiency and growth.[47]

The division between mutual and stock forms was not always clearly maintained. Some of the early stock companies were 'hybrids' in that they shared profits with their policyholders. The Mecklenburg Life Assurance and Savings Bank, founded in Schwerin in 1853, began with a joint stock of 100,000 thalers in 500 shares, but aimed to convert to the mutual form as soon as its business became 'self-sustaining'. Ten per cent of annual profits were to be transferred to an amortization fund, employed to buy back the original shares at par, while 60 per cent were to be divided among the policyholders, after having been placed in a reserve for five years. The remaining 30 per cent were to be paid as dividends to shareholders.[48]

During the second half of the century, demand for life insurance was boosted by rising household incomes, tax relief on premiums, fear of epidemic disease, and by the introduction of Bismarck's social insurance schemes, discussed below. Table 6.4 shows the expansion of life insurance in Germany between 1850 and 1910. Growth in the number of policies remained in double digit figures, but between 1879 and 1910 the average size of a policy declined. Mutual companies grew much slower than stock companies, and their share of total policies fell from 41 to 21 per cent. Their share of the total amount insured, however, did not decline so precipitously, indicating that in contrast to the stock companies, the average size of policies sold by mutuals was increasing before the First World War. These are trends that possibly reflected underlying changes in German society and business, and would merit serious research.[49]

By the early 1870s many German life insurance companies were also transacting accident and employers' liability insurance. This market was directly stimulated by state interventions. The Imperial Liability Law of 1871 made large areas of German industry liable in the event of workplace injuries. This greatly increased the demand from employers for private accident insurance.[50] Compulsory contribution employment-based health insurance was introduced in 1883, followed by statutory accident insurance in 1884 and state disability and old age insurance for workers in 1889. The health scheme

---

[47] In Prussia, for example, the Berlin Life Insurance Company of 1836 was granted a fifteen-year exclusive right to sell life insurance in the state. Borscheid 1984, 64.

[48] Walford 1878, 295–6.

[49] Writing in 1984 Borscheid remarked how German life insurance awaited its great scholarly interpreter. Thirty years later this sadly remains true.

[50] Stadlin 2010, 44.

Table 6.4. The growth and distribution of life insurance in Germany, 1850–1910

	All companies			Joint-stocks		Mutuals	
	No. of policyholders ('000)	No. of policies ('000)	Insurance in force (mRM)	No. of policies ('000)	Insurance in force (mRM)	No. of policies ('000)	Insurance in force (mRM)
1850	37		143				
1879	574	789	2,151	468	1,153	321	998
1910		10,686	13,538	8,452	7,909	2,234	5,629

Source: Borscheid and Drees 1988, 61, 63, 65.

of 1883 entailed a system of sickness funds based locally, or at particular firms or guilds, with separate funds for construction workers and miners. Employers were required to provide insurance for all workers earning below 2,000 marks, although those earning more were allowed to buy into the scheme. Premiums were paid in a 2:1 ratio by the employee and employer. Insured workers were entitled to free medicines and medical treatment and to cash payments worth up to half the wage through to the thirteenth week of incapacity.[51] Originally the scheme applied only to certain categories of industrial worker, but from 1901 coverage was gradually extended to other occupational groups. These statutory schemes helped spread the understanding of life and health insurance, stimulated the growth of private companies supplying accident insurance to employers, and kick-started the provision of private industrial assurance for the German working class. A turning point in the latter was marked in 1911 by the creation of the *Volksfürsorge*, a project of the cooperative and free trade union movements, which in turn elicited a response from thirty private life insurance companies that founded a joint industrial assurance venture of their own.[52] In sum, life, pension, health, and liability insurance grew by the end of the nineteenth century into a huge national business, insuring millions of Germans and comprising a range of public and private, cooperative, mutual and joint-stock organizational forms.

In contrast to much of eighteenth-century Europe, in colonial British North America there was no restriction or prohibition of life insurance. The market, however, remained tiny. Two corporations in Philadelphia, chartered in 1759 and 1769, provided life insurance on a not-for-profit basis for the widows and orphans of clergymen. There were also small fraternal societies that covered their members for the costs of burial. The first for-profit life insurance was sold by two stock companies chartered in Pennsylvania and Massachusetts in 1811 and 1818, respectively. Both were intended to provide an income for philanthropic bodies, namely the Orphan Society of Philadelphia and the Massachusetts Hospital in Boston. Neither company sold, or tried to sell, much life insurance, their policies being expensive because they employed pessimistic mortality assumptions.[53] Although it became the largest financial institution in New England, the primary business of the Massachusetts company involved managing deposits in trust.[54] Before the 1830s a few other companies were chartered to write life insurance, but most were soon wound up. Just two joint-stocks, the New York Life Insurance and Trust and the Baltimore Life Insurance, both incorporated in 1830, succeeded in expanding their businesses with more accurate mortality tables and rate structures, and with agency networks that extended beyond their home cities. By 1840

---

[51] Winegarden and Murray 1998.   [52] Arps 1965, 583–98.
[53] Murphy 2008.   [54] White 1955, appendix 3; Dalzell 1987, 81, 103–10.

Table 6.5. The growth of life insurance in the United States, 1840–1910

	No. of companies	Life insurance in force ($m)
1820	6	0.1
1840	15	4.7
1850	48	97.1
1860	44	173.0
1870	123	2,006.1
1880	58	1,522.7
1890	60	3,522.2
1900	84	7,573.0
1910	284	14,908.0

Source: Wright 2010, appendices 1, 2.

the New York company accounted for more than half of the $8.6m of life insurance sold in the US.[55]

The banking panic of 1837, however, reduced the enthusiasm of American investors for all types of new joint-stock projects. Between 1838 and 1846 only one new stock life insurer successfully raised a capital. Insurance promoters turned instead to the mutual form of organization. By the end of the 1840s seventeen new life mutuals had been formed.[56] As Table 6.5 shows, the initial growth surge occurred during this first heyday of the mutuals. Whereas the volume of life insurance grew eightfold in the 1830s, it increased by a factor of 21 in the 1840s.

Nevertheless, many of the new mutuals ran on shoestring budgets and inadequate reserves, and as growth slowed in the 1850s, several went bankrupt. This increased concerns about the viability of mutual forms of insurance. Some state legislatures, led by New York in 1849, introduced the requirement that all new life insurance ventures raise at least $100,000 of equity capital for the protection of their policyholders before commencing business. This resulted in the formation of some hybrid companies with part-mutual and part-stock financial structures. The legal stipulation about start-up capital, together with increasing taxation and regulatory restrictions on investments, also helps explain why new company formation slowed down in the 1850s. Sales remained weak, except in the urban south where there was a rapidly growing market in insuring slaves.[57]

---

[55] Murphy 2010, 4–6.   [56] Murphy 2010, 6.

[57] A further law in 1851 required all life insurance companies operating in New York, including those chartered prior to the law, to deposit $100,000 in US public stock, bonds, or mortgages on real estate with the state comptroller. Wright 2010, 247; Murphy 2010, 8, 117. On slave insurance before the Civil War, see Murphy 2005.

From the beginning of the Civil War through to 1870 there was a new boom in American life insurance. This was partly due to the fact that most companies accepted war-related risks, but it was also because of the improved image of life insurance in the contemporary press as legitimate and trustworthy.[58] By this time the technology of legal reserves had been established and sales systems had become extensive enough for life insurance to be affordable to larger numbers of people. Sales of new policies rose from $160m in 1862 to $1.3bn by 1870, an average annual growth rate of 30 per cent.[59] As Table 6.5 shows, the number of companies trebled in the 1860s and the volume of life insurance multiplied nearly twelvefold. Greater competition led to the temptation to be incautious in the struggle for market share. Some companies paid dividends and accepted premiums in the form of promissory notes or scrip, and overextended their operations and racked up management expenses upon this uncertain income. Others fell victim to outright fraud by clerks and directors. Public trust and confidence declined as bankruptcies increased and industry malpractices came to light.[60] Economic recession also took a toll on smaller companies, struggling with bad investments and rising expense and mortality rates. As Table 6.5 shows, 1870 marked the onset of a catastrophic collapse in company numbers and sales. The industry responded in several ways. First, there was a flight to quality that benefited the more cautious companies that insured only select lives and kept expenses and agents' commissions low.[61] Second, the market became more concentrated. By 1881 three giant New York corporations, one mutual and two stock, had come to dominate the industry with 40 per cent of the $1.7bn insured on American lives. We do not know the exact share enjoyed by mutual companies, but in that year four of the largest mutuals, including the market leader the Mutual Life, together insured 32 per cent of the total.[62] Third, the three New York giants led the first export drive of US insurance, aggressively marketing cheap tontine or deferred dividend policies to the consternation of European regulators and competitors.[63] Fourth, a small number of new companies emerged, such as the Prudential and the Metropolitan Life, which targeted lower-income families with cheap 'industrial assurance', comprising small policies and weekly door-to-door collections of premiums.[64]

---

[58] Budros 1989, 226; Wright 2010, 248–9.

[59] Measured in 1860 US dollars, Wright and Smith 2004, 23. Budros 1989, 248, suggests that by 1870 New York's life insurance industry had reached its peak density for the nineteenth century and that consequently the pool of investors 'must have been near exhaustion', although it is unclear how his data demonstrate this.

[60] Budros 1989, 227.   [61] Wright and Smith 2004, 33–4.

[62] Market shares calculated from Wright and Smith 2004, 35, tables 1–6.

[63] The Equitable Life of New York, chartered in 1859, began issuing these kinds of policies as early as 1868. Murphy 2010, 175. On US life insurance exports in this period see Wilkins 1970.

[64] Murphy 2010, 295–6.

On this basis the industry recovered. By 1894 $4.9bn was insured in the US, which represented some 46 per cent of world life insurance.[65] Complaints about the industry, though, never disappeared. By 1905 some two thirds of all policies were tontine or deferred dividend plans.[66] These gained a poor reputation for a high lapse rate and for delivering poor value.[67] It has been estimated that only about 40 per cent of holders of such policies received dividends at the end of their policy term. Some died before the expiry of their policy, but most allowed their policies to lapse. Industrial assurance too came under criticism for the fact that it was $-for-$ expensive compared to ordinary whole life insurance. Partly this was because working-class mortality was higher, but it was also because of high collection costs and management expenses. Many fraternal societies also appeared towards the end of the nineteenth century offering industrial assurance on a mutual basis. They competed successfully against their larger for-profit corporate rivals, mostly due to the informational and associational advantages and lower set-up costs that they enjoyed. Fraternals only faded in the early twentieth century after the federal government began to regulate them more closely.[68]

Following increased public clamour about the need to protect policyholders from the depredations of life insurance corporations, the State of New York established an investigating committee in 1905. The Armstrong investigation uncovered fraudulent accounting, bad investments, and the gross misappropriation of company funds for personal use by managers and directors. Numerous state legislatures followed New York in abolishing tontine policies and regulating investments, proxy voting, policy forms, lobbying practices, and the activities of agents. Henceforth, companies, regardless of their ownership structure, were required to issue dividends to shareholders and policyholders alike. Profits not returned in this way became limited to 10 per cent of a company's liabilities. The use of premiums as slush funds for investment schemes was prohibited.[69] These measures helped to repair public confidence, but they also stimulated structural change.[70] One consequence of the Armstrong report resulted from the support that it gave to the mutual form of organization. This helped to induce a wave of mutualization of large stock corporations, including the Prudential, the Equitable Life and the Metropolitan Life, that continued through the First World War and into the 1920s.[71]

---

[65] Calculated from data collected by the Actuarial Society of America, reproduced in *Insurance Critic* 22, 1894, 48.

[66] Murphy 2010, 175–6; Budros 1989, 228.

[67] Among many examples, see the attack on the 'mortuary tontine' scheme of the United States Beneficial Life Insurance Company of New York in *Milwaukee Sentinel* 30 August 1871.

[68] Stalson 1942, 445–61; Wright 2010, 249.

[69] Wright and Smith 2004, 43–4; North 1954; Ransom and Sutch 1987.

[70] Wright 2010, 250.   [71] Wright and Smith 2004, 70–2.

III

Given the partial, and in some areas still immature, state of historical literature on the German and American insurance industries, the above survey is inevitably incomplete. Nevertheless, the data already point to three general conclusions: first, that both industries were characterized by multiple organizational forms more or less from birth; second, that no single form ever consistently dominated all markets over time, regardless of whether one defines these markets by geography or by line of insurance; third, that many factors underpinned organizational choice. Identifying these factors and their relative importance, however, remains problematic without further research and so the following discussion must be tentative in nature.

What shaped organizational choice in German and American insurance? Was it determined by differentials in access to capital? Was organizational form the product of attempts to resolve principal agent and other internal governance problems, or external information problems relating, for instance, to levels of moral hazard among policyholders? Alternatively was organizational form shaped by adaptation to the changing nature of risk in different lines of insurance over time? Were certain forms crowded out of markets by the existence of private or state monopolies, or by discriminatory regulation, or were other political and cultural forces, such as mutualism, the most influential? All of these factors appear at different times and with varying degrees of significance in the history of both countries' insurance industries.

There were periods when financial crises, bankruptcies, a tightening of credit markets, and uncertainty among investors drove capital away from new stock company promotions to the benefit of mutual organizations. A good example of this was the reconfiguration of American life insurance following the banking crisis of 1837, whereby mutual companies rose to dominate the industry for the next two decades. The weak condition of the equity markets, however, is not the only explanation that has been put forward. Stalson has suggested that aggressive marketing campaigns using more effective agency networks helped the new mutuals of 1843 gain ground over the few existing stock companies. Zelizer has argued that more positive religious attitudes towards life insurance, whereby it was no longer regarded as an industry that undermined people's faith in providence, boosted the growth of mutual life insurance in the 1840s. Murphy rejects both these explanations. She argues that the mutuals constructed their businesses on foundations laid by the early stock companies, while also capturing the optimism of the new urban middle class by marketing life insurance as an investment, rather than simply as a compensation for the death of a breadwinner.[72]

---

[72] Stalson 1942; Zelizer 1983; Murphy 2008; Murphy 2010.

Whichever is the more accurate account of early US life insurance, variable access to capital seems but a partial explanation of the distribution of life insurance among mutual and stock forms of organization. Regardless of their form of organization and ownership, it was important for life insurers to invest their funds profitably and to distribute their portfolios across a wide range of assets. Because they were selling a financial product with a long time horizon, both mutuals and joint-stocks needed to ensure that investments generated sufficient funds to meet a rising volume of liabilities as policyholders aged and died. Companies that failed to manage assets carefully with this long-run liability curve in mind would have poor survival prospects.[73] This applied equally to life insurance in Germany. In periods when German capital markets grew slowly, as was the case before the 1860s, investment outlets became limited, which undermined the growth capacity of mutuals as well as stock companies, even the very largest, such as the mutual Gotha Life Insurance Bank.[74]

As noted in the introduction to this volume, the question of governance has been at the core of the economic theory of organizations. It has been argued that the historic competitiveness and survival of mutual insurance organizations depended upon good governance as much as good investments, in order to maximize policyholder value and preserve reputational capital.[75] However, the historical evidence from Germany and America for the managerial preference problem is, at best, ambiguous. The scandals that hit US life insurance in the early twentieth century afflicted mutual and stock companies alike. The greatest scandal involved the internal governance of America's largest joint-stock life insurer, the Equitable Life of New York.[76] The lavish lifestyle of the Equitable's vice-president, James Hyde, son of the company's founder, captured the attention of the gossip columnists and raised questions about how it was paid for. In 1904–5, on the eve of the Armstrong investigation, Hyde's rivals organized a coup against his 'personal proprietary regime'. This involved extending the Equitable's franchise to policyholders so that they could vote in board elections, a reform that the plotters described, inaccurately, as 'fully mutualizing' the company. Their logic was that if policyholders could vote, the field agents, controlled by Hyde's rivals, would be able to campaign for the reform slate of candidates who would then vote Hyde out of office. The struggle lasted six months and was characterized by the revelation of murky financial dealings on both sides. Once Hyde was ousted, he had to face the hostile questioning of the Armstrong committee and a string of lawsuits that drove him into exile for several years. In 1909 the Equitable fell under the control of Pierpont Morgan, who inaugurated a full mutualization that was

---

[73] Wright and Kingston 2012, 452–3. [74] Borscheid 1989: 35–6.
[75] Wright and Smith 2004, 11–12.
[76] Buley 1967, vol. 1, 587–699, vol. 2, 701–824; Beard 2003.

completed in 1914. The Equitable affair shows how a change in organizational form could be a means of rescuing a corporation from the consequences of severe governance problems. It also reveals how organizational choice might become a weapon in the hands of those involved in bitter internal warfare over corporate control.

Early US marine insurance may be seen as a good illustration of the role of asymmetric information problems in determining organizational forms, but here too scholars have recognized other factors at work.[77] In the 1790s private underwriters and brokers claimed that their system could more accurately assess the risks of shipping and insure them more cheaply than could the new stock corporations, and without the danger of monopoly control. By limiting their exposure on any single risk and by spreading their underwriting as carefully as possible across several different voyages, private underwriters believed that they could minimize losses. Writing for their own account, they required no costly governance structures to offset principal agent problems. Risk bearers and decision makers were one and the same, which gave them greater flexibility when determining policy conditions. Iterative business and social interactions between underwriters and shippers enhanced trust and helped the former obtain the information needed to assess risks and overcome moral hazard and adverse selection problems.

Notwithstanding these putative agency and information advantages, around the turn of the century US marine insurance rapidly moved from private to corporate underwriting. Most of the reasons for this related to historical contingency rather than agency or asymmetric information problems. First, the size of the private market was of critical importance. In the late 1790s there were about fifty underwriters in Philadelphia, compared to several hundred underwriters working in Lloyd's of London.[78] Numbers in other US ports were even smaller. For American merchants this increased the expense, time, and difficulty of finding new underwriters for each policy, especially if they had to seek additional cover on the other side of the Atlantic. When Alexandria merchants petitioned the Virginia legislature in 1797 to incorporate a new stock insurance venture, their primary argument was that the export trade from the port had outgrown the capacity of local underwriters, leading to the cost and inconvenience of finding insurance elsewhere, and to the drain of money out of the state.[79]

Second, the solvency and permanence of individual underwriters came into question, especially in wartime. During the 'quasi-war' with France between 1796 and 1800 over 2,300 American ships were captured by French privateers. This drove up rates and heightened concerns about the financial strength of underwriters. By overwhelming the market with systemic risks, wartime losses

---

[77] Crothers 2004; Kingston 2011.   [78] Kingston 2011, 173.
[79] Crothers 2004, 620–1.

undermined the information and cost advantages of the private underwriters and made them less competitive. Before the quasi war, Philadelphia underwriters charged 1.3 per cent less than the new corporations. At the height of the war in 1797–8 they were charging 2.8 per cent more.[80] American merchants turned to corporate insurers who could spread their risks among shareholders, who in turn could diversify their assets. The larger capital funds of the corporations also allowed them to smooth premium rate fluctuations, to absorb greater losses, and to offer more generous credit terms, which was an important benefit for the long-distance trade.[81] Furthermore, in the case of disputes a merchant was able to sue a corporation as a single legal entity, rather than having to chase down the many individuals who may have underwritten his policy in the private system.

Organizational choice was also shaped by gaps in the market and the emergence of new types of risk that existing insurers would not cover or could not price actuarially. The specialized 'class' mutuals in US fire insurance are an example of this. Class mutuals were so called because they wrote only one or a few classes of risk, such as the property of bakers, millers, and manufacturers. From the 1830s New England textile mill owners began to group together to establish mutual insurance companies because the existing stock companies refused to reduce premium rates on the safer types of mill.[82] They spread risks by reinsuring each other, charged lower rates, and returned premiums in the form of dividends when losses fell below expectations. This induced manufacturers to welcome mill inspections and to improve fire safety in their premises. The business of New England factory mutuals more than quadrupled from $93m to $407m between 1870 and 1885.[83] Numerous other specialized mutuals emerged outside New England textiles to write industrial and commercial risks that existing companies refused.

The joint-stock fire insurers fought back in various ways. In 1890 they established a syndicate, the Factory Insurance Association, to compete in the New England mill insurance market.[84] They offered discounts on premiums for mill owners who invested in fire protection measures such as sprinklers and water tanks, and they organized their own inspection system for special hazards such as electrical systems and boilers.[85] They also supported newspaper attacks on the reputation of the mutuals. Factory mutuals in Michigan and Missouri were accused of accepting the worst risks that stock companies would not touch and of failing to maintain sufficient funds to cover their

---

[80] Kingston 2011, 182.
[81] Crothers 2004, 621–2, 631–2. Crothers argues that the booster role in the Virginia economy played by corporate marine insurance credit was widely recognized at this time.
[82] Wright 2010, 250.   [83] *Insurance Critic* 14, 1886, 151.
[84] *Indicator* 9, 1890, 172, 244. The New England factory mutuals responded with an association of their own in 1894, *Insurance Critic* 22, 1894, 381.
[85] Wermiel 2000, 134–5.

liabilities.[86] Such attacks were aided by the fact that many local class and general mutuals got into difficulties because they accepted promissory 'premium notes' from their members in lieu of cash and then proved unable to enforce payment in the event of losses. The Philadelphia druggists' mutual fire insurance company, for instance, came to an end in 1891 for this reason.[87]

The story of the American class mutuals also makes it clear that to understand the coexistence of different organizational forms in insurance requires paying attention to the attitudes of regulators and public opinion.[88] Changes in public confidence in a particular form of organization were often influenced, or reflected, by regulators. In the late 1860s, for instance, a campaign was conducted against local mutual fire insurers in Missouri by newspapers and by Wyllis King, the state's first insurance commissioner. Prior to new legislation in 1869, it was claimed that such mutuals had been too easy to incorporate in Missouri. According to King, any five or more 'poverty stricken adventurers' had been able to procure a license and become a corporate body to do insurance upon the mutual plan, merely upon filing their articles of association with the county court. Members of such mutuals had been at the mercy of directors who ran the companies for their own benefit. Following a regulatory template provided by Massachusetts and New York, the new Missouri laws of 1869 established minimum levels of paid-up capital for stock companies as a condition of their incorporation and a minimum volume of membership applications and paid-in cash premiums before a mutual fire insurance company was permitted to commence business.[89]

Like their western counterparts, the eastern insurance press applauded the new regulatory system in Missouri.[90] In the face of this new tougher regulatory environment and public condemnation, did the mutual fire insurers in Missouri fade away? As indicated by Tables 6.1 and 6.2, the current state of research does not allow us to answer this and other questions about organizational trends in US insurance, let alone to explore the causal factors behind such trends. Were legislators merely catching up with structural changes in insurance and just reflecting shifts in public confidence in particular organizational forms, or did they provide the impetus for such changes? The same uncertainty about the direction of causality exists with regard to the populist support extended by press and regulators to local mutual and cooperative assessment insurance organizations in western states such as Wisconsin, Kansas, and Colorado during the 1880s and 1890s. Here such ventures were held up as people-friendly counterweights to the malevolent eastern stock

---

[86] *Insurance and Commercial Magazine* 8, 1879–80, 238–9; *Insurance Times* 20, 1887, 134.
[87] *Insurance Critic* 19, 1891, 433.   [88] Wright 2010, 263–5.
[89] *Western Insurance Review* II, 1868–69, 36–7; *Western Insurance Review* III, 1869–70, 245–7.
[90] *Spectator* II, 25 March 1869; *Spectator* III, 15 August 1869.

corporations that colluded over prices and squeezed the pockets of policy-holders for the benefit of shareholders and directors.[91] To what extent, however, did such support improve the business prospects of mutual and cooperative insurers in these states?

Three things can be stated with more certainty: first, that some regulation was, indeed, game changing; second, that in the US most proposals advocating public forms of insurance encountered stiff opposition from vested interests and were seldom realized; third, that, despite wide variations among the German states in their approaches to regulation, there was an embedded cultural propensity in Germany to regard state involvement in insurance as a viable proposition.

A good example of regulation constraining and reshaping organizational forms is the first life insurance legislation passed by New York. By the law of 1849 all new life insurance projects, regardless of their corporate structure, were required to raise at least $100,000 of equity capital before commencing business. Henceforth, all new mutual life insurers were compelled to be hybrids with a mixture of stock and mutual finance. A further law in 1851 required all life insurance companies, including those chartered prior to the law, to deposit with the New York state comptroller $100,000 in US public stock or in bonds and mortgage on real estate in the state.[92] As noted above, this forced those promoters, who wished to launch a purely mutual company, to issue shares. This, together with the profit-sharing policies increasingly offered by stock companies to their customers, ensured over the long term the near convergence of mutual and stock forms of organization in US life insurance, especially as regards the business practices of the largest companies.

In the years following the Civil War, and again during the Progressive Era, numerous voices were raised in the US in favour of public forms of insurance. In 1865, for instance, the insurance commissioners of Massachusetts proposed a voluntary state guarantee fund to 'insure' mutual fire insurance companies against excess losses. If a company's loss in any year should amount to more than 80 per cent of its cash premiums, the Commonwealth would make up the excess, in return for an annual contribution by each company scaled according to the size of their premium income.[93] This plan was intended to reduce the attrition rate of Massachusetts mutuals, whose number had fallen from sixty-two in 1857 to forty-eight by 1864.[94] The scheme was rejected by the legislature, but further projects for state and municipal insurance reappeared in Massachusetts and in other states, where they were met with equal hostility.

---

[91] For examples, see *Milwaukee Sentinel* 14 March 1887; *Emporia Weekly Gazette* 30 September 1897; *Denver Sunday Post* 25 September, 9 October, 13 November, 27 November 1898.
[92] Murphy 2010, 117.
[93] *10th Annual Report of the Massachusetts Insurance Commissioners* January 1865, ix–xiv.
[94] *10th Annual Report of the Massachusetts Insurance Commissioners* January 1865, xi, table I.

In Wisconsin, for instance, a proposal for the state insurance department to issue fire insurance policies directly, with premiums to be deposited in the state treasury and expenses to be covered by an annual tax, was rubbished by critics who argued that the plan could not be made to pay as the existing private fire insurance companies there operated with 'nothing very tangible in the way of net profit'.[95]

Robert Wright has neatly listed the main problems ostensibly associated with state insurance, namely that it distorts the market for private alternatives; that it redistributes revenue from taxpayers towards special interest groups; that it pays out more in benefits and charges less than actuarially fair premiums and is therefore inefficient; that it adapts too slowly to market changes, including changes in asymmetric information caused by the very existence of state insurance; and that it subsidizes risk taking or creates new risks in trying to reduce existing ones.[96] The claims of market distortion and inefficiency were the arguments that figured most prominently in nineteenth-century America. The large east-coast and foreign stock corporations spent a great deal of time, money, and effort trying to influence regulators, legislators, and newspaper editors. Attacks on non-stock forms of organization were chiefly launched with the interests of the stock corporations in mind.

It was different in Germany, where some form of state involvement remained the norm rather than the exception. This reflected a less liberal regime in which insurance regulation, before the establishment of the imperial supervisory office in 1901, was based on local police monitoring and licensing. However, it also reflected different cultural expectations in Germany of what the state could and should do. The history of Bavarian hail insurance provides a good illustration of this.[97] Peasant farmers in southern Germany were particularly vulnerable to crop damage caused by severe hail and windstorms. Hailstorm risk had certain special features. It was impossible to prevent and therefore *ex-ante* moral hazard was zero, while *ex-post* moral hazard was low as crop damage was fairly easy to assess. Insurers, however, faced large adverse selection problems, especially when farmers tended to know more about the frequency of hailstorms in their districts than did the underwriters. Equally, there was an adverse selection problem for the insured who could not be certain that insurers would be able to pay out on their claims. A new company's efficiency of loss adjustment and the level of payouts often provided the only reputational signals that customers could follow. Early premium rates often proved inadequate where the risk pool was too small and risks were inter-related.

---

[95] *Spectator* VIII, February 1872, 111, citing a proposal published in the *Milwaukee Sentinel*.
[96] Wright 2010, 259–60.
[97] The following account is based on Oberholzner 2006. I am most grateful to Frank Oberholzner for generously providing me with a copy of his paper.

Between 1770 and 1873 there were repeated, but abortive, attempts in Bavaria to establish a state hail insurance scheme along the lines of the regional and national fire insurance institutions. Obstacles included an absence of data on hailstorms, a lack of a template for actuarial pricing, and political divisions between those advocating compulsory versus voluntary schemes. In 1831 the idea of a state organization was put on hold when a law was passed that permitted the formation of regional hail insurance associations as private initiatives. The first such association, the Hagel-Assekuranz Verein (hereafter HAV), was licensed in 1833 in the Isar district of Bavaria. The initial aim of the HAV's founders was to create a hybrid mutual-stock institution with members paying an annual subscription, for a minimum of five years, in proportion to the value of their crops insured, together with equity capital raised from investors. The share issue, however, was unsuccessful so the HAV was compelled to take out a loan to supplement members' subscription income.

One problem was that the HAV's rates took no account of the relative vulnerability of different crops to hail damage. Another was that its risk pool remained too small. Despite efforts to remedy both these deficiencies— operations were extended to the whole of Bavaria in 1840—the HAV suffered chronic balance sheet problems, with persistent heavy losses and too limited income. Its response was to tighten policy terms, to increase levels of excess, and to raise subscription rates. The company also repeatedly lobbied the Bavarian legislature for powers of compulsory insurance and against the unregulated entry of other private insurers. None of this worked. Having reached a peak membership of 17,000 in 1838, the HAV entered a long period of decline. The Bavarian state bailed it out in 1846 with a one-off grant to meet a huge shortfall on its liabilities. In 1853 the company reverted to issuing *post-hoc* calls to cover losses. By 1855 it had just 839 members left. In the following year, despite the HAV's objections, the government permitted private hail insurers from outside the state to operate in Bavaria. Between 1856 and 1872 four stock and four mutual companies commenced writing hail insurance, but they were cautious about the high rate of loss and did only a limited amount of business. As late as 1884 the private hail insurers together insured just 6,100 policies in Bavaria.

By the 1880s, therefore, after 110 years of experimentation, Bavaria had still not resolved the optimal organizational form to supply hail insurance to its farmers. Neither state schemes, quasi-monopoly mutual or hybrid institutions, private not-for-profit mutuals, nor private for-profit stock companies could handle the high hailstorm risk environment of south German agriculture, the low demand for the product at the prevailing prices, and the poor access to corporate capital or credit, and turn a satisfactory profit. During the 1860s and 1870s, politicians and economists reopened the debate about a national hail insurance scheme and whether it should be voluntary or compulsory.

Eventually, the voluntary principle was embedded in the law of 1884 that established a state mutual hail insurance institution, with a start-up capital of 100,000 gulden derived from surpluses from the state fire insurance chamber and from other transfers from the state treasury. *Post-hoc* calls were prohibited and no agencies were permitted in order to reduce costs. Premium rates were to be calculated from the existing data for tax relief awarded to victims of hailstorms and the premiums were to be collected by local community administrations. The insured were guaranteed to receive 80 per cent of their insured losses. Although membership was voluntary, by abolishing the existing tax relief for victims of hailstorms, the law effectively drove farmers into the new state institution in large numbers. This helped to solve the risk distribution problem that had bedevilled earlier ventures such as the HAV. Although it had to compete with private companies, the new national hail insurer quickly captured the majority of the business in Bavaria, with 28,500 out of 44,500 policies by 1887. By 1900 almost 126,000 farmers insured over 194m RM with the state institution. Thus it provided a large number of farmers with affordable hailstorm cover, helped spread the risk of hail damage across the whole of Bavaria, and raised levels of consumer trust in this branch of insurance.

IV

The US and Germany today represent the two largest non-life insurance markets in the world, together accounting for 41 per cent of global premiums. In life insurance the countries are ranked first and sixth respectively, accounting for one quarter of the world market.[98] Their insurance histories, therefore, are of enormous importance to any understanding of the rise of the global economy.

Agency and governance issues and capital markets affected the means by which insurance developed in these two countries at different times. Their organizational histories, however, also suggest the importance of historical contingency, in the guise, for example, of warfare and political economy, and path dependency, in the shape, for example, of inherited cultural and social norms. Both factors could influence the reputational capital of one form relative to another. The story of Bavarian hail insurance, where over a long period priority was repeatedly given to public and mutual schemes and private stock companies were generally marginalized, illustrates the role of cultural expectations in helping to shape the organizational structure of the industry.

---

[98] Calculated from *Sigma* 3, 2012, appendix tables V, VII.

Cultural preferences may also have played a role in shaping life and non-life insurance in the US. The existing data, though far from complete, provide evidence from different states of peculiar regional distributions of organizational types, and changes in these distributions over time, patterns that are worth exploring through further research.

There is plenty of evidence from Germany and the US for the significance of the intervention of regulators and legislators and for the impact of public insurance on the private market for life and non-life insurance. In an era before full nationalization, state schemes often had the effect of spreading the understanding of insurance among wider sections of the population rather than crowding out private insurance. The German social insurance systems introduced in the 1880s, for example, helped drive the gross premiums earned from life insurance in Germany from 78m RM in 1880 to 620m RM in 1910.[99]

The absence of public insurance schemes, which was often the result of political as well as economic circumstances, could also benefit particular forms of insurance under certain historical conditions, especially where the private market was underdeveloped, although the precise transmission mechanism remains unclear.[100] The early history of health and accident insurance in the US, for example, shows the beneficial effect on mutuals of an absence of crowding out. In 1901 there were 107 mutual sickness and accident insurance organizations earning $2.96m from premiums and assessments. By 1914 there were 195 earning $12.92m. This growth was the result of the lack of state or federal social insurance schemes. By 1900 between 25 and 50 per cent of US workers had some form of sickness cover through insurance plans provided by these types of institutions or by trade unions.[101]

Finally, the changing nature of risk, and the challenge of insuring new and uncertain technologies, also clearly played a factor in shaping organizational choice in our period and beyond. The rise of factory mutuals in the US and state hail insurance in Bavaria are examples of this. In the latter case, the technological challenge to generate a viable risk pool defeated all forms of private and public insurance until the state intervened to create a large national institution. In the former, the new mutual forms emerged as a response to the inability of existing mutual and stock fire insurers efficiently to underwrite the novel risks associated with American industrialization.

---

[99] Calculated from Borscheid and Drees 1988, 86–8. Cf. Borscheid 2001, 317.
[100] Wright 2010, 240.   [101] Wright 2010, appendix 5.

Part II

Mutual Insurance Organizations in Uncertain Environments

7

The World Insured South Africa

Early Insurance Activities of Insurance Companies in South Africa, 1820–1910

Grietjie Verhoef

The history of insurance in South Africa is closely linked to the overseas expansion of the British insurance industry. The penetration into the British colonial markets was the result of the prevalence of the insurance industry in Britain. Roman Dutch law, which was the prevailing 'common law' of the Dutch colony at the Cape since 1652 and later in the unified South Africa, did not recognize the specific contract of insurance. When British colonial authority was established in 1806, British insurance practice followed the growing need for risk management. The proliferation of British insurance concerns from the 1820s was the natural development of commercial practice following business and people. Since short-term insurance was the dominant insurance form in Britain, fire and property casualty insurance was the first to penetrate the colonial markets. No Dutch 'indigenous' insurance concerns were marginalized by the introduction of British insurers, since there were none. A lucrative insurance industry developed as inhabitants of the colony developed the need to protect themselves against risk to life and property.[1] The predominance of British forms of insurance introduced a strong business-oriented approach to the insurance industry, while concepts of mutual interest, confidence, and trust that characterized mutual insurance organizations, emerged from local interest groups only about twenty-five years after British joint-stock insurance companies started their business in the Cape Colony. Mutual insurers were latecomers to the market, but soon established a strong presence there.

---

[1] Cummins and Venard 2008, 297, 317.

This chapter will investigate the formative years of the insurance industry in the British colonies preceding the formation of the Union of South Africa in 1910. The prevailing economic conditions in which these insurance concerns emerged will be explained as illustrative of the incentives to engage in the industry. Finally, the chapter explores the preferred organizational form of early insurance enterprises.

COLONIAL ECONOMIES: CONDITIONS FOR INSURANCE ENTERPRISES

The Cape of Good Hope was the refreshment station of the Verenigde Oostindische Compagnie (VOC). Between 1803 and 1806 the Cape Colony was administered by the Dutch Government (the Batavian Government), after which Britain finally conquered the colony in 1806. From the Cape Colony British influence spread to the Natal Colony, acquired and proclaimed in 1842, and the two Boer republics after the South African War of 1899–1902. Wheat, wine, and sheep/wool farming, and later for a brief period also ostrich feathers, contributed to the relative wealth of the Cape economy. Exports of those commodities were primarily destined for British markets.[2] The entire region depended on agriculture and by 1860 agricultural exports valued £21m. The boom in agricultural and trading activities in the Cape and Natal led to the formation of numerous small high dividend-paying local unit banks. Excessive speculation, drought, and a downturn in the business cycle towards the early 1860s caused the collapse of the small banks and insurance companies. The financial markets became consolidated in the hands of the British imperial banks after 1862. Conditions were exacerbated for the colonies and the republics by the depression in the Cape Colony during the late 1880s.[3] When the discovery of diamonds in 1867 and gold in 1886 revolutionized the economic attraction of the South African market, the British institutions were aptly positioned and sufficiently capitalized to provide the capital needs of the expanding railway infrastructure development, mining expansion, and subsequent industrial manufacturing.[4]

The predominantly Dutch-speaking Voortrekkers of the eastern parts of the colony rejected British domination and in 1838 moved into the interior and formed independent republics. These republics were relatively poor, agricultural economies with small white populations—around 15,000 in the Orange Free State by the early 1850s and around 60,000 on the eve of the discovery of

---

[2] Viljoen 1951; Houghton 1976, 8–13.
[3] *Post Magazine and Insurance Monitor* 7 July 1899, 13.
[4] Viljoen 1951, 197–203.

diamonds. In the Transvaal the white settler population was only around 30,000 before the discovery of gold. The mineral discoveries attracted British attention and after two wars of independence Britain secured control of the entire sub-region, leading to the consolidation of the British possessions in the Union of South Africa in 1910. Economic opportunities emerged through the control of the mineral rich markets and the sea route around the southern tip of Africa to the east.[5] Only towards the beginning of the twentieth century did efforts commence to create an integrated market.[6]

With British colonial control came the settlement of post-Industrial Revolution populations, post-Adam Smith citizens of the British Empire, who were well acquainted with the urban life and liberal ideas of the post-French revolution era.[7] The introduction of the silver shilling in 1825 as legal tender at the Cape Colony gradually eliminated the exchange in more than ten other coins/currencies.[8] British administration set the pre-conditions for economic growth—infrastructure was constructed, harbours improved, banks set up, and manufactured goods imported for the sophisticated domestic market. The first insurance business at the Cape started soon after the arrival of British settlers in 1820. Under the British Governor, Lord Charles Somerset, who arrived in April 1814, a deliberate policy was followed to ensure that the Cape Colony had a British character. He encouraged British settlement, especially of merchants. On the eastern frontier Somerset wanted British settlement to provide defence for the Colony. The eastern region of the Colony had been cleared by the British colonel John Graham by force following attacks by the indigenous population. Britain suffered from high unemployment after the Napoleonic wars and emigration to its empire offered some solution. To support the military block houses set up between the two eastern frontier centres, Grahamstown and Cradock, Somerset wanted scattered small settler villages. The Colonial Office was slow in reacting to Somerset's request, but after an attack by a Xhosa prophet Makanda on Grahamstown the matter received greater urgency. This emigration scheme was the first organized initiative of its kind in the British Empire. Some 90,000 people applied to emigrate to the Cape Colony.

This was the first attempt by the British Government to people its empire with British subjects. Early in 1820 4,000 British settlers arrived in the district of Albany in the eastern Cape. They were organized in small parties, some under the leadership of wealthy men, others only under the leadership of adult males. Most of the leaders were either farmers or tradesmen, but none of the settlers had previously owned land in Britain. Between 5,000 and 6,000 settlers immigrated to the Cape Colony, but in 1823 the government

---

[5] Hussey 1963; Wilson and Thompson 1971; Müller 1983; Davenport and Saunders 2002.
[6] Kenwood and Lougheed 1999.   [7] Müller 1974, 146–56.
[8] Arndt 1928, 176–8; Sayers 1952, 63–8.

terminated further assisted emigration.[9] After 1837 another 5,000 British artisans and labourers from England and Ireland immigrated to the Cape Colony. After the Voortrekkers (the Boers who had emigrated out of the Cape Colony since 1838 and who had settled on the eastern coast of southern Africa before British occupation in 1845) left the Natal Colony in 1848, around 4,500 British colonists were taken there.[10] After 1858 further British-supported immigration to the Cape Colony occurred, bringing to around 12,000 the number of new British immigrants who had settled on the eastern side of southern Africa between 1858 and 1863.[11] The lack of farming experience, subsequent crop failures, and adverse climatic conditions led many to leave the land and settle in nearby towns such as Port Elizabeth and East London. Although the numerically stronger British settler population strengthened the colonial population, they were very insecure in terms of livelihood and social stability. The threat to life and property posed by the indigenous population created a market for insurance.

The colonial economy was just beginning to open up as the colonial authorities only granted permission for the opening of the first privately owned bank in 1836, thus paving the way for the development of a contested financial services environment. As the Natal Colony developed and British settlers moved there, Cape merchants and businessmen extended their sights to the east coast. With the growing British settler population agricultural activities, forestry, and trading in consumer goods developed. Soon banks, trust companies, and other financial services were established.[12] The European population was still very small—around 18,000 towards the end of the first decade of the nineteenth century.[13] A relatively sparsely populated European community offered only a very limited market for insurance. The market for insurance services developed later when the European population increased and it became more reasonable to expect potential policyholders to be able to fulfill their obligations in keeping up with premium payments. As explained by Keneley in this volume (see Chapter 8), mutual confidence between the issuer of an insurance policy and the policyholder constituted a prerequisite for the development of an insurance industry. The European population in the Cape Colony, and subsequently the Natal Colony, gradually created a critical mass for financial services to enter the market—and insurance companies followed ordinary banks and building societies. By 1861, more than thirty banks and more than twenty insurance companies operated in the Cape. The banks were small local unit banks tailored along the British banking system, but the insurance business was conducted from head offices in London.[14] The

---

[9] Davenport and Saunders 2000, 44–5.   [10] Viljoen 1951, 182–3.
[11] Viljoen 1951, 183.   [12] Mann 1859; Webb and Brookes 1967.
[13] Viljoen 1951, 183. Only after the passing of the Cape Immigration Act in 1903 were accurate records of net immigration kept in the Cape Colony. See Wickins 1983, 17.
[14] Solomon 1983, 137–8; Jones 1996, 10–13.

insurance companies began exploring the potential of the colonial markets by sending out agents rather than opening up branches or offices immediately.

The first insurance agents from Britain started business in the Cape Colony in 1806. Alexander Macdonald arrived in the Cape in 1799. He and John Houghton were appointed by power of attorney by the *Phoenix Assurance Company of London* on 6 August 1806. Their business was to sell fire insurance, at that time the most widely held insurance contract in the Colony. The other form was marine insurance, capturing the risks of the 170 ships calling at the Cape port annually.[15] The *Phoenix* even translated the application forms for their policies in Dutch to serve the needs of the predominantly Dutch community. The overseas principal was referred to as the 'Home Office' and this office sent agents or representatives to conduct their business outside Britain. Knaggs noted that 'the *Norwich Union Fire Society* had come to South Africa as early as 1874, when Sir Arthur Owen Horwood...and James Whiley, one of the original 1820 settlers, had been granted the agency in Port Elizabeth'.[16] In the absence of any notable indigenous insurance industry, British insurance companies followed British citizens and business and came to dominate the South African market. A market for insurance took shape gradually as the environmental, social, economic, and market factors conducive to the emergence of such a market converged towards the late nineteenth century in the British colonies of southern Africa.

The early insurance companies' primary business was fire, marine, life, and, only to a limited extent, accident. The latter was slow in developing.[17] The fertile soil for the development of mutual insurance companies was the existence of a tradition of friendly societies in the Cape Colony, which had an unmistakable British origin in community self-help.[18] From friendly societies colonists could make a natural transition to mutual insurance companies. Towards the end of the nineteenth century three local companies, namely the *South African Mutual Life Assurance Company* (established 1845), the *Southern Life Association* (established 1891), and the *Industrial Life Assurance Company of South Africa* (established 1894) secured more life business than the twenty-two foreign companies collectively.[19] The majority of companies selling different types of insurance in the Cape Colony were private stock

---

[15] The term 'assurance' was the correct term used to refer to that class of business in which the sum assured is bound to be paid sooner or later, as distinct from types of contract where the sum insured may never have to be paid. This implies that life business was referred to as 'assurance' and non-life business, such as fire, marine, or accident provisions as 'insurance'. Throughout history the two terms have been used interchangeably, with the result that 'assurance' has become the 'old-fashioned' term. In this chapter I use 'insurance' for both categories of insurance. See Miller 1968, 2.

[16] Knaggs 1990, 25.

[17] *Post Magazine and Insurance Monitor* 12 July 1897, 432.

[18] Verhoef 2006, 609–11; Verhoef 2007, 20–2.   [19] Spyrou 1955, 326.

companies. The English companies dominated the fire business until the 1930s. They benefited from their British experience in providing fire cover for residential, industrial, and mining needs. The fire insurance stock companies organized themselves into associations in Cape Town, Durban, Port Elizabeth, and Bloemfontein, later called the Council of Fire Insurance Companies (established 1907), modelled on the Fire Offices Committee of London. This was done to promote uniform and sound practices in fire business throughout the country.[20] Although there were no excessive fire catastrophes in South Africa during the second half of the nineteenth century, insurance companies quoted different tariffs and competed keenly until the tariff associations were established.[21] British insurance companies had long colluded on tariffs, for example for the cotton risks of Lancashire. Local companies in the Cape Colony quoted lower tariffs for their far less risky environment, thereby undercutting the English business. The highest risks developed in the gold mining industry towards the end of the nineteenth century, which were typically reinsured in London. The associations contributed to the development of a sound market, good underwriting standards, sound insurance practices and procedures, and general engineering standards in the Cape and Natal markets. Because of the size of potential fire claims and the unpredictability of fire calamities distributed unevenly among policyholders, this type of insurance is not typically accommodated in mutual associations. As will be seen below, some companies quoted for fire and life assurance, which afforded them access to the life premiums to balance fire risks.

DEVELOPMENT OF THE COLONIAL MARKETS

Soon after the permanent establishment of the British administration at the Cape Colony in 1806, many British insurance companies set up business in the colony, dispatching representatives on a temporary basis or soliciting the services of local residents. The *Africa Insurance Record* commented: 'It has often been said that wherever you find two or three Britishers met together you will find an insurance agent, and it would appear that such was the case with the 1820 settlers, for shortly after their arrival on the 1st February 1826,

---

[20] Spyrou 1955, 327. The Cape Town Fire Tariff Committee formed in 1894 and the Johannesburg Fire Tariff Assurance Association in 1898. *Post Magazine and Insurance Monitor* 1 January 1898, 13; Vivian 2001, 23–4.

[21] Schweizerische Rückversicherungsgesellschaft 1964, 406; *Post Magazine and Insurance Monitor* 1 January 1898, 12–13. As described below, British companies were not the only ones to offer fire insurance in the Cape Colony. A fire in Cape Town in 1858, however, did alert the 'London offices transacting business in the colony' to agree on an increase in rates for private houses. Quoted by Trebilcock 1985, 318.

the *United Empire & Continental Life Assurance Association* (acquired subsequently by the Eagle)... announced in the Cape Town press that it had established a branch in South Africa.'[22] The settlement of the British immigrants of 1820 was the most important impetus for the development of an insurance market in South Africa. Although three older insurance companies had long been active in the British market, namely the *Sun* (from 1710), the *Royal Exchange* (from 1720), and the *Phoenix Assurance* (from 1782), it was the *Alliance British and Foreign Life and Fire Assurance Company*, established in 1824, that pioneered the serious expansion of business to the Cape Colony. This company announced in the Government Gazette in August 1826 that it had dispatched agents to the colony. These agents, Nisbet and Dickenson, were authorized to 'assure against Fire' on behalf of the Alliance of London.[23] The *Alliance* published three classes of fire insurance, namely private dwellings (at 5s per cent), private warehouses (at 7s.6d per cent) and warehouses partly constructed of timber, containing hazardous goods such as hemp, flax, pitch, turpentine, etc. (at 10s.6d per cent).

The early British insurance companies attracted business in the Cape Colony because they had an established business model and were sufficiently capitalized. In the colonial market these companies used the same risk and mortality tables applicable to the British market. As late as 1894 the Government Actuary, James McGowan, reported:

> Companies assuring the lives of persons resident in the Colony are, it must be admitted, working in the dark as regards the rates of mortality which prevail here. Until we have a compulsory Births and Deaths Registration Act in operation, we cannot even surmise how the death rates here compare with those in other countries. Owing to the finer climate one would imagine that the mortality here would be more favourable than in England, and if this be the case, the Foreign Companies must benefit, as they charge their ordinary Home rates for lives resident in the Colony.[24]

Furthermore, these companies had the advantage of a long-standing knowledge of the British market, which to a degree was duplicated in the British colonies. Risks were not altogether different. The British companies' 'healthy capital' base afforded them the opportunity to test the potential of the new colonial markets, while balancing risks in the colonial market by their established home portfolios. The favourable economic conditions in the Cape Colony and the imperial preference trading policy linked colonial fortunes to those of the mother country. As Britain looked upon the Cape Colony as the bulwark of British influence, British insurance companies were eager to

---

[22] Quoted in *Review* (10 March 1951): 209.

[23] *Cape of Good Hope Government Gazette* 21, 1074, 11 August 1826.

[24] Cape of Good Hope: *Return under the Life Assurance Act, 1891, for the Year ended 31st December 1892* 11 April 1894, 9.

pursue the promise of the new market.[25] As British citizens settled in the colony, these companies were favourably positioned to enter that market: the colonists were British, might be familiar with the companies' British perform-ance, spoke the same language, and shared the same culture. While the settlers were at the beginning of forming a new community, the fostering of relation-ships of trust would take time. In the immediate vicinity of Cape Town the British population trusted British firms, while in the more remote eastern frontier of the colony the settlers' existence was still very uncertain. At that time it made good sense to seek risk protection from companies from the mother country.

By the 1830s the Cape Colony capital markets were emerging, with private banks, boards of executors, and building societies offering financial services. A definite savings propensity had developed, because by 1823 deposits had reached Rds 1.4m (Rds = Riksdaalers—the Dutch currency still in use in the colony).[26] In 1831 the Cape of Good Hope Savings Bank, the first private bank, opened for business and soon opened branches in small towns in the interior such as Grahamstown, Somerset East, Stellenbosch, and Graaf Reinet. In 1838 the Eastern Province Bank opened for business in Grahamstown and in 1847 the Port Elizabeth Bank opened in the port town.[27] The first trust company or board of executors was established in Cape Town in 1834 by twenty-two residents. Between 1834 and 1899 thirty similar trust companies were formed in the Cape Colony.[28] Building societies followed in the later 1850s. By the 1830s these capital markets indicated a relatively high savings ratio and opportunities for stock companies to engage in profitable business. No sys-tematic data exist on total savings in the Cape Colony before 1850, but a recent study has calculated that by 1850 that total had reached £130m.[29]

In this market the first insurance company was established on colonial soil as the *South African Fire and Life Assurance Company* in March 1831 by local capital. A capital of £20,000, was raised 'which amount is guaranteed for the security of the assured by a highly respectable body of Proprietors, including much of the wealth of the Colony'. Cape businessmen, wheat and wine farmers, and the professional community of Cape Town enjoyed a high standard of living and were always seeking new business opportunities.[30] The fire rates, published in three classes, were cheaper in each category than the *Alliance*. These rates were advertised as 'lower than similar institutions in the Cape Colony', thereby pointing to the growing competition with foreign companies.[31] For life policies rates were quoted for a person thirty years of age, for one year at £2.6.9d per annum, for seven years £2.7.9d per annum, and for

[25] Robinson et al. 1961; Packenham 1992.   [26] Arndt 1928, 488.
[27] Arndt 1928, 489–91.   [28] Ehlers 2002, 4–5, 29.
[29] Greyling and Verhoef 2012.   [30] See Giliomee 2003, 117–18.
[31] *Grahamstown Journal* 6 October 1836.

life £3.9.2d per annum. Profits were to be distributed after five years and divided amongst shareholders. This private company appointed prominent people as agents in a number of locations, such as Grahamstown, Uitenhage, Swellendam, Port Elizabeth, Graaff Reinet, Beaufort, George, Clanwilliam, Stellenbosch, Worcester, and Paarl. The agents as well as the directors of the company were from both the English-speaking and the Afrikaans-speaking communities. Under conditions of uncertainty—this was the first local insurance company—prominent businessmen took the risk and could claim a growing sense of local loyalty by the impressive growth of the company. Despite this being a private stock company, the local support showed an awareness of an identifiable local colonial identity emerging. Success with this company would encourage confidence to venture into similar enterprises.

Competition soon developed between local and foreign insurance companies. At the fifth annual general meeting of the *South African Fire and Life* specific reference was made to the company as a local and not a 'foreign office', that claims were immediately assessed and adjusted and 'paid out in the Colony', and that capital was retained 'in the Colony'.[32] The *Alliance* announced in 1833 that its life insurance department would accept risks on female lives as well as on the lives of emancipated slaves of both genders. The *South African Fire and Life* followed suit and added that it would offer life cover to all 'coloured persons'. Strong competition between these companies resulted in the lowering of rates quoted on life insurance in the mid-1830s.[33] The competitive market soon lured new entrants. In December 1835 the *Cape of Good Hope Fire Assurance Company* was floated in Cape Town. The capital was £20,000 divided into 400 shares of £50 each. The directors were all Englishmen and a 'Baron von Ludwig'. This company only insured against fire, but quoted lower rates and stated that its competitiveness followed from 'Economy with regard to rates of premium, and Security in respect to the number of Proprietors'. The rates were stated to be much lower than those hitherto quoted in the Colony, which was expected to enhance the profits of the company. The distribution of shares amongst 'so many' shareholders was put forward as enhancing the 'field of responsibility, and consequently extends the security to the Public'.[34] These three companies dominated the insurance market for the next few years. The remarkable enterprising nature of these companies was that they could sustain good business in a sparsely populated colony, where a total of 145,042 inhabitants (as recorded in the official census of 1834–35) lived in an area stretching twenty-eight hours by horse-drawn cart between Cape Town and Swellendam.

Competition led to a reduction in premiums by *Alliance* in 1838 and the declaration of healthy bonuses to policyholders.[35] New forms of insurance

---

[32] *Grahamstown Journal* 6 October 1836.   [33] Hirsch 1962, 39–41.
[34] *Grahamstown Journal* 21 July 1836, 5 October 1836.   [35] Hirsch 1962, 43.

were introduced as the need arose. When a company was formed in 1838 to purchase a steamboat for cargo transport between the harbours of Cape Town and Port Elizabeth, the *Cape of Good Hope Fire and Life* seized the opportunity to set up a company to issue marine insurance. A joint-stock company was established under a trust deed for the purpose of providing insurance against sea risks to the entire settler community.[36] The introduction of marine insurance in South Africa was not a British initiative, but the *Equitable Marine*, established in 1849, followed by the *Colonial Assurance Company* in 1874, extended the provision. These companies competed with well-established overseas marine underwriting of hull and freight business. By 1898 eight companies wrote marine insurance, but relative to fire and life assurance, it was of minor concern.[37] The insurance industry was driven by business opportunities—if profits were to be made, the public was to be assured that it was in their interest—securing their assets against risk and offering an investment opportunity to entrepreneurial spirits in the colony.

Initial success encouraged market entry. The market became all but saturated but profits were good. The *South Africa Fire and Life* paid out only £6,645 between 1833 and 1839 while the *Alliance* extended its geographical reach by sending agents to the Eastern Cape. In 1838 the first insurance company established by Dutch businessmen entered the market. *De Protecteur Fire and Life Assurance Company* was established in Cape Town with capital of £40,000. The company promised to pay claims within three months, which indicates that this might have been a cause of dissatisfaction in the colony.[38] Although *De Protecteur* was Dutch owned, policies were issued in English and Dutch. The directors were well-known local leaders such as Hofmeyr, Blanckenberg, and Van Reenen, and Servaas de Kock was the secretary. The insurance industry at the Cape Colony was not monopolized by British interests or English-speaking colonists, since Dutch-speaking directors served on the board of directors of the *South African Fire and Life* and the auditors to that company were Hohne and Redelinghuys, a Dutch audit firm of Cape Town.[39] Insurance activities in the Cape Colony served local communities and specific regional interests. There was no reason to change the corporate form of organization from joint-stock to mutual, because the owners were well-known members of the community and trusted leaders in business. They had access to capital and delivered on their promises. The three leading companies, the *Alliance*, the *South African Fire and Life*, and the *Cape of Good Hope Fire and Life* seemed to be in keen competition, but closer analysis of their rates actually indicate a degree of collusion or agreement not to undercut each other.

---

[36] Hirsch 1962.   [37] Spyrou 1955, 328–9.   [38] Verhoef 2010, 147–8.
[39] *Grahamstown Journal* 6 October 1836; Hirsch 1962, 25.

Favourable economic conditions supported a steady flow of new entrants into the market. New entrants appear in the Cape Town area as well as in the Eastern Cape. The *Eastern Province Fire and Life Assurance Company* was established in 1843 and the *Equitable Fire and Life Assurance and Trust Company* in Cape Town in 1846, though the latter also dispatched agents to country districts as far as Swellendam, Caledon, Worcester, Port Elizabeth, etc.[40] To gain a competitive advantage the *Equitable* introduced, alongside its life and fire business, also a trust department, to conduct the administration and management of estates and other properties.[41] It also cut its rates on both fire and life business to attract policyholders, with considerable success. The *Cape of Good Hope* soon revised its rates downward as well, but not the *South African*. In 1844 another competitor entered the Cape Colony—the *Alfred Home and Foreign Life Assurance and Mutual Annuity Association* of London. The *Alfred* was the first company to quote 'without profit' life tables, but it failed in 1873. Little further innovation in terms of products characterized the insurance market in the Cape Colony. The most important development was the annexation by the British Government of the Natal Colony in 1842, which led to the expansion of insurance business into that market.

THE AWAKENING OF A PEOPLE

In the decades after the end of the Napoleonic Wars settlers in the Cape Colony grew increasingly impatient with the authoritarian colonial administration, which refused them the civil liberties that British citizens had grown accustomed to. A group of 'radical democrats' in the Cape Colony waged campaigns calling for the freedom of the press and a degree of political participation. These efforts paid off when independent newspapers were allowed in 1827 and the *South African Commercial Advertiser* (1827), the *Zuid-Afrikaan* (1830), and the *Grahamstown Journal* (1831) appeared regularly. After the abolition of slavery in 1838 the greatest obstacle to representative government in the colony was removed. The settlers stepped up their campaign for political participation—similar to developments in French Canada and New South Wales in Australia shortly before. The newspapers became the battleground for representative government and voiced a growing awareness among the settler community of their interests as citizens, their civil rights, and their agency in promoting their own well-being. A local 'nationalism' developed, which could foster community action, of which mutual organizations represented a familiar manifestation. Public leaders, such as

---

[40] *Grahamstown Journal* 23 October 1839, 31 August 1843, 11 January 1844.
[41] *Natal Witness* 27 February 1846.

John Fairbairn (editor of the *SA Commercial Advertiser*), emphasized mutuality as a strategy to empower themselves and secure their future. During the repetitive frontier wars in the Eastern Cape during the 1830s and 1840s settlers were increasingly calling for cessation, or for the move of the seat of government to the Eastern Cape—agitation that suggested their taking agency of their own future and a desire to control their own destiny.[42] The mutual form of organization also offered a new selling point to local entrepreneurs wanting to champion the establishment of more insurance companies, especially since mutual companies did not need much start-up capital.

Those promoting the mutual form of insurance appealed to the trust and sense of community that had been shaped by the political agitation and the insecurity on the Eastern Cape frontier to encourage fellow settlers to join forces in their own interest. A sense of shared destiny, trust of fellow settlers, and a joint agency in the future of the colony created fertile ground for the development of a mutual insurance company. It is interesting that the mutual insurers were only life assurers. A single-product mutual concern could be justified as including members of similar disposition with a strong identity of interest, a shared social context, a relative homogenous type of risk, and a desire to strengthen the sense of community in opposition to distant British commercial interests or the Imperial Government.[43]

Mutualism in insurance was an important innovation in the Cape Colony. It occurred at very much the same time, the mid-1840s, as the formation of mutual life assurance companies in the United States of America.[44] In 1845 prominent Cape Town businessmen met to consider the formation of the *Mutual Life Assurance Society of the Cape of Good Hope* (later renamed *South African Mutual Life*). Their model was the Scottish Equitable Mutual Life Assurance Society and the concept was mutual benefit, with profits not going to shareholders but to holders of policies. In the founding meeting the benefits of the mutual form of organization were explained at length. The emphasis was placed on benefits to bereaved individuals, but also to the community at large. The promoter, John Fairbairn (himself a Scottish immigrant), wrote in the *Commercial Advertiser* that the Bible commanded provision by the head of a family for his dependents, stating that, 'to provide for his own household is a condition of salvation. The neglect of this duty is a denial of the faith; and the professing Christian who has this guilt to answer for is in a worse condition than the infidel or heathen'.[45] The 'considerable profits driven out of similar associations' would not occur in a mutual organization where all proceeds of investments would accrue to policyholders. The local community

---

[42] Davenport and Saunders 2000, 101–4; Giliomee 2003, 1117–22; Pretorius 2012, 95, 527.
[43] See the discussion of the USA's emerging market for mutual insurance since the early 1840s in Hansmann 1996, 273–4.
[44] Klerk 1978, 90.   [45] See Hirsch 1962, 26.

of policyholders would benefit from direct access to their accumulated benefits and immediate attention to claims in case of death. In the promotional essay by Fairbairn on a mutual assurance company the first mention was made of the potential benefits accruing to residents of the colony, as opposed to the benefits of assurance going to the overseas shareholders of stock companies. There is no trace of public complaints about agency problems or complaints of excessive cost to policyholders in the Colony of insurance sold by foreign companies.[46] No reference can also be found to concerns about the non-payment of claims causing settlers to distrust the foreign stock companies, which Hansmann has suggested was a greater possibility in stock companies than mutual entities.[47]

A more credible explanation for the emergence of a desire for mutual action in life assurance was put forward by Birchall, who suggested that there is a causal relationship between the choice of a mutual form of organization and the nature of social relationships between the individual and the community. The idea that individual and collective well-being can be acquired through mutual dependence, and a sense of joint destiny, leads to the preference for the mutual organizational form.[48] In the Fairbairn articles, and in the context of an emerging insistence on the recognition of their civil liberties in the Colony and their interests as distinct from those of people in Britain, the emerging Cape settler community was ready to pursue their own collective interests. Developments leading to representative government for the Cape Colony in 1853 and subsequent responsible government in 1872 strengthened the awakening of a collective social responsibility and the potential collective advantages of mutuality. This sense of community also helps explain why not many mutual assurers entered the market—the dominant *SA Mutual* could serve the collective interests of the relatively small Cape Colony.

In the spirit of the collective interest of potential policyholders, the founders of the *SA Mutual* presented a detailed and transparent outline of what the company offered. A full list of premiums for full life cover was published from ages fourteen to fifty-five. These accorded with the principles and rates of the Scottish Equitable Life Assurance Society. All profits were to be divided every three years and allocated to all policyholders.[49] The concept of the mutual benefit of policyholders and the direct advantage of policyholders' general welfare to the society at large was an important source of security to colonists in a society peripheral to the metropolitan centre and subject to the greater insecurity of a rural economy. Soon more mutuals appeared: on 21 June 1845 a

---

[46] Hansmann 1996, 274, 357n.

[47] Hansmann 1996, 266–8. Cf. the similar conclusions about insurance in colonial Australia drawn by Keneley elsewhere in this volume.

[48] Birchall 2001, 3–5.

[49] *Grahamstown Journal* 26 June 1845, 17 July 1845; Macintyre 1898, 80–1; Van Selm 1945, 1–3.

meeting established the *Eastern Province Mutual Life Assurance Company*.[50] The *SA Mutual* put the concept of mutuality to good use in competition with other insurance companies in the Cape Colony. It advertised that it was prepared to reduce premiums by 5, 10, 15, and 20 per cent, and even more on policies that had run for a corresponding number of years. The company added: 'By this resolution the assured will in effect participate in the profits in a ratio increasing at the expiration of every five years'. The *SA Mutual* was established in April 1845 and by June of the same year it advertised mortgages to property owners, stating that it had money on hand to invest. The *Equitable Fire Assurance and Trust Company* (formed a year later) even closed down its life department and shared its offices on 12 Heerengracht Street, Cape Town with the young rising mutual company.[51] The *SA Mutual* (later known as *Old Mutual*) transacted a relatively small amount of business during its establishment years, but survived the serious banking crisis of the 1860s.[52]

More foreign insurance companies commenced business in the Cape Colony, Natal, and the two Boer Republics. Access to capital was extremely limited in the Boer Republics and Natal was perceived to be an extension of the Cape market. In 1845 the *Royal Insurance Company* of Liverpool was the first Home Office to dispatch a full-time representative to the Cape Colony.[53] In 1846 the *Equitable Fire Assurance and Trust Company* was formed. A trust company formed the core of this business, while a fire department wrote fire insurance. Agencies were opened in Port Natal and several Cape towns.[54] By 1849 the *Equitable* also offered marine insurance. As a local concern it advertised the fact that it was 'a Colonial Institute, all its Funds are invested in South Africa'.[55] In 1847 the *Professional Life Assurance Company* of London sent an agent to the Cape Colony. The *Natal Fire Assurance Company* was established in 1850 to write in fire insurance in Natal.[56] In the latter fire insurance was also part of the business of a trust company, which engaged extensively in the discounting of bills, accepting deposits, opening accounts with private parties, and the administration of insolvent and other estates.[57] This developed as a standard combination in Natal because of the lack of banking institutions and the shortage of currency there.[58] In 1851 the *Church of England Life, Fire and Trust and Annuity Institution* of London started business in the Cape Colony, with the Bishop of Cape Town as its patron. This company offered low rates and conducted business until 1893, when it was finally wound up.

---

[50] *Grahamstown Journal* 17 July 1845.   [51] Hirsch 1962, 26.

[52] Arndt 1928, 290–4; Jones 1996, 25.

[53] See Schweizerische Rückversicherungsgesellschaft 1964, 406; Vivian 2001, 19–22.

[54] *Natal Witness* 27 February 1846.   [55] Macintyre 1898, 108.

[56] *Natal Witness* 4 May 1849, 3 May 1850, 25 April 1851, 17 October 1851.

[57] *Natal Witness* 7 May 1852.   [58] Webb 1992, 26–7.

The local insurance companies remained the dominant players. The *Equitable* and *De Protecteur* continued to cut rates slightly under those of the *Cape of Good Hope* to dominate the market. For five consecutive years *De Protecteur* allocated 50 per cent of its revenue in the form of bonuses to all types of policyholders.[59] By 1851 the *SA Mutual* alone had already accumulated funds in excess of £30,000 with an annual revenue of £4,500. The promoter of the *SA Mutual*, Fairbairn, put his public prominence to good use in promoting his mutual insurance company. He epitomized the growing settler 'nationalism', which supported the growth of the company. In 1849 Britain attempted to send convicts to the Cape Colony to be liberated there on tickets of leave. Fairbairn led a large gathering of citizens objecting to the landing of the ship in Table Bay. The agitation succeeded in preventing the landing of the crew as well as the felons on board the *Neptune* (282 persons) and the ship was forced to proceed to Australia. Fairbairn was later sent to London by the Cape Town City Council to impress on the Colonial Government that the Cape Colony was not in favour of any similar actions in future. In response, the Colonial Office offered a guarantee that no more convicts would be sent to the Cape Colony.[60] After the 1850s more competition would develop in the Cape Colonial market as a result of improved information flows to Britain. More ships frequented Table Bay en route to Australia and India, which increased contact with the remote colony and led to greater expectations of participation in the lucrative market. The *Unity Fire Insurance Association* established itself in the Cape Colony. Later, in 1853, the *Guardian Assurance and Trust Company* of Port Elizabeth was established and in 1856 competition was further fuelled by yet more rate reductions by the *South African Fire and Life*.[61]

During the 1860s sheep farming prospered and wool exports from the Cape Colony rose substantially. In Natal the sugar industry was established and Indian indentured labour imported to supplement local labour supplies. General agricultural conditions improved, but a lack of railway connections pand weak road access hampered commercial exchange. The newly found wool wealth was short-lived, since a collapse in international wool prices by 1862 resulted in a collapse in the Cape wool industry. The relative prosperity of the agriculture in the Eastern Cape led to the emergence of more local insurance concerns, such as *The Union Fire and Marine Insurance Company* in Grahamstown in 1860 and the *Commercial Union Assurance Company Limited* of London, which opened for business in the Eastern Cape in 1861, with the specific objective of insuring the risks of merchants trading agricultural commodities to and local products from the Eastern

[59] Spyrou 1955, 325; Hirsch 1962, 26.
[60] Van Selm 1945, 12; Hirsch 1962, 27; Müller 1973, 157–8.
[61] Van Selm 1945, 20–1.

Table 7.1. Paid-up capital of South African insurance companies, 1857

Name	Paid-up £/s/d per share	Market value of shares
South African Fire and Life	£10.0.0	£100.0.0
Cape of Good Hope Trust and Assurance Company	£10.0.0	£14.0.0
De Protecteur	£5.0.0	£20.0.0
Equitable	£5.0.0	£17.10.0
Cape of Good Hope Marine	£10.0.0	£26.0.0
Commercial Marine and Fire	£5.0.0	£5.10.0
Port Elizabeth Fire	£2.0.0	£2.0.0
Eastern Province Fire and Life Assurance	£5.0.0	£25.0.0
Frontier Fire Assurance	£2.0.0	£2.16.0
Guardian of Port Elizabeth	£2.0.0	£2.2.0

Source: Hirsch (1962), 27.

Cape region.[62] Some new foreign insurers entered the Cape Colony during the 1860s, such as the *London and Lancashire Fire Insurance* Company in 1862, but the explosion in the insurance market came in the 1880s after the discovery of diamonds in 1867 and 1871, and again after the discovery of gold in 1886.[63]

In the period between the establishment of the first insurance companies in the Cape Colony during the 1820s and the boom following the mineral discoveries, insurance was conducted primarily on a private equity basis. Only two insurance companies were mutual. Profits were reasonable, but not exorbitant. The main business was fire and life insurance, with limited marine insurance. Table 7.1 shows the paid-up capital of the South African insurance companies by 1857.

The local insurance companies were well capitalized and competed most in the fire industry where rates were low. Foreign companies conducted their business through agents, while local fire insurers had the upper hand.[64] In life insurance local companies also dominated the industry, although the life business was limited as a result of the small and sparsely populated white population.[65] No product innovation occurred, since the British insurance model remained the benchmark. While accident insurance was introduced in Britain in the 1860s, it only came to the Cape Colony in the 1890s.[66] Local companies offering marine insurance all had their risks underwritten in London, which meant that there was no native marine insurance in South Africa by the 1890s. The local companies attempted to gain an advantage over foreign companies by advertising that their policies had no additional premium for residents of the colonies, thus undercutting foreign companies

---

[62] *Grahamstown Journal* 21 February 1860, 19 June 1860; Macintyre 1898, 51.
[63] Vivian 2002, 138–45.   [64] Macintyre 1898, 9–10.
[65] Macintyre 1898, 7, 21.   [66] Macintyre 1898, 17–20.

that attempted to add extra risk to local policies. As we have seen, one strategy of the local industry that characterized its formative years was the combination of trust business with insurance. This enabled managers to supplement insurance income with revenue from the administration of estates, a strategy indicative of the strong profit motive behind engagement in the market.

MINERALS AND ECONOMIC TRANSFORMATION

Insurance activities increased by compound rates after the mineral discoveries. Foreign firms from Australia, New Zealand, the Netherlands, Germany, and more from Britain opened branches in the Cape Colony, the ZAR, the Orange Free State, and the Natal Colony. Insurance companies from the Cape Colony and Natal expanded their business into the ZAR and the Orange Free State. Railways were built to the mines on the Witwatersrand and communication of prospects travelled fast. In 1893 the *Post Magazine and Insurance Monitor* noted: 'South Africa is the space to which the Companies are turning with great activity. Branches and agencies are covering the area of explored territory, and we shall not be surprised to find English Offices' agents in Uganda'.[67] Foreign insurance companies were required to pay a license fee of £500 and a deposit that varied among colonies. In the Cape Colony, Natal, and the Orange Free State £10,000 was demanded, while the Transvaal required a deposit of securities to the value of £10,000. Furthermore, a tax of 2.5 per cent on premiums recovered was payable in the Cape.[68] These measures were not taken too kindly to, as the *Post Magazine and Insurance Monitor* described them as 'the avaricious desire of native legislation to impose taxes on foreign companies'.[69] Similar deposit requirements were in place in Canada and the United States, described by the *Review* as 'and so on with a lot more of such rubbish'.[70] The reason for the imposition of the tax was to protect local companies against the growing competition of English and other foreign companies, especially in fire insurance. The tax introduced in the Cape was under the terms of the Cape Colony Stamp Act of 1887, requiring payment of 6 per cent of premium income and later extended to the other colonies.[71] This

---

[67] *Post Magazine and Insurance Monitor* 1, 7 January 1893, 13. (This was a British publication.)

[68] *Post Magazine and Insurance Monitor* 14 December 1895, 862; *Review* 9 September 1903, 543, 5 December 1903, 700, 9 December 1904, 768. (*Review* was also a British publication.)

[69] *Post Magazine and Insurance Monitor* 1, 5 January 1895, 13. See also a court case contesting liability to pay such tax, referred to in *Post Magazine and Insurance Monitor* 3 June 1899, 392–3.

[70] *Review* 9 December 1904, 768.

[71] *Post Magazine and Insurance Monitor* 14 December 1895, 862; Vivian 2001, 21.

tax offered the Colonial Government a welcome source of revenue, because there was a substantial degree of competition in the Cape market, especially in fire insurance.[72] More than twenty-one local insurance companies were taken over by thirteen foreign companies.[73] After the mineral discoveries, more than twenty UK companies extended their business to Johannesburg. Australian, American, and New Zealand insurance concerns also attempted to benefit from the rapidly growing urban population and the high risks in the mining industry.[74] Despite the expansion of foreign interest in the local insurance market, by 1895 three colonial companies had secured more business in the Cape Colony than the twenty-two foreign companies. These were the *SA Mutual Life Assurance Company* (established 1845), the *Southern Life Association* (1891), and the *Industrial Life Assurance Company of South Africa* (1894). The *Southern Life* was a mutual life insurance company because, as its founder chairman J. M. Stephen explained, only one local mutual had engaged in the market to insure lives and protect inhabitants against fire and accident risks. A strong emerging 'nationalism' was apparent in his motivation for a second local mutual: South Africans were capable of providing superior assurance services to their own people, capable of managing such business profitably and in the interest of policyholders. He stressed that the colony did not need foreigners to render such services, since local capacity and expertise existed, while the economic growth of the country promised a secure future to such enterprises.[75]

The most important development of the post-mineral discovery period was the promulgation of legislation to regulate the insurance industry. In 1891 the first legislation was passed in the Cape Colony, providing for the registration of insurance companies. The Life Assurance Act, no. 13 of 1891 required all life assurance companies to register and submit an annual statement of policies in force. Every five years an actuarial report was required. Companies not incorporated by an Act of Parliament, or registered under the Joint Stock Companies Limited Liability Act of 1861, had to submit articles of association or a Charter of Incorporation to the government. In 1893 the Accident Insurance Act added the requirement that a duty of £50 was payable by each company in respect of the different classes of accidents insured.[76] Foreign

---

[72] *Post Magazine and Insurance Monitor* 11 August 1894, 573.

[73] Including the *Royal Exchange Assurance Company of London*, the *Guardian Fire and Life Assurance Company of London*, the *Commercial Union Assurance Company*, the *Sun Insurance Office*, the *British and Foreign Marine Insurance Company*, the *London and Lancashire Insurance Company*, the *Manchester Fire Assurance Company*, and the *South British Fire and Marine Insurance Company*.

[74] *Post Magazine and Insurance Monitor* 12 July 1897, 432; Vivian 2001, 21–4; Spyrou 1955, 325–7. See also *Summaries of Returns Deposited with the Treasury by Insurance Companies during the Year ended 31 December 1924*, 5–8.

[75] Bulpin 1996, 5.   [76] Macintyre 1898, 48–50, 52.

companies were required to deposit £10,000 with the Colonial Treasurer (section 14 of the Stamp Act). This was required of all classes of insurance business. Section 11 of the Stamp Act also required all foreign companies to take out annual licenses, the fee for which was 'sixpence per pound sterling, or fraction of pound sterling, on the premiums received during the preceding year'. The minimum payment was £30 and the maximum £500.[77] Statutory regulation had the advantage of providing statistics on the industry that hitherto had been absent. In the Natal Colony no legislation existed before the end of the century, but annual license duties were required. The ZAR, under Act no. 12 of 1892, and later also the Transvaal Colony, demanded the deposit of securities with the government of £5,000 in the case of fire or accident business or both, and £10,000 for life assurance by all insurance companies with head offices outside the republic. Annual returns were also required that reported the total amount of insurance in force, the total amount of new business, premiums received, and assets and liabilities. An annual license duty of £20 was payable.[78] In the Orange Free State Ordinance no. 10 of 1891, *The Regulation of the Admission of Assurance Companies into the Free State* set out requirements for registration. Foreign insurance companies had to deposit £5,000 for fire or accident business and £10,000 for life business, with annual license fees of three pence for every £ received in premiums, to a minimum of £20. Annual returns on policies in force, policies lapsed and new policies were required.[79]

This regulatory environment aimed less at controlling the industry than securing revenue to the colonial governments. From the annual submissions to the colonial treasurer in the Cape Colony since 1891, the size of the industry can be established.[80]

The growth of the local insurance industry is reflected in Table 7.2. These statistics are for the life insurance of inhabitants of the Cape Colony only. They were taken to be only the European population, which was around 377,000 in 1891 and 2 million by 1909. It does therefore not include the business written by these companies in the other colonies. Local companies issued 49 per cent of policies in 1891 and the foreign companies 51 per cent, but by 1907 the ratio was 70:30. The significance of this ratio is that the

---

[77] *Cape of Good Hope, Colonial Secretary's Ministerial Division: Returns under the Life Assurance Act, 1891, for the Year Ended 31st December, 1893:* sections 7 and 8: 3; See *Post Magazine and Insurance Monitor* 14 December 1895, 862.

[78] *Returns under the Life Assurance Act, 1891, for the Year Ended 31st December, 1893:* section 12: 5. See also *Post Magazine and Insurance Monitor* 14 December 1895, 862; Macintyre 1898, 54–5.

[79] *Returns under the Life Assurance Act, 1891, for the Year Ended 31st December, 1893:* section 13: 5. See also *Post Magazine and Insurance Monitor* 14 December 1895, 862; Macintyre 1898, 56, 58.

[80] Similar reports are not available for the Boer republics or the Natal Colony for this period.

Table 7.2. Performance of life insurance companies, Cape Colony, 1891–1907 ('000)

	1891	1893	1895	1897	1899	1901	1903	1905	1907
No. of policies	18,814	22,534	27,821	31,873	36,123	49,720	66,716	83,010	84,560
Foreign	9,518	12,526	13,184	15,157	16,995	18,524	22,268	23,253	24,939
Local	9,296	10,008	14,637	16,716	19,140	31,196	44,442	59,737	59,621
Sums assured	8,734	10,181	10,806	12,233	13,193	14,766	18,213	19,815	20,936
Foreign	4,340	5,590	5,762	6,505	7,217	8,111	9,979	9,938	10,491
Local	4,394	4,591	5,044	5,723	5,976	6,654	8,234	9,876	10,444

Source: Cape of Good Hope, Colonial Secretary's Ministerial Division: Returns under the Assurance Act, 1891, for the Years Ended 1891–1907.

number of foreign firms was substantially higher than the number of local firms. In 1891 there were sixteen foreign companies and two local companies competing in the Cape insurance industry. This ratio remained highly in favour of foreign companies by 1907: then the number of foreign companies was thirty and there were five local companies, a ratio of 6:1. The value of policies or sums assured differed between the local and foreign companies. The average value of policies issued by local companies was £175 and the average by foreign companies £420.

Local companies insured on average smaller policyholders, being the majority of colonial inhabitants. Foreign companies insured the wealthier inhabitants. Local companies were thus developing the social base of insurance, which in the long run would strengthen their market share. By 1900 the ratio of total life insurance issued in the Cape Colony was still 45:55 in favour of foreign companies.[81] By 1909 this ratio had more than reversed. A more remarkable observation was that the average sum assured per head (of the European population) in the Cape Colony was £23 in 1891, compared to £19 in Australasia, £12 in the UK, £9 in Canada, and £10 in the United States. By 1909 the figure rose to £31 in the Cape Colony, with only New Zealand at a higher level per head at £32. The average per policy in the Cape Colony was £411 in 1908, but £246 in New Zealand.[82] The insurance industry in the Cape Colony experienced strong growth towards the end of the first decade of the twentieth century, which was a direct consequence of the mineral discoveries. The insurance companies that extended their business to the ZAR/Transvaal Colony and the OFS/Orange River Colony, were all active in the Cape Colony, or established offices in that colony as a basis for their operations in the areas of new wealth.

The majority of insurance companies were joint-stock limited liability companies. Only two mutual companies were active in life insurance: *SA Mutual* and the *Southern Life Association*. Foreign mutuals, such as the *Mutual of New York* and the *Colonial Mutual* (established in 1873) from Melbourne, attempted to enter the local market, but their business was limited. The leading local companies, however, were predominantly mutual in organization and they displayed dynamic growth, responding to the emerging settler identities and trust in local fellow policyholders and managers.

It was primarily in the Cape insurance market that new life products were developed by the *SA Mutual*. At a special meeting of its board of directors it was decided to revise the table of whole life rates and adopt a new table which reduced the rates for younger ages and increased them from forty years upwards. The company also decided to issue policies of which the premiums

[81] *Review* 9 December 1903, 700.
[82] Cape of Good Hope, Colonial Secretary's Ministerial Division: Returns under the Assurance Act, 1891, for the Year Ended 1908.

were limited to a certain number of payments instead of being payable over the whole life. The next innovation was to issue 'Endowment Assurance'. This provided for the commencement of premiums in infancy, with policies payable at the age of fourteen or twenty-four years of age. The *SA Mutual* also decided to issue policies on joint lives payable at the decease of either life, depending on the date of death of the first policyholder. The company also commenced issuing annuities. It was decided that no policy would become forfeitable so long as the surrender value thereof was sufficient to pay one year's premium together with a moderate fine thereon. The limits on free travel were also extended, clearly taking into account the opening up of economic and commercial incentives in the interior.[83] These life products were developed in conjunction with the needs of the members. The board of directors were all policyholders and, constitutionally, had no more power than any other policyholder in the mutual organization. The close association between its members and the organization was partly responsible for the steady growth of the company. In the Cape Colony industrial insurance was also introduced to the working classes in 1894 by the *Industrial Assurance Company of South Africa*. This type of insurance was a life product with small premiums payable on a weekly basis and paid out at death. No sick benefits were included. These types of policies occupied a position between the provisions of friendly societies and ordinary life assurance.[84]

The expansion of the insurance industry after the mineral discoveries commenced in the Cape Colony, where the industry was well established. That was also the location of greatest competition, but when opportunities opened in the interior, the established Cape firms expanded operations to the Transvaal and the Free State/Orange River Colony. The *SA Mutual*, the *Southern*, and various foreign insurance companies opened branches in Bloemfontein and Pretoria and/or Johannesburg.[85] In the Orange River Colony firms from Port Elizabeth and the Cape Colony extended their services and some local enterprises were established. In Bloemfontein the *Bloemfontein Board of Executors and Trust Company* was established and engaged in fire assurance, while the *Port Elizabeth Fire and Marine Assurance Company* opened a branch for business.[86] The US *Equitable Life Assurance Society* and the *Northern Assurance Company* of London also extended their business into the Free State.[87] By 1907 more than thirty insurance companies submitted returns to the Transvaal Colonial authorities, none of them locally

---

[83] Van Selm 1945, 28–9.

[84] Cape of Good Hope, Colonial Secretary's Ministerial Division: Returns under the Life Assurance Act, 1891, for the Year Ended 31st December 1893, 6.

[85] Van Selm 1945, 23–6; Bulpin 1996, 9–13. See also *Post Magazine and Insurance Monitor* 12 June 1897, 432.

[86] *Friend of the Free State and Bloemfontein* 1 April 1880, 5 April 1880.

[87] *Friend of the Free State and Bloemfontein* 19 September 1890, 25 December 1878.

incorporated.[88] These were either foreign or Cape companies. The foreign insurance companies with offices in the Cape Colony simply extended their operations to the interior by following their business clients.

CONCLUSION

The insurance industry developed gradually along the slowly expanding commercial frontier in South Africa, from the Cape Colony to the Natal Colony and then following the business explosion of the mineral discoveries into the ZAR/Transvaal Colony and the Orange Free State/ORC. The British insurance industry was almost duplicated in the colonies. Market access was not subject to any specific barriers and the use of British mortality tables benefited them. Despite the existence of friendly societies in the Cape Colony, mutual insurance societies were late to enter the market and did not dominate it. The strong foreign presence was partly responsible for this phenomenon. Businessmen heading up limited liability private stock companies spearheaded the majority of the early insurance companies. They were driven by profit and return on investments, while a sense of social responsibility and a local 'nationalism' gained ground towards the middle of the nineteenth century. The political maturity of the Cape Colony after the establishment of representative government in 1853 gave the colony greater constitutional sovereignty and in 1872, when responsible government was granted, the confidence of the Cape settler community grew in stature. These developments epitomized the development of a local identity, local confidence, a sense of social entitlement, and collective community interests distinct from the home interests. These social developments coincided with the economic prosperity of the Cape Colony and the entrepreneurial spirit among local businessmen, professionals, and community leaders.

The decision to form the first mutual life assurance company in the 1840s occurred around the same time as similar developments in the US market and five years before the first mutual life assurance company was formed in Australia (see Chapter 8 by Keneley in this volume). The introduction of insurance into the Cape Colony was a business venture, but as the colonial community developed a more distinct identity, the interests of local inhabitants moved to the foreground. Mutual organizations reflect the development of an awareness of the economic value of cooperation. This was visible in the Cape Colony towards the middle of the nineteenth century, when the anti-convict campaign bore fruit and the colony was granted representative

---

[88] National Archives of South Africa: T 20/4–67: Submissions in Terms of the Insurance Law of the Transvaal Colony, 1906.

government. Social values for the benefit of members of the community were developing and can explain the profoundly better performance of the *SA Mutual* compared to other life insurance companies in the Cape Colony by the end of the century. A similar sense of community developed among inhabitants of the Eastern Cape around Port Elizabeth, Grahamstown, Swellendam, and East London. The second mutual insurance company was established in that region, displaying the shared values of community benefit. Despite the 'world coming to insure South Africa' with the large number of foreign insurance companies from the United Kingdom, Germany, the British Commonwealth, the USA, and even India, the local mutual insurance companies outperformed the market. The distance between foreign shareholders created an agency problem for those companies. During the formative years of the insurance industry in the Cape Colony local agents could address local concerns, but the profits went towards non-nationals or foreign shareholders. This was an important argument put forward by the promoters of the *SA Mutual* when mobilizing support for their new mutual concern. When the mineral discoveries opened opportunities in the interior, the local mutual sustained its superior performance and expanded into those markets.

8

Business Strategies under Conditions of Uncertainty

The Rise of Mutual Life Insurers in Colonial Australia

Monica Keneley

During the late 1990s Australia witnessed a series of demutualizations of life insurance companies. This trend represented the end of an era in which, for over 150 years, these firms had been the leading players in the life insurance market. Australian mutuals grew to be more than economic entities; they became part of the fabric of Australian society supporting a range of economic, social, and cultural activities. The mutual form of organization proved remarkably successful in the Australian context. A large part of the success of these institutions lay in the manner in which they were able, from an early stage, to synthesize the needs of the community with their own business interests.

Mutual life insurers formed in the mid-nineteenth century. The first, the Australian Mutual Provident (hereafter AMP), was established in 1849 but it was not until the late 1860s that other such organizations appeared. Between 1869 and 1881 twelve mutuals opened their doors for business. The popularity of mutual associations was reinforced by the failure of stock companies to provide the types of insurance products consumers wanted. This chapter seeks to explain why the mutual form of organization was the preferred form at this time. In doing so it will address the question of how the Australian experience fits theoretical explanations for the rise of mutuals. It argues that whilst such models explain part of the story, a range of other economic and institutional influences have also played a role in the growth of the mutual culture. In respect to Australia, a number of environmental and market influences determined the make-up of the life insurance market. The chapter identifies four groups of influences that account for the rise and popularity of mutual life insurers in Australia. It is argued that whilst economic and social factors provided the context and underlying rationale for the emergence of mutuals, it was the environmental and market forces that were the drivers creating opportunities for establishment and growth.

THEORETICAL EXPLANATIONS OF MUTUALITY

Academic debate surrounding the emergence of mutual institutions has focused largely on the issue of market failure. Hansmann has argued that the mutual form of organization emerged in response to problems associated with market operations.[1] The costs of ownership and the costs of contracting were identified as two key issues. Ownership costs arise from agency problems associated with the separation of ownership and control. In respect to insurance companies, an incentive/contracting conflict has been argued to exist between managers of stock companies and policyholders.[2] Contracting problems include the costs associated with asymmetric information, uncertainty, and opportunism. In a mutual organization, the absence of the need to consider shareholder interests allowed premiums to be set at a level that would offset the risks involved.[3]

Hansmann suggests that if we are to understand the popularity of mutual structures in insurance markets (particularly life insurance markets) we must not only consider ownership and contracting issues.[4] We must also understand the origins of the industry in the nineteenth century. Three factors influenced the spread of mutual insurers at this time. These were the problems of long-term contracting under conditions of uncertainty, asymmetry of information between policyholders and insurance companies, and the need to avoid problems of adverse selection.[5] The policyholder in taking out a life insurance policy must have a degree of confidence that the insurer will be able to fulfil their obligations. Poor information is another issue affecting consumers when deciding on the most appropriate type of life insurance policy. This problem can be ameliorated under a mutual structure where the policyholder has ownership rights. From the insurer's perspective there must also be an assurance that the policyholder will fulfil their own obligations to continue to make premium payments over the long term. In the nineteenth century, when actuarial knowledge was relatively rudimentary, investment portfolio

---

[1] Hansmann 1996, 265.   [2] Fama and Jensen 1983, 337–41.
[3] Hansmann 1985, 129–32; Mayers and Smith 1986, 77–8.
[4] Hansmann 1985, 126.   [5] Hansmann 1985, 129.

diversification limited, and mortality rates higher, there was a much higher risk of market failure. Mutuals became popular alternative providers because the structure of these organizations allowed them to set rates high enough to cover worst-case scenarios. In the event that the risk was overestimated, the resulting surplus could be returned to policyholders in the form of bonuses.[6]

Economic methodologies provide some insights into the emergence of mutual insurers, but they do not account for their popularity over time. Many of the constraints associated with the stock company structure were likely to become manifest in financial mutuals as they expanded and the association between members and management became increasingly separated. To understand the nature of the mutual insurer it is necessary to look beyond the economic rationale and consider the broader social context in which these organizations were formed. Birchall suggests that a reason for the appeal of mutuals is the connection they draw between the individual and the community.[7] He argues that mutuality is essentially a sociological construct. It connects the individual with the rest of the community laying down the rights and responsibilities conditional to membership of a group.

Economic and social factors explain the contextual setting in which mutual insurers formed but they do not provide the whole story. This chapter argues that two other types of influences need to be taken into account in any explanation of the emergence of mutual organizations. Figure 8.1 represents a schematic illustration of a proposed model explaining the influences on organizational types in the life insurance market. Although this model is intended to explain the Australian experience it may also be applicable in the analysis of the development of other financial markets, particularly in settler societies. Verhoef (see Chapter 7 in this volume), for example, tracks the development of mutual life offices in South Africa under similar conditions and highlights the role of social and community influences in the growth of these organizations.

The model assumes that four key parameters have influenced the foundation and growth of mutual life insurers in Australia. *Economic* factors are those associated with the ownership and contracting problems explained above. *Social* factors include social and moral codes of behaviour. Insurance mutuals formed in the nineteenth century as self-help organizations for the protection of members and their families. Their foundations are linked to those of other self-help organizations such as friendly societies.

Environmental factors refer to the prevailing economic and regulatory structure of the country in which the market is located. These include the

---

[6] Hansmann 1985, 134.   [7] Birchall 2001, 3.

Monica Keneley

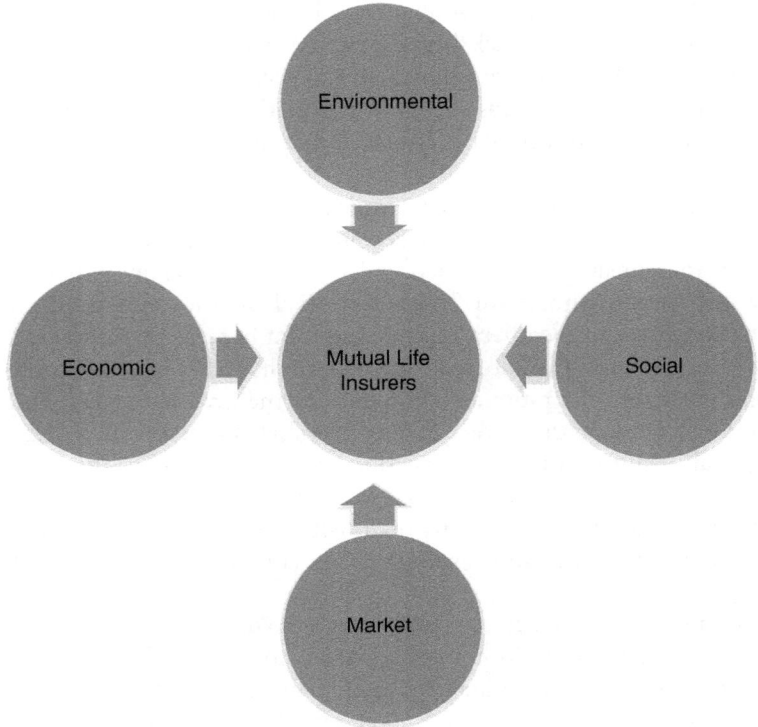

Figure 8.1. Factors influencing the emergence of life insurance mutuals

maturity of the economy, its size and geographic boundaries, population and trade constraints, the degree of urbanization, income distribution, and systems of government. In the mid-nineteenth century the economies of the Australian colonies were relatively immature. It was not until the latter half of that century that economic growth, spurred on by the effects of gold rushes in two key colonies, Victoria and New South Wales (hereafter NSW), resulted in a growing level of economic sophistication. Environmental factors refer to the ability of the economy to support a robust financial services sector and generate demand for insurance products.

Market factors relate to the specific state of the market, its structure, stability, and relationship with other insurance markets. What was the nature of the product and how was it sold? What factors encouraged or impeded the supply of life insurance and how were mutuals able to capitalize on or deal with these issues? British firms played a leading role in the development of property and liability insurance markets in the colonies. They were less successful in the life insurance market. The influences of market forces explain, in part, why this was the case.

THE EARLY LIFE INSURANCE BUSINESS 1830-50

The first Australian insurance company recorded as doing business in the colonies was established in 1835.[8] The colony of New South Wales (the major colony) was forty-seven years old at that time.[9] It had an estimated population of less than 100,000 and its economy was still very much based on the convict system. The Australian economy was a 'settler' economy. The stimulus for growth was primarily extensive relying on natural resources.[10] During the 1820s and 1830s, wool production drove economic development. This was significant to the ongoing development of the economy as wool production had weak regional forward linkages in terms of value added. This had the effect of limiting the capacity for industrial growth and focusing it in major urban centres such as Sydney (NSW) and Melbourne (Victoria). These were commercial cities and existed to facilitate the production of wool and other primary products.

In terms of insurance markets, the early colonial economy offered little scope or security. Population, although increasing, was small, limiting the demand for risk products. Major population centres were few in number and underdeveloped whilst the dependence of the economy on a small number of staple products left it susceptible to economic cycles.

In the early years of the colonies, life insurance was sold, firstly through agents of British companies operating in Australia and later through local fire insurance companies or branches of British offices. This initially tied the sale of life insurance to the fortunes of the fire insurance market. Early agencies included representation from the Eagle British and Colonial Life Assurance Company (1827) and the Alliance British and Foreign Life and Fire Assurance Company (1833).[11] In the 1830s local insurance companies first started to appear. Although many nominally sold life insurance, the main focus of these companies was on either fire or marine. Eleven indigenous insurance companies were recorded as trading between 1831 and 1840; this number had fallen to nine by 1851.[12] British and other overseas companies trading in Australia were also few in number. One was recorded as trading between

---

[8] Pursell 1964.

[9] The colonial system of government was progressively introduced into Australia as population centres became established in specific locations. In 1788, when the first convicts arrived, the colony of NSW constituted the eastern half of the continent. The western half was known as New Holland. By 1825 the British had laid claim to whole of the continent and there were three penal colonies: NSW, Western Australia, and Tasmania. South Australia was established as a free colony in 1836. Victoria separated from NSW in 1851, followed by Queensland in 1859. At this time there were six independent colonies which were later to become states at federation in 1901. These were NSW, Victoria, Tasmania, South Australia, Western Australia, and Queensland.

[10] McLean 2004.   [11] Gray 1977, 12-14.   [12] Pursell 1964, 157.

Table 8.1. Early Australian insurance companies, 1831–51

Company	Business	Established	Type of insurer	Location	Wound up or absorbed
Australian Marine Assurance Co.	Marine	1831	P	Sydney	Wound up 1843
Tasmanian Fire and Life Co.	Fire and life	1835	P	Hobart	Absorbed by the Alliance 1892. No evidence of life policies sold
Union Marine Assurance Co.	Marine	1835	P	Sydney	Wound up 1846
Australasian Fire and Life Co.	Fire and life	1835	P	Sydney	Restructured as a marine insurer 1843
Hobart Town and Launceston Marine	Marine	1836	P	Hobart	Wound up 1883
Derwent and Tamar	Fire, life, marine	1838	P	Hobart	Dropped life 1850
Van Diemen's Land Life Assurance	Fire, life, marine	1838	P	Hobart	Wound up 1850
Sydney Alliance	Fire	1840	P	Sydney	Wound up 1840
Mutual Fire Insurance Association	Fire	1840	M	Sydney	Wound up 1843
Mutual Indemnity Assurance Co.	Marine	1840	M	Sydney	Wound up 1840
Melbourne Fire and Marine	Fire and marine	1840	P	Melbourne	Wound up 1843
Cornwall Fire and Marine	Fire and marine	1841	P	Launceston	Absorbed by CU 1898
Sydney Fire Insurance Co.	Fire	1844	M	Sydney	Wound up 1855

P = Proprietary; M = Mutual
Sources: Pursell 1964; Gray 1977; Nobbs 1978.

1831 and 1840 and this had increased to four by 1851.[13] Table 8.1 traces the fortunes of early local insurers.

Table 8.1 highlights several key issues that influenced early insurance markets. The first is the limited number in existence. Thirteen local companies have been identified as being in operation for at least some of the time between

---

[13] Pursell 1964.

1831 and 1851. A small number of agencies of overseas companies, principally British, were also in existence. Although there is no accurate data it is unlikely that there were more than eight overseas insurers with agencies in Australia.[14]

The second feature of the market evident in Table 8.1 is its limited geographic spread. The majority of companies (seven) were located in the largest population centre (Sydney). Four were located in Hobart, the capital of Tasmania, leaving one other company in Tasmania (Launceston) and one in Melbourne.

The third aspect evident in the table is the small number of companies purporting to sell life insurance. Four companies nominally stated that they sold life insurance though there is evidence to suggest that not all of them did.[15] None of these companies were selling life insurance by 1850. Two had been wound up, a third restructured, and the fourth did not sell this type of insurance.

The fourth feature revealed by Table 8.1 is the instability of the market. Of the twelve companies listed, six were wound up before 1850 and another two restructured. A catalyst for company failure was a sharp contraction in colonial economies in 1842–3 as a result of a downturn in the pastoral industry. This depression highlighted the weaknesses of local firms that were launched by entrepreneurs with little experience of the insurance business and little capital backing. Promoters of new insurance companies typically raised capital by subscription from investors after advertising in the local newspaper.[16] Access to such funds was limited and levels of paid-up capital often quite low. An assessment by the agent for Sun Insurance Office was that many of these local firms were essentially bubble companies with few capital assets.[17]

The failure of early insurers to flourish in either the life or fire insurance markets can be attributed primarily to environmental and market factors. The colonial markets were underdeveloped. Urban centres were growing but the population base was small. Essential infrastructure was absent increasing the risks attached to fire and other types of hazards. Without effective communication and transportation systems insurance companies were locked into the market in which they established. Even with sufficient capital it would have been difficult to expand and branch out as their British counterparts were doing. The market itself was unstable and undercapitalized. The rapidity with which insurance companies appeared and disappeared did nothing to engender consumer confidence. Moreover, the sales system which relied principally on the buyer approaching the seller or the seller's agent did not generate the volume of business required to build a steady income stream. There was clearly an issue of market failure in the provision of life insurance products. However, there is also a question about the level of demand for such products.

---

[14] Nobbs 1978, 242.   [15] Gray 1977, 20.   [16] Gray 1977; Blair 1991.
[17] London Metropolitan Archives (hereafter LMA), MS 31522, Sun Foreign Agency Memorandum Books, vol. 25, Victoria 3, 1870s.

Nobbs makes the point that to many colonists, life insurance practice was one of the obscurities of the time.[18] They had only a vague understanding of how it worked.

It was against this background that the first mutual life insurance association, the Australian Mutual Provident, was established in 1849. The driving forces behind the formation of this institution were social rather than commercial. The AMP was formed by three prominent Sydney philanthropists with a view to establishing a mutual self-help mechanism to provide against old age, illness, and death. They were concerned that not only were existing life products inadequate for the purpose, but the people most in need of such security did not see the value of the investment as protection for their families. The words of the society's prospectus sum up the intent of these gentlemen. It was established for the 'express purpose of rendering Widows and Orphans free from all risk of suffering and penury' and for a 'means of providing for old age . . . by all who wish to avoid the humiliation of dependence on the bounty of strangers'.[19]

BUSINESS EXPANSION 1860S TO 1880S

The fortunes of the colonies changed with the discovery of gold in the 1850s. The gold rushes initiated a prolonged period of expansion and growth giving rise to increased immigration, industrialization, and urbanization. The population of the colonies more than trebled between 1850 and 1860 from just over 405,000 to 1.46 million.[20] The significance of the gold rushes for insurance markets, particularly life insurance, was twofold. First, it led to a sustained growth in population, particularly in major urban centres. Second, it provided a capital base upon which the country began to industrialize.[21] Between 1850 and 1860 real GDP grew at an average rate of 12.8 per cent.[22] In the 1860s the Australian colonies began to move beyond a primary base and develop the economic infrastructure that would sustain a more complex market environment.

Population increase and the associated urban development were accompanied by the industrialization of major city centres.[23] Colonial economies were no longer totally dependent on the fortunes of the wool market for prosperity. In addition, by the mid-1850s the colonies had also attained self-government and were developing their own administrative and regulatory bureaucracies.

---

[18] Nobbs 1978, 270. [19] AMP Archives, Sydney, *AMP Prospectus*, 1856.
[20] Gray 1977, 11. [21] Butlin 1964, 32.
[22] McLean 2004, 332. [23] Linge 1979.

The growing sophistication of colonial economies and the expansion of the population, most of whom were concentrated in urban areas, created an environment in which insurance companies could flourish. During the 1860s and 1870s overseas insurers (the majority of which were British) increased their presence in the Australian colonies. At the beginning of the 1860s there were eight foreign insurers with a presence in Australia. A decade later this number had risen to twenty-four.[24] Eight of these were identified as selling life insurance in the late 1860s. These were the Alliance, European, London, Liverpool and the Globe, London and Lancashire, Northern, Queen, Standard, and the Royal.[25] However, none appear to have continued this line of business beyond 1890.[26] British companies that operated in Australia in the 1860s and 1870s did so through agencies. For the most part insurance was only an adjunct to the main business of the agent, and life insurance an even smaller proportion.[27] The preoccupation of overseas companies at this time was with fire insurance. Local insurance companies also increased in number in the 1860s and 1870s. Sixteen appeared between 1861 and 1871 and a further eighteen in the following decade.[28] Of that number, however, only four were recorded as selling life insurance.

It is evident from the foregoing discussion that there was a significant gap emerging in the provision of life insurance in the colonies. Neither local nor overseas insurers were committed to this line of business. Moreover the fire insurance market was chronically unstable, which did little to instill confidence in consumers looking for long-term insurance contracts.

The AMP remained the only mutual and dedicated life insurer for two decades. From 1869 a number of new mutuals opened for business. All were keen to capitalize on the AMP's business model by adopting a mutual structure. However, there were varying degrees of commitment to the social and philanthropic foundations of mutuality that had motivated the formation of the AMP. Mutuality became more of a commercial decision in the 1870s compared with the more idealistic motivations that had driven the founders of the AMP. Seven mutual associations appeared between 1869 and 1876. Table 8.2 lists these companies. An interesting point of note is that in at least five of the seven cases establishment was driven or strongly influenced by men working in the insurance industry.

Variations in mutual structures are evident amongst these seven associations. Some like the Australian Widows' Fund (AWF) and the Australasian Temperance and General (T&G) had an affiliation with a religious or friendly

[24] Pursell 1964, 157.
[25] LMA, MS 31522, Sun Foreign Agency Memorandum Books, vol. 23, June 1867.
[26] Gray 1977, 22.
[27] *Australasian Insurance and Banking Record* (hereafter *AIBR*) 1877, 391.
[28] Pursell 1964, 157.

Table 8.2. New mutual companies in Australia, 1869–78

Company	Year of establishment	Location	Connection
Mutual Life Association of Australasia	1869	Sydney	Protest against policy restrictions of AMP
National Mutual Life Association	1869	Melbourne	Associated National Insurance Company
Mutual Life Association of Victoria	1870	Melbourne	Associated with Jacques Martin (insurance broker)
Australian Widows' Fund	1871	Melbourne	Established by Jacques Martin (insurance broker)
Colonial Mutual Life Association	1873	Melbourne	Established by Jacques Martin (insurance broker)
Australasian Temperance and General	1876	Melbourne	Related to Independent Order of Rechabites
City Mutual Life	1878	Sydney	Established by James Garvan (already in the insurance business)

society. The AWF was modelled on the Scottish Widows' Fund and had links to the Presbyterian Church. The T&G was linked to a friendly society and one expressed purpose was to encourage temperance amongst its members by discounting premiums for abstainers. Previous attempts by the Independent Order of Rechabites to sell insurance to its members had not proved successful. The decision was taken to establish an insurance company for that specific purpose.

The National Mutual Life Association (NMLA), on the other hand, came about when the directors of the National Insurance Company (NIC) decided to branch out into life insurance. Instead of establishing a proprietary company it was thought that a mutual structure was more likely to be successful because of its growing public popularity.[29] The success of the AMP, which by this time had been in business for two decades, struck a chord with the public. Not only had it proved a reliable provider, it also paid bonuses to policyholders, the amount of which increased over time as the surplus generated grew. Nobbs cites the popularity of mutual insurance principles as one of the influences on this decision.[30] The founders of the NMLA were well-known businessmen rather than the philanthropists and clergymen that had driven the establishment of the AMP. The relationship between the NMLA and the NIC was taken one step further when it was decided that the NMLA would

---

[29] Robson 1969, 6.   [30] Nobbs 1978, 284.

operate out of the same office as the NIC and use its same administrative and sales resources.[31]

The Colonial Mutual Life Association (CML) was the brainchild of Thomas Jacques Martin, who, as is evident from Table 8.2, had his fingers in a number of pies. Jacques Martin was one of those larger-than-life characters.[32] The manager of the Sun, in his report on conditions in Victoria in the 1870s, described him thus:

> He is only 38 but has 'lived' twice that time. Everyone admits he is a wonder. He is agent for the Standard of New Zealand, the Swiss Lloyds (Marine Insurance), has a building society and a life company . . . (which) appears to me that he will make a big success or a big failure. Probably he doesn't care which.[33]

Martin's vision was to create an insurance company structured on a federated basis. It was intended to be an international life insurer with branches overseas as well as in the Australasian colonies.[34]

The business of the CML grew at a rapid rate. The number of policies increased from 1,203 in 1875 to 2,905 in 1879.[35] Much of the early success of the CML can be attributed to Martin's business acumen and ability to enlist high-profile identities to the cause. The first General Committee consisted of key political leaders, including judges of the supreme court and speakers and presidents of the legislative assemblies in the various colonies.

The two other mutual insurers, the Mutual Life Association of Victoria and the City Mutual, did not grow as strongly or quickly as the NML or CML. They remained smaller and more regionally based and failed to capture market share in what was becoming a very competitive environment. The City

---

[31] Nobbs 1978, 288–9.

[32] Martin was born in Liverpool in 1839 and immigrated to Australia with his family in 1854. From an early age he embarked on a series of entrepreneurial activities. His first position was an agent with the Northern Insurance Company (UK). He then became a director of the Australian Insurance Company. At the age of twenty-one he founded his own insurance agency and broking firm. He acted as agent for a number of overseas and local insurers including the London and Lancashire, the Colonial Mutual Fire Insurance Company (no connection to CML), and the North German Fire Insurance. In 1859 he founded the Mutual Life Association with Robert Thomson and was a director of that organization for ten years. In 1870 he established the Australian Widows' Fund, reportedly suggested to him by his mother. Soon after he founded the Colonial Mutual, intending to put into practice his concept of a federated organization with self-governing branches. He was also involved in a number of import/export businesses and was Portuguese Consul for Victoria for a time. He died of pneumonia aged fifty-seven in 1896. Commonwealth Bank Archives, Sydney, CML Papers, Anon (n. d.), Unpublished History of the Colonial Mutual.

[33] LMA, MS 31522, Sun Foreign Agency Memorandum Books, vol. 25, G. R. Manvell's Report, 27 May 1877.

[34] Nobbs 1978, 312.

[35] Colonial Mutual Life Association, Annual Reports of the Colonial Mutual Life Assurance Society, Melbourne, 1876, 1880.

Mutual continued, while the Mutual Life Association of Victoria merged with the NML in 1896.

After 1880 interest in establishing mutual institutions waned. Gray attributed this to the fact that the market was already supplied by a number of mutual societies and there was not the impetus for philanthropists to support additional projects.[36] However, it is evident from the discussion above that recent entrants were motivated more by commercial rather than philanthropic concerns. In this case it is likely that the extent of competition and the growing size of the three major mutuals, the AMP, NML, and CML, acted as a deterrent for other potential entrants modelled on a mutual structure with no capital base. The structure of the life insurance market established at this time was to dominate for the next seventy years. For all intents and purposes the life insurance market remained basically mutual until after the Second World War, when an influx of overseas competitors began to challenge the status quo.

FACTORS INFLUENCING THE ORGANIZATIONAL STRUCTURE OF AUSTRALIAN LIFE INSURERS

Theoretical explanations for mutuality revolve around agency problems and contracting problems, as discussed in the second section. The schematic model applied in this chapter suggests that there are other equally relevant issues influencing the governance structures of life insurers. The argument here is that social, market, and environmental pressures are also important factors in the emergence of mutual insurers.

Economic Factors

It has been claimed that important reasons for the mutualization of insurance companies were the perception that stock companies charged a substantial premium on insurance policies and that an incentive/contracting conflict existed between managers of stock companies and policyholders.[37] Whilst it is difficult to establish whether stock companies were able to charge a premium on policies in a bid to put shareholders' interests above that of policyholders', it seems unlikely that this occurred on any scale. Table 8.3 presents a snapshot of premium rates. Whilst the rate charged by the stock company

---

[36] Gray 1977, 48.
[37] Mayers and Smith 1986, 73–7; McNamara and Rhee 1992, 221–3.

Table 8.3. Annual premium for a £100 life insurance policy at age twenty: five Australian companies in 1875

Insurance company	Rate £
Australian Alliance	1.17.0
Mutual Life Association	1.16.2
National Mutual	1.16.9
Colonial Mutual	1.16.4
AMP	1.16.8

Source: company prospectuses 1876.

(Australian Alliance) is slightly higher, there is not a significant difference between it and the mutuals.

There is some evidence, however, that conditions of uncertainty may have been a barrier to the provision of all types of insurance by stock companies. The Sun's manager, G. R. Manvell, instructed his Melbourne office that moral risk was worse in the Australian colonies and that increased caution in accepting policies was needed.[38] Insurances on the property of squatters were declined because of the opportunity for fraud that could occur in remote locations.[39] Overseas insurers such as the Sun were particularly wary of colonial conditions. The Victorian agent, for example, was instructed in 1878 to limit business as much as possible to Melbourne and within a ten-mile radius of Geelong.[40]

The issues of moral hazard and adverse selection were common to both mutual and stock life insurers. Mutuals such as the AMP attempted to minimize this risk by being overly cautious in accepting policy applications. From the early years of their operation, the society was very particular about whom it issued policies to. All policies had to be approved by the principal board of directors, who, as they stated, 'exercised great caution in accepting lives'.[41] Medical examinations were a requirement of any policy application. With the introduction of canvassing agents, medical referees were employed to travel with agents as they toured the countryside in an attempt to minimize the risk attached to policy applications. This type of activity suggests that it was not necessarily the issue of participating contracts that acted to reduce

[38] LMA, MS 31522, Sun Insurance Office Foreign Agency Memorandum Book, vol. 26, Victoria 4, entry for 17 January 1878.

[39] LMA, MS 31522, Sun Insurance Office Foreign Agency Memorandum Book, vol. 24, entry for 20 September 1867.

[40] LMA, MS 31522, Sun Insurance Office Foreign Agency Memorandum Book, vol. 26, Victoria 4, entry for 17 January 1878.

[41] AMP Archives: Sydney, First Annual Report of the Directors of the Australian Mutual Provident Society, 1849.

moral hazard in mutuals. Instead, mutuals were extremely aware of the issue and took specific steps to minimize the risk involved, even though it would have been associated with higher costs of service provision.

Social Factors

The mutual insurers that emerged in the Australian colonies in the mid-nineteenth century were a reflection of that colonial society. At this time the colonies, flush with funds generated by the gold rushes, were growing at a rapid pace. A new social structure was emerging as each of the colonies gained self-government. An emerging middle class was reflective of new social attitudes. One observer of Victorian society in 1880 summed up these prevailing attitudes: 'The spirit of independence is strong within them, and they thought it would be a fine thing to show the mother country, and the world generally, that they are capable of providing for themselves'.[42] A key element that formed the basis upon which mutual life insurers operated in the nineteenth century rested on the fact that they were not seen as charitable institutions. Instead, they were based on the concepts of individual responsibility and self-help. Members, in taking out a policy, earned an entitlement to certain benefits in the eventuality of death or disability. This was the reward for practising restraint and economy during their lifetime.

The growing individualism of Australian colonists led them to accept responsibility for their own risks. However, there was also a philanthropic rationale behind early mutual life insurers such as the AMP. Mutual life insurers were regarded as instruments for the betterment of society by their founders. The Chief Justice of NSW, Sir Alfred Stephens, summed up the role of the AMP when he stated at the 1864 annual general meeting that it was established 'not for commercial purposes, not with the object of making money, but for the purposes of benevolence and of extended usefulness'.[43] The intention of the founders of the AMP was to provide an opportunity for the 'industrious classes' to make provision for old age and death. In reality it was the more affluent middle classes that took advantage of the opportunity.

Much of the rhetoric associated with the early stated goals of the AMP in relation to relieving the conditions of the widows and children of the deserving poor was missing in the later foundation of other mutuals. These organizations were established on a much more commercial footing. It was implicitly recognized that mutual insurers were there to help those prepared to help themselves. The goal had become not so much to ensure the protection

---

[42] Cited in Cannon 1975, 189.
[43] AMP Archives: Sydney, Minutes of Annual General Meeting Held on 4 February 1864.

of the vulnerable but to educate them in the need to ensure that they protect themselves.

The popularity of mutuals in the mid-nineteenth century reflected the underlying values of colonial society. In a curious blend of social forces, a culture of self-help was combined with a growing egalitarian sentiment, which upheld the view that everyone had the opportunity to advance. Mutual aid societies were seen as one way in which the individual, with the assistance of the group, could improve their future prospects and reduce the risk of future suffering and penury.

Environmental Factors

The Australian economy boomed for three decades from the 1850s, first as a result of the discovery of gold, but then by a pastoral boom and the expansion of private- and public-sector investment. Industrialization and urbanization further encouraged sustained growth in GDP. Although real GDP fell from its high of 12.8 per cent in the 1850s, it grew at a sustained rate of 4.8 per cent in the 1870s and 1880s.[44] More significant for the life insurance market was the level of GDP per capita at this time. McLean suggests that Australians had possibly the highest standard of living in the world from 1850 to 1890. Using an index of the USA as 100, real GDP in Australia was 155 in 1870. This can be compared with the United Kingdom at 133, Canada at 66, and New Zealand at 127.[45] This high standard of living was reflected in an increasing demand for life insurance. The sale of new policies grew at an average of 8 per cent during the 1880s. The rate of growth in new policy sales was between 2 and 4 per cent in Britain at this time.[46] In 1880 the AMP sold 30 per cent more policies than the top-selling British firm the Gresham. In a list comparing the sale of new policies by British and Australian offices published in that year the Colonial Mutual ranked seventh and the National Mutual thirteenth out of sixty-seven.[47]

The colonial economies were maturing in the 1870s and 1880s, allowing a deepening of financial markets. This provided an environment in which life insurance companies could develop investment portfolios that would secure policyholder funds. Security remained the cornerstone of life office investment strategies as dictated by Bailey's canons.[48] The booming property market

---

[44] McLean 2004, 332.   [45] McLean 2004, 331–2.
[46] Gray 1977, 151.   [47] *AIBR* 1881, 97.
[48] In 1862 Bailey delivered an address to the Institute of Actuaries in London that set down the principles that should be applied by life insurance offices. These became known as Bailey's canons. The canons were: (1) the prime consideration in any decision should be the security of the capital invested; (2) within this context the second consideration was to obtain the highest possible rate of interest; (3) whilst ensuring that a small proportion of funds was held in convertible assets, the bulk of funds were to be invested in non-convertible securities; and (4) capital should be employed to aid the life insurance business. Bailey 1862, 142–7.

provided a ready outlet for mortgage lending, which constituted the main avenue for the investment of life offices' funds. The average rate of interest earned by Australian life offices in the early 1880s was over 6 per cent, compared with rates in Britain of between 4 and 5 per cent.[49] The provision of loans provided a growing source of investment income during this period. The AMP, for example, generated enough income from interest alone to cover all policy claims and three quarters of management expenses.[50] Higher returns on investment also meant that Australian mutuals could pay higher bonuses, a fact that was not lost on the policyholding public.

Whilst the growth of colonial economies provided a market in which local life insurers could flourish, the diverse regulatory environments between colonies acted as an impediment. Legislation to regulate the life insurance industry was enacted in the Australian colonies in the 1870s and 1880s.[51] Legislation could not be applied beyond colonial borders, leading to a multitude of differing legislative requirements. This created complications for those companies wanting to trade beyond colonial borders. A particular issue of concern was the deposit requirements imposed under each act. Deposits ranged from £5,000 to £10,000 in the various colonies. These sums were not large compared to the requirement under the British Life Insurance Act of 1871. However, life offices were required to pay multiple deposits if they wanted to expand beyond one colony. Regulation became a barrier to trade. Only the larger established life offices were in a position to expand nationally. Those offices were by and large the mutual offices.

Market Factors

The influx of new firms into the life insurance market slowed after the mid-1870s. Aside from the eight mutuals there were four indigenous stock companies in operation in the 1880s. As Table 8.4 indicates the market for life insurance was highly concentrated with the top five firms accounting for over 82 per cent of new premiums in 1885. Stock companies accounted for less than 2 per cent of these premiums.[52]

In addition, there were a further five British insurers with agents nominally selling life insurance, although this was not their core business.[53] By 1890 this number had fallen to three and it is unlikely that they had sold any new

---

[49] Keneley 2006, 105.   [50] Spratt 1968, 133.

[51] New South Wales was the only colony not to pass legislation regulating the behaviour of life insurers. The resulting market distortion became a problem in the 1920s when a number of undercapitalized stock companies entered the market.

[52] Keneley 2005, 5.

[53] These were the London and Lancashire, Standard Life, Royal, Queen, and the Northern.

Table 8.4. Australian life insurance firms in 1885

	Date established	Head office	No. of new premiums	% of new premiums
AMP	1849	Sydney	8,857	30.8
National Mutual Life (M)	1869	Melbourne	4,512	15.7
Australian Widow Fund (M)	1871	Melbourne	3,705	12.9
Colonial Mutual Life (M)	1874	Melbourne	3,563	12.4
Mutual Assurance of Vic (M)	1870	Melbourne	3,052	10.6
Mutual Life of Australasia (M)	1869	Sydney	2,624	9.1
City Mutual Assurance (M)	1878	Sydney	1,823	6.3
T&G Mutual Life (M)	1876	Melbourne	250	0.9
Australasian Alliance (P)	1862	Melbourne	365	1.3
Adelaide Life and Guarantee (P)	1866	Adelaide	1	0.0
Citizens Life Assurance Ltd (P)	1886	Sydney	N/A	
Victorian Life and General (P)	1859	Melbourne	N/A	
Total			28,751	

P = Proprietary company; M = Mutual association
Source: *AIBR* 1885.

policies in the previous ten years.[54] British insurers suffered a number of setbacks in the 1870s that impacted on their Australian interests. The collapse of the Albert Assurance Company in 1869 and the European Assurance Company in 1872 resonated in the colonies.[55] This was a key factor in influencing the introduction of insurance company regulation in the colonies. It reinforced a growing preference amongst colonialists to do business with local firms. Further problems for British insurers attempting to sell in the colonies occurred with the passing of the British Revenue Act in 1884. One of the measures introduced with this act was the requirement that probate duty be paid on life policies sold by British companies in the colonies.[56] This encumbrance on the sale of life insurance further weakened the appeal of overseas companies in the Australian market.

British composite companies had not been able to make the transition from the fire insurance market to the life insurance market as they had in the United Kingdom. One reason for this was their persistence in using the agency system to sell policies. Long after the mutuals had introduced the travelling agent, British companies were still tied to the agency system. One problem was that they had yet to establish fully functioning branches from which travelling agents could be managed. Another problem was that British companies were not prepared to pay the market rate of commission.[57]

The unstable nature of the fire insurance market was both a distraction for composite insurers and a deterrent for consumers. The fire insurance market

---

[54] Gray 1977, 23.   [55] *AIBR* 1877, 15.
[56] Gray 1977, 23.   [57] *AIBR* 1887, 15; Gray 1977, 22.

was fiercely competitive and the agency system was an important source of this competition as firms attempted to outbid each other for good agents.[58] Collusive agreements were made and broken at frequent intervals leading to market instability. There was an ongoing battle between indigenous insurance companies and their British counterparts for control of the market. This conflict also spilt over at times into a clash between the British companies themselves, a reflection of the battles being fought in the home market.[59] It was not until large operations such as the Commercial Union began to open branches in the colonies in the early 1880s that the overseas companies got the upper hand.

The fate of local fire insurers was sealed with the advent of a sharp depression in 1890. In the preceding decade a land boom, particularly in the colony of Victoria, had fuelled speculative investment. This bubble burst in 1889. Unwise mortgage investments on the part of local firms left them vulnerable to the ensuing collapse in land prices. As a consequence twenty-three of the thirty-four local fire companies in existence at the time exited the market or were absorbed by other firms.[60] Foreign participants also found conditions in Australia challenging. Trebilcock traces the fortunes of the Australian agency of the Phoenix Assurance Company in the mid-nineteenth century where underwriting surpluses were negative for most of the 1880s.[61]

It was against the background of increasing demand for life insurance, and an inability of private companies to provide effective alternative supply, that mutuals thrived. However, being in the right place at the right time was not the key to their success. To fully understand why mutuals were able to maintain a large market share over an extended period of time it is necessary to look at how they developed insurance products and by definition insurance markets.

MUTUALS AS ENTREPRENEURS

A feature of mutual life insurers in Australia in the nineteenth century was the entrepreneurial spirit of their managers. Australian mutuals developed a reputation for liberalization and innovation in terms of policy development. They were associated with the introduction of new sales methods. In addition their actuaries were at the forefront of the development of the actuarial profession not just in Australia but internationally.

---

[58] Keneley 2002, 58.
[59] LMA, MS 31522, Sun Insurance Office Foreign Agency Memorandum Book, vol. 26, Victoria 4, entry for 11 September 1887.
[60] Pursell 1964, 159; Keneley 2002, 63.   [61] Trebilcock 1998, 292.

The issue of sales was a central problem facing the AMP in the first decade of its existence. The society struggled to expand its life insurance business in its early years. It took nearly ten years to sell the first 1,000 policies. The directors attributed much of the early inertia to the 'apathy on the part of the poorer classes', who they claimed were ignorant of the principle of mutual life insurance.[62] To overcome problems associated with the sale of life policies the AMP searched for innovative ways of marketing their product. A key problem was that the AMP, as with other insurance companies, relied on the agency system to sell their product. For most agents, life insurance was a sideline to their core business and as a consequence the volume of business grew erratically. The *Australasian Insurance and Banking Record* (*AIBR*) described local agents as 'people with little acquaintance with the subject, apathetic in promulgating a knowledge of it [and] fully occupied with their own business'.[63] Life insurance continued to be 'bought' not 'sold', and until a new method of selling was introduced the sale of policies would continue to be problematic. The solution appeared in 1860 when the board of directors decided to try an experiment and appointed Benjamin Short as the first full-time insurance salesman.

Short, who had recently arrived from Britain, was an evangelical lay preacher.[64] The same skills he brought to the pulpit were adapted to his new career. His approach to selling was to travel the country lecturing not only on the benefits of life insurance but on a host of other topics. At a public meeting he would entertain his audience and then sign up members at the end of the proceedings.[65] Short was so successful that for a time in the 1860s he was selling four out of every ten policies sold by the AMP.[66] The society was quick to perceive the benefits of this approach and extended it to develop the travelling agent (or canvassing agent) system. Agents were employed solely by the AMP to travel the countryside with the express purpose of signing up life insurance proposals. Eventually travelling agents were replaced with more permanent full-time agents with designated territories. It was the shift from part-time agencies to canvassing agents, however, which marked a turning point in the marketing of life insurance. The practice of providing entertainment as a means of selling insurance became more widespread as competition increased with the entrance of new mutuals. The use of the public lecture as entertainment spread to incorporate numerous topics. Short himself lectured on subjects such as 'Happy Homes and Happy Marriages' and 'How to Be Successful'. Others looked for topics that would astound their audiences. Figure 8.2 represents an advertisement for one such lecture evening presented on behalf of the City Mutual.

---

[62] AMP Archives: Sydney, First Annual Report of the Directors of the Australian Mutual Provident Society, 1849.

[63] *AIBR* 1877: 391.   [64] Short 1994; Blainey 1999, 34.

[65] Short 1994, 31.   [66] Blainey 1999, 35.

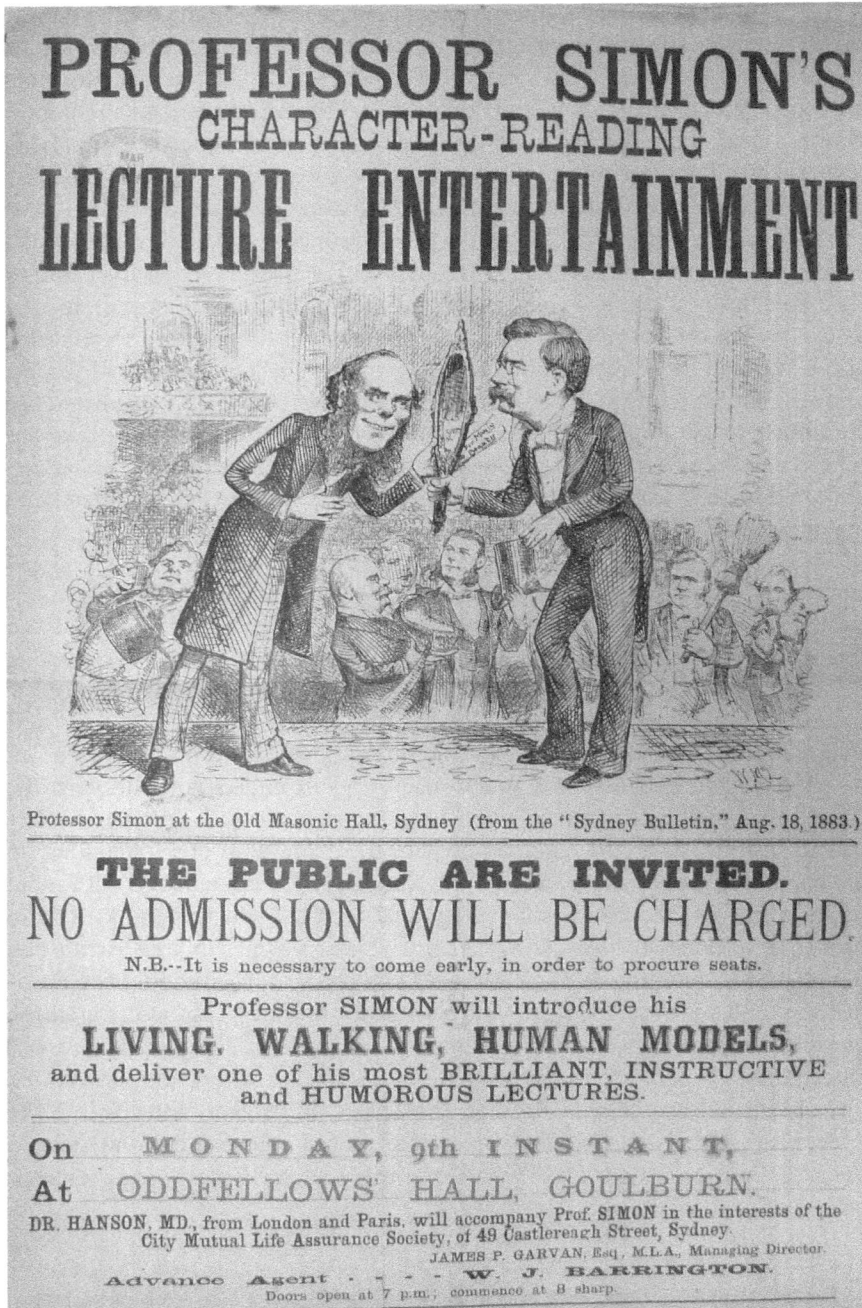

Figure 8.2. Professor Simon's character-reading lecture entertainment

The introduction of canvassing agents also contributed to the development of the organizational structure of the life office. Following the model adopted by Australian banks, the branch system was used as a method of expansion into new markets and as a means of competing with rival firms. As the sales system grew and became more geographically widespread the management of agents became more complex. To overcome problems associated with managing and monitoring the canvassing agents, geographic divisions within the branch were created. In this way mutuals were able to spread their sphere of influence into outback Australia, establishing a presence in country towns and regional centres. Control remained centralized but distribution was localized, enabling life offices to take advantage of local knowledge and local business networks.

Product development was another competitive tool utilized by the mutuals. Early life insurance policies, including those issued by the AMP, contained comprehensive restrictions, which if transgressed voided the policy. Exclusions such as going to sea or place of residence were common constraints on policies as were loadings for other forms of risk. The AMP Prospectus of 1856 listed a range of other prohibitions such as voluntarily entering the army or navy, becoming a gold miner, habitual drunkenness and 'collision with (attack by) aborigines'.[67]

The influx of new mutual offices in the early 1870s provided an incentive for policy reform. The Mutual Life Association (MLA), for example, is said to have been formed after a group of yachtsmen sailing on Sydney Harbour realized that their life insurance policies would become void if they sailed outside the Sydney Heads.[68] This association was the first to offer policies with no restrictions on residence, occupation, or habits. The 1875 Prospectus lists the advantages of an MLA policy that included no restrictions on residence in Europe and any of the Australasian colonies, travel between Europe and Australasia, employment in mining operations, and belonging to a volunteer corps in the colonies.[69]

Policy reform became an important competitive force in the 1870s. As new mutuals emerged they searched for angles that might increase their public appeal. The National Mutual is a case in point. A key platform in its formation was the introduction of the principle of non-forfeiture. Previously a lapse in premium payment had voided a life insurance policy. The non-forfeiture system allowed for the continuance of the policy in the absence of payment for as long as its available surrender value.[70] This condition was to become a feature of all policies in time and eventually mandated by law. Other companies introduced similar policy adjustments very quickly. In 1875 the

---

[67] AMP Archives, Sydney, *AMP Prospectus*, 1856.   [68] Gray 1977, 33.

[69] Mutual Life Association of Australasia, *Prospectus and Table of Rates*, 1875, Sydney.

[70] National Mutual Life Association, *Prospectus and Table of Rates*, 1878, Melbourne. This scheme was said to have been the vision of John Templeton, the NMLA's accountant and appointed actuary.

AMP proclaimed new policy regulations that listed eight areas of reform to policy restrictions.[71] Other companies such as the Colonial Mutual, Australian Widow's Fund, and Mutual Life of Victoria followed suit.

The development of policy conditions was also associated with the development of actuarial standards and the actuarial profession in Australia. Mutual life offices were the training ground for actuaries in the colonies, and the actuaries employed by offices such as the AMP went on to become leaders in the profession.[72] Further improvements in policy conditions and the distribution of the surpluses generated by the operation of the life offices occurred as actuaries developed more accurate mortality tables and valuation methods. An outcome was reform of the method of calculating and distributing the surplus. By 1881, offices such as the AMP were advertising annual bonus payments instead of the previous practice of quinquennial payments.

A further measure taken to expand the attractiveness of life insurance was the introduction of loans to policyholders. The National Mutual introduced loans on policies in 1871. A loan would be granted on the condition that the policyholder take out a policy for twice the amount advanced.[73] Loans on policies grew to become a small but significant item in the life office investment portfolio. With interest charged generally higher than market rates, they provided income to the firm as well as a service to members.

The actions of mutual insurers in developing sales systems and product improvements were further cemented through an astute use of advertising to expound not only the reliability of the mutual office but the material advantages it brought to its members. McFall and Dodsworth make the point that the construction of a market for life insurance depended on convincing the public that the product was worthwhile and the seller trustworthy.[74] Australian mutuals followed the methods engaged by their British counterparts. Pamphlets, newspapers, and magazines emblazoned with company crests and mottos extolled the benefits of life insurance products. The construction of grand office buildings reinforced the message of probity and respectability.[75] Although stock companies emulated the initiatives introduced by mutuals they were not able to increase their share of the market.

CONCLUSION

Mutuals were the market leaders in the Australian life insurance market for over 100 years. The longevity of this form of organizational structure owed its

---

[71] AMP Archives: Sydney, AMP, *Prospectus and Table of Rates*, 1875.
[72] Bellis 1997.   [73] Nobbs 1978, 295.   [74] McFall and Dodsworth 2009, 49.
[75] McFall and Dodsworth argue that insurance companies established an image of prudence and rectitude particularly through office architecture. McFall and Dodsworth 2009, 31.

success in large part to the manner in which the early mutual life insurers were able to develop their market potential and respond to demand side pressures.

Theoretical explanations for the existence of mutual associations suggest that market failure in the form of informational and ownership issues are important considerations in the emergence of these organizations. The history of Australian mutuals indicates that these factors are only part of the explanation. The explanatory model developed in this chapter suggests four types of influences on the form of organization that appeared in Australian life insurance in the nineteenth century. These were economic, social, environmental, and market factors. Economic factors revolved around information and ownership problems. Social factors highlighted the particular societal ethos at the time in respect to the role and responsibility of the individual to provide for future contingencies. These forces provided the context for the emergence of mutuals. Mutuality resolved problems associated with policyholder versus shareholder interests and reduced those associated with moral hazard. It also provided a self-help mechanism that not only satisfied the prevailing social code, but also fulfilled a philanthropic function—a means of helping those unable to help themselves. This was certainly a key rationale behind the establishment of the AMP in 1849. However, other later mutual life insurers took a decidedly more commercial approach to their operations.

Economic and social factors are insufficient in themselves in explaining the preference for mutual life offices in Australia. They provided the context but it was the environmental and market factors that afforded the opportunity. The maturing of the Australian economy, the growing affluence of its population, and the deepening of financial markets provided a climate in which mutual life offices could flourish. Market factors also worked in favour of mutual structures. The fire insurance market was unstable, rocked by periodic price wars and company collapses. Composite companies were unable to build a presence in the life insurance market. The instability in the fire insurance market, and the failure of overseas and local fire insurers to make the transition to the life insurance market, created the space for mutuals to expand and develop.

Mutualism was a business strategy that appealed to a particular cohort of the population at a particular time. Wealthy and middle-class colonists looking to protect the future and to hedge against risk were attracted to the mutual life insurance product. However, mutual life insurers would not have been so successful over a sustained period of time without the entrepreneurial outlook of their managers. Innovative approaches to sales, product development, support for actuarial advances, and use of the media all combined to cement the position of these firms in the Australian psyche. As these institutions grew into the twentieth century they developed an iconic status as symbols of how far the country had advanced from its convict heritage. Almost every country town of moderate size had a mutual life office presence. In regional areas and country towns mutual life offices provided employment, they supported local firms, and were a source of funds for farming, pastoralism, and business. Nationally they were significant sources of government finance and played a key role in the financial sector. They were also important supporters of economic development projects such as land development schemes and infrastructure renewal. In addition they were key contributors to philanthropic and community projects, being among the first to develop a corporate social responsibility platform.

The demise of mutuals in the 1990s was the closing of a chapter in Australian history. It reflected not only a realignment of the Australian life insurance market but the end of the mutual era.

9

Support for Mutual Insurance Companies during the Franco Dictatorship (1939–75)

Jerònia Pons Pons

In the Spanish insurance market in 2010 there were a total of 287 insurers operating in the direct insurance business. Of these, fifty-five were social benefit mutual societies and another thirty-five also had the mutual legal form. In spite of the process of concentration that the Spanish insurance sector has undergone, an important group of mutuals has stood the test of time. The mutual form has been the legal form chosen on numerous occasions in the history of insurance as the way to deal with the uncertainty caused by changes to the legislative or fiscal framework. This situation was especially complex in historical periods when such decisions were in the hands of authoritarian governments. This chapter aims to contribute to the historical debate over whether political ideologies can determine, or at least influence, the organizational form of companies. In this case, we focus on the insurance sector in the context of the Franco dictatorship. Although the importance of mutuals in the sector had started to become evident in Spain before the Civil War, their number increased during the first decades of the Franco regime until it reached over 50 per cent of companies by 1950. There were 256 mutuals operating in the Spanish insurance market in 1950, out of a total of 511 insurance companies. Their large number did not give mutuals predominance in the sector in general, as they only accounted for 21 per cent of premiums, although they did achieve higher percentages in some branches such as industrial accident and, later, automobile insurance.

The chapter has two main objectives: first, to study how government policy in the early years of the Franco era was able to influence the diffusion of mutualism through legislative and fiscal measures. In particular, some of the first decisions will be analysed, such as Larraz's tax reforms or the law on mutual societies of 1941. These, although they initially caused enough uncertainty to prompt a small wave of demutualizations, led to a growth in this type of organization in the medium term. From the mid-1940s, insurance legislation, reinforced by the insurance law of 1954, established deposit and reserve requirements that always favoured mutuals over joint-stock companies, thus promoting this growth. The volume of deposits and reserves collected are compared with premiums and also different forms of investment are related to corporate form, in order to determine investment patterns and establish whether these were politically influenced. Franco's governments also promoted mutuals for purely political motives in certain branches, such as industrial accident insurance, or as part of their social policies with the creation of workers' mutuals (*Mutualidades Laborales*), organizations that operated in parallel with the social security system and were linked to the world of labour and trade unionism. Their growth in certain branches and their specialization in automobile insurance are also explained.

The second objective of the chapter is to examine the reaction of the mutuals, and especially their top executives, in the light of these circumstances. In some cases it is possible to analyse how executives took advantage of the benefits of mutual organization and their preferential treatment to acquire shares and control stock companies, in order to carry out insurance activities that could not be done through mutuals or to defend their private interests. These activities explain the interest of the senior management of the largest mutuals in maintaining the mutual system, as their conversion into stock companies may well have entailed an important loss of control and power for these top managers.[1]

THE PRECEDENTS: THE DEVELOPMENT OF MUTUALISM IN THE SPANISH INSURANCE MARKET (1908–39)

Since the nineteenth century, and throughout different historical periods, the Spanish institutional framework has been conducive to the development of insurance companies in the legal form of mutual societies. Between 1815 and 1869 the lack of national capital, and legislative hurdles to the creation of joint-stock companies without government authorization, fostered the creation of friendly societies writing fire insurance in the principal Spanish provinces.[2] The first mutual was created in Madrid in 1822, then the model subsequently spread to Valladolid and Seville (1832), Burgos (1833),

---

[1] Mayers and Smith 1992; Lamm-Tennant and Starks 1993; Smith and Stutzer 1995.
[2] Matilla Quizà 2010; Guillém Mesado 2010. This mutual form was widespread throughout Europe in the nineteenth century. Pearson 2010a, 7–8.

La Coruña (1835), Barcelona (1836), Malaga (1840), San Sebastián (1842), Valencia (1844), a second mutual in San Sebastián (1847), Gerona (1857), Bilbao (1860), and Palma de Mallorca (1862).[3] Mutuals also developed in other areas of insurance. There were tontine societies, for example, which were dedicated to the accumulation of capital until, after a predetermined period, the resultant capital was shared out among survivors.[4] Mutuals were also created in the world of agriculture (in crop, hail, and livestock insurance) and were disseminated all over Spain, although their survival was always precarious. Livestock insurance was perhaps the most outstanding of these cases.[5] 'Conscription mutuals' ('mutuas de quintas') were likewise developed for exemption from military service.[6]

Meanwhile, in the face of the uncertainties related to the risk of sickness, death, industrial accidents, or old age in the nineteenth century, caused or exacerbated by the spread of industrialization, industrial workers created friendly societies to meet these needs on the basis of solidarity. These mutuals were located in the areas of greatest economic growth: the region comprising Catalonia and Valencia, the Basque Country, and Madrid. The process of creating friendly societies expanded from 1880 onwards, first of all in urban areas and later in rural areas where small and medium-sized family farms predominated. The model did not spread, however, to the areas of large agricultural estates (Eastern Andalusia, Extremadura, and Castile-La Mancha).[7] Later, it was the large companies of the second industrial revolution (mines, railways, electrical, and chemical companies) that created mutuals to provide the first social welfare programmes for their workers.[8] Finally, the law on industrial accidents of 1900 promoted the creation of industrial accident mutual societies among industrial employers.[9] Between 1900 and 1931 some forty-five employers' mutuals were created, twenty of them in Catalonia, the most industrialized region of Spain. This number multiplied with the extension of employers' liability to agricultural workers from 1931 onwards, and the adoption of compulsory insurance from 1933. The result of the mandatory nature of this insurance was that in just two years there were 155 employers' mutuals in the industrial sector and seventy-eight in the agricultural sector.[10]

Thus, the mutual form was used extensively in Spain, both in the field of commercial insurance and in social insurance programmes. In 1908, when the first Spanish law on private insurance was passed, there were thousands of

[3] Maestro 1991; Larriñaga and Lázaro 1996; Reina 1999; De Mateo Avilés 2000; Alonso Olea 2010; Pons Pons 2010.
[4] Bahamonde 1981.   [5] Burgaz and Pérez Morales 1996.
[6] Sales de Bohigas 1970.
[7] Castillo 1994; Castillo and Ortiz de Orruño 1997; Maza Zorrilla 2003; Castillo and Ruzafa 2009; Pons Pons and Vilar 2011; Vilar and Pons Pons 2012.
[8] Aubanell Jubany 2002; Martínez Vara 2006; Pérez Castroviejo 2010.
[9] Pons Pons 2006, 2011.   [10] Pons Pons 2006.

mutuals resulting from different historical processes in different branches. This law was a first attempt to rationalize and bring order to the insurance market. To this end, a substantial number of insurers, mainly mutuals that were assumed not to have profit as their goal, were excluded from the obligations established by the legislation. The legislator intended that the law clearly distinguish between those mutuals arising from worker, employer, and citizen solidarity, which had promoted a solidarity-based insurance against sickness or fire risk, for example, and for-profit mutuals, even though the latter's profits were subsequently distributed among members in the form of rebates or reduced premiums. However, this distinction proved very complicated in practice and the legislation was eventually restricted to certain types of companies. Article 3 excluded mutuals from the provisions of the law, subject to depositing a copy of the statutes and a policy model with the Inspectorate General of Insurance and with the obligation to submit a copy of their annual balance sheets. The following were specifically excluded: a) friendly societies; b) mutual associations without a fixed premium that only operated on a local, municipal, or provincial scale and were not profit seeking (mutuals, therefore, that in principle functioned by means of a special levy); and c) transport insurance companies.[11] In 1915, there were 1,740 mutuals in Spain excluded from the law of 1908. These were consequently not subject to the deposit or reserve requirements, or the mandatory investment of these reserves, which were obligatory for other insurance undertakings (national and foreign insurance companies and some mutuals classified as 'commercial'). According to Article 124 of the Commercial Code, a mutual was considered to be a commercial company in two cases: a) if it was engaged in commercial activities unrelated to the aim of the mutual and b) if it was a fixed premium mutual society.[12] Of the 1,740, the majority (1,065) were friendly societies, which covered sickness, disability, retirement, industrial accidents, and death. Of the rest, forty-five were fire insurance mutuals, fifty-seven operated in livestock insurance, and three in crop insurance. There were also thirty-four industrial accident mutuals among those excluded.[13] Such a large number of mutuals were excluded because, in theory, they were benefit societies and were not pursuing profit. They were also exempted under the tax system. In the tax on

---

[11] The companies operating in this branch, mainly writing marine insurance, were not subject to the provisions of this law until the Royal Decree of 13 August 1920. The law did not explain why this type of company was excluded. Perhaps the reasons lay in the long tradition of marine insurance companies and to the fact that they were already regulated by successive commercial codes. However, in 1920 it was decided that they could not be excluded from the audit of the supervisory bodies created after the 1908 law and that they had to abide by the same rules as other insurance companies.

[12] Fernández Junquera 1975, 45.

[13] 1917 report on insurance enterprises subject to the provisions of the Law of 14 May 1908. Comisaría General de Seguros.

industrial corporations known as 'Contribución de Utilidades' of 22 September 1922, specifically under Tax Rate III according to which insurance companies were taxed, 'insurance mutuals that do not have the nature of commercial companies' were excluded. In practice, all mutuals, whether excluded or not, were exempt from paying taxes under Tax Rate III of the industrial corporation tax. Only mutuals that were regulated under the law of 1908 were included in the official statistics of the Directorate General of Insurance.

For decades, the premiums of the mutuals excluded from the 1908 law were not included in the official statistics of the sector, and the authorities governing the insurance business exerted little control over them. In practice, the majority of mutuals operating on a local or provincial scale were excluded, as were some of those operating regionally. Before the Civil War (1936–39) only those functioning on a national scale and the largest regional operators appeared in the official statistics of the Directorate General of Insurance. In these statistics, mutuals were most numerous in fire and industrial accident insurance. They accounted for 19 per cent of all insurers operating in the fire branch and 73 per cent in the industrial accident branch (Tables 9.1 and 9.2).

Other insurers joined this excluded group over time, including burial insurance companies, sickness insurance societies created by doctors, and some involved in other types of insurance activity that in essence were businesses, but which took advantage of this not-for-profit mutual category to avoid paying taxes or complying with the reserve and deposit obligations of the 1908 law. The confusion and lack of clarity in the activities of these mutuals continued until after the Civil War.

THE EARLY YEARS OF THE FRANCO REGIME AND THE CREATION OF AN INSTITUTIONAL FRAMEWORK FAVOURABLE TO MUTUALISM (1939–59)

The Franco regime, as to be expected of an authoritarian regime, used paternalistic social policies as a form of propaganda, in order to offer a friendly face of the regime and with the intention of disguising the repression that was being applied at political and social levels.[14] Within this policy, mutualism was one of the forms used as propaganda for the professional solidarity that the regime advocated in the face of the class struggle. For this reason, the authorities promoted mutuals both directly and indirectly in the world of social insurance and, in this context, also expressed support for the mutuals that

---

[14] Molinero 2005.

Table 9.1. Insurance mutuals and total number of insurers in Spain, 1915–35

Branch	1915		1920		1925		1930		1935	
	Mutuals	Total	Mutuals	Total	Mutuals	Total	Mutuals	Total	Mutuals	Total
Life	0	22	0	23	0	26	2	31	2	42
Industrial accident	12	28	14	31	17	38	22	51	85	116
Personal accident and public liability	0	16	0	22	0	30	2	42	5	47
Fire	7	53	7	60	9	75	15	87	18	93
Transport					1	53	2	51	2	47
Sickness and burial	1	45	1	61	1	74	3	76	5	73
Theft	0	1	0	2	0	6	1	15	1	31
Plate glass	0	11	1	11	1	13	2	18	2	18
Livestock	0	12	0	11	0	10	0	8	0	7
Hail	0	2	1	3	1	3	1	4	3	6
Other branches	0	2	0	3	0	5	0	6	0	8

Source: Memoria Estadística de Seguros, financial year 1951. Dirección General de Seguros.

Table 9.2. Number of mutuals per branch of insurance as percentage of total number of insurers, Spain, 1915–50

Branch	1915	1920	1925	1930	1935	1942	1945	1950
Life	0	0	0	6.4	4.8	6.1	4.4	6.2
Industrial accident	**42.8**	**45.1**	**44.7**	**43.1**	**73.3**	**71.3**	**67.4**	**63.5**
Personal accident and public liability	0	0	0	4.8	10.6	8.1	13.8	18.0
Public liability	—	—	—	—	—	15.5	14.3	16.5
Fire	**13.2**	**11.6**	**12.0**	**17.2**	**19.3**	**27.1**	**26.4**	**29.0**
Transport		1.9	3.9	3.3	3.3	4.8	5.6
Sickness and burial	2.2	1.6	1.3	3.9	15.9	15.9	18.9	20.7
Theft	0	0	0	6.7	7.9	7.9	6.8	7.8
Plate glass	0	9.1	7.7	11.1	17.4	17.4	12.1	11.5
Livestock	**0**	**0**	**0**	**0**	**46.1**	**46.1**	**33.3**	**28.6**
Hail	**0**	**33.3**	**33.3**	**25.0**	**50.0**	**50.0**	**50.0**	**38.1**
Other branches	0	0	0	0	0	18.7	10.7	8.8

Source: Memoria Estadística de Seguros, financial year 1951. Dirección General de Seguros.

operated in commercial insurance. During the first decades of the Franco era the institutional framework, both fiscal and legislative, favoured the insurance mutuals. In the legislative field this was done by allowing the survival of thousands of mutuals that carried out small-scale insurance operations, and which were not regulated by the authorities responsible for controlling the insurance sector. They operated without mandatory reserves or deposits. While it is true that the majority remained restricted to a very limited geographical area and had a low volume of business, their persistence nevertheless hampered market concentration. In the more developed branches where mutuals predominated, sickness or hail insurance, for example, the deposits required were far less than in other branches. These lower requirements prolonged the life of a great number of small, barely solvent mutuals. As far as taxation was concerned, a special system was established for commercial mutuals (regulated by the law of 1908) whereby taxes were based on premiums rather than on profits, unlike the taxation of stock companies and foreign companies.

Partly due to this protection, the number of mutuals subject to the insurance law of 1908 increased in the first two decades of the Franco dictatorship (Table 9.3). The 256 mutuals in 1950 (49 per cent of all insurance enterprises operating that year) grew to 266 in 1960 (44 per cent). The premiums of the mutuals remained at 20 per cent of the market share. The market was still fragmented in spite of attempts to reduce the number of insurers operating in the sector.[15] These figures only included the mutuals that were governed by the insurance law of 1908, that is, those operating as commercial enterprises.

[15] Pons Pons 2010.

Table 9.3. Number of enterprises per corporate form and per branch in the early years of Francoism

Branch	1942				1945				1950			
	A	B	C	D	A	B	C	D	A	B	C	D
Life	27	19	3	49	49	19	3	68	60	15	5	80
Industrial accident	21	16	117	164	43	17	124	184	62	20	141	222
Personal accident	35	22	5	62	58	23	13	94	74	26	22	122
Public liability	28	21	9	58	52	20	12	84	70	26	19	115
Fire	43	43	32	118	66	40	38	144	78	42	49	169
Transport	34	25	2	61	56	24	4	84	62	22	5	89
Sickness and burial	58	–	11	69	73	–	17	90	96	–	25	121
Theft	20	15	3	38	38	17	4	59	52	19	6	77
Plate glass	12	7	4	23	21	8	4	33	36	10	6	52
Livestock	6	1	6	13	11	1	6	18	14	1	6	21
Hail	4	3	7	14	5	3	8	16	10	3	8	21
Others	12	1	3	16	24	1	3	28	30	1	3	34

Notes: A = national companies; B = foreign companies; C = **mutuals**; D = total insurance enterprises
Source: Memoria Estadística de Seguros, financial year 1951. Dirección General de Seguros.

With regard to legislation, the intention during the first years of the Franco regime was to further organize the sector, above all by identifying social welfare organizations (which always adopted mutual or non-profit civil association forms) and separating these from commercial companies. Many businesses masqueraded under these forms (mutual and associative) in order to avoid control and circumvent tax regulations. To combat this, a law on mutuals was passed on 6 December 1941. The law provided that henceforth associations that offered insurance of a charitable or social welfare nature would be considered as mutuals or 'montepíos' (similar to friendly societies). This law did not apply to mutual-type undertakings that offered insurance that was not of a social welfare nature, and these would remain subject to the 1908 law. This was, therefore, another attempt to revise the classification of mutuals that had been in effect since 1908. From 1944 onwards, the government published a list of 'montepíos' and mutuals that had been entered in the register of the Directorate General of Insurance. A total of thirty-seven lists were published, the last of these on 23 November 1955. From 1944 to 1955, a total of 2,165 insurance enterprises were enrolled that did not have to abide by the private insurance law of 1908, nor by the recently passed law of 1954.[16]

---

[16] This law replaced the private insurance law of 1908. It regulated the insurance business in all its facets (it increased the minimum share capital, deposits, and reserves required for the companies, revised the insurance contract, etc.). The 1954 law continued with the exclusion of an important group of mutuals. First, it continued to exclude the 'montepíos' and free mutuals

They were basically civil servants' mutuals, those related to large companies, employers' industrial accident mutual, and mutual associations of professionals. However, in the case of some of the insurers that joined this group (some employers' mutuals and doctors' associations, for example) it was not so clear that they were not, in fact, running lucrative businesses. On the other hand, many of the mutuals linked to workers and trade unions (principally the socialist trade union UGT) disappeared in the years after the Civil War, in many cases due to political purges of their boards of directors and members.

In conjunction with this attempt to reorganize the insurance market by excluding non-profit organizations, in order to prevent the fragmentation of the sector the state passed the tax reform law of 16 December 1940 (Larraz's law). This new fiscal regulation established that insurance mutuals, whatever their profits, would no longer be exempt and would pay the minimum contribution paid by insurance companies within the category of tax rate III of industrial corporations. In practice, all mutuals had to pay 0.75 per cent of premiums received, plus another 0.42 per cent municipal surcharge.[17] The application of this law, however, posed problems. Discussion centred on whether the new law applied a minimum contribution (a percentage of premiums, not of profits) to all the mutuals that had been exempt up until then, or whether this only applied to those that made profits. This matter became the subject of debates and legal claims. The Supreme Court ruled eventually in favour of those who argued that this tax measure should only apply to for-profit mutuals.[18]

Subsequently, the tax reform law of 26 December 1957 repealed the previous legislation. The payment of a fixed contribution or licence tax was established for all insurance entities, which would replace the contribution hitherto paid under tax rate III of the tax law. However, the subsequent regulation of 13 May 1958 allowed mutual insurance companies to continue paying taxes in accordance with the system of minimum contributions based on premiums. A special regime for mutuals was thus maintained. The main consequence was that mutuals were not taxed on their profits under corporation tax, and were not subject to pay the licence tax contribution of the industrial tax.

subject to the law on mutual societies of 1941. Moreover, it added to the list of those excluded the compulsory mutuals that had been created by some groups, mainly liberal professionals (lawyers, doctors, etc.) and the workers' mutuals system of social insurance introduced by the Franco regime.

[17] These are the percentages that the management of Mutua General de Seguros informed the board of directors that they would have to pay after the implementation of the law. Minutes of 7 June 1941 of the Board of Directors of Mutua General de Seguros, Book 2.

[18] Sentence of the Supreme Court of 19 October 1955, included in Fernández Junquera 1975, 50.

In short, with regard to taxation, after the Civil War Larraz's tax reform had obliged the mutuals to pay taxes, although its implementation created controversy as to whether the taxes should be on premiums or on profits. The tax was applied to premiums although the courts in 1955 ruled in favour of applying this tax to profit-making mutuals. Finally, the regulation on the 1957 tax law, implemented in 1958, continued to impose a special regime for mutuals based on taxation of premiums.

Mutual insurance activity during this period was concentrated above all in three branches. The industrial accident branch had the greatest presence of mutuals. Employers' mutuals had played an important role here since its creation in 1900. In 1949 and 1960 mutuals accounted for 70 and 66 per cent respectively of all insurers, and in both of these years they took around 42 per cent of premiums. In fire insurance mutuals comprised a third of all companies in 1950 and 1960, but only collected around 6 per cent of premiums. These were either small local mutuals, some of them founded in the nineteenth century, or employers' industrial accident mutuals that had generally begun their diversification process with fire insurance, one of the branches with fewer actuarial requirements, and where they operated as commission agents by reinsuring a substantial part of the risk.

In sickness insurance, mutuals accounted for 27 per cent of insurers and took 37 per cent of premiums in 1949. By 1960, after the impact of the 1954 insurance law, they comprised only 20 per cent of insurers, yet the percentage of premiums they collected had increased significantly to 52 per cent. It must be noted that many of these mutuals collaborated in the management of the compulsory sickness insurance scheme created by the state, an activity that they supplemented with private insurance. There was government intervention in this branch, which was extremely fragmented, as, from the law of 1954, it was no longer permitted for insurance to be undertaken by civil associations (doctors' associations), which had to become stock companies.[19]

In 1966 the industrial accident branch disappeared from private insurance business, following the implementation of the basic law of social security passed in 1963. Insurance mutuals, in order to continue with accident insurance, had to separate this activity from the rest of their insurance operations. They were obliged to create two different businesses, namely an employers' mutual that continued as a collaborating organ of the social security system and a commercial mutual that operated in other branches.[20] From this point, when commercial mutuals lost a large part of their accident business, they

---

[19] The orders of the Ministry of Finance and governance of 14 June 1955 also had an effect in this sense, Pons Pons 2000, 428–38.

[20] The regulation on the collaboration of employers' mutuals of 6 July 1967 obliged mutuals that operated in other branches to create two separate entities, one that continued managing industrial accident cover and another that would be responsible for all other business.

Table 9.4. Mutuals as percentage of number of companies and premiums per branch of insurance, Spain, 1949–70 (%)

	1949		1960		1970	
	A	B	A	B	A	B
Life	8.4	5.9	4.5	4.8	5.4	5.6
Industrial accident	70.0	42.4	66.3	42.4	–	–
Personal accident	16.9	6.6	18.9	8.1	23.8	10.3
General public liability	9.8	4.1	12.0	2.8	8.9	3.6
Automobile third party	14.0	4.8	18.8	9.9		
Voluntary					26.4	16.2
Compulsory					26.7	17.4
Fire	33.5	6.6	37.9	7.2	41.4	7.9
Transport	5.9	8.9	7.4	10.7	6.3	12.4
Sickness and burial	27.4	37.6	20.2	52.4	9.2	6.1
Burial			9.5	0.4	5.1	0.1
Theft	9.2	2.9	7.9	3.3	7.8	2.4
Plate glass	11.4	22.7	15.3	22.9	16.2	6.0
Livestock	33.3	13.9	21.4	7.6		
Hail	47.0	83.5	20.0	51.1	24.5	52.1

Notes: A = % of companies; B = % of premiums
Source: *Revista del Sindicato Vertical del Seguro*, 1950, 1961, and 1971.

concentrated on automobile insurance. They gained increasing weight in this branch, accounting for 26 per cent of the total number of companies operating in both voluntary and compulsory automobile insurance, with an average of 17 per cent of premiums (Table 9.4).

The loss of the industrial accident branch for the private insurance business coincided with the passage of compulsory automobile insurance.[21] Insurance mutuals, most heavily affected by this loss as industrial accidents had been the original basis of their foundation, saw their best future prospects in automobile insurance and concentrated on this new branch.[22] The growing importance of automobile insurance premiums was accompanied by an increase in the number of mutuals, including ones that specialized in this branch. In the 1970 ranking of top companies there were five compared to the two in the 1960 ranking. We find Mutua Madrileña Automovilística in seventh position, Mapfre ninth, Musini, the state-owned mutual, tenth, and Mutua General de Seguros in eleventh place. Mutua Nacional del Automóvil also joined this list in nineteenth place. Together the five accounted for 8 per cent of the market (Table 9.5).

[21] The law 122/1962 of 24 December, the implementation of which was postponed until 1 June 1965.
[22] In 1957 industrial accident insurance accounted for 75 per cent of Mapfre's premiums, Tortella Casares et al. 2009, 379. In the case of Mutua General de Seguros, industrial accident accounted for 67 per cent of total premiums in 1966.

Table 9.5. Position of the mutuals in the Spanish insurance company rankings of 1960 and 1970

1960				1970			
Company	LF	MS %	B	Company	LF	MS %	B
1. La Unión y El Fénix	SA	6.96	11	1. La Unión y El Fénix	SA	6.19	14
2. Banco Vitalicio de España	SA	3.48	10	2. La Estrella	SA	3.93	13
3. Plus Ultra	SA	3.21	13	3. Plus Ultra	SA	2.70	13
4. El Ocaso	SA	2.95	6	4. Banco Vitalicio de España	SA	2.67	11
5. Mutua General de Seguros	**M**	**2.94**	**8**	5. Santa Lucía	SA	2.00	4
6. Fed. Mutualidades de Cataluña	**M**	**2.69**	**1**	6. Ocaso	SA	1.80	7
7. Santa Lucía	SA	2.06	4	**7. Mutua Madrileña Automovilística**	**M**	**1.75**	**12**
8. La Equitativa, R.D.	SA	1.73	7	8. Catalana	SA	1.73	14
9. Sociedad Catalana de Seguros	SA	1.62	12	**9. Mapfre**	**M**	**1.67**	**14**
10. Bilbao	SA	1.59	16	**10. Musini (INI)**	**M**	**1.64**	**10**
11. General Española de Seguros	SA	1.55	11	**11. Mutua General de Seguros**	**M**	**1.58**	**8**
12. Cervantes	SA	1.48	8	12. Galicia	SA	1.49	9
13. Occidente	SA	1.39	12	13. Bilbao	SA	1.44	15
14. Nacional Hispánica Aseguradora	SA	1.39	10	14. Nacional Hispánica Aseguradora	SA	1.41	12
15. Unión Levantina	SA	1.39	7	15. Cervantes	SA	1.39	13
16. Hispania	SA	1.31	7	16. Mare Nostrum	SA	1.35	13
17. Caja de Previsión y Socorro	SA	1.27	6	17. Minerva	SA	1.27	12
18. Aurora	SA	1.25	9	18. La Equitativa	SA	1.16	8
19. Zurich	SA	1.20	7	**19. Mutua Nacional del Automóvil**	**M**	**1.15**	**2**
20. La Vasco Navarra	SA	1.19	9	20. Unión Levantina	SA	1.14	10
Total top 20		42.65				39.46	

Notes: LF = legal form of the company; M = mutual; SA = stock company (sociedad anónima); MS = market share; B = number of branches.
Source: *Revista del Sindicato Vertical del Seguro*, extraordinary edition (1961) and (1971).

Mutuals had expenses in automobile insurance, including commissions and administrative costs, which were lower than those of Spanish stock companies (Table 9.6). Furthermore, over time they achieved an accident rate a few points lower than that of commercial companies.[23] One of the key elements may have been specialization in this branch, with the emergence of mutuals

---

[23] Lamm-Tennant and Starks 1993.

Table 9.6. Claims, commissions, and administrative costs in Spanish voluntary automobile insurance, 1965–70

Year	Spanish commercial companies		Insurance Mutuals	
	Commissions and administration costs as a % of premiums	Claims as a % of premiums	Commissions and administration costs as a % of premiums	Claims as a % of premiums
1965	14.34	31.64	11.43	32.58
1966	15.30	46.04	9.36	41.34
1967	15.83	49.59	9.87	50.18
1968	15.77	55.62	9.69	55.10
1969	15.74	60.00	9.15	55.65
1970	16.06	65.71	9.39	55.09

Source: Memoria estadística de seguros privados, financial year 1970.

such as Mutua Madrileña Automovilística in Madrid and Mutua Nacional del Automóvil in Barcelona. This concentration on automobile insurance led to increased efforts to achieve reductions in the accident rate, commissions, risk selection, the hiring of professionals for the adjustment of claims, advertising, etc.[24]

THE FRANCO REGIME'S DIRECT PROMOTION OF MUTUALISM

Throughout the 1960s and until the end of the Franco era the special tax regime for mutuals was maintained. The tax reform law of 11 June 1964, and the revised text of this law published on 23 December 1967, did not change this. Indeed, a form of levy on insurance premiums to be collected in Spain by mutual insurance companies was established in article 52 of the law. The levy was 1.3 per cent in the life, accident, and transport branches and 4.1 per cent in the fire branch.

Apart from the maintenance of a special fiscal system for mutuals, different governments during the Franco period took decisions that favoured mutualism, both in the fields of private and social insurance. Essentially, mutuals were allowed to participate as private companies in the management of the social insurance programmes that were being regulated by the state. In particular, the government permitted them to manage compulsory sickness insurance schemes from 1944 onwards, created workers' mutuals (*Mutualidades Laborales*) as a parallel system to the general regime of social insurance, and gave employers' mutuals the right to continue managing industrial

[24] For the example of Mapfre, see Tortella Casares et al. 2009, 109–10.

accident insurance when the law on social security was passed in 1963. Finally, the state actually contributed directly to strengthening mutual companies with the creation of a mutual within the state's industrial group INI (Instituto Nacional de Industria).

In the law of 14 December 1942, by which compulsory sickness insurance was passed, it was established that the management of this insurance was handed to the National Welfare Institute, and also to the workers' mutuals (*Mutualidades Laborales*) created by the Franco regime itself. However, whether it was due to pressure from the mutuals, which had been offering this type of provision for decades, or whether it was because of the National Welfare Institute's lack of infrastructure and personnel to cover this new insurance, a decree of 2 March 1944 permitted company funds, mutuals, and doctors' associations to make special agreements with the National Welfare Institute to cover the cash benefits and healthcare provisions of this new insurance. Stock companies, however, were excluded. The management of this activity, with the mandatory creation of local offices and branches, benefited some mutuals, which increased their private insurance business. As a result of this activity, Mutua General de Seguros appeared fifth in the ranking of insurance companies in 1960, with 2.94 per cent of the market share. This mutual had been founded by employers in 1907 to insure against industrial accidents. In 1945, it accounted for 26 per cent of compulsory sickness insurance premiums. Next, in sixth position, came Federación de Mutualidades de Cataluña with 2.69 per cent of premiums.[25] From 1949 onwards, the deficit in the management of compulsory sickness insurance increased due to rising pharmaceutical expenditure and medical fees and the financing of the hospital infrastructure. In addition to these factors, the collaborating bodies (with many mutuals among them) were accused of putting their commercial interests first (camouflaged in the part of the premiums that could be kept as administration costs). A financial adjustment of compulsory sickness insurance was attempted in 1949, by increasing premiums by 1 per cent, by the mandatory extension of the insurance to workers with annual incomes up to 18,000 pesetas, and by introducing a new proportional system for contributions. However, these measures did not solve the financial imbalance. In 1954, the year in which the ten-year term of the contracts with the collaborating bodies expired, the National Welfare Institute raised the terms demanded of the latter to continue with the special agreements. Finally, in 1963, this insurance was incorporated into the public management of the social

---

[25] This federation had been created in 1896 under the name Unión y Defensa de los Montepíos de la Provincia de Barcelona. In 1917, now under the name Federation of Friendly Societies of the Province of Barcelona (Federación de Sociedades de Socorros Mutuos de la Provincia de Barcelona), it comprised 726 societies with 177,234 members. In 1924 it consisted of 641 organizations with 166,894 members. Rodríguez Ocaña 1990, 334.

security.[26] In short, difficulties in managing sickness insurance forced the government to take the private management of compulsory sickness insurance out of the hands of private enterprise and to manage the scheme directly through the National Welfare Institute.

As well as favouring employers' industrial accident mutuals in the management of compulsory sickness insurance, the regime created a new type of mutual which further complicated the already complex landscape of Spanish insurance. At first, workers' mutuals (Mutualidades Laborales) were created to supplement the National Welfare Institute's system of social insurance, as many workers were not covered by these compulsory insurances. Over time, they became another compulsory system parallel to that developed by the National Welfare Institute, a fact that complicated the social insurance system even more. Although they were established earlier, the period of greatest development of worker mutualism began in 1954, with the publication of the regulation entitled 'Reglamento General de Mutualismo Laboral'. Under this regime, Spanish workers belonging to a series of professional groups and employed by others were incorporated. Some groups of immigrants were also included in the scheme. Furthermore, the administrative staff of the single party of the dictatorship, the so-called 'FET y de las JONS', was also included, as well as personnel of the labour syndicate 'Organización Sindical y del Mutualismo Laboral'.[27] The inclusion of senior officials, excluded from the compulsory sickness insurance scheme and from other social insurance programmes, reinforced the regime's idea of disseminating an inter-class system that crossed class barriers and ran counter to the class struggle, which the regime intended to eliminate. Mutualism enabled the enhancement of 'solidarity' between classes and 'fraternity' between producers (workers, in the language of the regime) and employers.

State intervention in the industrial accident branch was different, but here too it favoured employers' mutuals. This branch had been in the hands of private insurance (stock companies and mutuals) until the basic social security law of 1963. In 1960 this branch accounted for 29 per cent of all private insurance premiums. In 1963, while the law was going through parliament, political lobbyists close to the government, mainly belonging to Opus Dei, supported excluding stock companies from this activity, while continuing with its management by insurance mutuals. Velarde, in his analysis of the problems in the industrial accident insurance market in Spain, defended this position.[28] His arguments were based on the fact that the main Spanish insurers were linked to the large banks and so employers took out insurance with the financial group they were dependent on. Moreover, stock companies used accident insurance in order to try to get employers to take out policies for

---

[26] Vilar and Pons Pons 2013. [27] De la Calle Velasco 2010.
[28] Velarde Fuertes 1963.

other types of insurance (fire, civil liability, etc.). Furthermore, he added that stock insurers' production costs were higher, in the region of 21 per cent of insurance premiums. For these reasons, he defended the proposal to assign the management of accident insurance to the mutuals. With the support of statistics, Velarde, Guindos, and Lázaro reinforced the idea that mutuals had lower administration costs.[29] They argued that the commercial companies were more inclined to deliberate about the nature of a risk when it came to taking out a policy, and that their costs were higher because they spent more on advertising, administration, and agency commissions. It is certainly true that the expenditure on commissions and administration costs were much higher for stock companies than mutuals in this branch. In 1960 commissions and administration costs in industrial accident insurance accounted for 20.12 per cent of premiums for commercial companies, while for mutuals they only represented 7.04 per cent.[30]

Supported by these arguments, commercial companies were thus excluded from the industrial accident branch under the new social security law. Employers' mutuals, however, were allowed to continue. The basic social security law was implemented by the order of 27 April 1966 and employers' industrial accident mutuals were permitted to collaborate with workers' mutuals in the management of this type of insurance. The most common explanation for their durability in the business was their mutual nature, although the fact that they also benefited from the pressure successfully exerted by the employers' lobby, linked to mutuals close to government circles, should not be ruled out. In this way, through their mutual organizations, employers were allowed to continue managing industrial accident insurance as collaborating bodies in the social security system, and have continued to do so to the present day.

The participation of mutuals in private insurance was boosted by the Francoist institutions when the National Industry Institute (INI) created an insurance mutual to insure the activity of public companies. The INI was created on 25 September 1941, at the height of autarky, to stimulate industrial development.[31] During its first decades, national companies were created in various sectors (electricity, defence, automobile, etc.). From 1963 this industrializing role was abandoned, the institute reduced its contributions to nationalized industry, and the deterioration of some of its companies set in. In this context, and in view of the volume of insurance transactions carried out by INI companies, the institute decided to create the Mutualidad de Seguros del INI (Musini). The founding board met on 23 December 1966 and the procedures for its constitution were initiated. Each mutualist, that is to say each associate company, had to provide capital of 100,000 pesetas. On 15 February

[29] Velarde et al. 1963.
[30] *Memoria Estadística de Seguros Privados*, financial year 1960.
[31] Martín Aceña and Comín 1994.

1968, it was authorized to begin operations and on 30 April 1968 the first extraordinary constitutive meeting took place with the attendance of some of the entity's fifty mutual members. All of these were companies belonging to the INI: the shipyards in Cadiz, ATESA, Hidroeléctrica de Galicia, Empresa Nacional Adaro, ENASA, Empresa Nacional Calvo Sotelo, Empresa Nacional Petróleos de Aragón, Empresa Nacional Santa Bárbara, and Iberia, among others. The aim of Musini was to reduce the insurance costs of public companies and establish a system of coinsurance and reinsurance with other insurers. In this way, direct relations between public industrial groups and insurance companies were eliminated. To achieve this, public companies had to abstain from extending insurance policies already contracted and to replace them with policies taken out with the mutual.[32] In 1970, shortly after the start of its activity, Musini had entered the ranks of the principal insurance companies and had 1.64 per cent of the market share.

In sum, in spite of the initial support for the mutuals during the first stage of the Franco regime, there remained considerable uncertainty among the mutuals' boards of directors regarding their future, due to political pressures in favour of the state assuming exclusive control over certain social insurance programmes. This constant threat led mutuals to search for different strategies to deal with the situation.

THE CAPACITY TO ADAPT TO INSTITUTIONAL CHANGE: DEMUTUALIZATION OR THE CREATION OF BUSINESS GROUPS

On various occasions during the forty years of the Franco dictatorship, the boards of directors of the most important insurance mutuals raised the possibility of altering the legal form of their company in response to legislative or fiscal changes. This dilemma presented itself for the first time after the tax reform of 1940 and the law on mutuals of 1941. Although with time it proved to be bad judgement, the boards of directors of some mutuals, mainly employers' industrial accident associations, were afraid that the fiscal and legislative changes would limit their mutuals' insurance activities. Many of them had diversified beyond industrial accident insurance and considered their operations in branches of private insurance to be at risk. In view of this fear, two very different options emerged. One group of mutuals demutualized, adopting the legal form of the stock company. However, the boards of the

---

[32] Mapfre Global Risk Archive, Madrid, Minutes of the Board of Directors of Musini, 23 December 1966, 11 June 1967.

largest, Mutua General de Seguros and Mapfre, for example, opted for a strategy of continuing with their mutual legal form, while at the same time creating stock companies, linking share ownership individually to senior management and to the mutual itself. In this way, the mutual and its directors controlled companies that could carry out operations that, at that time or in the future, were prohibited for mutuals.

A demutualization process took place between 1942 and 1944 and affected a small group of mutuals. At least four mutuals became stock companies during this period. In 1942 Mutua Balear, created in 1923 in Mallorca, became Mare Nostrum.[33] In the same year, Hermes converted into Hermes S. A. and Mutualidad Sevillana de Seguros C. I. A. (Comercio, Industria, Agricultura), created in 1933, was transformed into C. I. A., Compañía Anónima de Seguros y Reaseguros.[34] A little later, in 1944, Mutualidad Gallega de Seguros, which had been operating since 1901, converted into Galicia S. A.

Other mutuals adopted a different strategy in the light of the uncertainty as to whether recent institutional changes would limit their activity in certain branches. Their strategy involved the creation of stock companies where the shareholders were the parent mutual itself and the executives most closely involved in its management, or members of the board of directors.[35] The examples below relate to mutuals whose origins lay in industrial accident insurance, but which had diversified or were in the process of initiating operations in other branches. In the case of Mapfre, following the proposals of its president, Isidro de Gregorio, Campo S. A. was constituted on 4 February 1943. This commercial company was to operate in the branches of life, fire, industrial accident, personal accident, public liability, transport, and reinsurance. The majority shareholder of Campo was Isidro de Gregorio, who was also its director general, and who simultaneously maintained his responsibilities at Mapfre. As well as the president, several directors and executives of Mapfre were the main shareholders. Fearing the possible nationalization of accident insurance, Mapfre's directors transferred the best risks to Campo S. A. With this strategy, the shareholding directors and executives protected their insurance and the commercial company's business rather than the parent mutual's insurance policies.[36]

In the following years there was great confusion between the activities of both companies, which shared head offices and employees. Only from 1949 onwards, and amidst great difficulties, did the two companies begin to

---

[33] Converted on 24 February 1942. *Anuario Financiero y de Sociedades Anónimas* 1950; Pons Pons 1998.

[34] They converted into stock companies on 24 July and 6 July 1942, respectively. *Anuario Financiero y de Sociedades Anónimas* 1950.

[35] Mayers and Smith 1992.   [36] Hernando de Larramendi 2000, 231–2.

dissociate and separate their activities. Finally, Campo S. A. was acquired by the Plus Ultra company.[37]

A similar case was that of Mutua General de Seguros. In the mid-1940s, the new board of directors that took control after the Civil War, instead of converting it into a stock company, created a group of companies linked to the mutual. This was part of an expansion plan in which majority control of the share capital of a series of insurance companies was envisaged. Operations that were prohibited or complicated for mutuals could then be carried out through the group. Article 5 of the decree of 29 September 1944 on commercial reinsurance operations covering Spanish risks, for instance, prohibited companies of a mutual nature from carrying out reinsurance operations.[38] The group of companies linked to Mutua General de Seguros was developed during the second half of the 1940s and comprised a reinsurer, La Compañía General de Reaseguros S. A. (REASE), CRESA, and the old company, La Constancia. The latter had been a target of the Allies' 'Safe Haven' programme after the Second World War, which aimed to immobilize all German assets and investments in other countries. After intervention, the shares of the German company Mannheimer ended up with Mutua General de Seguros.[39] Control of these companies was acquired through the individual purchase of shares by the board of directors and also by the mutual itself. These companies used the production structure (agents and representatives) and the technical and administrative apparatus of the parent mutual, which reduced their costs. Their portfolios were captive, with little independence from the mutual when it came to coinsurance activities. Moreover, La Compañía General de Reaseguros S. A. assumed part of the reinsurance ceded by Mutua General de Seguros. This strategy was a failure, however, due mainly to the fact that operations carried out by these companies were carried out in the interests of the mutual and its principal directors. REASE was dissolved by the directorate-general of banks, markets, and investors in January 1959. CRESA's shares were sold in 1955. The shares in La Constancia that Mutua General de Seguros had (22,659 of the 26,038 comprising the share capital) were sold in 1960.

The creation of business groups comprising companies linked to Mapfre and Mutua General de Seguros was undertaken by the executives and directors of these mutuals with the intention of growing without losing control of the business. This power could be at risk if they converted into stock companies and increased their capital base. Under this formula, stock companies linked

---

[37] Tortella Casares et al. 2009, 71–2.

[38] *BOE* (official state gazette), 19 October 1944, 7872–3.

[39] This company was created in Barcelona on 26 October 1906 by Pedro Hors Baus, Francisco de Asís Oller Padrol, and José Ferrer Arimón. Over the following decades a German company, Mannheimer, acquired part of its shares and became the majority shareholder in 1931. Frax and Matilla 2010.

to the mutuals were able to operate in branches such as reinsurance at this time, which presented difficulties for mutuals. However, in both cases they failed because the top directors and executives of the mutuals were allowed to own large portions of the share capital of these companies. This led to a conflict of interests because there was no clear separation between the assets and the personnel of these entities.[40] At times the directors of mutuals put their own interests as owners of the subsidiary companies first, to the detriment of the parent mutual. An important part of agency and administration costs, for instance, were passed on to the administrative apparatus of the mutual. Furthermore, directors put the interests of their mutual at risk by giving priority to reinsurance operations with the captive undertaking that offered few guarantees due to its lack of capital and limited business, instead of reinsuring externally with companies that could offer them advantageous premiums and greater security. Moreover, in many operations the subsidiaries proved to be mere intermediaries, commission agents who pushed up the mutual's costs, costs that could have been saved by contracting directly.

Nevertheless, this strategy, modified in order to avoid previous mistakes, was taken up again by Mapfre in the 1970s with the creation of the Mapfre group. This time, however, the mutual reserved branches with a high volume of transactions (automobiles) for itself and created various stock companies with separate assets and an independent legal structure (Mapfre Industrial and Mapfre Vida) that were able to obtain external financing for their growth. According to amendments to the company statute in 1965, directors and executives were not allowed to participate in the capital of these companies. With these measures in place, Mapfre's directors intended to prevent conflicts of interest and to prevent executive participation in commercial companies from leading to the interests of these companies being put before the mutual's own interests. This strategy enabled them to maintain control of the mutual while at the same time securing for the stock companies of the group financing for future growth.[41]

CONCLUSIONS

The Franco dictatorship promoted the mutual form both in private insurance and in public social insurance directly through its own initiatives, and also indirectly by creating an institutional framework that was favourable to the development of mutualism. In this sense, the regime introduced legislation that allowed the continuation of small mutuals that operated with

[40] McNamara and Rhee 1992.   [41] Tortella Casares et al. 2009, 121, 34.

scant control of their activities and only the largest mutuals were governed by the private insurance law. On the other hand, the tax system changed, eliminating the levy that existed prior to the Civil War, but imposing a special tax system for mutuals.

Directly, the Franco regime created workers' mutuals (*Mutualidades Laborales*) in the field of social welfare and especially favoured the employers' industrial accident mutuals that had been around since the beginning of the century but which now enjoyed a boom period of growth. It was a period of confusion, when the boundaries between public and private insurance were unclear and when mutuals played a prominent role. The state allowed employers' industrial accident mutuals to manage the public compulsory sickness insurance scheme, and when industrial accident insurance business was removed from the private sector, they continued to manage this, although henceforth as collaborating bodies of the social security system.

It was a confusing time because, in spite of two decades of support, the uncertainties grew for mutuals, due to fears that the state would introduce the public management of all social insurances and limit their activity in certain branches. The mutuals sought different strategies to deal with the situation. A few converted into stock companies. However, those that survived in the long term and came to play an important role in the sector maintained the mutual form. Managers of these mutuals looked for other ways forward, in particular the creation of a group of companies controlled by the mutual, which created or acquired firms in the form of joint-stock companies. The model was not always successful, especially in the first experiments during the autarkic economic period. Nevertheless, when it was implemented in the late 1960s, this system allowed them to grow, to maintain control and avoid being taken over by larger companies, and to secure financing that was difficult to obtain in their mutual form.

Part III

The Performance of Different Organizational Forms

10

The Development of the Mutual Form and Its Influence on the Life Insurance Industry

Evidence from Japan during the Period 1881 to 1935

YingYing Jiang

The modern insurance system in Japan was imported from Western countries after the Meiji Restoration. Many Japanese insurance companies were formed by taking foreign companies as models in and after 1879, in which year the first Japanese company, Tokio Marine, was established. None of these domestic companies adopted the mutual form even though there were no specific legal restrictions on the choice of corporate form before June 1899, when the Amended Commercial Law required that newly organized insurance companies could only adopt a stock form.

The mutual form was legalized soon after the first Insurance Business Act came into effect in July 1900. However, given the fact that stock companies were more numerous than mutuals over the pre-World War Two period, entrepreneurs seemed to prefer the stock form to mutual form. For instance, there was only one short-lived mutual company in non-life insurance, Toa Fire, founded in 1909 and dissolved in 1915. In contrast, mutual and stock forms coexisted for a long period in the life insurance business, though the latter outnumbered the former. The coexistence of stock and mutual companies began in October 1902, when the first mutual company, Dai-ichi Life, was organized. There were seven mutual companies at most in the ordinary life insurance business, compared to twenty-seven or more stock companies.

In terms of the number of companies, the stock form was therefore dominant in life insurance. However, the emergence of the mutual form might be regarded as of great significance, considering that two mutual companies eventually joined the ranks of the Big Five, despite their late entry to the

market. These two were Dai-ichi Life and Chiyoda Life. The latter was
established in April 1904 as the second mutual company. Both successfully
expanded their market share and from the late 1920s became the industry
leaders. The stock companies among the Big Five were Nippon Life, Teikoku
Life, and Meiji Life. In competition with the two big mutuals, these stock
companies suffered a decrease in market share, and Teikoku Life and Meiji
Life were eventually overtaken by their mutual rivals.

Hansmann argues that the mutual form is effective in solving the problem
of contract failure inherent in the long-term life insurance policy, which
results from the uncertainty of the future and the asymmetry of information.[1]
In other words, the assignment of ownership to the policyholders is a solution
to such problems. Moreover, it suggests that the survival of a mutual company
essentially requires the owners to conduct the control of the firm without
incurring excessive costs.[2] This implies that the analysis of organizational
form in the insurance business should be conducted in a comprehensive way.

This argument could possibly be applied to the pre-World War Two
Japanese life insurance industry. Given that the industry was underdeveloped
in this period, a mutual company might seize the advantage of being able to
resolve the problem of contract failure, which might be very severe due to the
lack of reliable data and expert knowledge in the industry. Moreover, in such
circumstances one might expect that well-managed mutual companies would
flourish. Indeed, the five smaller mutual companies eventually merged into
one company in November 1933 due to a slump in business.

However, although in theory the mutual form may be deemed to be more
appropriate for this nascent market, most contemporary entrepreneurs still
chose to enter the business by adopting a stock form of organization. More
than twenty new stock companies were founded after the mutual form became
legal, compared to just seven mutual companies. Furthermore, none of the
existing stock companies attempted to mutualize, despite the fact that mutualization was made legal by the Insurance Business Act.[3] This indicates that the
stock companies must have been able to employ some effective measures to
oppose the mutual companies.

The purpose of this chapter is first, to examine the marketing strategies
adopted by the Big Five life insurance companies, in order to clarify the factors
responsible for the success of the mutual form. Second, this chapter will try
to provide an explanation for the coexistence of two different organizational
forms in the pre-World War Two Japanese life insurance market. Third, it will
discuss whether the mutual form was more appropriate for the life insurance
business during this period.

[1] Hansmann 1985, 129–32.   [2] Hansmann 1985, 134–5.
[3] By contrast, the demutualization of an insurance company was forbidden by the Insurance
Business Act until 1995.

The chapter consists of five sections. In the second section, the marketing strategies adopted by the major stock companies before the emergence of mutual form will be discussed. The marketing strategies and the performance of mutual companies will be examined in section three. The impact of the appearance of mutual companies will also be analysed. The fourth section will discuss whether the mutual form was more suited for the market. Finally, the results will be summarized.

STOCK COMPANIES IN THE EARLY STAGE OF THE LIFE INSURANCE INDUSTRY

Distinctive Characteristics of Early Japanese Life Insurance Companies

The first attempt to establish a modern Japanese life insurance company was made by Norikazu Wakayama, a former government officer. He planned to found a stock company that assigned a profit-sharing right to its policyholders by selling with-profits products. Unfortunately, this plan was not well understood by potential investors and the project was eventually abandoned due to the failure to raise capital. After that, Wakayama projected a mutual company, the Nitto Life. His new plan was approved by the governor of Tokyo in September 1880. Nevertheless, the company was dissolved in June 1881 after it failed to gather the 100 policyholders required to start business as a mutual.[4]

Wakayama's initiative, however, had some influence on other entrepreneurs. With one exception, all of the projected companies before June 1899 were designed to take the stock form, after which the mutual form became illegal according to the Amended Commercial Law. The one exception was a company plan that appeared in May 1890, but this ended in failure.[5] Moreover, many of the stock companies founded after the Nitto Life's dissolution had adopted the idea of giving policyholders the right to participate in profit sharing.

[4] Association of Life Insurance Companies 1934, vol. 1, no.2, issue 2, 133–4. Mori and Miura each provide a different explanation for the dissolution. According to their analyses, the failure to raising a start-up capital was the main cause. See Mori 1929, 57; and Miura 1929, 51–2. On the other hand, Mizushima provides an analysis that supports the interpretation above. Given the circumstances of Japanese society and economy at that time, the purchase of insurance possibly was only affordable for the well educated or the wealthy. Since Wakayama had failed to convince some of those wealthy people to invest in his first company plan, it was probably very difficult to persuade those people to buy insurance from his company. Mizushima 1977, 28–31.

[5] A brief introduction to this issue can be found in 'History of Japanese Life Insurance Industry' (*HonpoSeimei HokenGyoShi* in Japanese), *Insurance and Banking News Report* (*Hoken GinkoJiho* in Japanese), Tokyo, 1933, 209.

Table 10.1. Sales performance of with-profits policies in Meiji Life, 1881–1900

	Whole life policies		Endowment policies			Whole life policies		Endowment policies	
	(A)	(B)	(A)	(B)		(A)	(B)	(A)	(B)
1881	402	220	19	0	1891	3,054	25	282	0
1882	584	109	24	0	1892	3,704	20	411	0
1883	402	15	13	0	1893	3,755	27	433	0
1884	717	10	20	0	1894	4,241	32	1,059	0
1885	226	7	32	0	1895	6,081	19	1,496	0
1886	650	14	25	0	1896	4,543	15	1,342	0
1887	978	25	53	0	1897	4,056	18	1,731	0
1888	1,368	44	66	0	1898	4,251	28	1,907	0
1889	2,276	40	133	0	1899	5,509	15	2,327	0
1890	2,946	32	139	0	1900	6,715	21	2,774	0

(A) Number of new contracts of without-profits   (B) Number of new contracts of with-profits

Source: Ministry of Commerce and Industry of Japan 1881–1932.

For instance, Meiji Life, one of the Big Five companies and the first modern Japanese life insurance company, announced itself in its prospectus as a hybrid organizational form between a stock and a mutual, despite the fact that it was registered as a stock company in July 1881. The company emphasized a so-called mixed-principle policy in its sales promotion, which enabled not only the shareholders but also the policyholders to share in its profits.[6] The company practised this principle by selling the ordinary with-profits whole life policy, although in fact they sold more without-profits policies (see Table 10.1).

Similarly, Nippon Life, another of the Big Five, which was founded in July 1889 as the third modern life insurance company, advertised itself as a composite mutual and stock organization, though it too was approved as a stock company. Its with-profits policyholders were eligible to participate in the company's profit sharing under certain conditions, which were quite different from those of Meiji Life, as we discuss later in this chapter. Moreover, the types of with-profits products in Nippon Life were more varied than those of Meiji Life. In addition to ordinary whole life insurance, Nippon Life developed four more types of with-profits products, which included two types of endowment insurance and two types of whole life insurance products.

Furthermore, a stock company like Kyosai Life, which was formed in April 1894 by the famous and successful banker Zenjiro Yasuda, even put a strict restriction on stock dividend payments, in addition to a product strategy that focused only on with-profits products.[7] It is notable that Tsuneta Yano,

---

[6] See Article 5 of the company prospectus in Sugiyama and Shimura 1981, 24–6.

[7] Association of Life Insurance Companies 1934, vol. 1, no. 2, issue 2, 106–7; Yasuda Mutual Life Insurance Company 1980.

Table 10.2. Total value of policies in force of top three Japanese life insurance companies, 1888–1902

	Meiji Life		Teikoku Life		Nippon Life	
	(A)	(B)	(A)	(B)	(A)	(B)
1888	2,577,400	84.01	490,600	15.99	–	–
1889	3,609,300	68.73	1,416,700	26.98	225,800	4.30
1890	4,670,000	53.94	1,986,300	22.94	2,001,100	23.11
1891	5,558,000	43.57	3,133,900	24.56	4,065,920	31.87
1892	6,694,400	38.78	5,301,700	30.71	5,265,600	30.50
1893	7,638,700	33.62	8,175,300	35.98	6,850,350	30.15
1894	8,958,900	29.92	10,375,300	34.66	8,732,070	29.17
1895	10,627,700	24.46	13,272,300	30.55	10,766,030	24.78
1896	11,884,300	19.57	16,686,300	27.47	13,120,000	21.60
1897	12,921,300	16.12	19,256,700	24.02	16,826,840	20.99
1898	14,049,200	14.10	20,952,300	21.02	20,861,050	20.93
1899	15,804,300	13.18	22,889,800	19.09	23,991,990	20.01
1900	18,041,200	13.56	26,073,200	19.60	27,523,110	20.69
1901	19,934,500	14.43	27,335,200	19.79	30,221,940	21.88
1902	23,392,200	15.43	31,307,850	20.65	32,708,770	21.58
			(A) = Amount (yen)		(B) = Market share (%)	

Source: Ministry of Commerce and Industry of Japan 1881–1932.

a well-known enthusiastic advocate of mutualism and the promoter of Dai-ichi Life, belonged to the management of Kyosai Life until June 1898. Yano's presence presumably facilitated the adoption of the mutuality principle in this company.

By contrast, some stock companies did not have such mutual characteristics at all. Instead of selling with-profits products, they simply adopted an aggressive low-price policy to compete with their rivals. Teikoku Life is a typical example of such companies. It was formed in March 1888 as the second modern life insurance company. Until 1901, the company successfully expanded its market share without selling any with-profits products and it had remained in the top group of companies since its foundation (see Table 10.2).

THE PURPOSE OF SELLING WITH-PROFITS POLICIES IN STOCK COMPANIES

Meiji Life and Nippon Life pioneered the sales of the with-profits policy by Japanese stock companies.[8] Their design of with-profits products was imitated

---

[8] It was said that the reason Nippon Life began selling the with-profits policy was because of a gentleman's agreement between the management and Dr Rikitaro Fujisawa, who provided the first Japanese Life Table for the company.

by many companies. However, these types of with-profits products were radically different from those developed by the mutual companies that appeared later. The characteristics of Meiji Life and Nippon Life can be briefly summarized as follows.

Meiji Life did not include any provision for a policy dividend in their contract. There were no specific terms that stipulated the terms of a policy dividend, such as the expected amount of the dividend or its calculation method. According to an announcement made by Meiji Life, the distribution of the policy dividend would be carried out only if there was a surplus in each four-year settlement term. A policy had to last for more than four years in order to receive a dividend payment. The amount of dividend was calculated as an interest on the premium difference between with-profits and without-profits policies, and the interest rate was decided by the management.

By contrast, the policy dividend in Nippon Life was to be distributed when there was a surplus in each eight-year settlement term. In other words, a duration of more than seven years was a minimum requirement for receiving a policy dividend. Moreover, the insured amount also became one of the conditions. For instance, only with-profits policies with more than 500 yen insured qualified for a dividend payment, with the exception of cumulative whole life insurance, where over 130 yen insured in the first year was required.[9] The method of calculation was not disclosed but according to the company's sketchy announcement, the dividend amount was calculated proportionally by taking each type of policy's premium as a measure.

In both companies, the financial resources for the policy dividend were the same as those for shareholders, yet the latter was distributed each year. This put the managers into a difficult situation if they really intended to consider the benefits of policyholders. In practice, however, the managers were not confronted with such problems since the pre-requisites for the policy dividend virtually restricted the possible access to profit sharing for the policyholders.

For instance, the policy dividend in Meiji Life was essentially designed as an uncertain interest on the premium difference, which was decided *ex post* by the managers. However, this design made the product less attractive to consumers, which was partly proven by the poor sales of the with-profits policies (see Table 10.1) .On the other hand, Nippon Life had a large number of policyholders from the primary industries, and most of them could only afford policies with a small insured amount. The average insurance in Nippon Life remained less than 500 yen before 1906.[10] Moreover, given the requirement of a seven-year duration to qualify for the policy dividend, the share of

---

[9] There were four categories in this cumulative whole life insurance, namely 110 yen, 130 yen, 150 yen, and 200 yen. Nippon Life Insurance Company 1992a, 174.
[10] Nippon Life Insurance Company 1992a, 277, 279–80.

company profits that was finally allocated to the policyholders as dividend would be consequently small.

In sum, the policy dividend rate was not determined in advance in both companies. All issues concerning the policy dividend, such as the decision about whether or not to carry out a distribution and the calculations on which it was based, were totally entrusted to the management. Therefore, these with-profits products were fundamentally different from those sold by the mutual companies established later. Selling a with-profits product in these stock companies was no more than a marketing strategy. In other words, it was intended to mitigate the negative images of their pursuit of profits and to promote the insurance business by advertising a form of mutualism.

This strategy was effective to some extent at this early stage of the life insurance industry. The rapid growth of Nippon Life, in particular, can be attributed to this marketing strategy. By selling several types of with-profits products, Nippon Life overtook the existing companies in market share (see Table 10.2) and became the leading company from 1899.

The with-profits policy, however, did not become a mainstream product before mutual companies entered the market.[11] Market competition had been mainly focused on the premium level of each product. Policy dividends were not an effective means of competition. They were not predetermined, which made them less attractive, although the with-profits product was developed as a differentiation strategy.

Table 10.3 shows the premium rates for the ordinary whole life insurance of three major stock companies, which were announced at the time of their establishment. A simple low-price policy assisted the Teikoku Life to win the competition over market expansion between itself and Meiji Life (see Table 10.2).

Table 10.3. Premium rates for ordinary whole life policies—three Japanese companies in 1934

Annual premiums per 100 yen insured

Entry age	Without-profits			With-profits	
	Meiji	Teikoku	Nippon	Meiji	Nippon
15	1.6	1.5	1.5	1.8	1.5
20	1.8	1.7	1.7	2.0	1.7
25	2.0	1.9	2.0	2.2	2.0
30	2.3	2.2	2.3	2.6	2.3

Source: Association of Life Insurance Companies 1934, vol. 1, no.2, issue 2, 192, 858, 1048.

[11] In some stock companies of the period, with-profits and without-profits products were differentiated not simply by the product names—since they were sometimes given the same name—but also by the contract conditions such as the sum insured or contract period.

Likewise, Nippon Life had given due consideration to the setting of prices for each type of its products. In the without-profits type of policies, the price differences between the Nippon Life and Teikoku Life were apparently smaller than that between the Meiji Life and Teikoku Life. On the other hand, in the with-profits product line, Nippon Life adopted a lower premium policy than Meiji Life. Undoubtedly, such pricing strategy helped the Nippon Life achieve the success in expanding its market share.

THE EMERGENCE OF THE MUTUAL FORM AND ITS INFLUENCE

The Entry of the Mutual Company into the Market

In October 1902 Dai-ichi Life started its business in the Tokyo area as the first Japanese mutual company.[12] This company was founded by Tsuneta Yano, who was a well-known promoter of the mutual form and who was also involved in establishing the Insurance Business Act.[13] The board of directors appointed a count named Yasutoshi Yanagisawa as the first president of Dai-ichi Life. This was simply intended to use the social influence of the nobility to advance the business. After Yanagisawa resigned in September 1915, Yano became the president and held that position for about ten years. He resigned from the presidency in 1926.

Yano played a central role in the company's management. Following his conservative principles of management, he placed more importance on saving expenses and improving the quality of management rather than blindly pursuing the expansion of market share. Two specific measures were taken by Yano in order to lower his company's expense ratio. The first was to specialize in the sales of large-value policies, namely only to sell policies with a sum insured of not less than 1,000 yen, except in some special cases where 500 yen was allowed. Considering that the industry average sum insured per policy was 252 yen in 1901, and about 94 per cent of policies in force in the same year were those for an amount less than 500 yen, Yano's product strategy seemed very bold. In fact, the average sum insured per policy in Dai-ichi Life was not only far larger than the major stock companies, but also bigger than its mutual

[12] Several unsuccessful attempts were made to establish a mutual company after the mutual form became legal in July 1900. The reasons why these projects did not get approved are unknown, but it was probably because the authorities were very cautious in approving a mutual company's formation. For a brief discussion of this issue, see Iwama 1926, 9.

[13] See Chapter 2 by Yoneyama in this volume.

Table 10.4. Average sum insured per policy in major Japanese life insurance companies, 1903–12

	Meiji	Teikoku	Nippon	Dai-ichi	Chiyoda
1903	415	464	393	1,237	-
1904	423	515	400	1,197	865
1905	442	518	413	1,615	834
1906	492	649	479	1,924	964
1907	530	670	520	1,714	948
1908	543	635	535	1,716	977
1909	573	622	597	1,902	1,039
1910	646	693	619	1,973	1,125
1911	656	869	656	1,912	1,250
1912	870	891	685	1,769	1,356

Source: Dai-ichi Mutual Life Insurance Company 2004.

rival, Chiyoda Life, although it was gradually raised over time in these companies (see Table 10.4).

The second measure was to employ a less costly distribution system. The most popular distribution system in those days was agency system. The agencies at the time mainly consisted of local notables such as successful businessmen or local bankers. Given that the life insurance business was not yet well known, the agency system seemed to be an effective means for selling policies by utilizing the social influence and creditability of those notables. Besides selling policies, the agencies were also engaged in premium collection and received a commission fee for each service.

Nevertheless, there were several problems associated with the agency system of the time, which could be attributed to the fact that the insurance business was only a side business for most agents. For instance, it could be difficult to set a reasonable commission rate capable of maintaining the motivation of agents to sell policies over time. If the commission rate was set too high, the cost of policy acquisition would increase, which could lead to a deterioration in cost efficiency and eventually impose a burden on policyholders.

In practice, the commission for selling a policy was generally set at 3 to 5 per cent of the amount of the new policy, and for premium collection it was set at 5 per cent of premiums collected. As the policies in force increased, however, some agencies became more interested in the premium collection than in sales. This was considered to be one of the main causes of the decline in the cost efficiency of the agency system at that time, which was manifested in the increase in the expense ratios of the companies.

As shown in Table 10.5, all three major stock companies were confronted with such problems from the end of the 1890s and they failed to make effective improvements over a long period of time, although overall the expense ratios in Meiji Life and Teikoku Life increased more rapidly than those in Nippon Life during the early 1900s.

Under these circumstances, Yano decided not to employ the agency system for his new venture. Instead, he chose to recruit professional staff to engage in selling policies, the so-called 'sales agent' system. With regard to the premium collection business, he either assigned a special staff to conduct it, or asked the policyholders to deposit money into the bank account designated by the company.

All these efforts focused on expense savings paid off. As shown in Table 10.5, the expense ratio in Dai-ichi Life was not only much lower than that in the three major stock companies but also generally lower than that in Chiyoda Life, since the latter employed the agency system at the same time. However, Yano's management policies and strategies enabled Dai-ichi Life to achieve a stable and sustainable growth and eventually to become the second largest company from 1934 onwards (see Table 10.6).

In contrast to Dai-ichi Life, the mutual form was not the only choice considered by the promoters of Chiyoda Life, the second mutual company formed in 1904. Since most of its promoters were graduates of the Keio Gijyuku School, as were the promoters of Meiji Life, the same stock organization form adopted by Meiji Life was taken for granted from the outset. This was understandable given that Ikunoshin Kadono, who played a leading role in Chiyoda Life's establishment and later became its first president, had studied under Yukichi Fukuzawa as well as Taizo Abe, the central figure in Meiji Life's foundation and also its first president.[14] Fukuzawa was the principal of the Keio Gijyuku School and one of the first Japanese to introduce the Western insurance system into Japan. Many of his pupils became involved in the insurance business.

However, after due deliberations, Kadono convinced the other promoters of Chiyoda to adopt the newly legalized mutual form. In an interview for the 25th Anniversary Memorial of Chiyoda Life's Foundation, Kadono explained that his decision was made by taking a historical perspective on the development of organizational form in the insurance business. Given the fact that the limited partnership was eventually replaced by the stock company, which appeared later and was generally considered a more advanced organizational form, Kadono believed that it was natural to view the newly emerged mutual company in Japan as an evolutionary organizational form as well, one that probably would become more prevalent in the future.[15] Thus it can be argued that the decision about corporate form in Chiyoda Life resembled a strategic choice by its early entrepreneurs.

Due to the different backgrounds to their foundations, there was a wide difference in the management strategy between these two mutual companies. In contrast to Yano's conservative management style, Kadono conducted a more aggressive sales promotion policy by building a dual distribution system in pursuit of rapid expansion in market share. Alongside the same sales agent

---

[14] On the foundation of Meiji Life, see Yoneyama 2010, 107–9.
[15] Chiyoda Mutual Life Insurance Company 1955, 9–10.

Table 10.5. The transition of the expense ratio in the major Japanese life insurance companies, 1889–1918

	Meiji	Teikoku	Nippon	Dai-ichi	Chiyoda		Meiji	Teikoku	Nippon	Dai-ichi	Chiyoda
1889	16.16	72.93	—	—	—	1904	24.88	28.65	23.10	33.30	44.77
1890	15.94	35.23	24.66	—	—	1905	27.19	25.29	25.19	25.42	29.95
1891	15.84	34.68	26.82	—	—	1906	30.80	23.17	21.33	21.11	21.73
1892	14.98	29.93	20.27	—	—	1907	32.27	27.66	25.16	18.24	19.49
1893	15.84	23.69	18.15	—	—	1908	29.95	26.26	28.07	17.51	19.16
1894	19.09	19.99	18.23	—	—	1909	30.41	25.17	25.45	16.93	17.73
1895	19.76	17.79	18.26	—	—	1910	30.32	26.33	23.69	16.48	16.42
1896	19.12	18.55	20.72	—	—	1911	33.29	24.97	22.83	18.87	15.45
1897	20.47	18.30	33.69	—	—	1912	28.99	23.46	24.98	17.72	15.95
1898	22.62	20.11	27.13	—	—	1913	27.13	22.24	24.98	17.51	15.83
1899	24.06	21.61	21.55	—	—	1914	26.40	22.79	17.44	16.70	15.33
1900	26.56	23.31	22.51	—	—	1915	23.55	24.59	18.54	12.27	14.25
1901	28.93	27.67	23.19	—	—	1916	23.75	25.09	17.73	12.64	15.22
1902	30.01	30.98	26.27	—	—	1917	24.87	26.84	18.45	12.63	17.87
1903	28.76	31.55	24.37	657.26	—	1918	23.93	29.01	22.99	14.66	21.58

Note: Expense ratio = (expense/premium income) * 100
Source: Ministry of Commerce and Industry of Japan 1881–1932.

Table 10.6. Changes in market share of major Japanese life insurance companies, 1910–35

Year	Meiji	Teikoku	Nippon	Dai-ichi	Chiyoda	Total
1910	13.84	12.32	15.97	2.45	6.70	51.29
1911	13.17	12.27	15.22	2.81	6.84	50.30
1912	12.52	12.19	14.85	3.00	6.90	49.47
1913	11.45	11.60	14.51	3.05	6.65	47.27
1914	10.97	10.95	14.06	3.08	6.38	45.44
1915	10.94	10.17	14.35	3.22	6.47	45.15
1916	10.85	10.43	14.56	3.37	6.75	45.96
1917	10.75	10.77	14.17	3.45	7.17	46.31
1918	9.70	10.56	14.17	3.49	7.45	45.37
1919	8.71	10.56	14.29	3.68	7.23	44.47
1920	8.25	9.94	14.01	4.22	7.19	43.62
1921	8.06	9.44	13.96	4.80	7.37	43.64
1922	8.52	9.01	13.86	5.38	7.75	44.51
1923	9.07	8.80	14.05	5.99	8.12	46.03
1924	9.50	8.47	13.98	6.35	8.24	46.55
1925	9.75	8.21	13.26	7.01	8.78	47.00
1926	10.06	7.73	12.58	7.70	9.48	47.55
1927	10.46	7.49	12.13	8.68	10.26	49.03
1928	10.96	7.32	12.12	9.38	11.05	50.82
1929	11.16	7.34	12.88	10.13	11.61	53.12
1930	11.34	7.58	13.73	11.05	11.87	55.58
1931	11.63	7.96	14.15	11.97	12.59	58.29
1932	11.74	8.42	14.13	12.64	13.01	59.94
1933	12.24	8.94	14.74	13.17	13.19	62.29
1934	12.51	9.21	15.30	13.53	13.34	63.89
1935	12.55	9.48	15.80	14.06	13.60	65.49

Note: The calculation was based on the total sum insured of policies in force at the end of each fiscal year.
Source: Ministry of Commerce and Industry of Japan 1881–1932.

Table 10.7. Changes in market share of Japanese mutual life insurance companies, 1921–32

	Kokko	Tokai	Horai	Chuo	Nippon Ishi Kyosai
1921	2.50	2.06	1.04	0.85	0.70
1922	2.49	1.99	0.86	0.90	1.00
1923	2.29	1.89	0.82	0.90	1.15
1924	2.06	1.78	0.75	0.85	1.23
1925	2.17	1.64	0.75	0.81	1.30
1926	2.13	1.48	0.79	0.75	1.40
1927	1.98	1.31	0.74	0.69	1.42
1928	1.80	1.10	0.71	0.61	1.38
1929	1.68	0.93	0.77	0.55	1.37
1930	1.46	0.79	0.72	0.44	1.27
1931	1.37	0.68	0.60	0.37	1.23
1932	1.26	0.66	0.50	0.34	1.07

Note: The calculation of market share was based on the amount of policies in force at the end of each fiscal year.
Source: Ministry of Commerce and Industry of Japan 1881–1932.

system employed by Dai-ichi Life, Chiyoda Life also introduced the agency distribution system, which was criticized by Yano for its high costs. Consequently, Chiyoda Life achieved a more rapid growth than Dai-ichi Life during the first few years after its establishment (see Table 10.6).

Besides Dai-ichi Life and Chiyoda Life, there were five more mutual companies established during the period 1908–20: Kokko Life, Tokai Life, Horai Life, Chuo Life, and Nippon Ishi Kyosai. Most of them failed to expand their market shares as successfully as Dai-ichi Life and Chiyoda Life. As shown in Table 10.7, the business performance of these companies remained stagnant. Eventually, they were combined into one company in November 1933.

Changes in the Market Brought about by Mutual Companies

Soon after the mutual form was legalized, some stock companies started to redesign their product strategies, which can be regarded as counter-measures taken against the forthcoming mutual companies. For example, in 1901, for the first time since its inception, Meiji Life clearly specified provisions relating to the policyholder dividend such as dividend rates and the method of funding the dividend reserves. According to these provisions, the policy dividend rate became predetermined, and the reserves for the policy dividend would be recorded as ordinary expenses in order to secure the funds necessary to ensure the dividend payments.[16] Moreover, in 1912 it also increased the variety of its

[16] Sugiyama and Shimura 1981, 76–7.

with-profits provision as its second and third types of with-profits products, limited-payment whole life insurance and endowment insurance, were developed.

A similar counter-measure taken by Teikoku Life was to launch its first with-profits product in January 1902, which was modelled on some tontine insurance schemes popular in America.[17] Its policy dividend was deferred for five years and only distributed to those policyholders who survived during the dividend period. The president of Teikoku Life, Arinobu Fukuhara, explained that the motive for issuing such a with-profits policy was an essential marketing strategy.[18] He also believed that a future mutualization might become inevitable for the further development of the company.[19]

As a result of successive changes to the product strategies of major stock companies, with-profits products eventually prevailed in the life insurance market as indicated in Table 10.8. The market share of with-profits products followed an upward trend in contrast to the downward trend of without-profits products. This suggests that most of the stock companies gradually modified their product strategies and shifted their leading products from the without-profits to the with-profits type.

For their part, the mutual companies undertook an intensive publicity of mutuality in their sales strategies. They laid great emphasis on explaining the difference in organizational form between themselves and other companies. For instance, Dai-ichi Life produced a pamphlet titled 'The Characteristic of Our Company' in order to introduce the mutual company and mutuality in general. In the pamphlet, the high stock dividend rates of some leading companies were used to make the comparison between the two organizational forms transparent. Using this example, they argued that the only purpose of the stock company was to satisfy its shareholders by maximizing the dividend, though some stock companies were also advertising benefits to policyholders by selling a with-profits product. In contrast to the stock company, however, people would become owners of a mutual company only by purchasing a policy. The mutual company considered their policyholders first and all profits were paid back to the policyholders under the so-called actual cost principle.[20]

Furthermore, competition among mutual companies was concentrated on the policy dividend. It commenced between Dai-ichi Life and Chiyoda Life and then extended over the whole industry. In practice, until 1905 both

---

[17] As is well known, tontine-type policies became very popular from the late nineteenth century in America. However, their sale was prohibited from the very beginning of the twentieth century due to problems such as the illegal diversion of policy dividend reserves and the exaggerated advertisement of anticipated dividends that occurred in some insurance companies.

[18] Asahi Mutual Life Insurance Company 1990, 262–4. Fukuhara was the founder of Shiseido, a major Japanese cosmetics company and one of the oldest cosmetics companies in the world, established in 1770.

[19] 'A Conversation with Arinobu Fukuhara', Hoken Jiho, 25 November 1901, 15.

[20] For further information, see Dai-ichi Mutual Life Insurance Company 1987, 57–8.

Table 10.8. Changes in the main products of the Japanese life insurance industry, 1910–35

	(A-1)	(B-1)	(A-2)	(B-2)		(A-1)	(B-1)	(A-2)	(B-2)
1910	54.52	45.48	71.19	28.81	1923	3.91	96.09	14.07	85.93
1911	48.51	51.49	67.27	32.73	1924	2.92	97.08	12.72	87.28
1912	43.87	56.13	62.68	37.32	1925	4.64	95.36	11.67	88.33
1913	36.89	63.11	57.20	42.80	1926	4.25	95.75	10.70	89.30
1914	29.65	70.35	52.46	47.54	1927	3.03	96.97	9.85	90.15
1915	19.27	80.73	41.71	58.29	1928	1.33	98.67	8.83	91.17
1916	20.24	79.76	39.49	60.51	1929	0.92	99.08	8.02	91.98
1917	12.38	87.62	35.25	64.75	1930	0.71	99.29	7.58	92.42
1918	5.46	94.54	25.42	74.58	1931	0.89	99.11	7.22	92.78
1919	4.13	95.87	20.93	79.07	1932	0.84	99.16	6.91	93.09
1920	4.58	95.42	18.21	81.79	1933	0.76	99.24	6.47	93.53
1921	4.55	95.45	16.59	83.41	1934	2.29	97.71	6.10	93.90
1922	4.98	95.02	15.29	84.71	1935	2.06	97.94	5.54	94.46

Notes: (A-1) Share of without-profits policy calculated on the number of new contracts; (A-2) share of without-profits policy calculated on the number of contracts in force at the end of year; (B-1) share of with-profits policy calculated on the number of new contracts; (B-2) share of with-profits policy calculated on the number of contracts in force at the end of year.
Source: Ministry of Commerce and Industry of Japan 1881–1932.

mutual companies employed the same dividend policy as Teikoku Life, a five-year deferred distribution system. From 1906, however, Dai-ichi Life began to adopt an annually cumulative dividend distribution system in which policyholders were able to estimate the dividend amount simply by multiplying the paid-up premiums, the duration, and the dividend rate together, although the distribution period remained set at five years.

The introduction of this new distribution system accelerated Dai-ichi Life's growth as shown in Table 10.9. A remarkable increase in the growth rate of new contracts can be observed, whereas Chiyoda Life began to experience a drop in growth rates.[21] Then, as a counter-measure, Chiyoda Life introduced the same cumulative dividend distribution system but shortened its distribution period to three years in 1910 and raised the policy dividend rate to 4 per cent in 1912, which was 1 per cent higher than Dai-ichi Life. In response, Dai-ichi Life raised its dividend rate to 4.5 per cent in 1917. After this, it maintained a more sustainable growth than other companies, as shown in Table 10.9. Chiyoda Life adjusted its dividend rate to the same level as Dai-ichi Life's in 1925.

Stock companies came up with different measures against the fierce policy dividend competition brought about by the mutual companies. Some of them refused to participate in this competition and insisted on a low-premium strategy, despite the fact that with-profits policies had already become their

---

[21] The decrease in 1914 and 1915 shown in Table 10.9 was caused by World War One.

Table 10.9. Percentage increase in the number of new contracts of major Japanese life insurance companies, 1907–32

	Meiji	Teikoku	Nippon	Dai-ichi	Chiyoda		Meiji	Teikoku	Nippon	Dai-ichi	Chiyoda
1907	30.09	88.20	4.30	18.82	18.84	1920	-6.37	-27.07	-4.48	19.35	-7.10
1908	-7.86	-8.42	37.43	11.31	14.88	1921	-12.76	-18.24	-4.85	20.53	-3.77
1909	12.85	-7.99	-6.47	-4.07	7.26	1922	34.46	-11.68	-0.77	6.42	10.85
1910	0.91	21.93	6.94	26.00	-3.30	1923	0.91	-5.84	-2.33	11.96	-4.90
1911	7.24	20.79	26.04	88.55	9.85	1924	21.42	29.29	11.48	10.40	10.31
1912	-14.12	27.75	4.78	23.29	8.11	1925	2.52	10.86	-9.81	34.22	39.71
1913	-1.41	-2.04	13.71	46.91	-1.23	1926	3.21	-16.62	-13.03	13.45	15.93
1914	-7.41	27.93	-25.86	-29.00	-19.57	1927	-5.45	1.30	-3.76	19.87	0.07
1915	-21.27	-55.36	-23.90	-23.37	-22.14	1928	10.43	14.36	36.25	16.20	28.26
1916	8.61	43.08	7.36	20.81	28.27	1929	3.27	13.59	28.55	13.40	11.06
1917	35.78	56.32	26.82	39.90	74.91	1930	14.41	19.55	24.02	15.77	-10.10
1918	-7.70	20.91	60.06	40.05	61.32	1931	30.53	25.78	7.59	22.49	42.75
1919	13.12	50.70	33.33	78.56	20.60	1932	-5.23	15.34	-7.73	1.89	10.08

Note: data calculated as (N2 - N1)/N1*100, where N1 = number of new contracts issued in the previous fiscal year; N2 = number of new contracts in current fiscal year.
Source: Ministry of Commerce and Industry of Japan 1881–1932.

leading products. They argued that there was no big difference between their low-premium policy and the high-dividend policy of mutual companies since the latter would require a high premium in the first place. Moreover, taking into consideration the long term of life insurance, the former rather than the latter strategy would be better since it ensured a low up-front premium payment.[22]

Meiji Life and Nippon Life were typical companies adopting a low-premium policy. The policy dividend rate in Meiji Life was 2.5 per cent to 3 per cent on average during the period 1921–8, and it had been much lower than this before 1921, whereas the average dividend rate of the high-dividend policy group was about 4.5 per cent in the same period.[23] An insurance policy with a 3 per cent dividend rate was introduced for the first time by Nippon Life in 1925, which was designed to compete against the cumulative dividend policies sold by Dai-ichi Life and Chiyoda Life. Due to its unintelligible distribution rules, however, the sales results were less than stellar and eventually it was withdrawn in 1931.[24]

Nippon Life proved more passive than Meiji Life in adopting the policy dividend as a measure against mutual companies or other high-dividend policy stock companies. For instance, the policy dividend period in Nippon Life was set for eight years until 1915, while it was no longer than five years in most companies regardless of their organizational form. Undoubtedly this hampered Nippon Life's business performance to some extent, as shown in Table 10.9.

In response to this situation, Nippon Life shortened the dividend period from eight years to five years in 1915, and in 1920 the accounts processing system was changed to secure financial resources for the policy dividend payment, in each case by amending the articles of incorporation. Nevertheless, all these measures seemed to have a very limited effect on improving its business performance and competing with the high-dividend policy of mutual companies (see Table 10.9).

The other group of stock companies headed by Teikoku Life took part in the policy dividend competition.[25] These companies eventually employed the same policy dividend method and dividend rates by following Dai-ichi Life and Chiyoda Life. Moreover, Teikoku Life launched a new with-profits

---

[22] This issue provoked a great response and ultimately it was related to the difference in organizational form: that is to say that, the issue of high dividends versus low premiums was essentially equivalent to the issue of mutual versus stock companies. An interview on this topic with directors from various life insurance companies was published in 'The Development of Life Insurance Industry and Its Future', *Kokumin Shinbun*, 22 March 1927.

[23] For more details, see Yui and Tatsuki 1982, 428.

[24] Nippon Life Insurance Company 1992a, 499–500.

[25] Besides Teikoku Life, Jinju Life and Daido Life were also major members of this high-dividend-paying group. Both the latter companies were middle sized.

product with a dividend rate of 5 per cent in 1927. This product attracted great public attention since its rate was the highest in the industry during the pre-World War Two period. As a result, Teikoku Life achieved a relative better performance in sales compared to Meiji Life and Nippon Life for several years after the launch of this product (see Table 10.9).[26]

In this period, many newspapers published articles that discussed the issue of high-dividend competition, declaring that the Japanese life insurance industry had entered a high-dividend era.[27] Some newspapers reported the high shareholder dividends paid by life insurance companies, whereas most stock companies in other industries were unable to distribute a dividend due to the financial crisis at the end of the 1920s. Consequently, critics argued that life insurance premiums were set too high, which enabled insurance companies to make excessive profits, since the basic mortality tables used in premium rate calculations varied among companies and there was no authoritative Japanese experience mortality table available until 1931.[28]

It is possible, however, that these media reports also pushed the low-premium policy companies to amend their strategies to some degree. For example, Nippon Life started a yearly dividend distribution system in 1929, and Meiji Life raised its policy dividend rate from 3 per cent to 3.5 per cent in 1930. Soon after, Nippon Life also developed a product with a dividend rate set at 3.5 per cent. With these strategic changes, market competition finally converged on the policy dividend.

Diversification of Distribution Systems Stimulated by Mutual Companies

The agency system was the major distribution system used by stock companies before the mutual companies appeared. Most of their agents were either local notables or local bankers in the early days. Apparently it was intended to utilize their social influence and credibility to sell policies since the life insurance business was not yet widely known. The gradual growth achieved by each company proved that the agency system was effective in selling insurance.

Agents were also engaged in collecting premiums. They would earn 5 per cent of the amount of premium collected as a commission, while the commission in the case of selling a policy was set at 3 per cent to 5 per cent of the

---

[26] The decline from 1920 to 1923 was caused by the Spanish influenza and the Great Kanto Earthquake in 1923.

[27] For instance, 'Life Insurance Industry Is Now in a High-Dividend Era', *Tokyo Asahi Shinbun*, 2 December 1928; 'A Noticeable High-Rate Dividend Competition in the Life Insurance Industry', *Tokyo Asahi Shinbun*, 8 December 1928; 'The High-Premium Trend of with-Profits Policy', *Osaka JijiShimpo*, 4 December 1928.

[28] 'Bloated Profits in Insurance Business', *Osaka Asahi Shinbun*, 11 July 1927.

Table 10.10. The sales performance of agencies in Nippon Life, 1914–27

	No. of agencies	Index A	Index B		No. of agencies	Index A	Index B
1914	615	80.25	73.95	1921	751	73.09	65.44
1915	644	78.04	72.42	1922	789	73.63	63.01
1916	674	74.91	69.99	1923	880	73.47	63.58
1917	690	74.91	71.03	1924	915	73.26	65.08
1918	708	76.74	72.80	1925	980	76.48	69.54
1919	718	74.45	68.86	1926	1044	73.75	68.07
1920	733	72.45	65.71	1927	1116	70.96	67.80

Notes: Index A = ratio of the number of new policies sold by the agencies; Index B = ratio of the amount of new policies sold by the agencies.

Source: Nippon Life Insurance Company 1992a, 497.

sum insured. However, the insurance business was merely a subsidiary occupation to most of these agents. Many tended to become more interested in premium collection than in selling policies as the number of insurance policies in force increased, and this caused a deterioration of cost efficiency in the agency distribution system from a sales point of view. Indeed, as shown in Table 10.5, most stock companies began to face a problem of high expense ratios from the late 1890s, calculated by dividing expenses by premium income. One example of the decline in efficiency, as can be seen in Table 10.10, was the sales performance of agencies in Nippon Life, which did not improve as much as might have been expected with the increase in their number.

By contrast, mutual companies adopted a different distribution strategy, namely the 'sales agent' system. In this system, the agents specialized in selling policies and were paid on a piecework basis. All things being equal, the cost efficiency associated with sales agents in this case should have been better than that in the agency system. In fact, as shown in Table 10.5, the expense ratios observed in Dai-ichi Life and Chiyoda Life were lower than that in the other three major stock companies, despite the fact that Chiyoda Life also employed the agency system.

As Chiyoda Life and Dai-ichi Life continued to successfully increase its market share, and market competition became more intense in response to the high-dividend policy by mutual companies, the stock companies started to reorganize their distribution systems. Eventually they decided to shift their major sales channels from the agency to the sales agent, having failed to significantly improve the operational efficiency of their agencies.

For example, Meiji Life accomplished such a distribution system reform in December 1920, after which its expense ratio improved (see Table 10.11). Similarly, Teikoku Life completed the conversion of its major sales channels in June 1924. Here an improvement in the expense ratio was subsequently

Table 10.11. The transition of the expense ratio in the major Japanese life insurance companies, 1919–32

	Meiji	Teikoku	Nippon	Dai-ichi	Chiyoda
1919	26.61	30.69	20.89	17.09	21.76
1920	26.66	30.09	24.65	19.77	22.65
1921	21.52	22.24	21.68	18.38	19.74
1922	22.08	21.68	21.58	18.92	18.35
1923	21.31	22.39	21.89	18.08	21.80
1924	20.87	22.97	15.50	16.75	18.91
1925	21.05	23.21	19.36	17.33	20.60
1926	21.43	21.44	19.50	16.82	21.06
1927	20.48	22.09	20.72	16.71	19.10
1928	20.87	18.95	23.33	15.99	19.31
1929	19.52	19.68	17.09	15.49	19.38
1930	17.92	20.30	25.76	15.09	16.42
1931	18.15	21.37	22.89	14.85	19.87
1932	18.61	21.48	21.73	14.00	19.29

Note: Expense Ratio = (Expense/Premium Income) * 100.
Source: Ministry of Commerce and Industry of Japan 1881–1932.

observed as well. By contrast, Nippon Life started recruiting professional sales agents in April 1914 after establishing new internal rules, and consequently achieved a remarkable improvement in its expense ratio (see Table 10.5). At that time, however, the sales agent system was only developed as a supplementary distribution channel. Its full-scale development in Nippon Life began from 1926.[29]

The Impact of Mutual Companies on the Insurance Business

After mutual companies entered the market, significant changes in the marketing strategies of stock companies occurred. First, stock companies began announcing the dividend rate of their with-profits policies in advance. Second, they gradually shifted their main product from the without-profits to the with-profits type. Third, most stock companies participated in price competition by means of the policy dividend. These adjustments enabled policyholders to have a greater opportunity to participate in a company's profit sharing, something which eventually led to a reduction in the cost of purchasing insurance.

Moreover, the policy dividend rates in the stock companies were either approximately equal to or higher than those in the mutual companies. This resulted in a reduction in the amount of profits payable to their owners, the shareholders. Given that their goal was to maximize the profits of shareholders, the stock

[29] Nippon Life Insurance Company 1992a, 447–8.

companies had thus deviated from their original purpose. The differences between the stock and mutual company had gradually become more ambiguous.

Furthermore, the fierce price competition provided more incentives for the stock companies to engage in improving their expense efficiency, since they tended to have a higher expense ratio than the mutual companies, possibly caused by the different distribution systems. Once they introduced the same distribution system employed by the mutual companies, some improvement in the expense ratio was observed. This allowed the stock companies to provide insurance at a lower cost and thus become more competitive.

Given that these innovations in the market were introduced by the mutual companies, the mutual form seemed more appropriate for the insurance business during this period. Mutuality appeared to deliver a competitive advantage because all profits arising from the insurance business were eventually delivered to policyholders as their ownership interests, whereas only shareholders were entitled to those profits in the stock company.

In fact, all stock companies with good business performance either maintained shareholder dividend rates at a certain level or raised them to a higher level while undertaking policy dividend competition with the mutuals. For example, Teikoku Life raised its shareholder dividend rate from 16 to 20 per cent in 1918, and then to 25 per cent in 1932. Nippon Life also raised its shareholder dividend rate from 15 per cent to 25 per cent in 1917, and also issued a bonus dividend to shareholders several times in and after 1918.

In despite of all the aforesaid advantages of the mutual form, only two mutual companies succeeded in expanding their market share. This suggests that the stock form of company may have had a better management control system than the mutuals, since the disadvantages it faced in the policy dividend competition with the mutuals may have been overcome by imitating the marketing strategies of the latter.

However, those strategic imitations could be a double-edged sword. They probably caused a deviation of company goals and serious conflicts of interest between shareholders and policyholders. Why, then, did shareholders yield to those management decisions? Did shareholders monitor their management effectively? In the following section, we discuss this issue in more detail.

MANAGEMENT CONTROL OF OWNERS

Ownership Concentration in the Stock Company

The stock companies formed in the early years had a relatively wide spread of ownership. At the time of their establishment, they intended to set their share price at as reasonable a level as possible to make their stock affordable for more people, so as to attract them into the insurance business to become first an investor and then a policyholder. For instance, the share price of Teikoku Life was set at one half the level of the pioneering company, Meiji Life.[30] Likewise, Nippon Life set it at one half of that of Teikoku Life. Furthermore, Nippon Life restricted the numbers of shares that could be purchased by each investor, except for some promoters of the company.[31]

As the insurance business developed, speculative investors appeared and attempted to take over or merge insurance companies by buying up their stocks.[32] Believing that the development of their companies would be adversely affected by such speculative activities, the management of insurance companies introduced loyal shareholders arrangements, which were aimed at building a stable stockholder structure by collectively purchasing floating stocks or conducting stock buybacks from the speculative investors. In most cases, such stock purchase operations were undertaken by third parties who had personal connections with the management of the insurance companies.

One example is that of Jinshiro Hiramatsu, the president of Hiramatsu Bank and known as a risk-loving banker, who in 1886 secretly bought up 187 shares of Meiji Life, which accounted for 18.7 per cent of its total issued shares, and thereby became one of its largest shareholders.[33] This news undoubtedly surprised the management of Meiji Life. Hiramatsu continued his aggressive buying and selling of Meiji Life stocks, which increased concerns that Meiji Life's management might become destabilized. This alarm eventually led to the introduction of a loyal shareholders arrangement in Meiji Life. In response to a request from Meiji Life, Hisaya Iwasaki, the third president of Mitsubishi Zaibatsu (a financial clique), purchased 337 shares, including those owned by Hiramatsu, and thereby became Meiji Life's top shareholder.[34]

In contrast, a loyal shareholders arrangement in Teikoku Life was undertaken as a preventive measure against such speculative takeovers. Its management initiated a first and second intensive stock buyback in 1904 and 1906, respectively. They collected 37.2 per cent and 51.1 per cent of issued shares respectively. In 1909 a third buyback was carried out, and consequently 60.5 per cent of its shares were concentrated among its seven directors and four advisors.[35] Similar actions were undertaken by Nippon Life as well. As shown

---

[30] Teikoku Stock Life Insurance Company 1939, 15–16.

[31] Each investor was not allowed to buy more than fifty shares. Nippon Life 1992a, 136–9.

[32] Speculative takeovers and mergers in the life insurance business reached a peak around 1901. See Ogawa 1987.

[33] The total number of shareholders at the time of the foundation in 1881 was eighty-three, and the top two shareholders owned 250 and fifty shares, respectively. Thus, the appearance of a shareholder with 187 shares was viewed as an unexpected threat to the company's management. The Hiramatsu Bank was a private bank established in 1882. During the 1880s it provided both banking and securities services, which was considered unique in Japan at that time.

[34] Sugiyama and Shimura 1981, 48–9.

[35] See Asahi Mutual Life Insurance Company 1990, 225–8.

Table 10.12. Transition in the number of shareholders in Nippon Life, 1890–1911

	Total number of shareholders	Total number of issued shares		Total number of shareholders	Total number of issued shares
1890	438	12,000	1901	332	12,000
1891	441	12,000	1902	307	12,000
1892	431	12,000	1903	293	12,000
1893	413	12,000	1904	256	12,000
1894	395	12,000	1905	247	12,000
1895	392	12,000	1906	231	12,000
1896	385	12,000	1907	226	12,000
1897	381	12,000	1908	219	12,000
1898	383	12,000	1909	207	12,000
1899	364	12,000	1910	204	12,000
1900	353	12,000	1911	201	12,000

Source: Nippon Life Insurance Company 1992b.

in Table 10.12, its total number of shareholders was successively reduced as stock acquisition by the management proceeded.

As a result, however, insurance stock ownership became highly concentrated among a few large shareholders from the early 1900s, and no significant change occurred in this situation during the pre-World War Two period. For example, in Nippon Life the ratio of shareholding by its five major shareholders rose from 31.5 per cent in 1900 to 47 per cent in 1911.[36] Similarly, in Meiji Life 64.2 per cent of shares were owned by thirteen shareholders in 1901, while in 1914 73.9 per cent of shares were concentrated among twelve shareholders. In Teikoku Life 89.4 per cent of shares were held among twenty-five shareholders by 1936.

The managers of these companies were either appointed by the large shareholders or were large shareholders themselves. Under such circumstances, managerial decisions undoubtedly favoured the largest shareholders, since ordinary shareholders had very limited influence. Indeed, few ordinary shareholders attended general meetings. For instance, Teikoku Life held its general meeting ninety-three times during the pre-World War Two period, but on seventy-one occasions fewer than twenty shareholders attended, and most of them were directors of the company.[37]

The management of the stock companies, therefore, was firmly under the control of their large shareholders. The imitation of the product strategies of mutual companies was compatible, above all, with large shareholders' interests. Although it may have resulted in a reduction in their immediate benefits,

[36] The five major shareholders were Hirose Keiretsu, Kataoka Keiretsu, Konoikei Keireitsu, Yamaguchi Keiretsu, and Okahashi Keiretsu. All of them were among the founding shareholders.
[37] Asahi Mutual Life Insurance Company 1992, 94.

it was also indispensable to sustain their companies in the face of competition, which might be expected to bring them long-term profits. Thus most of them chose to share profits with the policyholders rather than withdraw from the business. This motive also helps to explain why there was no organizational conversion conducted by any stock company during the period, despite the fact that this was legalized by the Insurance Business Act.

Many stock companies, however, managed to prevent sudden changes in the number of shareholders or speculative stock trading by maintaining stock dividends at a certain level, or by increasing their capital through new allocations to shareholders. Considering the fact that most life insurance stock companies at the time were unlisted, with the exception of a small and short-lived venture named Meikyo Life that went public in 1896 and dissolved in 1902, those measures taken by stock companies appear to have been fairly effective. Thus, the aforesaid management decisions in pursuit of the long-term development of their companies do not seem to have caused a severe conflict of interests between the large shareholders and ordinary shareholders.

Management Control in the Mutual Company

In the pre-World War Two period it was difficult for the owners of mutual companies, the policyholders, to engage in corporate management since their knowledge of the insurance business was very limited. For this reason, policyholders showed little interest in participating in management. The system designed for them to control the management was not effectively utilized. For instance, the general meeting of policyholders in Chiyoda Life could not even make a quorum from 1924, something which only required 150 members.[38]

Under these circumstances, company success greatly depended on the self-discipline of the management. As successful mutual companies, Dai-ichi Life and Chiyoda Life both had key persons who played a leading role in management discipline, most notably Tsuneta Yano and Ikunoshin Kadono, respectively. Both of them had specialized knowledge of the insurance business and wide personal relationships in the economic and political world. Their companies never experienced difficulties in raising funds.

Such specialists were absent in the other mutuals that failed to expand their market share. In these companies, neither their promoters nor managers had abundant expert knowledge of the insurance business. Most of these companies were confronted with management failures, as evident in the frequent replacement of managers in Chuo Life or the scandals of managers in Tokai

---

[38] Chiyoda Mutual Life Insurance Company 1955, 357.

Life. Poor management ability also caused the sluggish growth of Kokko Life, a mutual company established with the support of some Japanese nobles.[39]

CONCLUSIONS

The pioneering life insurance companies in Japan preferred a mixed principle imported from Western insurance companies. They appealed to the interests of policyholders by selling a with-profits policy, while at the same time adopting the stock form of company organization. However, in practice, their policyholders did not get enough opportunities to participate in company profit sharing since the requirements for receiving a policy dividend were very rigid. The policy dividend was not determined in advance and its calculation standards were hard for policyholders to understand.

After mutual companies entered the market, these stock companies were forced to change their marketing strategies. The most important change was to assign a substantial profit distribution to policyholders. This was a response to the mutual companies' success in expanding their market share by promoting mutuality in the form of a with-profits policy with a predetermined rate. Simplifying the calculation standards of the policy dividend to make them easier for policyholders to understand also enabled mutual companies to compete with the stock companies more effectively. The stock companies eventually adopted a version of the high-dividend policy of the mutual companies.

With the inevitable assimilation of the mutual companies' product strategies, the organizational differences between the stock company and mutual company became ambiguous. In other words, the stock company came to more closely resemble the mutual company. From this perspective, the mutual form seemed more suited to the pre-World War Two life insurance market than the stock company form. As Hansmann suggests, however, any evaluation of an organizational form should be conducted from a comprehensive viewpoint.[40] Thus, we need to consider the fact that the mutual form was not so popular in Japan in this period and that only two mutuals succeeded in expanding their market share.

Through an analysis of actual management conditions, we find that the mutual form in Japan tended to have a higher cost associated with ownership, in other words, the corporate control system for owners was dysfunctional. Only those mutual companies with an effective substitute for strong corporate governance systems, namely the existence of powerful company founders and

---

[39] See Iwama 1926 for more details.   [40] Hansmann 1985, 1996.

managers, achieved business success. By contrast, the stock companies had relatively effective corporate governance systems due to the fact that their ownership was concentrated among a few large shareholders.

This also helps to explain why the stock companies did not turn to mutualization despite the fact that their product strategies had virtually transformed them into a form similar to the mutual companies. This was because large shareholders believed that those strategic changes might still bring them profits over time. In other words, the mutual form had product advantages that derived from its mutuality principle. However, the imitation of mutual product strategies by the stock form of company increased the profit-sharing possibility for policyholders and thus enabled them to purchase their insurance at a reasonable price.

11

Growth Performance and Organizational Forms

The Case of Swedish Life Insurance, 1890–1950

Magnus Lindmark and Lars Fredrik Andersson

FROM JOINT-STOCK FIRST-MOVERS TO THE PREVALENCE OF MUTUALITY

The first Swedish life insurance company, *Skandia* (a joint-stock), was established in 1856. The entry of Skandia meant that the few mutual call-and-deposit types that existed at the time were faced with a radically different type of competition. *Skandia* was huge, not only in comparison with the existing life funds. It was by far the largest Swedish company. A novelty was also the use of modern actuarial techniques. As a composite life and fire insurance company, *Skandia* invested life insurance funds in mortgage loans, for which the collateral was property, fire insured with the company. The company was the first domestic company based on actuarial methods in the Swedish life insurance market. Small funds, such as the Widows and Pupils' Fund (1783), existed and a number of foreign companies, such as the *Alliance Assurance Company* and the *Deutsche Lebensversicherungs Gesellschaft*, were established in the Swedish market from the mid-1820s.[1]

Skandia was followed by two other composite companies (combining fire and life insurance) in 1866 (*Svea*) and in 1884 (*Skåne*). These companies shared similar company statutes and organization. Independently of the three composite companies, six additional joint-stock life insurance companies entered the market in the late nineteenth and early twentieth centuries and another two were formed in the inter-war period. The life insurance market was entirely controlled by stock companies until the 1890s. The first mutual life insurance

---

[1] Bergander 1967.

company (*Allmänna lif*) was established in 1887.[2] Up until the First World War seventeen mutual companies entered the life insurance market. During the war and the inter-war period eight additional companies were formed.

The entry of mutual and stock companies in the late nineteenth and early twentieth centuries increased the number of companies from ten in 1890 to twenty-four in 1920. During the 1920s the number of exits (sum of genuine exits, mergers, and takeovers) was for the first time larger than the number of entries. This consolidation phase continued in the 1930s and the number of companies decreased to seventeen by the late 1930s. The aggregated firm demographics show that the number of mutuals exceeded the number of stock companies already by the late nineteenth century. In the 1920s, the number of mutuals was twice the number of stock companies. Although the consolidation phase of the late 1920s and early 1930s meant that the number of mutuals declined, there remained more mutual companies than stock companies.[3]

From the turn of the century, the mutual companies took a jump-start and the stock insurers embarked on a journey of lost market shares until the mid-twentieth century. Measured as the share of total premium incomes, the mutuals increased their market share from 8 per cent in 1890 to 40 per cent in 1910. During the following two decades, the mutual expansion was somewhat slower. In 1930 mutual companies controlled half the life insurance market. Between 1930 and 1948 mutuals expanded more rapidly. In the years following the Second World War, the mutual expansion reached its maximum market dominance. The tide turned during the post-war period and stock insurers have today a very strong position in the Swedish life insurance market.

The Swedish life-insurance market therefore offers a good example of changes and choices of organizational form in the insurance market. In this chapter we address this issue by focusing on the change in organizational structure during the period 1890 to 1948. The aim is to explain the mechanism governing this change. A key issue is to uncover the determinants of comparative advantages of mutual and stock organizational form during the period of study. By explaining this issue, we believe this study can contribute to a better understanding of the mechanism governing the organization of life insurance markets. The following section outlines some of the theoretical arguments about the competitive advantages of stock and mutual organizational forms and their relation to more general changes in the insurance market. We then uncover key characteristics of the financial structures in mutual and stock companies. The third section provides an empirical analysis of how growth performance was related to organizational form.

[2] Lönnborg 1999.
[3] *Försäkringsväsendet i riket, 1888–1912*. Stockholm: Civildepartementet, Försäkringsinspektionen; *Enskilda försäkringsanstalter, 1912–1930*. Sverige Officiella Statistik, Stockholm: Statistiska Centralbyrån 1912–1950.

AGENCY THEORY AND THE HISTORICAL CONTEXT

Contemporary insurance economics uses various hypotheses based on agency theory and theories of asymmetric information in order to explain the choice of organizational form. Sometimes such theories have also been used in historical studies, either as analytical frameworks or for the testing of hypotheses. We believe that the use of such theories may help to enhance the analysis and the understanding of insurance markets. When applying such theories it is important not to overlook the historical context and to realize that many of the concepts used today may have had another meaning or interpretation historically. By applying a critical view of concepts and theories, historical studies help us to understand more of what is unique for historical periods, but also what is more universal in firm behaviour.

According to the theoretical literature on organizational forms it is argued that the competitive advantages of mutual and stock companies arise due to their different abilities to handle information asymmetry and/or agency problems. Given such competitive advantages, the change in the market share of each organizational form (as shown in Figure 11.1) may be seen as the aggregated outcome of a selection mechanism. Following Nelson and Winter, such a process can be considered evolutionary, in the sense that the capitalist economy inherits competing firms that differ in some characteristics that influence individual prospects of selection.[4] The selection in terms of survival, growth, decline, and exit may be the outcome of successful adaptation to the business environment where, for example, mutual organizational forms have competitive advantages in an environment characterized by unknown risk distributions, where the 'club-like' cooperative structures reduce the risks of adverse selection and potential for growth.[5] A key issue of selection is the firm's ability to adapt to changes in its business environment and how firm-specific outcomes are related to organizational form.

One basic theoretical idea is that mutual forms have a competitive advantage in handling information asymmetry problems (moral hazard and adverse selection).[6] The more difficult the risk assessments (and a priori pricing of risks) are in a market, the higher is the likelihood of significant information asymmetry. This, in turn, increases the probability for the dominance by mutual forms. This so-called *informational hypothesis* holds that mutual insurers are successful in such markets because their 'club-like' cooperative structures reduce the risks of adverse selection (e.g. by restricting access to the risk pool to low-risk types) and moral hazard (e.g. by imposing social sanctions in the event of vexatious claims).

---

[4] Nelson and Winter 1985.   [5] Smith and Stutzer 1990, 1995; Skogh 1999.
[6] Smith and Stutzer 1990, 1995.

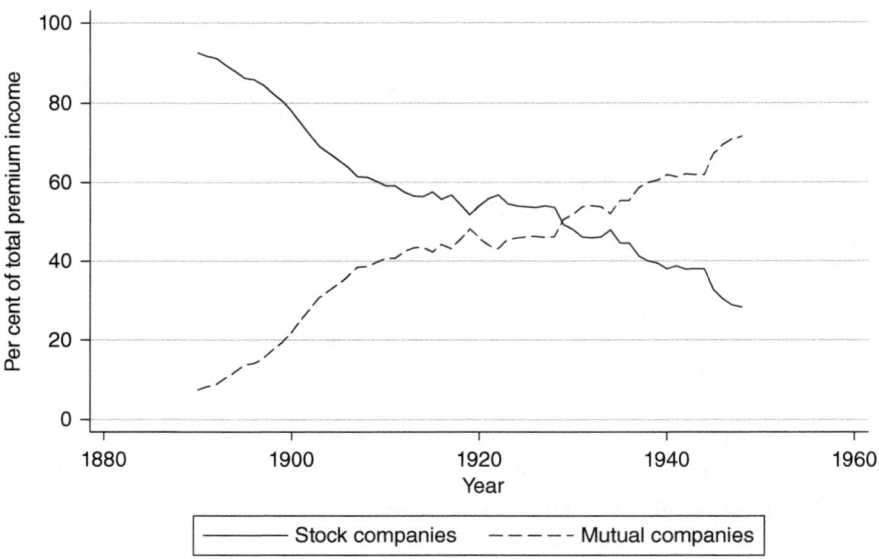

Figure 11.1. Organizational structure of the Swedish life insurance market, 1890–1948

Sources: Calculations are based on *Försäkringsväsendet i riket 1890–1912*; *Enskilda försäkringsanstalter 1912–1950*.

If the *informational hypothesis* is to explain the stock company first-mover phenomenon in Swedish life insurance markets, the latter are expected to be characterized by low-information asymmetry problems. A priori pricing would be fairly easy. The hypothesis, however, is not fully convincing when the historical reality of mid nineteenth-century Sweden is considered. To start with, the Swedish joint-stock first movers were established in a period when mortality was high and actuarial techniques were poorly developed. The composite companies, for instance, used British mortality tables. The non-life business also suffered from high risks and undeveloped statistical tools making large reserves and reinsurance a necessity. Due to investments in water and sewage systems, both fire frequency and mortality rates eventually declined from the mid-nineteenth century. Clean water prevented both epidemics and facilitated fire control. In Stockholm, where the *Skandia* was based, the construction of water and sewage systems was initiated in 1861. Insurance companies were active in promoting the installation of water and sewage systems in the city of Norrköping and Linköping. Proactive measures by life insurance companies to prevent tuberculosis also led to investments in sanatoriums.[7]

[7] *Försäkringsföreningens tidskrift* 1912, 71, 1919, 143.

Theoretically speaking, the motivation for such lobbying must have been to facilitate risk assessment and reduce problems of a priori pricing. According to the *informational hypothesis* this would have further reduced the competitive advantage of mutual organizations. It also exemplifies how insurance companies can be involved in a feedback loop process with its business environment. As the business landscape changes due to the actions of insurance companies, the risk environment also changes, which affects the relative competitiveness of organizational forms. In the case of the late nineteenth century, and drawing from the *informational hypothesis,* stock companies should have benefited over mutual organizations. Instead, what we see from the stylized facts in Figures 11.1 and 11.2 is that mutual organizations increased their market share during a period when mortality risk was reduced. Moreover, the mutual companies were not small organizations with club-like characteristics. Stylized facts presented in Table 11.4 below reveal little difference in size between stock and mutual companies.

A competing theoretical argument is that mutual organizations are best suited for lines of business such as life insurance, where long-term commitment and trust are important. If this hypothesis is to explain the rise of mutual organizations, it must be shown that mutual companies were more successful in creating bonds of loyalty and trust. The argument could find support in the advertisement of mutuals as non-profit organizations.[8]

The so-called 'managerial discretion' hypothesis claims that mutual organizations compete best in lines requiring less managerial discretion in risk selection and other choice decisions where the need for individualized underwriting is low, and/or where long time horizons are involved. If the opportunity for managerial intervention is limited, this will also eliminate potential owner-policyholder conflicts. Since this conflict dimension is not present in a mutual company, this will result in lower agency costs which give mutual forms a comparative advantage over stock companies.[9]

The *managerial discretion* hypothesis may be consistent with the stylized fact of declining mortality rates, especially in the wake of sanitary measures after 1860. As a priori pricing becomes less difficult, the scope for managerial discretion is also reduced. And when life expectancy increases, the time horizon of contracts will also be extended. Both these trends reduce managerial discretion. This means that the high agency costs in the first mover stock company are falling. At some level of falling mortality, mutual organizations start to appear. How the emergence of mutual organizations depends on falling agency costs is not fully clear. The theory says more about in what market segment one can expect one form to hold a larger share than the other.

[8] Hägg 1998.   [9] Mayers and Smith 1981.

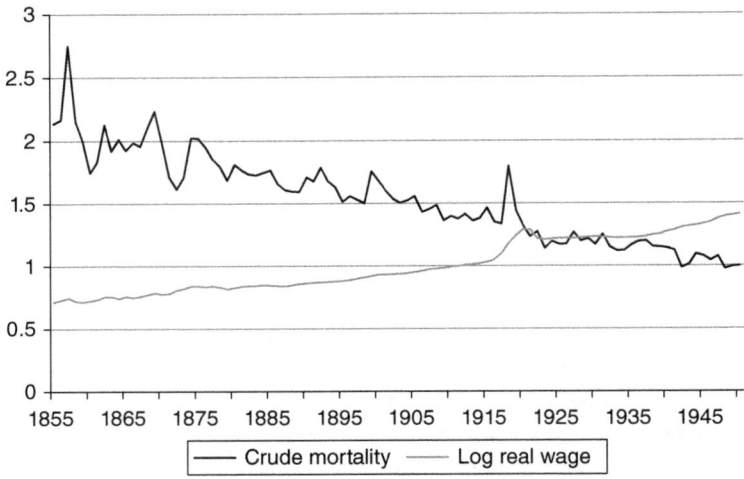

Figure 11.2. Crude mortality rate (deaths per 100 inhabitants) and log real male wage for blue-collar workers (1910–12 = 1) in Sweden, 1855 to 1950

Source: Historisk Statistik för Sverige 1999; Edvinsson et al. 2010.

One explanation could be that mortality is inversely correlated with income, but only when income levels are low.[10] By the turn of the century male real wages were on average 2.6 times higher than in 1855. The general development is shown in Figure 11.2. Once the majority of the population had reached the income level where the income-mortality relationship disappeared, it became possible to insure the mass of the population.

Andersson, Eriksson, and Lindmark have argued that income growth was a key determinant for the rise of household life insurance savings.[11] The diffusion of life insurance towards working-class households also meant that income growth had a larger impact during the late nineteenth and early twentieth centuries compared to the mid-nineteenth century. The expansion of insurance among lower income groups also instigated a change in the supply of policies. As shown in Figure 11.3, the real average policy size declined substantially from the late nineteenth century.

The transition of the Swedish life insurance market—from the few to the many—illustrates the growing ambition to supply life insurance products forthe less well off. Traditional ordinary life insurance companies, however, were slow to adapt to the changing business environment. Mutual industrial life insurance companies, which appeared in the late nineteenth century, supplied smaller policies that met the growing demand from the emerging wage-labour class. In Table 11.1, the differences in policy size between the two

---

[10] Dowd et al. 2011.   [11] Andersson et al. 2010.

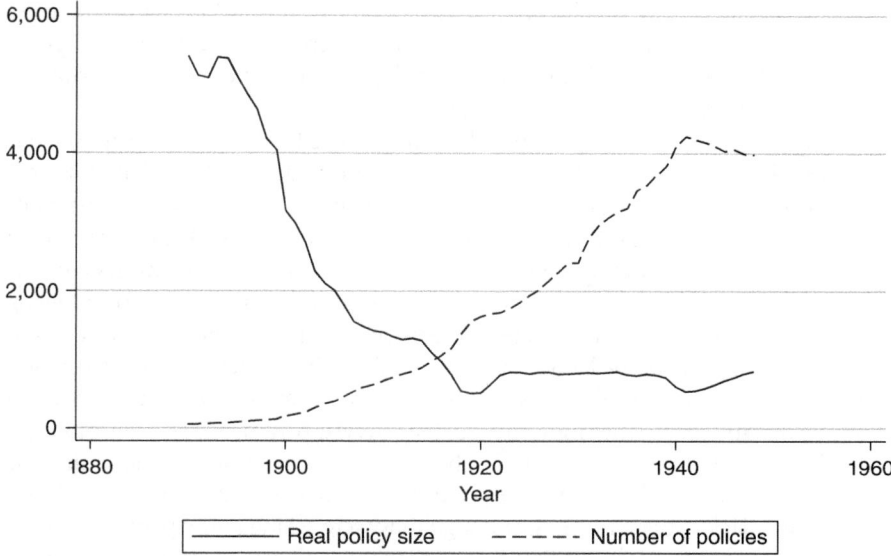

Figure 11.3. Real average policy size (SEK in 1890 prices) and number of policies in thousands in the Swedish life insurance market, 1890 to 1950

Notes: Calculations based on; *Försäkringsväsendet i riket 1890–1912; Enskilda försäkringsanstalter 1912–1950.*

Table 11.1. Real policy size in SEK (1890 prices) and number of policies, Swedish life insurance, 1890–1948

	Real policy size				Number of policyholders			
	1890	1910	1930	1948	1890	1910	1930	1948
	Panel A Stock companies							
mean	5,766	2,632	2,092	1,476	6,222	32,626	92,132	157,270
median	5,576	3,184	2,243	1,572	7,736	23,004	66,676	88,588
max	7,539	3,708	3,011	2,060	11,886	89,791	279,906	474,269
min	4,877	478	641	554	468	6,609	18,217	40,133
st. dev.	864	1,247	890	565	4,246	28,136	86,720	154,346
	Panel B Mutual companies							
mean	3,274	1,354	978	1,045	2,870	35,369	135,729	239,685
median	3,385	1,346	865	802	1,869	16,558	79,932	172,202
max	4,928	2,448	1,871	2,577	5,107	220,185	666,386	830,280
min	1,509	349	321	411	1,635	5,011	4,033	7,487
st. dev.	1,712	700	515	697	1,941	59,787	177,532	229,194

Source: Calculations based on *Försäkringsväsendet i riket 1890–1912; Enskilda försäkringsanstalter 1912–1950.*

organizational forms are shown. It is clear that the mutual companies focused on smaller premiums, while stock companies were oriented towards higher-income classes. Thus, life insurance developed into what became known in Sweden as small and large life insurance.

Trygg and *Folket* (later renamed *Folksam*) and later *Sveriges Privatanställdas Pensionskassa* (hereafter *SPP*) were among the most successful in selling low-cost life insurance policies and eventually grew to join the largest Swedish insurance companies. Whether this was due to their mutual form or some other organizational characteristic remains an open question. Workplace representatives (*arbetsplatsombud*) and a local organization created the organizational framework allowing policyholder influence. These developments occurred from the 1890s in tandem with the formation of the labour unions. Certainly, the mutual form of association appealed to workers and also drew on a rural organizational tradition. It is also worth noting that the cooperative movement of the interwar period, of which *Folksam* was a part, was a reaction to cartelization. The step to collective insurance, as in the case of *SPP* and later *Folksam* and *Länsförsäkringar* (*LF*), was therefore short. Stock companies lacked these features, although they were selling participating policies.

It could, however, be hypothesized that mutual organizations, as relative latecomers, adapted more efficiently to the changing business environment. Newly established life insurance companies will initially have a comparatively low claims-to-premiums ratio. While stock companies benefited from their ability to mobilize capital in the risky environment of the period 1850 to 1880, mutual solutions became competitive as capital requirements dwindled due to falling mortality and rising wages at the time of industrialization and after. Accordingly, mutual companies could more efficiently utilize the benefits of falling mortality rates, rising wages, and lower capital requirements, while the early stock companies were hampered both by their higher capital costs and their orientation towards high-income segments of the population.

The stylized facts suggest that the timing of entry and the business strategies of mutual companies were well adapted to the changing business environment. Such advantages, rather than the informational and governance advantages emphasized by traditional agency explanations of organizational forms, delivered growth and an expanding market share for Swedish life mutuals at the expense of their stock rivals.

REDUCED NEED FOR EXTERNAL CAPITAL AND ORGANIZATIONAL CONVERGENCE

The composite (life and fire) joint-stock insurance companies entered a market with a less well-known risk distribution. The uncertainties and difficulties of underwriting the lesser-known risk distribution placed a high

Table 11.2. Owner capital as a proportion of total liabilities (per cent) in Swedish stock companies

	Non-composite companies			Composite companies		
	Age = 1	*Age = 5*	*Age = 10*	*Age = 1*	*Age = 5*	*Age = 10*
Mean	83	62	25	95	83	70
Median	85	55	30	97	82	63
Max	96	99	38	99	95	90
Min	58	45	3	88	73	59

Note: Owner capital is the sum of stock capital and guarantee capital.
Source: *Försäkringsväsendet i riket* 1890–1912; *Enskilda försäkringsanstalter* 1912–50.

demand on capital. *Skandia*, therefore, was heavily capitalized, having a substantial share of equity capital long after entering the market. Insurance practices were also in other regards less developed. The lack of domestic reinsurance and the high cost of foreign reinsurance may also explain the heavy capitalization.

To some extent the composite form may have stabilized short-term fluctuations in claims experience at the company level as the shorter-term fluctuations in fire insurance could be balanced by the longer-term fluctuations in life insurance. Such methods of risk portfolio management, however, were abandoned with the 1903 Insurance Act, which prohibited new companies from writing both fire and life insurance, though the existing composite companies (Skandia, Svea, and Skåne) were permitted to continue to combine life and fire until the Insurance Act of 1948.[12] Although the risk management strategy of the composites may have been effective in the mid-nineteenth century, the demand for owner capital was high. As Table 11.2 shows, the owner capital share of total liabilities was on average 95 per cent in the first year, 83 per cent after five years, and 70 per cent after ten years. The next generation of stock companies (non-composite companies) used significantly less owner capital to start up their businesses.

As the prevalence of contagious infectious disease decreased, incomes rose, and mortality declined further, it was realized that life insurance companies could be founded with much less initial capital than previously. After all, in the mutual company, the life insurance savers provide the funds. Before that happened, a new type of stock company emerged in the *Thule* and later the *Victoria*. The statutes of both companies placed an absolute limit on their dividends. In Thule, the dividend share of owner capital fluctuated between 1.2 and 2.4 per cent while the policyholder's bonus as a share of reserves fluctuated between 1.1 and 1.9 per cent during the period 1873 and 1898.[13] This limitation of the dividend and the bonus to policyholders can be interpreted as an adjustment to mutual business practices.

[12] Larsson 1991; Larsson et al. 2005.   [13] Thule 1900.

Table 11.3. Guarantee capital share of total liabilities (per cent) in Swedish mutual companies

	Age = 1	Age = 5	Age = 10	Age = 1 if year <1903	Age = 1 if year >1903
Mean	35	10	6	38	32
Median	33	12	3	36	23
Max	72	31	26	72	71
Min	0	0	0	0	0

Note: Owner capital is the sum of stock capital and guarantee capital.
Source: *Försäkringsväsendet i riket 1890–1912; Enskilda försäkringsanstalter 1912–1950.*

Although the earliest mutual organizational forms were based on club-like characteristics (such as the Allmänna Änke-och Pupillkassan and Assurans-förening 401), the first mutual companies were of a similar size as the joint-stock companies.[14] To meet the regulatory requirements of entering the market, financial strength was a key issue. To overcome the potential problem of weak solidity, most mutuals used guarantee capital, namely a guarantee to cover claimant losses in the case of bankruptcy.[15] The guarantee capital could be obtained from different sources such as foundations, companies, or private individuals. The most common arrangement seems to have been for a stock holding company (*förlagsaktiebolag*) to provide the guarantees. The average mutual company had a 35 per cent share of guarantee capital in the first year. Soon after entry into the market, the guarantee share decreased as reserves started to accumulate. Table 11.3 shows that after ten years of business the average guarantee capital share fell to only 6 per cent.

The issue of solidity was an intensively debated issue in the life insurance industry in the late nineteenth century. The leading stock companies claimed that many of the mutual companies were technically insolvent. To mobilize against the mutuals, one strategy was to enforce an insurance regulation that imposed minimum standards on the solidity of companies. Following such an initiative, one might expect that the guarantee capital would have increased after the passing of the Insurance Act of 1903. From Table 11.2, however, it is hard to find evidence for a legislative effect. Mutual companies founded before 1903 had on average a guarantee share equal to 38 per cent, while mutuals that commenced after 1903 had a lower share guarantee capital on average.

The Insurance Act of 1903 seems not to have changed the gap in the financial structure between mutual and stock insurers. Stock companies re-tained a higher share of owner capital and thereby faced a potentially higher capital cost for running the business. To examine how such differences, along with other firm-specific factors, affected the development of the insurance market, the following section provides an analysis of growth performance.

---

[14] Bergander 1967.   [15] Bergander 1967.

ANALYSIS OF GROWTH PERFORMANCE

In this section the growth performance by organizational form is examined. The analysis is based on a panel data design where all domestic mutual and stock companies are included for the period 1890 to 1948. The panel is unbalanced (not all firms existed during all years) and includes 1,098 observations. To account for the growth pattern a set of independent and explanatory variables are used.

Three variables are used as growth measures: premium growth, amount insured, and number of policies insured. The reason for having three measures is to check for potential bias in a single measure and to indicate differences in growth patterns between the organizational forms. The growth rate is measured in real terms. Premiums and amount insured are deflated by a consumer price index and the number of policies is already a volume measure. All three growth measures are calculated as the annual absolute growth weighted by company size.[16] This calculation method is one way of overcoming the size bias inherent in measuring firm growth rates.

Drawing from the theoretical literature, it may be argued that growth rates are a purely stochastic process. One of the best-known propositions is Gibrat's proposition that the proportionate organic (or internal) growth rates of firms are independent of their size.[17] Gibrat's law, however, is not fully conclusive. Later research on financial markets has shown that size matters. Following Cummins, size is expected to be positively correlated with growth if economies of scale are present. A negative correlation is also plausible, reflecting late-comer advantages, meaning that initially small companies enter the fastest growing market segments.[18]

Growth performance may also be related to age. Following Choi, age is expected to be negatively correlated with growth as young firms grow faster than older firms.[19] This also relates to the stylized facts presented previously showing a number of first-mover disadvantages as the market conditions changed during the nineteenth century.

From the stylized facts on policy structure and growth, we also expect that average policy size will be negatively correlated with growth. This is because lower average premiums reflect the fact that a company is engaged in the growing wage-earning working-class segment of the market. Industrial life insurance companies experienced high growth rates, which may indicate that small premiums promote growth.

Previous studies have shown that reinsurance increased the capacity to underwrite new business in fire insurance.[20] If a similar mechanism applies in life insurance, one would expect that companies that ceded a large

---

[16] See Ahmad and Petersen 2007.   [17] Gibrat 1931.
[18] Cummins et al. 1999.   [19] Choi 2010.   [20] Kader et al. 2010.

Table 11.4. Descriptive statistics of independent and explanatory variables

Variable name	Variable description	Mean value		t-test
		Mutual	Stock	Sig.
Premium growth	Growth* in real premium income (1890 prices)	0.022	0.009	**
Amount growth	Growth* in real amount insured (1890 prices)	0.021	0.010	**
Policy growth	Growth* in number of policies insured	0.023	0.015	**
Age	Age of company	19.04	40.66	**
Company size	Size of company by number of policies insured	10.37	10.35	
Policy size	Real policy size (1890 prices) in log scale	6,794	7,645	**
Reinsurance	Share of premiums ceded to reinsurer	0.087	0.113	**
Claims ratio	Claims expenditure in relation to sum insured	0.011	0.019	**
Leverage	Premium income in relation to assets	0.208	0.107	**
Real wage	Real wage of industrial workers (1910–12 prices)	7,405	7,036	
Mortality	Crude mortality rate (death/population)	0.013	0.013	

Note: Growth * is calculated according to the US-firm growth index (t1−t0)/(t1+t0)/2. The level of significance (sig) is denoted ** at the 1 per cent level and * at the 5 per cent level.
Sources: Försäkringsväsendet i riket 1890–1912; Enskilda försäkringsanstalter 1912–50.

proportion of their business to reinsurance expanded more rapidly than companies that reinsured less.

Table 11.4 provides descriptive statistics of growth variables by organizational form. All three growth measures (premiums, amount insured, and growth in the number of policies) are significantly higher for mutual than for stock companies. Mutual companies were on average younger than stock companies and issued smaller policies. Stock companies reinsured more and had significantly higher claims ratios (expenditure on claims as a proportion of sums insured). Stock companies also had significantly higher leverage positions (premiums to total assets), indicating that those companies were more highly capitalized.

Correlation analysis also provides support for difference across organizational forms. Table 11.5 shows that stock companies had lower growth rates across all growth measures. The highest correlation is for policy numbers (−0.17) and the lowest for the amount insured (−0.13), while premium growth lies in between (−0.15). The growth figures are not directly correlated to policy size or reinsurance. In the former case, an indirect relation is possible due to the significant and positive correlation between policy size and the stock company dummy. The same also holds for reinsurance, since it is positively correlated with the stock form of organization. Across all growth measures a

Table 11.5. Correlation matrix of growth measures and explanatory variables

Variables	[1]	[2]	[3]	[4]	[5]	[6]	[7]	[8]	[9]	[10]	[11]	[12]
[1] Premium growth	1											
[2] Amount growth	0.64*	1										
[3] Policy growth	0.38*	0.56*	1									
[4] Stock company	-0.15*	-0.17*	-0.13*	1								
[5] Age	-0.27*	-0.37*	-0.4*	0.51*	1							
[6] Company size	-0.18*	-0.26*	-0.32*	-0.01	0.54*	1						
[7] Policy size	-0.03*	-0.01	0.04*	0.5*	0.05*	-0.45*	1					
[8] Reinsurance	0.02	0.02	0.02	0.28*	-0.11*	0.07*	-012*	1				
[9] Claims ratio	-0.32*	-0.42*	-0.42*	0.44*	0.79*	0.44*	0.02	-0.14*	1			
[10] Leverage	0.43*	0.46*	0.47*	-0.34*	-0.55*	-0.34*	-0.16*	0.1*	-0.59*	1		
[11] Real wage	-0.02	-0.04*	-0.29*	-0.07*	0.53*	0.61*	-0.47*	-0.06*	0.5*	-0.32*	1	
[12] Mortality	-0.01	0.05*	0.29*	0.08*	-0.49*	-0.59*	0.49*	0.03*	-0.47*	0.32*	-0.9*	1

Sources: Försäkringsväsendet i riket 1890–1912; Enskilda försäkringsanstalter 1912–50.

negative relation to company size can be established. Claims ratios and growth are also negatively associated. In turn, the three growth measures are positively and significantly correlated with leverage. The two macro variables are not directly related to growth rates, but may have had an impact on growth due to the close relation with the other explanatory variables.

As most of the relations between the explanatory variables are significant at the 5 per cent level, a variance inflation test (VIF) is applied to control for multicollinearity. The computing of the VIF showed a test statistic of 6.88 for mortality and 6.46 for real wage (correlation coefficient equal to -0.9). After removing mortality, the VIF dropped to 2.5, which is below the commonly recognized threshold.[21]

In the multivariate analysis we have used separate models for the growth variables and measures to make sensitivity comparison possible. In order to perform robust tests, a number of specification tests were applied in order to find the most preferable multivariate model. The Breusch and Pagan Lagrangian multiplier test for random effects shows that a panel data regression is more appropriate than pooled OLS. The Hausman test shows that fixed effect is more efficient than a random effect. The Wooldridge test for autocorrelation in panel data shows no autocorrelation. A Modified Wald test shows the presence of heteroskedasticity. To control for heteroskedasticity, robust standard errors are applied.

As the fixed-effect model imposes time-independent effects, time-invariant variables (organizational form) are omitted. To overcome this omission, the firm/company fixed-effect component is retrieved and compared for each organizational form (mean value of firm fixed effect for stock and mutual companies). As only a t-test is available to test the difference in the fixed effect between organizational forms, a random effect model was also applied in order to explicitly test for the impact of organizational form. Both the random and the fixed-effect models were first run in a base line setting where the impact of organizational form and macrovariables on firm growth was tested exclusively. In a second step, firm-specific variables (age, company size, policy size, reinsurance, claims experience, leverage) were included in order to test how the differences in firm characteristics across organizational form (see Table 11.4) affect growth performance. By differentiating the analysis in these two steps, the impact of differences in key components associated with organizational form may be more fully examined.

Table 11.6 reports the results of the multivariate analysis. In the baseline model, mutual companies had a positive association with growth performance, while stock companies had a negative association. The average fixed effect of mutual companies is positive (0.005) and negative for stock companies (-0.006 to -0.007). A t-test of difference in group means (stock versus mutual) shows

---

[21] Kennedy 2003.

Table 11.6. Multivariate analysis of real growth by premium, policies, and amount insured

Panel A Fixed-effect model

	Baseline model	Firm-effect model	Baseline model	Firm-effect model	Baseline model	Firm-effect model
	Premium growth		Amount growth		Policy growth	
Mutual (M) fe	0.005 *na*	−0.025 *na*	0.004 *na*	−0.023 *na*	0.004 *na*	−0.0003 *na*
Stock (S) fe	−0.007 *na*	0.037 *na*	−0.007 *na*	0.033 *na*	−0.006 *na*	0.0005 *na*
M_fe (-) S_fe	0.012 ***	−0.062 ***	0.012 ***	−0.057 ***	0.010 ***	−0.0008
Age		−0.002 **		−0.002 **		0.000
Company size		−0.015 **		−0.015 **		−0.011 **
Policy size		−0.010 **		−0.007 **		−0.010 **
Reinsurance		−0.031 **		−0.005		−0.039 **
Claims ratio		−0.730 **		−0.957 **		−0.574 **
Leverage		0.079 **		0.057 **		0.047 **
Real wage	0.003 ***	0.012 **	0.000	0.015 **		0.000
Constant	0.066 ***	0.264 **	−0.015 **	0.185 **		0.120 **
R-square						
Within	0.010	0.312	0.020	0.419	0.15	0.279
Between	0.080	0.375	0.040	0.538	0.02	0.143
Overall	0.020	0.164	0.010	0.231	0.09	0.183

Panel B Random-effect model

	Baseline model	Firm-effect model	Baseline model	Firm-effect model	Baseline model	Firm-effect model
	Premium growth		Amount growth		Policy growth	
Stock company	−0.015 **	0.021 **	−0.0005	0.035 **	−0.007	0.005
Age		−0.001 **		−0.001 **		0.000
Company size		−0.007 **		−0.009 **		−0.007 **
Policy size		0.005		0.003		−0.006 **
Reinsurance		−0.023 *		−0.013		−0.030 **
Claims ratio		−0.831 **		−1.097 **		−0.539 **
Leverage		0.108 **		0.076 **		0.057 **
Real wage	0.003 **	0.006 **	0.000	0.010 **	0.003 **	0.000
Constant	0.069 **	0.097 **	−0.008 **	0.087 **	0.009	0.071 **
R-square						
Within	0.010	0.286	0.019	0.398		0.275
Between	0.047	0.456	0.043	0.699		0.195
Overall	0.024	0.254	0.004	0.307		0.245

Note: ** denotes significance at the 1 per cent level, * denotes significance at the 5 per cent level.
Sources: Försäkringsväsendet i riket 1890–1912; Enskilda försäkringsanstalter 1912–1950.

that the differences in the fixed effect are significant at the 1 per cent level for all baseline models. The random-effect models also show a negative but less significant impact of stock companies on growth performance.

To control for the significant differences in company characteristics reported across organizational form in Table 11.4, the firm-effect model was applied. The firm-effect model takes into account the fact that stock companies were older, reinsured more, supplied larger policies, experienced higher claims, and were less leveraged compared to mutual companies. When running the firm-effect model, it becomes clear that most of the key stock characteristics are negatively associated with growth. The regression results show that age, policy size, reinsurance, and claims experiences had a negative association with growth, while leverage had a positive association.

Stock companies had a disadvantage in the timing of the emerging mass market. The aged stock companies were slow to adapt to the rapidly growing segment of smaller life insurance policies as indicated by the negative associations between age and policy size and growth performance. Mutual companies were more successful in expanding their business towards the industrial life mass market by supplying smaller policies, using a more extensive sales network and workplace representation, and by establishing a close relationship with the labour unions. By selecting such a business strategy, Swedish mutuals seem to have benefited more (than stock companies) from the growth in real wages and the decline in mortality. Another major disadvantage was the financial structure. Stock companies were tied up with more reinsurance and reserves; precautionary measures that became less preferable when mortality declined rapidly from the late nineteenth century through to the mid-twentieth century.

After controlling for the disadvantages in targeting the growing mass market and in their financial structure, the regression analysis shows that stock companies inherited some positive growth components. Such a positive effect may have been associated with corporate governance structures, underwriting techniques or other characteristics bound to the stock form of organization. To uncover the competitive advantages of such characteristics, however, further research is needed.

CONCLUSIONS

This chapter has examined mechanisms governing the organizational structure of the Swedish life insurance market during the period 1890 to 1948. From a small share of the market in the beginning, mutual companies expanded their business and controlled 70 per cent of the market at the end of the period. Taking a point of departure from the theoretical literature on the field, this study cannot find evidence to support the argument that mutual companies were more successful than stock companies in controlling for informational asymmetries. None of the mutuals were run according to 'club-like' cooperative structures or other arrangements for controlling for moral hazard and adverse selection. Many mutual companies did not use a medical examination, while stock companies did. An apparent advantage with the mutual organization form at the time was the general movement towards cooperative contracts and arrangements in the labour market (unions, health and sickness insurance), in consumers associations and in non-governmental organizations. Mutuals could indirectly appeal to this movement through marketing, but also directly by working together with unions. By associating with such values, mutual companies could gain trust for the long-term commitment inherent in life insurance. The establishment of mutual companies was facilitated by the low capital requirements needed to start up a life insurance business. By using only a small share of guarantee capital in the balance sheet, the barriers of entry became low. During the two decades following the first entry of a mutual company, eighteen mutual companies were established while only three stock companies were established. By the 1920s mutuals were twice as numerous as stock companies.

The mutual companies expanded their business more rapidly than stock insurers. Their growth rate was higher on average during the period 1890 to 1948. When analysing the mechanism behind the high growth figures it seems clear that the timing and business strategies of the mutual organizations provided them with an advantage compared to the stock companies. Stock companies had a disadvantage in the timing of the emerging mass market as their business model was rooted in the ordinary life insurance business patronized by high-income segments. The traditional stock companies adapted slowly, while mutual companies offered small life insurance policies for the growing wage-earning working class in need of financial protection for old age and dependence. The organizational capabilities of large sales networks and door-to-door sales further delivered growth in the expanding life insurance market. The competitive advantages of mutuals were not rooted in informational or governance advantages, but rather in the timing and the business strategy that were well adapted to the business environment in Sweden during the period from the late nineteenth century to the mid-twentieth century.

Part IV

Demutualization

12

An Attempt by a Black Mutual Life
Insurance Company to Demutualize

The Case of Golden State Mutual of Los Angeles

Natsuki Kinoshita

This chapter explores the decision-making process undertaken by a racially constituted mutual life insurance company in the United States with the intent to demutualize. It examines, through the analysis of several factors that influenced its thinking, the experience of one black mutual life insurance company—the Golden State Mutual Life Insurance Company (GSM). GSM was selected for this case study because the company was the largest black life insurer, and the only black mutual insurer in the American West to have made the attempt to demutualize.

Life insurance companies founded specifically by blacks for black communities emerged in the United States in the 1890s. Although one of the roots of life insurance companies owned and run by a racial group came from insurance services provided by black fraternal associations that were based on a spirit of mutual aid, both mutual and stock insurers, among black life insurance companies, were evolved from fraternal associations and chronologically, in fact, black stock insurers preceded black mutual insurers. Black stock insurers were founded in the southern states from the 1890s to the first decade of the twentieth century and by the 1920s some of them had spread throughout the country. Indeed, from the 1920s to the 1940s, black mutual insurers (apart from the North Carolina Mutual Life Insurance Company, founded in Durham, North Carolina in 1899) were established almost exclusively outside the South. GSM, like other black mutuals, was a company founded by migrant black communities that settled in urban areas of the American North and the West of the early twentieth century. In contrast to the former black communities of the South, the newly emerging black communities in the North and the West were characterized by their strong consciousness of being 'new blacks'.[1]

A black community in Los Angeles, California, founded GSM in 1925 and during the years before the Second World War the company expanded its business to black communities scattered throughout the state. In the late 1930s and the early 1940s, the company opened branch offices in Texas and Illinois, but outside California the amount of business remained small. Since, throughout its history, the business in California has accounted for about 90 per cent of its total activity, GSM can be described as a life insurance company for California blacks. After the remarkable business development during wartime fed by massive black migration into California from the southern states, the company underwent a transformation from a small life insurance company for a local community with a small black population to a larger company for the black ghetto with a huge black population. As the economic and social situation of California blacks gradually worsened in the 1950s, GSM's business began to stagnate and, though the company struggled to reorganize and introduced new systems in management, agency operation, and marketing, their attempts resulted in failure. By the 1960s, the economic and social situation for blacks had become so aggravated that riots broke out in many black communities across the country consecutively. In 1965, the Los Angeles black community experienced one of the worst of these riots. Known as the '1965 Watts Riots', they critically damaged GSM as a business and led to despair about its future. After the turmoil, the Los Angeles black community experienced increasing unemployment and deepening poverty, and the previous sense of community completely broke down.[2]

In 1968, three years after the riots, GSM began to work out a plan to demutualize.[3] At that time, few companies in the US insurance industry had converted from mutual to stock companies, and it was not until the 1990s that the largest life insurance companies, such as the Prudential, Metlife, and John Hancock, undertook to demutualize.[4] Since GSM was not riding any wave of demutualization, its attempt to demutualize in 1968 was a rare case, and a question therefore arises, which this chapter seeks to answer: why did GSM make an attempt to change its corporate form in the late 1960s? This chapter also intends to examine what the plan to demutualize by a black mutual life insurance company meant in the historical context of the changing racial situation in post-war America, and why in the end it had to be aborted.

---

[1] Flamming 2005, 49–50; Baldwin 2007.   [2] Kinoshita 2010a, chapters 2, 3, and 4.
[3] *Golden State Mutual Life Insurance Co. Records* (hereafter *GSMR*), Box 13, Folder 1.
[4] Keneley and Verhoef 2011, 137.

PRIOR STUDIES: LIFE INSURANCE BUSINESS
HISTORY OF THE UNITED STATES

In prior studies of the history of the US life insurance business, its corporate form has not been a major topic; although several studies do refer to the corporate forms of the life insurance companies, most do so only in part and in passing. In the field of business history, Keller examines the rise from the late nineteenth to the early twentieth centuries of big business in the US life insurance industry, concentrating on the so-called 'Big Five'. Through a wide range of perspectives, Keller explains the process by which, up to the beginning of the twentieth century, life insurance companies consolidated their power.[5] Although his study covers the history of the largest companies, Keller does not place any emphasis on the corporate forms of big business. Stalson focuses on historical changes of marketing techniques in the US life insurance industry since the beginnings of the insurance business, and yet though he mentions a different marketing approach through the adoption of corporate forms, especially amongst mutual life insurance companies, he does not develop this theme.[6] Zelizer analyses US life insurance business history from the perspective of religious and cultural values, but does not discuss corporate forms.[7]

Recent studies of life insurance history have been more interested in the corporate forms of companies. A study of the Guardian Life Insurance Company of America by Wright and Smith discusses how corporate forms affect the business performance of companies in several industries. Focusing on the issue of trust between clients and companies, they present various arguments about corporate forms and explain the advantages of the Guardian Life's choice to remain a mutual.[8] More recently, Murphy has described how mutual life insurance companies developed in the US during the 1840s and ended up surpassing stock companies. Mutual companies successfully convinced emerging middle-class Americans of the rationality and profitability of buying life insurance policies.[9]

Several studies have dealt with black life insurance companies. Weare and Gloster each have examined the history of the North Carolina Mutual (NCM), the largest black life insurance company, but their studies simply describe the development of the NCM as a business up to the latter half of the twentieth century.[10] Henderson examined the history of the Atlanta Life Insurance Company, the second largest black life insurance company, and she described in detail how, in the historical context of Georgia at the beginning of the twentieth century, the Atlanta Life settled on its corporate form.[11] As well as

---

[5] Keller 1963.   [6] Stalson 1942.   [7] Zelizer 1983.
[8] Wright and Smith 2004.   [9] Murphy 2010.
[10] Weare 1973; Gloster 1976.   [11] Henderson 1990.

these accounts of companies based in the southern states, two studies focus on companies located in Chicago: Puth examines the Supreme Liberty Life Insurance Company and Weems examines the Chicago Metropolitan Assurance Company.[12] The most recent study of the black life insurers outside the South concerns the Golden State Mutual by Kinoshita.[13] Although most of these studies look at larger companies in both non-black and black life insurance, few of them analyse the companies through the perspective of corporate form, for though some studies explain why each company has chosen its own type of corporate form, they do not elaborate this in detail. Yet each type of corporate form makes a difference to the company's business strategy and to its relationship with the local community, as the next section goes on to explain.

THE CHARACTERISTICS OF BLACK LIFE INSURANCE COMPANIES BY CORPORATE FORM

The location of black communities in the US ensured their different characteristics, and this determined the organizational forms of black life insurance companies. Many of the black stock insurers did business in the South, where the great majority of the black populations worked in the agricultural sector and were relatively poor. In each community, the main stockholders were a small number of upper-class blacks. Alonzo F. Herndon, the largest stockholder in Atlanta Life, acquired most of the stock of the company when it converted to a business corporation from a fraternal society led by church elders. Herndon was a famous barber, one of the most successful and richest businessmen in black business history.[14]

So while in the South the stock insurance companies were in the hands of a very small number of the black upper class, by contrast, black mutual insurers founded their businesses in communities where the proportion of black middle and lower-middle classes was on a more equal footing. Although examples of black mutual insurers in black communities can be found as far south as the NCM, they developed largely elsewhere: in Chicago, New York, and Los Angeles.[15]

A comparison of the financial statements of black stock and mutual insurers reveals the difference in their business structures and strategies. Reflecting the economic status of their policyowners, black stock insurers mainly sold industrial life insurance policies (see Table 12.3 below). In addition, the

---

[12] Puth 1976; Weems 1996.   [13] Kinoshita 2010b, 2010a.
[14] Henderson 1990, 17–19; Bristol 2004.   [15] Stuart 1969.

death rate of blacks in the stock insurers' sales territories was higher than in communities serviced by black mutual insurers, while the average premiums, the lapse rate, and the expense rate of the black stock insurers were all in excess of such rates amongst black mutual insurers.[16]

While black stock insurers were doing their business within the higher-risk segment of the black population of the United States, black mutual insurers enjoyed a stable position based on black middle-class and lower-middle-class communities that could afford to buy more ordinary life insurance policies and keep their contracts longer. Dedicated social and political activities by black mutual insurers on behalf of their communities bonded the communities and the companies together tightly. Their community-conscious activities, such as encouraging white-collar job creation for young blacks and financing mortgage loans for black families, made their relationships trustworthy and reliable.[17]

THE CASE OF THE GOLDEN STATE MUTUAL

The Formation and the Development of the Golden State Mutual

When, in 1925, the Golden State Mutual Life Insurance Company, now the largest black life insurance company in the American West, was established in Los Angeles, California, it began life as a small assessment mutual life insurance company, the smallest-scale life insurance organization authorized by the Insurance Code of the State of California.[18]

Since the black population in California grew only modestly up to the outbreak of World War Two, GSM devoted itself to local markets. The home office was located in Los Angeles, which had the largest black population in the state. They had several district offices in other Californian conurbations with black populations.[19] In the early years, the company sold life and accident and health insurance policies not only to blacks but also to Mexicans.[20]

As war industry production increased, so the black population of California grew from 124,306 in 1939 to 463,172 in 1950.[21] This changed the scale of

---

[16] Data from *Best's Life Insurance Reports* (annual). Alfred M. Best Company.

[17] Weare 1973, 77–83, 59–160; Weems 1996, 56–70.

[18] GSMR, Box 1, Folder 3, 'A Brief History of the Foundation, History and Objectives of the Now "Golden State Mutual Life Insurance Company"', 4.

[19] GSMR, Box 1, Folder 8, Executive Committee Book, 1926–30; Box 2, Folder 3, Minutes, 1925; Box 3, Folder 4, Executive Committee Book, 1928–30.

[20] GSMR, Box 3, Folder 4, Executive Committee Book, 1928–30; Box 3, Folder 3, Executive Committee Book, 1931–7.

[21] De Graaf 1962, 182.

business for GSM: the company's reserves increased from about $300,000 in 1939 to nearly $4 million dollars in 1950; both the amount of life insurance in force and the number of policyowners showed tenfold increases during the same period—from $5.8 million to $58 million (life insurances in force) and from 15,000 to 150,000 policyholders.[22]

The Demutualization Planning of GSM (1968)

From March to July 1968, the company's senior officers discussed a plan to demutualize. The company records show why and how in the late 1960s GSM tried to change its corporate form.[23] This section discusses that plan.

Planning proceeded as follows. In the early phase, the company consulted the commissioner of the California Department of Insurance about the conversion plan.[24] Since they received a positive response from the commissioner, a selected number of company officers continued to discuss in detail several matters that would follow from the conversion. The company then began discussing the demutualization procedures with some experts from a law firm (Lawler, Sterling, and Kent), the Securities Exchange Commission, and a consulting actuaries office (Milliman and Robertson, Inc.). After receiving technical advice concerning legal procedures, the directors, executive officers, and other key officers held further intensive discussions.[25]

The company's demutualization plan may be summarized briefly. First, they planned to establish a holding company, named the Golden State Financial Corporation. The next step was to convert the Golden State Mutual into a stock life insurance company, the Golden State Life. The directors anticipated that the Golden State Life would be capitalized at $5 million.[26] As a final step, they designed a group of businesses to be compiled through the acquisition of existing companies and the creation of new companies. While it was agreed that after conversion the main business of the group would continue to be life and health insurance, the company planned to launch a business that would provide other financial services as well.[27]

As a legal requirement, at least two thirds of the life policyowners of GSM had to approve the plan to transform the company into a stock corporation.[28]

---

[22] *GSMR*, Box 4, Folder 8, Company Growth since 1925.

[23] *GSMR*, Box 13, Folder 1 contains all the records concerning the planning for demutualization.

[24] *GSMR*, Box 13, Folder 1, Letter from Edgar J. Johnson to Norman O. Houston, 8 March 1968.

[25] *GSMR*, Box 13, Folder 1, Letter from C. W. Ferguson to Norman O. Houston, 29 April 1968, et. fol.

[26] *GSMR*, Box 13, Folder 1, Letter from Ivan J. Houston to Norman O. Houston, 24 May 1968.

[27] *GSMR*, Box 13, Folder 1, Special Officers Meeting, 30 May 1968.

[28] *GSMR*, Box 13, Folder 1, Letter from Ivan J. Houston to Norman O. Houston, 24 May 1968.

At that time, the company held approximately 200,000 life insurance policies and 50,000 health insurance policies. In the process of a conversion, it was not necessary to take those who held health insurance policies into consideration; they would be treated as clients rather than policyowners. After the exclusion of 30,000 paid-up life insurance policies, the company calculated that 133,000 votes would be needed to approve demutualization. For this, the full cooperation of the agents was indispensable because more than 70 per cent of the life insurance policies were industrial or monthly debit ordinary life, which meant that the agents kept a record of such clients, including their names and addresses.[29]

The promotion of this new project and the public relations that it entailed were contemplated cautiously. All the participants in planning the demutualization knew that not only the company but also the policyowners and their agents had to be behind such a huge project. They were concerned that, in a conversion to a stock company, the change of ownership of such a community-based insurance company as GSM might not please everyone, especially if the policyowners thought that they would be affected adversely. For a successful implementation, they planned to emphasize that as many eligible people as possible would be able to acquire shares or benefits from stock rights. They also intended to stress that the transformation to a stock corporation would produce 'real Black Financial Power' and eventually bring benefits to the entire community.[30]

FACTORS IN THE DECISION MAKING

This section analyses the several factors that influenced GSM's decision to demutualize: these factors were market specific, community specific, political specific, and firm specific.

Market-Specific Factors

In August 1959 the *Los Angeles Tribune* published an article entitled 'Little Chance of Survival for Negro Insurance Companies Seen'. The article, written by an insurance specialist, analysed the then current conditions of the black life insurers. 'Today', it argued, 'the walls of racial separation ... are tumbling down ... The time is not far off when Negro insurance companies in order to

---

[29] GSMR, Box 13, Folder 1, Special Officers Meeting, 11 June 1968.
[30] GSMR, Box 13, Folder 1, Letter from Ivan J. Houston to Norman O. Houston, 24 May 1968; Holding Companies, 28 May 1968.

Table 12.1. Deaths per 1,000 US population, 1900–43

	1900	1910	1920	1930	1940	1943
Black	29.4	25.5	20.1	18.3	13.8	12.8
White	14.6	17.1	12.4	10.8	10.4	10.7
Other	11.9	19.4	–	–	–	–
All	15.0	17.6	–	–	10.7	10.9

Sources: US Department of Commerce, Bureau of Census, Negro Population 1790–1915. Washington: Government Printing Office 1918, 305; Negroes in the United States 1920–1932. Washington: Government Printing Office 1936, 445; Murray 1947, 71.

survive will be obliged to merge with one another or their white competitors will slowly but surely absorb most of them'.[31]

Black life insurers faced even fiercer competitive situations in the post-war life insurance business world when, in the early 1950s, non-black life insurance companies began entering the market formerly reserved for blacks. The primary reason that they did so was the remarkable improvement in the health of the black population. Table 12.1 shows how, by the early 1940s, the difference in death rates between blacks and whites had gradually narrowed. Between 1900 and 1943, the health of black people improved markedly, as deaths per 1,000 populations of blacks dropped by more than 50 per cent.

A further reason was the growing economic power of blacks after the war. The urbanization of blacks had given them the opportunities to get better-paid jobs, and this had created a growing lower-middle class in black communities that could be treated as good customers by corporate America. In the 1950s it was clear that racially oriented companies no longer secured a racially segmented market.[32]

The entry of non-black life insurance companies into the market previously open to black clients threatened black life insurance companies. The non-black companies 'head-hunted' (or 'cherry-picked') competent black agents from black life insurance companies and consequently some black life insurers lost both agents and policyowners. In 1943 only fifty-five non-black life insurance companies sold life insurance policies to blacks; by 1957 the number had jumped to 104 and the number of non-black life insurers who adopted the standard rate for blacks also increased.[33]

An increase in the number of black life insurers also spurred competition amongst themselves. In 1930, there were only fifteen legal reserve black life insurance companies, but in the post-war period the number of the legal reserve black life insurers increased to fifty. Yet, at the same time, traditional burial associations and fraternal societies for black people collapsed and

---

[31] *Los Angeles Tribune*, 14 August 1959.
[32] Puth 1976, 146–7.   [33] Puth 1976, 170.

Table 12.2. Total amount ($1,000) and distribution of insurance in force (%) of life insurance companies in the USA, 1930–74

	Ordinary	Group	Credit	Industrial	Total insured ($1,000)	
1930	73.9	9.2		16.9	106,412,506	100.0%
1945	67.1	14.7		18.2	151,975,159	100.0%
1950	63.7	20.4	1.7	14.3	234,168,000	100.0%
1955	58.2	27.2	4.0	10.7	372,332,000	100.0%
1960	58.0	29.9	5.3	6.7	586,448,000	100.0%
1967	54.0	36.2	6.2	3.6	1,079,821,000	100.0%
1974	50.0	41.8	6.4	1.9	2,144,580,000	100.0%

Source: Institute of Life Insurance, American Council of Life Insurance, Life Insurance Fact Book, for each year.

disappeared. Many smaller black life insurers, including associations, were merged with larger black insurers.[34]

In the 1950s and 1960s black life insurance companies failed to sell a new form of insurance that was expanding and growing fast within the US life insurance industry—group life insurance. Table 12.2 shows that in 1960 group life insurance in force in the United States accounted for approximately 30 per cent of the total. In the black business community, however, few companies were able to buy life policies for their employees because most of them were running small businesses in such limited fields as barber shops or grocery stores. Tables 12.3 and 12.4 show that both black stock and mutual insurers were unable to develop group life insurance business until the early 1970s. Subsequently, however, group life insurance amongst black life insurers increased sharply: this is explained below.

As a result, black life insurers in the early 1960s accounted for only a minimal proportion of life insurance in the United States, for although in 1963 the amount of assets of the leading twenty black life insurers amounted to more than $300m dollars, this accounted for less than 1 per cent of the total assets of all US life insurers.[35]

The plan to demutualize GSM was therefore intended to help the company survive in the fiercely competitive environment of the racially oriented insurance business in the late twentieth century. Since there were more restrictions on mutual companies than on stock companies, mutual companies had far less flexibility, as, for example, in financing, investing in non-insurance business, and in mergers and acquisitions. Around 1960 many smaller black life insurance companies were on the verge of bankruptcy. Most of them, however, were stock companies. In 1968 GSM found an opportunity to merge with a black stock insurer—the Mammoth Life and Accident Insurance Company.

---

[34] Weare 1973, 281; Puth 1976; Walker 1998, 312.   [35] Walker 1998, 312.

Table 12.3. Total amount ($) and distribution of insurance in force (%) of black stock insurers, 1930–74

	Ordinary life			Group	FEGLI and SEGLI	Other	Industrial	Total insured ($)	
	Total	Life and end.	Term						
1930	35.6	25.6	2.5	0.6	0.0	6.9	64.4	72,245,496	100.0%
1945	15.6	15.0	0.4	0.1	0.0	0.0	84.4	351,798,965	100.0%
1950	19.0	17.4	1.1	0.1	0.0	0.4	81.0	523,776,867	100.0%
1960	27.3	21.8	5.1	0.4	0.0	0.0	72.7	672,419,474	100.0%
1967	35.0	26.8	6.2	1.0	0.5	0.4	65.0	876,662,000	100.0%
1974	76.0	8.8	2.7	55.5	9.5	0.0	24.0	2,663,475,000	100.0%

Notes: FEGLI = Federal Employees' Group Life Insurance; SEGLI = Service Employees' Group Life Insurance.; End = Endowment insurance.
Source: Alfred M. Best Co., Best's Life Insurance Reports, for each year.

Table 12.4. Total amount ($) and distribution of insurance in force (%) of black mutual insurers, 1930–74

	Ordinary life			Group	FEGLI and SEGLI	Other	Industrial	Total insured ($)	
	Total	Life and end.	Term						
1930	36.7	25.0	11.6	0.0	0.0	0.0	63.3	38,877,186	100.0%
1945	45.2	43.2	0.9	1.1	0.0	0.0	54.8	121,129,051	100.0%
1950	44.6	40.8	2.9	0.9	0.0	0.0	55.4	267,934,108	100.0%
1960	46.8	35.9	9.3	1.6	0.0	0.0	53.2	649,450,437	100.0%
1967	65.1	37.3	13.3	1.8	12.5	0.2	34.9	1,028,415,000	100.0%
1974	88.2	14.2	3.9	56.7	13.2	0.1	11.8	4,051,690,000	100.0%

Notes: FEGLI = Federal Employees' Group Life Insurance; SEGLI = Service Employees' Group Life Insurance; End = Endowment insurance.
Source: Alfred M. Best Co., Best's Life Insurance Reports, for each year.

Unlike other troubled companies, Mammoth Life was a relatively large company that covered a broader-based southern market. Yet, although GSM was willing to buy the Mammoth Company in order to bolster their California-only business, which was then in decline, mutual companies were not supposed to merge with stock companies, and GSM would therefore have to change its corporate form if it were to have any chance of accomplishing the merger.[36] If it was to have any flexibility in the black life insurance industry, the company deemed it necessary to demutualize.

Community-Specific Factors

In post-war America black communities experienced many changes, most conspicuously in the North and the West where the majority of the black mutual insurers were located. The first change involved a redistribution of the black population. In the greatest migratory movement since the 1910s, the exigencies of wartime redistributed the black population all over the country. California was the most popular destination and received the largest number of black migrants: from 1940 to 1950 the black population of California grew by 272 per cent, and that of Los Angeles by 160 per cent.[37]

Within the black communities themselves, cultural diversity and differentials in socio-economic status were growing. The black community of Los Angeles illustrates this well. In pre-war Los Angeles, the black community was monolithic in economic status and cultural values. Most of its members were employed in the service sector and were classified in economic terms as lower-middle class. Many soon abandoned the culture of the southern states and began to adopt middle-class values and enjoy a new urban life.[38] Those who migrated in wartime, by contrast, had more difficulty in adjusting to the new life. Owing to a decline in job opportunities after the war, they were forced to settle in an economically lower class and were condemned to reside in a huge ghetto.[39]

The changing characteristics of the Los Angeles black community affected the influence of GSM's leadership within the community, both in civil rights activities and in their business public relations. Whereas before the war GSM leaders had played an important role in organizing and managing the Los Angeles Branch of the National Association for the Advancement of Colored People (NAACP), after the war the middle-class leadership failed to reorganize the new NAACP to meet the demands of a lower-class community.[40] The close relationship between GSM and NAACP was finally dissolved, except

---

[36] *GSMR*, Box 13, Folder 1, Letter from Robert C. Tookey to Norman O. Houston, 12 June 1968; Special Conference, 20 June 1968.
[37] De Graaf 1962, 181–2.   [38] Flamming 2005, 36–59.
[39] Sides 2003, 43.   [40] Kinoshita 2010a, chapter 2.

for the involvement of an executive officer of the company, Norman B. Houston, who continued to commit himself to the association.[41]

The wider post-war gap between the economic classes inside the Los Angeles black community exerted an influence on GSM business and the company's relationship with the community deteriorated. With increasing poverty, lower-class blacks developed a feeling of antagonism towards middle-class blacks and the headquarters of GSM—a modern building on the city's more fashionable west side employing white-collar workers—epitomized the status of a successful middle-class black. While they were the major clients, the lower class sometimes showed a hostile attitude towards the company.[42] The post-war GSM had to do business in such bitter circumstances.

One other factor had an important impact on the business foundations of the company. In the 1950s, as noted above, blacks began buying life insurance policies from non-black life insurance companies, and both middle- and lower-middle class blacks were more likely to choose to buy from the non-black companies.[43] At the same time, such higher-class blacks were usually employed by non-black and relatively large companies or by government organizations that provided group insurance policies for their employees. This meant that black life insurers lost their low-risk clients who enjoyed economic stability and were in good health, and had to concentrate on business with high-risk clients who were economically unstable and whose health was poor.

In the early 1960s economic restructuring progressed in such US manufacturing centres as the urban areas of the North and the West. In Los Angeles massive plant relocations led to a rise in unemployment among black blue-collar workers, which worsened the economic, social, and even the health conditions of Los Angeles's black community.[44] Finally, in the mid-1960s, various cities experienced a sequence of racial riots, most of them in cities of the North and the West. One of the most serious and damaging of these riots, known subsequently as 'the 1965 Watts Riots', took place in a Los Angeles black community.[45] The riot and its aftermath gave a knockout blow not only to the already demoralized Los Angeles black community but also to the community-based business development vision of GSM.[46] The company realized that being a mutual company whose operations were based solely on the local black community would soon bring their business to an end. For a racial mutual company, a racial community's economic and social conditions were a matter of fundamental importance: the success of the business and the condition of the community were inextricably intertwined. Once a community

---

[41] Smith 2006, 64–5; *NAACPR*, Carton 82, Folder 30, The Following Release, 18 August 1965.
[42] *GSMR*, Box 37, Folder 6, A Memorandum, 23 May 1951.
[43] Weems 1998; *GSMR*, Box 37, Folder 7, The Challenge of 1954.
[44] Sides 2003, 180–2.   [45] Horne 1997.
[46] *GSMR*, Box 44, Folder 4, Performance Rating, October and November 1960.

underwent breakdown, the racial mutual company based on that community would inevitably suffer corresponding damage. Such a hopeless situation in the local community led GSM to develop their plans to demutualize.

Political-Specific Factors

The political status of black Americans gradually changed as the civil rights movement spread throughout the nation. A series of uprisings in black communities nationwide forced society to recognize the need for the radical improvement of the political and economic conditions of black people. Consequently, in the late 1960s, the federal government decided to adopt what became known as the ʾaffirmative action policyʾ. The policy was to give racial and ethnic minorities preferential treatment in the fields of employment, housing, educational opportunities, and other issues.[47] In business and industry, black-owned companies were targeted as agents of the policy and this gave them an unprecedented opportunity to do business with the federal and local government, or with major companies. Several of the larger black life insurance companies captured contracts for the group life and health insurance policies of employees of the government and a number of major companies. GSM insured employees of fourteen big companies that included three major automakers and Los Angeles County.[48]

Leaders of larger black life insurance companies had, since the late 1960s, been holding negotiations with key figures in the US Government who supported the affirmative action programmes.[49] Thus, around the same time that black life insurers faced a hopeless situation with regard to their own local black communities, they strongly believed in the possibility of new business development that the affirmative action policy would open up. Underwriting large-scale group insurance policies would unfailingly expand the scale of their business and secure their financial grounding. In the late 1960s leaders of the black life insurance companies were already calculating a strategy for the new era—providing new services in finance and investment.[50]

This provides a further reason for GSM's plans to convert to a stock company. In responding to the new situation in which black businesses now found themselves, the company knew, because of the strict legal restrictions on a mutual company, that to remain a mutual would impede the launch of their planned activities in finance and investment. The plan to demutualize was intended to help the company move quickly to capture an opportunity

---

[47] Weems 1998, 70–9.
[48] *GSMR*, Box 12, Folder 4, Report of Examination 1971, 16–17; *GSMR*, Box 6, Folder 6, SPEECH IDEAS FOR 50TH ANNIVERSARY, 8 March1974.
[49] Weems 2009, 67–8.   [50] *Los Angeles Sentinel*, 7 and 21 January 1965.

brought about by the new situation opened up for racial and ethnic groups in the United States.

Firm-Specific Factors

In the early 1950s GSM struggled to reorganize the company that during the war had experienced a considerable expansion in the scale of its business. In order to survive in the post-war competitive business world, the company attempted to transform what before the war had been a small firm with a family atmosphere into a fully-fledged life insurance company with professional personnel and an efficient business operation.[51] Unfortunately, the corporate reform did not work out. Throughout the first half of the 1950s the company's performance slowed down and by 1954 the company had become keenly aware of the current situation and of the bleak future of a racial life insurance company.[52] In response, it began to employ the slogan, 'KNOCK ON EVERY DOOR'. It recognized that 'Eventually, the Negro market will fade and become just a part of the regular American market ... Integration is here, but it is a two way street. We must get on it. It's time to stop leapfrogging over homes not occupied by Negroes. KNOCK ON EVERY DOOR'.[53]

During 1955-6 the slogan was used to promote a new bet-on-the-company policy—a monthly debit ordinary life insurance policy, called 'Budgeterm'. The big appeal of the new product was that policyowners paid less in premium payments but received more in policy claims. The strategy was designed to show that 'we were moving past the bounds of BUSINESS BY COLOR'. The company believed that if they sold an innovative product backed by better service, black life insurance companies could compete in a non-black market.[54]

Because of the harsh financial conditions, the promotion of a monthly ordinary life insurance policy necessitated a cut in payments to agents, and in selling Budgeterm the company introduced a new rule on the payment rate of commissions. The previous rate for collecting premiums on industrial life insurance policies had been 15 per cent, but the new rate of collecting premiums on the monthly debit ordinary life insurance policy was set at 10 per cent. Under GSM's previous policy of industrial life insurance, agents had been collecting premiums monthly, and in sales of Budgeterm agents would

---

[51] *GSMR*, Box 44, Folder 1, Messenger, 1949–51.

[52] Kinoshita 2010a, chapter 9, 81–99.

[53] *GSMR*, Box 44, Folder 1, Messenger, 15 December 1954.

[54] *GSMR*, Box 48, Folder 4, 1955 Budgeterm; video script, 22 September 1955; Training Script for Special Ordinary Policies to be Used with Flip Chart; The Facts of the Budgeterm Campaign.

be expected to collect premiums monthly as before but would get less commission.[55]

The sales of Budgeterm were so successful that ordinary life insurance in force in the company exceeded industrial life. Aside from a few black life insurers that sold only ordinary life, GSM became the first black life insurance company whose main insurance policy was ordinary life.[56] Yet, the company's triumph was short-lived. In 1957 GSM agents went on strike in protest at the company's new sales programme and the severe cut in their commission rate, about neither of which, they said, had they ever been consulted. Most GSM agents participated in the strike that lasted for some sixty days.[57] In response, the company ruthlessly fired the strike participants, whose length of service in GSM ranged from three to twenty-five years. This heated the conflict between the company and the agents. The agents' union, the Golden State Mutual Agency Club, first established in 1948, then proceeded to affiliate itself with the AFL-CIO (American Federation of Labor-Congress of Industrial Organizations) Insurance Workers International Union.[58] This made the company directors, who had no favourable opinion of union activities to begin with, even angrier.[59] Furthermore, in addition to the suspension of business during the strike, policyowners in the Los Angeles black community denounced the company's forcible measures. The company received many protest messages by telephone and letters from policyowners who supported the action of the agents.[60]

The disclosure of the internal feud gave the company a bad name in the community and critically damaged the reputation of a business that was based on a close relationship with each specific community. GSM realized that their business could only work successfully with the cooperation of agents and it was therefore obliged to give way to agents' demands. Without them, the company would easily lose all connection with the policyowners.

This experience forced the company to come to terms with the actual situation and reconsider its own position. From the very start of the business, GSM agents had played an important role in the development and stability of the company. They were the people who collected premiums in the community and communicated in person with policyowners in everyday life. The agents were the principal force in building up the business of a black life insurance company as a community project and they were the ones who had always supported the customer base of black mutuals whose business policy

[55] *Los Angeles Tribune*, 13 February 1957.
[56] Kinoshita 2010a, chapter 9, 100. The amount of life insurance in force of GSM reached more than $100m ($133m) for the first time in the company's history because of the successful Budgeterm sales.
[57] *Los Angeles Sentinel*, 21 February 1957.
[58] *Los Angeles Tribune*, 6 February 1957; *Los Angeles Sentinel*, 7 March 1957.
[59] *Los Angeles Tribune*, 13 February 1957.   [60] *Sun Reporter*, 9 March 1957.

was community consciousness. While community consciousness might have restricted the company's business strategies, bonding between agents and community had, since the birth of the company, laid a strong foundation for black mutuals. Yet, since the Budgeterm sales project had in fact failed to cut costs, the company came to believe that such strong links to the community might, in the new post-war business world, become a burden or present an obstacle to the company's urgent drive for fresh developments.

The company's new strategy aimed to reverse its poor post-war business performance, but it failed to do so thanks to one of the chief characteristics of mutual companies—a dedicated community relationship. Thus, when the core of a mutual company came to be considered a burden rather than an advantage for the business, demutualization seemed the only answer.

CONCLUSION

Aborting the Demutualization Plan

After long discussions lasting from March to July 1968, the company found it difficult to demutualize at that particular moment. There were several reasons for this. The first was the huge cost of obtaining proxies from two thirds of the estimated 133,000 policyowners. The cost would have to include actual payments to debit agents for cooperation in collecting the names and addresses of policyowners in debit to each agent. Besides, the company would need to ask debit agents to persuade their policyowners to approve the demutualization. Before that, the company would have to explain to the agents why it needed to convert to the corporate form and how the demutualization would not only benefit the business but GSM agents as well. The most troublesome task was to persuade the agents, and this involved tough negotiations with agent union leaders. The company was concerned that internal conflict might break out again if the negotiations broke down. It was likely that, if persuasion failed, the company might lose its business foundation, as well as the opportune moment for conversion.

The second reason was a shortage of appropriate personnel inside the company to handle not only the procedures needed for conversion, such as the exchange of stocks, but also to manage the business of finance and investment after they had converted to a stock company. This was the other side of the coin: after the war, GSM had focused on nurturing insurance specialists and had conducted intensive education programmes at every level of the company. As a result, the company maintained few specialists in finance and investment, unlike larger black stock insurers such as Atlanta Life that had been developing financial specialists since the early twentieth century. At the same time, they could look to no recent precedents: in the 1960s there were no cases of conversion from mutual to stock. Even the consultants employed by the company lacked the confidence to advise their clients. The company concluded that it would be premature to demutualize in 1968.

The third reason for doubting whether it would be possible to demutualize concerned the ownership and control of the company. This issue was import-ant above all for a company that had been run by and for a particular group or community. In the case of a mutual, the group legally owns it, and demutual-ization would fundamentally change the nature of a company that had until then been based on a particular group or community. In discussions of the demutualization plan, the company assumed that a certain number of policy-owners would become stockholders after conversion, but came to understand that in due course, as a stock company expanded its capital fund, stockholders and the particular group that constituted a community would no longer coincide.[61]

For a mutual life insurance company such as GSM, whose business base was on a particular group or community, group or community ownership of the company was an important feature of its corporate identity: this was some-thing that the management, agents, and policyowners implicitly agreed on. As the discussions progressed, GSM leaders realized that demutualization would not just mean a change of corporate form: it would threaten the company's corporate identity as it had evolved as part of the history of blacks in America. They concluded that the company's plans for future development would have to take account of the new situation in which black Americans and black business in the late twentieth century found themselves.

Since 1968, GSM, while adhering to community consciousness, made efforts to move forward in the difficult situation for black business that was brought about by changes in the socio-economic status of black Americans in the post-civil rights era. Along with becoming involved in community activ-ities, in 1974 the company established the 'Golden State Minority Foundation' to support disadvantaged young students, including non-black groups who were interested in having careers in the life insurance industry. In the late 1980s the company steered in a new direction to break the deadlock of the black lower-class market. The company started marketing to the black middle class and local non-black groups. An analysis of company officials, the first target group, traditionally covered by large non-black insurance compan-ies, revealed that they were not satisfied with the high price products. While the black middle class enjoyed increased economic power, the prices set by large companies exceeded what most of the black middle class could afford. GSM aimed to cater to the real demand of that group. First, the company

---

[61] *GSMR*, Box 13, Folder 1, Conference with Luckham and Tookey, 17 July 1968. The record of this conference contains three reasons, discussed above, to abort the demutualization.

developed an array of products. Second, it upgraded its sales force by fostering more professional skills and hiring more college graduates as agents. Third, GSM used professional American football star, Herschel Walker, for advertising. This popular celebrity spokesman enabled the company to have greater visibility and be recognized among potential customers nationwide.[62]

The second target group reflected an increasing non-black population in areas that the company covered. GSM, as a local mutual life insurer, has been dealing with the demands of multi-ethno-racial communities since the 1980s. To start with, the company hired non-black groups—Filipino, Korean, Chinese, Hispanic, and other groups of diversified origin—as agents and home office employees.[63] This attempt is ongoing: GSM, still a company mainly for blacks, is continually transforming itself as a local mutual life insurance company. Mutuality represents both one of a racial group and of a local coexistence.

What the Demutualization Attempt in 1968 Means in the History of Black Life Insurance Business

This chapter has analysed four factors that led one particular insurance company, Golden State Mutual, to contemplate demutualization and thus effect a radical change to its corporate form: these factors were the market, the local community, political issues, and firm-specific matters.

Like other black life insurance companies, GSM faced fierce market competition. During the post-war era, the national insurance market, which had formerly been segregated by race, became racially integrated. A business based on race could no longer succeed, while the restrictions imposed on GSM by being a mutual made it hard for the company to survive. GSM's plan for demutualization aimed to break free from these restrictions and do business with greater flexibility, thus responding to the competitive market of the late twentieth century.

At the community level, the influence of the market was critical to black mutual insurers. In contrast to the more stable situation of the early twentieth century, the black communities in which most black mutuals were located now underwent a period of economic instability and social unrest. This was partly caused by a split within black communities themselves, where the growing black middle and lower-middle class became new customers for

---

[62] *Black Enterprise*, June 1989, 13, 286, 295–8.

[63] I. J. Houston, 'Black Leadership in Los Angeles: Ivan J. Houston', *UCLA Oral History Program*, interviewer R. B. Hopkins, Tape 4, 7 February 1987; A. E. Flinck, Director of Marketing and PR, Golden State Mutual Life Insurance Company, interviewer Natsuki Kinoshita, 13 March 2008.

corporate America and black life insurers lost the most stable and developed segment of the entire black community. This especially damaged black mutual insurers whose business had been based on community solidarity provided by the economic stability of the black middle and lower-middle class. The social unrest that most affected the black mutuals reached its worst point with a series of black community uprisings in the 1960s. In Los Angeles, the 'Watts Riots' completely blew apart the existing social order and left GSM with a feeling of despair about its future development. For black mutual life insurance companies, economic and social stability and solidarity within the community had constituted the solid base of their business, and without this basis black mutuals could no longer remain in business.

A change in the political 'playing field' offered GSM the possibility of developing, should it be able to convert to a stock company. The late 1960s was actually a hopeful as well as a critical time for blacks. The success of the civil rights movement saw the legal improvement of the status of blacks, while the policy of affirmative action gave black businesses the opportunity for new developments. In the late 1960s, black businessmen began rethinking their strategies and some decided to leave the racial market for the national market, where they could do business with corporate America as well as with federal and local governments. GSM leaders also began to think about the possibility of taking advantage of this opportunity. If the company were able to benefit from the affirmative action programme, then their business and financial foundations would become sufficiently stable for them to expand and launch various business projects that would not be limited to the field of insurance only. Yet for the company to be able to do that, it would first have to free itself of the restrictions imposed upon it by being a mutual.

At the firm-specific level, a failure to reorganize forced GSM to consider changing its corporate form. The wartime migration of blacks to California expanded the business scale of GSM and immediately after the war the company became one of the largest black life insurers for a ghetto with a huge black population. When, later on, it needed to adjust to both internal and external changes, GSM attempted to reorganize its management arrangements, agency operations, and relationship with the community, but such efforts worked out negatively. In 1957 the GSM agency network rebelled against the management and the internal turmoil gave the company a bad reputation within the community. On the one hand, this taught the company that the success of their community-conscious business had been achieved because their agents made connections between the company and policy-owners. On the other hand, GSM saw that agents and their union could become an obstacle to the promotion of new business policies or strategies. In other words, the mutuality of a black mutual company that was based on a relationship between actors such as agents and policyowners could impede the launch of new programmes, even if these were seen as essential for survival.

Whereas mutuality had once been an advantage for black mutuals, it could, in the competitive business world of the post-war years, be a crippling cost or a debilitating constraint. In this sense, the company sought to devise a plan to convert to a stock company as a means of ensuring greater flexibility in the promoting of its business strategies.

Although serious discussions within GSM led the company to abort its plan to demutualize, the internal debates nevertheless gave the company the opportunity to rethink its vision of how to survive and develop in a post-racial society. In 1968, the year that GSM planned to demutualize, the American Management Association conducted a session 'Holding Companies, Mergers and Acquisitions in the Insurance Industry'. One of the topics discussed during the session was the matter of conversion from a mutual to a stock company, a trend which, at that time, had just begun.[64] As racial integration progressed, companies based on a racial community, such as black mutual life insurers, had to handle a new situation. They were faced with a choice: either to start again as a stock insurer, responding to the trend whereby insurance organizations moved into other business fields, or to preserve the community-based business as a mutual. Although GSM chose the latter, the word 'community' here no longer necessarily meant a black community. Towards the end of the twentieth century, the Los Angeles black community became a multi-ethno-racial community with a consecutive influx of Hispanic and Asian populations, while the number of black life insurance companies fell from forty-two companies in 1973 to twenty-three in 1993, and most of those that survived were very small.[65] Only three companies, including GSM, have managed to retain a certain level of business in the twenty-first century and, unlike two companies that expanded into multiple business fields or in other localities, GSM, which has remained a mutual, provides services for a local community in California.[66]

In the historical context of post-racial America in the late twentieth century, GSM's demutualization plan indicates that black mutual life insurers needed a new business strategy for survival in the new circumstances in which black Americans found themselves at the beginning of the 1950s. As long as the company saw that the previous business model of black mutuals was nearing its end, it would be asked to reidentify itself and, as a refashioned company, to present a revamped vision for the future.

As, from the beginning of the twentieth century, black communities began to spread widely across the country and formed communities in cities of the

---

[64] *GSMR*, Box 13, Folder 1, Letter from Norman B. Houston to Norman O. Houston, 28 May 1968.

[65] Walker 1998, 312–13.

[66] A. E. Flinck, Director of Marketing and PR, Golden State Mutual Life Insurance Company. Interviewed by the author, 13 March 2008 in Los Angeles.

North and West of the United States, so the black mutual life insurance companies that evolved to meet their needs sold insurance services that were indispensable; they provided not only a safety net or security but also maintained various community institutions that supported the rapid and remarkable development of urban black communities. Yet, during the post-war era, the situation of urban black Americans changed again and when a company does business for one racial group, then the changing social situation of that group will determine the company's business. GSM's attempt to demutualize shows clearly that a complex web of factors will influence the choice of corporate form. In the United States, especially, changing racial relationships matter to life insurance businesses. In the early twentieth century, a stable racial community gave racially based mutual insurers like GSM an advantage. In the post-racial society of the late twentieth century, however, mutuality based on one racial community might shackle them. Indeed, this seems to have been the eventual outcome. In the fall of 2009, the California State Insurance Commissioner ordered an intervention in the business operations of GSM to protect its policyholders from the consequences of the deterioration in its financial position. The GSM management lost control and its all-in-one insurance policies were transferred to another company.[67] This failure followed a long and ultimately fruitless struggle during the first decade of this century to adapt to serving a multiracial customer base in a post-racial society.

---

[67] Marc Lifsher, 'California Regulators Seize Struggling Golden State Mutual Life', *Los Angeles Times*, 1 October 2009.

13

The Insurance Demutualization Process Develops in Spain with Mapfre

Leonardo Caruana de las Cagigas

This chapter examines the story of Mapfre, a Spanish insurer that commenced as a mutual in 1933 and converted to a stock company at the beginning of the twenty-first century. Mapfre's board of directors considered that the conversion was consistent with trends in global markets, while still respecting the mutual culture of the company. It was clear that large 'insurer-financial' groups were setting the pattern in all markets. The United States was moving in that direction after the introduction of the Financial Services Modernization Act in 1999, while Japan followed suit. In Europe, intensive processes of mergers and acquisitions permitted the appearance of giants such as Allianz in Germany, Axa in France, Generali in Italy, and ING in the Netherlands, all large multinationals in world insurance.

Mapfre too proceeded to demutualize with the aim of becoming bigger. Even though Mapfre is relatively small when compared with the aforementioned giants in Europe, in Spain it is the leading insurer. In 2006 the process of demutualization commenced and it was completed in 2008. Critically, however, the new stock company was placed under the control of the Mapfre Foundation, which had been set up some time before to support social activities of public interest and was financed by the mutual company. Since 1965 the statutes of Mapfre required that in the event of the dissolution of the mutual the foundation would receive the majority of the shares and control over the insurance company.

Being controlled by a foundation as the majority shareholder, Mapfre can perhaps be held up as a model for other mutual companies elsewhere that wish to demutualize, but that also wish to retain their independence. If they create a foundation that takes control of the majority of shares, it is possible to survive as a stock company in an ever more globalized insurance market, while enjoying one of the primary advantages of a mutual, namely that it cannot be sold. To date, however, Mapfre is the only insurer that we know of that has followed this path. This makes Mapfre's history particularly instructive and so the focus of this chapter is on it. Its demutualization story begins in the 1960s when the earliest stages of its slow and gradual conversion to a stock company can be traced.[1]

WHY DEMUTUALIZATION?

Evidence of the benefits of demutualization is not clear. The economic literature provides many points of view that do not always converge. First, it is obvious that insurance companies face many similar challenges regardless of their corporate form, for example the challenge of developing new products, sales expertise, marketing innovations, and new technologies, and the need to reduce fixed costs and improve administrative management, know-how, risk management, financial capacity, etc. Nevertheless, some have perceived advantages in conversion from mutual to stock.

The main reason usually given for demutualization is to open a company up to a greater number of owners, with the aim of bringing more capital into the firm.[2] The board of directors of such a company may also consider it essential to increase the number of shareholders in order to improve management performance. The decision to convert, however, can create much anxiety. Lee, for example, notes the difficulty involved in developing financial institutions in less-developed countries and suggests that the mutual form of organization is more advantageous in such countries.[3] Worthington and Higgs argue that stock companies normally take greater risks in business than mutual companies.[4] This can raise a conflict between the interests of policyholders, who may not wish to see large risks taken in the investment strategy of the company, and shareholders, whose returns may benefit from such a strategy. Nevertheless, the search for improved performance has also been cited as a justification for demutualization. Serifsoy, in a piece of empirical research, found that demutualized companies had a higher technical efficiency than their mutual counterparts.[5] Aggarwal discusses the control of companies that move from mutual association to shareholder decision making and suggests that the main reason for demutualization is the rise of global competition and technological advances.[6] Lai, McNamara, and Yu have argued that demutualized insurers outperform non-demutualized companies after they go public.[7]

---

[1] For another account of the demutualization process in insurance with a longer-term perspective, see Keneley 2010.
[2] Viswanathan and Cummins 2003.   [3] Lee 2002.
[4] Worthington and Higgs 2006.   [5] Serifsoy 2008.
[6] Aggarwal 2002.   [7] Lai et al. 2008, 142.

MAPFRE: FROM ITS BEGINNINGS TO
ITS DEMUTUALIZATION

Mapfre's origins lay with the Association of Owners' Group of Rural Estates of Spain which started in August 1931. This organization sought to bring together Spanish farmers to improve the productivity of rural areas and to defend their own interests within the new political situation (the democratic period that had commenced in Spain after a dictatorship). A few years later, on 16 May 1933, they created a mutual insurance organization. The name Mapfre came from the first letters of the mutual's title: *Mutua de la Agrupación de Propietarios de Fincas Rústicas de España*. It was a response to the new Accident Insurance Law, passed on 4 July 1932. This made it mandatory for owners of farms to insure everyone working for them.[8] It was an initiative of the socialist labour minister, Largo Caballero, who viewed it as a means of better distributing economic benefits through the rural population, but it became an important sector for the private insurance industry, even in the period of the Franco dictatorship. Spain was still a largely agrarian economy and millions of peasants stood to gain an insurance policy under the new law.[9]

The constitution of their mutual was considered the best way of covering the new accident insurance risks. The first director of the company, Isidro de Gregorio y Villota, explained the reasons why the association opted for a mutual instead of a stock company form.[10] First, to create a mutual was a low-cost operation in comparison to the foundation of a stock company with its initial capital issue. Second, a mutual did not have to worry about generating profits for shareholders from the outset. Third, a mutual, especially with a small number of owners in its early days, could promise those owners a more direct involvement with the management and a better awareness of how their company functioned.

For a long time (1933–58) the firm was against asking for credits or having anything to do with banks. For the board of directors of Mapfre, and for many people in Spain during the republic and the early years under Franco, managers of banks were considered as evil and the capitalist system was considered not to be the correct system for economic growth in general, and in particular for Spanish society.[11]

In the 1960s a major change occurred in Spanish social attitudes towards capitalism.[12] This was also reflected in the Mapfre board room when it was

---

[8] Before 1932 the insurance of accidents was only mandatory in respect of workers in factories. That year the law was extended to all workers, including those in agriculture.

[9] Tortella Casares et al. 2009, 33.

[10] De Gregorio y Villota 1933.

[11] This belief was shared by socialists and communists and by those on the right, falangists, and carlists.

[12] The 'economic miracle' in Western Europe was one factor behind this change.

resolved to develop a finance arm of the business. The strategic step in this direction was taken on 27 May 1962 when the directors decided to take control of the company *Central de Obras y Crédito* (COC), with the purchase of shares worth 4,626 million pesetas. The aim was to offer finance for car purchases to any customers, but especially to Mapfre's own policyholders. Buying or developing a financial firm had been undertaken before by other major insurance companies in Spain, such as La Unión y el Fénix, the Life Insurance Bank, the Zurich or the Plus Ultra, and these companies had proved profitable. In some cases the solution had been to create direct subsidiaries for car finance, but Mapfre found it easier simply to acquire an existing company, namely the COC.

The board meeting of 25 April 1963 accepted what Joan Sardá, the famous economist of the Bank of Spain, had argued, namely that there were too few financial companies in the country.[13] The common practice for many people was to save up the full amount for large items and pay cash. Interest rates were abusive, and yet half the motor vehicles purchased were bought on finance because of their high price, around 100,000 pesetas, an amount equivalent to the annual salary of a company manager in Spain.

Following the purchase of COC shares, another market-oriented move was taken on 11 December 1963, when Mapfre started Muinsa (*Mutualidad de Inversiones*) for the purpose of investing technical provisions.[14] At the time insurance companies—both stock and mutual—faced rigorous regulatory conditions for any kind of financial investment. One solution to get around this restrictive system was to create a joint-stock vehicle to invest in the stock market without those restrictions. If an investment was made directly by an insurance mutual, that investment had to be supervised by the *Dirección General de Seguros*, the Spanish supervisor for all insurance companies, especially for equities listed on the stock exchange, so it was a slow and costly process.

The creation of an investment trust company (ITC) got around this snag in a legal manner, by making it possible to deposit shares in an ITC that could manage its portfolio securities without restrictions. In subsequent years during the 1970s, with the increasing investment needs of Mapfre, other ITCs (Muinsa Dos, Progesa, Mapinco) were created. Another strategic decision was to increase investment in real estate. During the 1960s and 1970s inflation was high in Spain, so stock market investments often led to losses, while real estate investment represented the classical form of risk diversification.

[13] Sardá noted that, although the Spanish economy remained very backward, its rapid growth would require the creation of new financial firms.

[14] The acronym comprised the two first letters of both names in the company title plus SA (Spanish for stock company). Technical provisions reflect the actual value or estimated liabilities in respect of insurance and reinsurance contracts entered into, as well as the costs associated with compliance with these obligations. They form part of the general liabilities of the insurer.

The final reform of the 1960s was the organization of a new company, Gram (*Grupo Asegurador Mutuo*), registered on 7 July 1965 as a stock company. The purpose of Gram was to take over all the operations that Mapfre, being a mutual company, could not handle, particularly those associated with credit finance, the underwriting of motor insurance that faced the problem of higher accident rates, and also reinsurance operations from which Mapfre was forbidden by law.[15]

The above account indicates that already in the 1960s this innovative mutual company was transforming some parts of its organization into a joint-stock form. This process would accelerate in the 1970s with the creation of the Mapfre Group (called Gama). Thus the mutual company transferred part of its business into two new stock companies: Mapfre Industrial and Mapfre Vida. All insurance business with industrial and other companies was to be managed by the former and all life insurance business by the latter.

The general reason for the change was that the CEO, Ignacio Hernando de Larramendi, was convinced of the predominance in the near future of major insurance groups, often associated with financial companies or multinational corporations. These major groups were formed from the recruitment of more qualified employees and the acquisition of other smaller companies. Their advantages lay in their ability to spread the high costs of acquiring modern equipment and opening new offices and the ability to reduce the costs of training staff. Additionally, the ability to grow in the life insurance sector, a sector most closely associated with the more developed countries, involved accumulating large reserves, something that only large financial groups could successfully do. The concentration of insurance into such groups with specialized branches was becoming a global phenomenon.[16]

To try to ensure Mapfre's position among the top insurance companies, the board approved the new organizational scheme that would convert the company into something totally new, aiming to prepare the firm to provide an efficient service to Spanish policyholders and open the door to international insurance markets. Greater competition was seen as inevitable, in other countries or in Spain, with the arrival of large multinational insurance companies. Under the Franco regime national companies had been favoured, and foreign companies had found it difficult to develop business. In 1930 foreign companies had controlled 34 per cent of insurance in Spain, but by 1954 this share had fallen to just 15 per cent.[17] In the early 1960s Spain had applied to join the European Common Market but was rejected. With the demise of

---

[15] Mapfre, *Memoria* (*Annual Report*) 1965.

[16] *Seguros: Revista del Sindicato Nacional del Seguro* 1973, 303–13.

[17] Market shares from Matilla and Frax 1996; García Ruiz and Caruana 2009; Pearson 2010b. The so-called period of autarky, 1939–59, proved rather disastrous, so the Franco regime moved to promote a more open economy from 1959.

autarchic policies during the final phase of the Franco dictatorship, however, managers of insurance companies began to prepare for an increase in competition from foreign insurers and with less government protection. This same process of change can be seen in Mapfre as it began in the 1960s to launch new companies organized as joint-stocks. The idea was to face the new challenges by creating a 'group', within which the parent mutual would keep for itself the most profitable sectors, such as motor insurance. Other sectors could be operated through stock companies under the control of the mutual, but with independent capital and legal status, thus giving them an opportunity to obtain external financial assistance to grow in Spain and abroad. At this stage Larramendi was already thinking that the mutual should become a multinational business. In addition, the successful experience of Mapfre Mutual Patronal after its segregation in 1966 convinced the board of directors of the advantages of specializing in particular branches.[18]

As a result, the establishment of the Mapfre Group was approved by the extraordinary general meeting of 1970 and was initially formed by three companies. The main company, Mapfre, remained a mutual. This operated mainly in the sector of automobile insurance, but also in any sector with a large volume of insurance policies, and more or less homogenous products that were relatively simple to insure. This included the insurance of private homes, small industries and businesses, personal accidents, and similar lines. The second company, noted above, was Mapfre Industrial SA, established as a joint-stock on 30 January 1970. The company Gram, which had suffered considerable losses due to the high accident rate in the lines covered by its operations, was merged into this new stock company.

The purpose of this new company was to operate in sectors that covered the typical risks of large companies, transport insurance, and reinsurance. These insurances required qualified specialists. Mapfre had neglected this area and, besides, as a mutual company, it was not in a position to negotiate coinsurance operations with limited liability corporations that would normally deal with insuring large risks. This organization scheme was based on tried and tested models from the United States, but there was no certainty as to whether it would work in Spain. The new scheme, however, was more customer-oriented. In sectors like transport insurance, the mutual form was often not even considered viable by Mapfre because of the high capital risks in that sector and the financial restrictions placed on mutual companies by the law in Spain.

The third company in the new group was Mapfre Vida SA, formed in 1969 to operate exclusively in life insurance, a line of business that required a network of highly skilled, competent, and autonomous salesmen. The Mapfre

---

[18] Fernández Pacheco 1995, 24. The Mapfre Mutua Patronal was created because in Spain all workers' accident insurance had to be under the control of the state social security and delivered through independent companies.

board considered that this business too could only develop adequately through a stock company. Its primary aim was to offer new life insurance products. What was beyond doubt was that the mutual funds system lacked the sufficient operational flexibility to meet the growth targets that Mapfre had set for life insurance. Furthermore, the expenses associated with new life sales accounted for around 125 to 150 per cent of first-year premiums. This required a solid financial infrastructure to avoid excessive reinsurance. Mapfre could only succeed in its growth strategy for life insurance by becoming a stock company, which would provide the capital to expand in proportion to the demand and increase in sales thanks to easier access to credit. An important matter to settle was the question of how to distribute the new company's risks. Because a modern insurance company needed to tailor its products to individual customers, it could not persist with the old mutual system of distributing profits a posteriori and aggregated by line of business. Moreover, mutual insurers were subjected to a tax on premiums that was higher than that levied on stock companies, which made them less attractive, especially in the life insurance business.

At the time the Mapfre Group was formed, the greatest difficulty was probably the coordination between the new companies within it. The board wanted to make clear that each company should have well-defined goals: a large volume of personal non-life insurance in Mapfre Mutualidad; business insurance in Mapfre Industrial, and life insurance in Mapfre Vida. Mapfre Mutualidad would be the visible head of the group and the owner of the majority of the capital of the other two companies. In addition, it would coordinate and provide other services to reduce expenses, and provide resources to enable the managers of the other companies to focus on the practical and commercial aspects of increasing their sales. The core of that coordination within the Mapfre Group would depend on four factors: a common financial administration, practical information, joint investment and financial policy coordination (except for Mapfre Vida because of its special characteristics), and regular auditing.

The organizational development of the Mapfre Group was the historical forerunner of the present-day Mapfre. With Mapfre Vida and Mapfre Industrial the firm would benefit from the stock form of organization, which would lead to improvements in the company's efficiency and its success. However, a stock company in the new open Spanish economy might also be exposed to predatory takeover attempts. The preferential agreements with the European Economic Community, signed in June 1970, marked a first move towards Spain's entry into the European Common Market and many Spanish insurance companies, poorly provided with capital, would end up being absorbed by multinational companies. That the transformation of Mapfre occurred under the aegis of the mutual parent company helped avert the danger of foreign competitors in the Spanish market taking over the business.

Further change in the company structure took place in the 1980s. A stumbling block in Mapfre's way to the top of the list of the insurance companies in Spain had been the crisis of the CIC (*Central de Inversión y Crédito*), previously called COC. Although it had improved significantly with its financial investments, and could become useful as a corporation to handle the main branches of the mutual company and ease its access to the stock market to finance future expansion, some members of the executive committee felt that its financial activities had little strategic value for the group and that future profits were uncertain. For those reasons it was decided to sell off eight financial companies of the CIC to the American giant *Citibank*.

Thus, Mapfre reduced its finance activities to strengthen its core insurance business. The shift toward a more cautious policy was also reflected in a preference for state bonds at the end of 1980, leading the group to buy a large volume of public debt (3,140 million pesetas) that exceeded by 114 million pesetas the amount required to meet its legal obligations regarding reserves. The economic environment was not a good one at the time and it seemed more reasonable to adopt a conservative approach to investments with a small financial risk. State bonds then enjoyed a higher return, so they were a convenient alternative to equities, with significant tax benefits.

Mapfre's auditor, *Arthur Young*, and Citibank's auditor, *Arthur Andersen*, both agreed that the CIC and its holdings had been evolving positively. However, just when everything seemed sound, the Bank of Spain warned foreign banks about buying financial companies in Spain. The warning had a wide-ranging impact, both nationally and internationally. The *Financial Times* of 10 March 1981 was of the opinion that the aim of the Bank of Spain had been to prevent the operation involving the CIC and criticized the fears that still existed in Spain about the entry of foreign capital.

Mapfre's reaction was to accept the official warnings. That meant the company would have to complete the work of organizational restructuring without outside help. The CIC's reorganization had begun in 1977 and the liquidation of its shares and its real estate agency had been completed, concentrating its activity in financial investments.

While negotiating the sale to *Citibank*, the executive committee had been working on the transformation of the CIC into the Mapfre Corporation. The plan was to convert the CIC into a holding company to handle the shares of the Mapfre group. Mapfre Corporación had been established, building upon the significant assets of Mapfre Vida and Mapfre Industrial.

To carry out this transformation, Mapfre once more contracted *Arthur Young* to carry out an audit. The first activities of Mapfre Corporación were presented already audited. In the annual report of 1982 an audit report was included in the accounts and income statements of all the consolidated companies of Mapfre Mutual Insurance and Mapfre Corporation. The report was one of the first published in Spain, because at that time there was no legal obligation to do so.[19]

Besides Mapfre there were other important investors in the corporation such as the *Caja Madrid* (8.5 per cent) and the *American Prudential Reinsurance Co.* (8 per cent). Mapfre Industrial, Mapfre Vida, and the Mapfre financial field (thirty-nine provincial and local companies throughout the country, which had been mainly engaged in car sales, with over 61,000 million pesetas in sales) would be integrated into the new corporation. Investment activity had been beset with losses since the oil crisis of 1973, but the equity was over 1,600 million pesetas of which the corporation had overall control (an average share of 76 per cent).

The properties of the CIC and its shares in industrial companies were transferred to Mapfre Investments (the former Inmobiliaria Mapfre, which had changed its name). As the name changed from the CIC to the Mapfre Corporación, the mutual company endorsed a major increase of its capital with the addition of the shares in Mapfre Vida and Mapfre Industrial. These produced some limited gains for the mutual company because they had maintained their book value. What took longer was the integration of the financial companies with the territorial infrastructure of Mapfre. With very few exceptions, they would no longer be financially independent.

In 1983 the management drew up a plan to incorporate all the finance companies of the former CIC into the Finanzas Mapfre. Each financial company operated in geographic areas that mapped closely onto the sub-centres of Mapfre itself, so it became necessary to concentrate the dispersed financial companies, which adopted the names of fifteen different Spanish regions. The fate of the financial offices of Guipuzcoa, Valladolid, Zaragoza, Cordoba, and Almeria remained undecided. The success of this restructuring of the finance business was remarked upon at the board meeting of 12 September 1984. The financial crisis of the CIC, which had commenced some nine years before following poor results from industrial and real estate investments during the mid-1970s, was regarded as over.

Another step in the lengthy and complex restructuring of the company was the creation of the organization called the Sistema Mapfre that served for the growth of the company until the establishment of Mapfre SA in 2007. The origin of this idea dates back to September 1983, just when the corporation had begun to write reinsurance. At a time of marked adjustments, the governing board had considered that the organization, adopted in 1970 for a medium-large company, had become inadequate for a large one, in particular because the greater scale of the business demanded that each of the branches of the company needed to be more self-directed or more independent.

---

[19] Mapfre 1983, 161.

The centralized coordination of the Mapfre Group, where the executive committees of the branches had been managed largely with the same personnel as those of the mutual company, ended up as a group of fully autonomous units under the Sistema Mapfre, which became operational on 1 January 1985.

The problem then was to coordinate the various autonomous operational units of the network. It was necessary to configure a legal and organizational infrastructure. The corporation had been under the supervision of Mapfre Mutualidad, which had been responsible for the smooth running of the entire business, with a criterion of efficiency for maximum profits, without forgetting its commitment to 'serving the community'. The establishment of the new system represented a move towards decentralization combined with a strict and efficient control over the employees and the general spending of the firm.

The Sistema Mapfre meant significant changes in the board of the company: Ignacio Hernando de Larramendi ceased to be the CEO of Mapfre Mutualidad and was appointed chairman of the supervisory board, responsible for supervising the company's entire network. He was also named President of the Mapfre Foundation and continued to run the Corporación Mapfre, which allowed him to pay special attention to international expansion. The person who assumed the new responsibilities was Julio Castelo Matran, appointed CEO of Mapfre Mutualidad and a member of the foundation representing the Mapfre mutual company. The general director of Mapfre Mutualidad, Manuel Ocón Terrasa, was also Chairman of Mapfre Finanzas, to ensure maximum coordination between the two companies.

The reports of the board meetings of Mapfre Mutualidad make it clear that the business model that used to configure the system was the one originated by the historic Japanese business conglomerates (*Zaibatsu*). During the 1980s it was common to find business managers exchanging the American business model for the Japanese one, and Mapfre's managers were no exception. The Japanese conglomerate had been characterized by knowing how to combine a wide range of business activities with the same culture into a single firm. The Sistema Mapfre was not to be very different. The two core companies, Mutual Mapfre and Corporation Mapfre, had very different juridical natures and objectives but coincided in the essential: to provide the best service in the insurance business. At the general assembly of 1983, which was held during the celebration of the 50th anniversary of the firm, the point was stressed that Japanese conglomerates had achieved their success thanks to good internal communications, so that decisions could be made collectively.

In 1984, to simplify the new organization, Mapfre Mutualidad bought shares of the corporation in Mapfre Finance, Mapfre Finance of the North, and Mapfre Finance of Guipuzcoa, companies that had emerged from the mergers of many local financial companies. The operations were carried out on the basis of their book value, simple transfers to reduce the corporation's workload and in turn allow its expansion.

Finally, the adoption of the new organizational structure realized Ignacio Hernando Larramendi's ideas about specialization and decentralization, albeit adapted to the new size of the company. Larramendi's principal aim was put into practice: namely to concentrate an activity in one sector, each with its own managerial accountability, without considering the need to cross-subsidize or ensure the stability of other sectors of the business. Sector managers were required to take care of their own sales performance and to work to improve their line of insurance—motor vehicle, life, transport, etc.—without any financial assistance from other parts of the group. That internal discipline, together with a critical attitude that had never been satisfied with excuses, was what led Mapfre to recognized standards of excellence in insurance management, especially in motor insurance and general insurance. Decentralization left in the hands of the large geographical network of offices across Spain all the responsibility of dealing with customers and planning strategies to increase sales. The decentralized and specialized structure improved the speed and accuracy of administrative information flows, focused attention on the customer, and helped minimize central administrative expenses. On this basis Mapfre proceeded to achieve spectacular growth.

The development of joint-stock companies, which had begun with the creation of the Mapfre group, was completed thirty-eight years later with the establishment of Mapfre SA. The company at the beginning of the new century had been strongly conditioned by its history during the last decade of the twentieth century. In the years of economic prosperity, following its traditional line, Mapfre had avoided simply targeting purely financial gains, because it had been more concerned with operational results than financial ones. Strict application of the rules in the selling of insurance policies had kept the technical results of Mapfre above the industry average, as it had relied relatively little on investment yields from the stock market. Furthermore, the expansion of Mapfre with direct insurance in Latin America had also been completed. After an initial success in acquiring companies in different countries, there had followed a reorganization of Mapfre in Latin America, which would not have been successful without the support and example of the Spanish Mapfre. This was the moment when the company finally ceased to be a mutual company. The change had been possible, to a large extent, because of the existence of the Mapfre Foundation, which had materialized many years before with the social commitment of the company manifested through activities of general interest financed by annual contributions by the group. In the event of the dissolution of the mutual company, the statutes of 1965 had designated the foundation to receive all the company's assets. The new organization announced in May 2006 provided for the integration of all the business activities of the group in a stock company to be called Mapfre SA, and transferred the majority control of the listed company to the Mapfre Foundation.

The new organizational scheme was developed by Alberto Manzano, Vice-President and former general secretary of the firm. He designed it to increase the group's financial capacity, to enable a more efficient and transparent management, to submit all of its business to the discipline of the market, and to compete in the global economy. The existence of the foundation as the major shareholder allowed the independence of Mapfre and its spirit of public service to be safeguarded. This was apparent over the years in various versions of its code of corporate governance, especially evident in a concrete and practical form in its 'enterprise culture' internalized by thousands of employees and managers.

The members of the mutual company (about 5 million people) were given the option of deciding whether they wished to maintain their links with Mapfre because it had offered them a choice between converting their participation into equity shares of Mapfre SA or receiving their cash value. The distribution was carried out without complication and in the end about 500,000 people chose to continue as shareholders of the group with its new organization.

One of the main motives of the corporate restructuring had been to make it easier for Mapfre to reconfigure its operational organization in order to increase its sales and improve its customer service. The new corporate organization was part of an effort of the board of Mapfre that was something quite new in corporate Spain, an attempt to preserve founding principles while translating them effectively as a multinational company into the modern world. The historical antecedents of this change were referred to by the chairman Jose Manuel Martínez in his report to the general assembly of 15 June 2006. Martínez pointed to the chairman's account, presented to the company's extraordinary general meeting of 28 February 1970, of how the Mapfre Insurance Group would develop in the future:

> It is considered appropriate to propose the creation of an insurance group to coordinate the insurance operations of mass risk coverage performed by the Mutual Funds Company . . . while insurances of very specific practical or commercial characteristics will be separated from it and dealt with by joint stock companies, co-ordinated with the Mutual Funds Company but with its own individual legacy and legal status best suited to the type of operations and customers. In this respect, it also must be noted that MAPFRE's willingness to extend its operations and its business methods in Latin America at the right moment, considering this expansion logical for an insurance group with a substantial internal importance, requires being able to provide a reinsurance service, which is also very convenient, [as it had also been] to keep the control of the Group within the Mutual Funds Company or companies with a foundational nature.

These major objectives of 1970 had been fulfilled, but it had also become apparent that the modernization of the company had been aimed at increasing the size of the business in a joint-stock form as Mapfre SA.

The process by which the company changed its legal status as a mutual company was not without difficulties, but it was successful. José Manuel Martínez, at the first General Meeting of Shareholders (26 March 2007), reported the conclusion of the project:

> I consider it necessary to stress that the agreements adopted at the Extraordinary General Meeting of our organization held last December 29 have been completed and implemented, along with an increase of capital amounting to €3.450 million, a change of the registered name from the previous one, (CORPORACION MAPFRE) to MAPFRE S.A., the adaptation of the statutes for the new situation and a modification of the members of the Board to suit the new prevailing conditions of all the business activities of MAPFRE. With this, MAPFRE S.A. now includes all the business activities of the SISTEMA MAPFRE.

The development of Mapfre had a high public profile, more than usual for a mutual company, for it had always been administered as a genuine public service institution. Furthermore, an alliance with the savings bank Caja Madrid, which commenced at the end of the twentieth century, significantly increased the volume of transactions, especially in life insurance. This became one of the largest bank–insurance collaborations in the Spanish market, which, without losing the autonomy and individuality of either organization, managed to increase the market share and territorial presence of both. Automobile insurance was omitted from the agreement, but it did include collaboration in international markets.

In 2006, once the new corporate organization of Mapfre had been announced, the organization had to redraft the agreements of the alliance, which were completed in 2008. The ownership of 100 per cent of subsidiaries would be held by Mapfre, the savings bank going on to be the second largest shareholder of Mapfre SA (after Foundation Mapfre), with a 15 per cent share in the listed company. In this way the commercial collaboration between the two groups was maintained, without reducing Mapfre's ability to establish partnership agreements with other commercial banks and savings banks. The year 2008 also saw the renewal of the code of good governance for Mapfre SA, preserving its institutional and business policies as well as defining the fundamentals of the business within a stock company framework. The new organizational structure is shown in Figure 13.1.

Finally, as a joint-stock the new company had the benefit of the Mapfre Foundation. After Spain joined the European Economic Community, many Spanish stock companies disappeared under foreign control. For example, the most historically important Spanish company, La Unión y el Fénix, fell under the control of the German company Allianz and its name and way of doing business disappeared. Two other big Spanish companies, La Estrella and El Banco Vitalicio, were acquired by the Italian company Generali, others by the biggest French company AXA (namely La Urbana, Aurora, La Polar, Abeille,

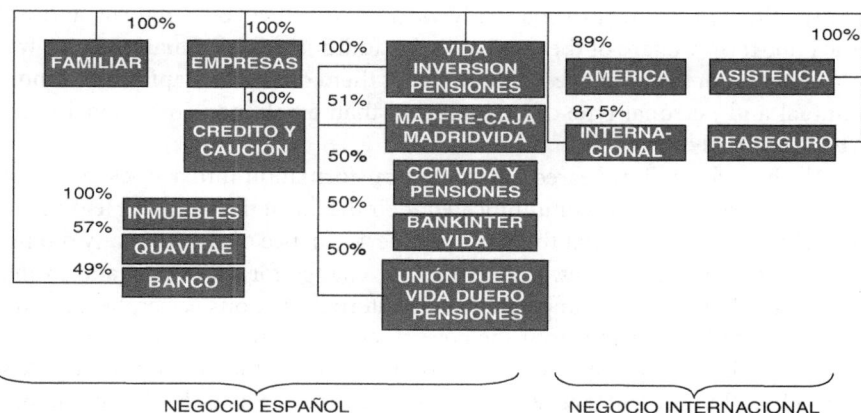

Figure 13.1. The new organizational structure of MAPFRE in 2008

Atlas, Unión Española, Minerva, Mare Nostrum, Seguros Industriales, Compañía Anónima (SICA), and Unión Condal).

There is an obvious risk that a joint-stock company can be bought out in any country of the world. For Mapfre the foundation continues to preserve the independence of the company and its own culture of doing things that has been so successful up to the present.

THE RESULTS OF THE DEMUTUALIZATION OF MAPFRE

The company had many fears about the process of becoming a joint-stock. First, there were thousands of members of the mutual that might not have accepted the conversion, even if the general assembly voted for it. Second, they could not predict how the market would react to the change. In 2006 more than 30 per cent of Mapfre's business was in the Americas, especially in Latin America, so the company also had to await the reaction there. For many members of the company the mutual form was a plus, because it did not have '*ánimo de lucro*', that is, it did not focus on economic gains and profits. Once the company became a stock company, however, profits were essential because the shareholders' dividends depended upon them. In a company with millions of clients, they may transfer their capital to another company, which could be the end of the firm. For many people a stock company was also less moral than a mutual, for in a mutual company the board of directors, it was claimed, were obliged to look after the interests of their members. By contrast, some felt that the managers of a stock company would be mainly concerned with the shareholders, who in turn may only worry about their own returns and not the long-term welfare of the company. An additional fear of management was the reaction of the employees. For many of them old-style Mapfre was a more mutual and personal type of organization than a cold and impersonal joint-stock company.

All these fears disappeared when the transformation into a stock company was complete. Very few communicated their dislike of the change. Helping the transition was the fact that the economic performance of the company did not suffer, nor did the services. Things did not change for the clients and profits increased. Finally, the change also made internal relations easier, because the possible conflicts arising from the coexistence of mutual and stock organizations within one group were now removed and information flows were smoothed. Investment overseas was also facilitated. Since the 1960s the primary strategic aim of Mapfre had been growth in Spain. From the 1980s that aim was extended to foreign markets. As a mutual under Spanish law it was not possible to develop abroad, so the foundation of the joint-stock Corporación Mapfre solved that problem. By the early twenty-first century Mapfre conducted more of its business outside Spain than in the domestic market.

CONCLUSIONS

This chapter has highlighted the fears that many medium-sized firms have of losing control of their decision making and being controlled or bought out by other companies, and through this, losing their specific form of management, which is part of their own company culture. In this sense, the story of Mapfre is to some extent also the story of Spanish business culture and organization. Probably its early development would not have been so successful if it had been founded as a stock company, because a large proportion of Spanish society did not trust the latter. Furthermore, the economic capabilities of a small company were few at the beginning, and financial institutions were weak in 1930s Spain. The growth of the company, however, and its subsequent ambitions to grow even further, made it necessary to access more funds, something that only the stock market made possible. The transition from mutual to stock company improved its development potential in Spain, with the creation of the Mapfre Group in 1970 that included two joint-stock companies for life and industrial insurance. Another move in the same direction was the transformation of CIC, the financial company of the group, into Corporation Mapfre, in order to make it easier to attract more investors and to finance investments outside Spain. System Mapfre was the next step in this process, which immediately followed the creation of Corporation Mapfre. The process was finally completed in 2008 with the establishment of Mapfre SA, with Foundation Mapfre holding over 50 per cent of the shares, essentially to avoid being 'conquered' by others. Certainly, one can assert that the performance of American, Japanese, German, French, English, and other foreign companies provide efficient models of how to offer services in the insurance world, but Spaniards can also claim that, in the form of Mapfre, they have their own particular model of organization that is well suited to the needs of a medium-sized and less-developed country. The foundation is the key institution in the Mapfre system that serves to preserve the company culture and way of doing business.

Bibliography

Adams, Mike, Andersson, Lars-Fredrik, Jia, Joy Yihua, and Lindmark, Magnus (2011) 'Mutuality as a Control for Information Asymmetry: a Historical Analysis of the Claims Experience of Mutual and Stock Fire Insurance Companies in Sweden 1889 to 1939', *Business History* 53: 1074–91.

Aggarwal, R. (2002) 'Demutualization and Corporate Governance of Stock Exchanges', *Journal of Applied Corporate Finance* 15: 105–13.

Ahmad, N. and Petersen, D. R. (2007) *High-Growth Enterprises and Gazelles: Preliminary and Summary Sensitivity Analysis.* Paris: OECD-FOR A.

Alborn, Timothy (2009) *Regulated Lives: Life Insurance and British Society, 1800–1914.* Toronto: University of Toronto Press.

Alonso Olea, Eduardo (2010) 'El mundo del seguro en Vizcaya. 1890–1936. Empresas y empresarios', in Jerònia Pons Pons and Mª Angeles Pons Brías (eds) *Investigaciones Históricas sobre el Seguro Español.* Madrid: Fundación Mapfre, 157–89.

Åmark, K. (1932) *Allmänna Brandförsäkringsverket 1782–1932 – Minnesskrift.* Stockholm: Victor Pettersons Bokförlag.

Andersson, L-F., Eriksson, L., and Lindmark, M. (2010) 'Life Insurance and Income Growth: the Case of Sweden 1830–1950', *Scandinavian Economic History Review* 50: 203–19.

Anon (1811) *Considerations on the Marine Insurance Laws.* London.

Anon (1813) *Observations on Marine Insurance.* London.

Anon (1960) *Thames and Mersey Marine Insurance Company Limited, 1860–1960.* Liverpool: privately printed.

Arndt, E. H. (1928) *Banking and Currency Development in South Africa.* Cape Town: Juta.

Arps, Ludwig (1965) *Auf Sicheren Pfeilern: Deutsche Versicherungswirtschaft vor 1914.* Göttingen: Vandenhoeck and Ruprecht.

Asahi Mutual Life Insurance Company (1990) *The Hundred Year History of Asahi Life: Volume 1 (Asahi SeimeiHyaku-nen-shi: Jo-kan* in Japanese). Tokyo: Asahi Mutual Life Insurance Company.

Asahi Mutual Life Insurance Company (1992) *The Hundred Year History of Asahi Life: the Book of Materials (Asahi SeimeiHyaku-nen-shi: Shiryo-hen* in Japanese). Tokyo: Asahi Mutual Life Insurance Company.

Asajima, Syouichi (2007) 'Actual Conditions of the Self-Insurance of Mitsui Bussan', *Monthly Report of the Institute of Social Science, Sensyu University* 526: 1–40 (in Japanese).

Association of Life Insurance Companies (ed.) (1934) *Collection of Historical Materials of Insurance in the Meiji and Taisho Era: Volume 1 (Meiji Taisho Hoken Shiryo: Dai-1-kan* in Japanese). Tokyo: Association of Life Insurance Companies.

Aubanell Jubany, Anna Maria (2002) 'La élite de la clase trabajadora. Las condiciones laborales de los trabajadores de las eléctricas madrileñas en el periodo de entreguerras', *Scripta Nova: Revista Electrónica de Geografía Y Cienicas Sociales* 6, 119.

Bahamonde Magro, Ángel (1981) 'El horizonte económico de la burguesía isabelina, 1856–1866', unpublished PhD thesis, Universidad Complutense de Madrid.

Bailey, A. H. (1862) 'On the Principles on which the Funds of Life Assurance Societies Should Be Invested', *Assurance Magazine and Journal of the Institute of Actuaries* 10: 142–7.

Baldwin, D. L. (2007) *Chicago's New Negroes: Modernity, the Great Migration, and Black Urban Life*. Durham, NC: University of North Carolina Press.

Bankoff, Greg (2008) 'Non-Institutionalised Forms of Risk-Spreading in the Philippines: Living without Insurance in a Dangerous Environment', paper presented to the Asia-Pacific Economic and Business History Conference, Melbourne.

Baranoff, Dalit (2003) 'Shaped by Risk: the American Fire Insurance Industry, 1790–1920', unpublished PhD thesis, Johns Hopkins University.

Bawcutt, Paul (1997) *Captive Insurance Companies*. 4th edition, London: Witherby.

Beard, Patricia (2003) *After the Ball: Gilded Age Secrets, Boardroom Betrayals, and the Party that Ignited the Great Wall Street Scandal of 1905*. New York: Harper Collins.

Bellis, C. (1997) *The Future Managers, Actuaries on Australia 1853–1997*. Sydney: Institute of Actuaries.

Bennett, C. (2004) *Dictionary of Insurance*. 2nd edition, Harlow: Pearson.

Berg, L. and Grip, G. (1992) *Branschglidningen mellan bank och försäkring. En översikt och introduction*. Stockholm.

Bergander, B. (1967) *Försäkringsväsendet i Sverige 1814–1914*. Stockholm: Försäkringsinspektionen.

Bernier, G. and Nathan, A. (2007) 'A Descriptive Analysis of Canadian Insurance Markets', in J. D. Cummins and B. Venard (eds.) *Handbook of International Insurance: between Global Dynamics and Local Contingencies*. New York: Springer, 403–53.

Best, A. M. (2010) *Best's Report on Global Mutual Insurance*. Bowdon: ICMIF.

Birchall, J. (ed.) (2001) *The New Mutualism in Public Policy*. London: Routledge.

Blainey, G. (1999) *A History of the AMP*. Sydney: Allen and Unwin.

Blair, M. (1991) 'The Choice of Ownership Structure in the Australian Life Industry', unpublished PhD thesis, University of Sydney.

Blomberg, N. W. (1964) *Framsteg: Folksams uppkomst och utveckling*. Stockholm: Kooperativa Förbundets Bokförlag.

Boenigk, Otto v. (1895) 'Zur Geschichte der Feuerversicherung', *Assecuranz Jahrbuch* 16: 5–27.

Bohlin, P. and Sjöblom, N. (2005) *Värdeöverföringar från livförsäkrings-aktiebolag som inte får dela ut vinst*. Lund: Lund University.

Boksjö, A. and Lönnborg-Andersson, M. (1994) 'Competitive and Collusive Institutions in the Swedish Insurance Market', *Scandinavian Insurance Quarterly* 2: 139–59.

Borscheid, Peter (1984) 'The Establishment of the Life Insurance Business in Germany in the Nineteenth Century', in W. Engels and H. Pohl (eds) *German Yearbook on Business History*. Berlin: Springer, 55–74.

Borscheid, Peter (1989) *Mit Sicherheit Leben: Die Geschichte der deutschen Lebensversicherungswirtschaft und der Provinzial-Lebensversicherungsanstalt von Westfalen*. Vol. 1, Greven: Eggenkamp Verlag.

Borscheid, Peter (1997) *275 Jahre Feuersozietäten in Westfalen: Vorsprung durch Erfahrung*. Münster: Westfälische Provinzial-Versicherungen.

Borscheid, Peter (2001) 'Vertrauensgewinn und Vertrauensverlust: Das Auslandsgeschäft der deutschen Versicherungswirtschaft 1870–1945', *Vierteljahrschrift für Sozial- und Wirtschaftsgeschichte* 88: 311–45.

Borscheid, Peter (2010) 'History of the Insurance Industry in Germany', in Leonardo Caruana (ed.) *Encuentro Internacional sobre la Historia del Seguro*. Madrid: Fundacion Mapfre, 43–68.

Borscheid, Peter (2012a) 'Middle East and Northern Africa: Overview', in Peter Borscheid and Niels-Viggo Haueter (eds) *World Insurance: the Evolution of a Global Risk Network*. Oxford: Oxford University Press, 349–72.

Borscheid, Peter (2012b) 'Far East and Pacific: Overview', in Peter Borscheid and Niels-Viggo Haueter (eds) *World Insurance: the Evolution of a Global Risk Network*. Oxford: Oxford University Press, 415–43.

Borscheid, Peter (2012c) 'Latin America and Caribbean: Overview', in Peter Borscheid and Niels-Viggo Haueter (eds) *World Insurance: the Evolution of a Global Risk Network*. Oxford: Oxford University Press, 559–77.

Borscheid, Peter and Drees, Annette (eds) (1988) *Historische Statistik von Deutschland, Band IV: Versicherungsstatistik Deutschlands 1750–1985*. St Katherinen: Scripta Mercaturae Verlag.

Boyce, Gordon (1992) '64thers, Syndicates and Stock Promotions: Information Flows and Fund-Raising Techniques of British Shipowners before 1914', *Journal of Economic History* 52: 181–205.

Bristol, Douglas (2004) 'From Outposts to Enclaves: a Social History of Black Barbers from 1750 to 1915', *Enterprise and Society* 5: 594–606.

Brown, Anthony (1980) *Cuthbert Heath, Maker of the Modern Lloyd's of London*. Newton Abbot: David and Charles.

Brundin, G. (1950) 'Skälighetsprincipen i skadeförsäkring', *Nordisk Försäkringstidskrift*, 1: 20–38.

Büchner, F. (1976) 'Die Entstehung der Hamburger Feuerkasse und ihre Entwicklung bis zur Mitte des 19. Jahrhunderts', in Hamburger Feuerkasse (ed.) *300 Jahre Hamburger Feuerkasse*. Karlsruhe: Verlag Versicherungswirtschaft, 1–50.

Bucht, O. (1936) *Försäkringsväsendets företagsformer från antiken till våra dagar*. Stockholm: Kooperativa Förbundets Bokförlag.

Budros, Arthur Louis (1989) 'The Making of an Industry: Organizational Births in New York's Life Insurance Industry, 1842–1904', unpublished PhD thesis, University of California Los Angeles.

Buley, Roscoe C. (1967) *The Equitable Life Assurance Society of the United States 1859–1964*. 2 vols, New York: Appleton-Century-Crofts.

Bulpin, T. V. (1996) *Die Southern*. Cape Town: Cape Publishers.

Burgaz, J. and Perez-Morales, M. (1996) *1902–1992. 90 años de seguros agrarios en España*. Madrid: Ministerio de Agricultura.

Butler, Richard J., Cui, Yijing, and Whitman, Andrew (2000) 'Insurers' Demutualization Decisions', *Risk Management and Insurance Review* 3: 135–54.

Butlin, N. G. (1964) *Investment in Australian Economic Development 1861–1900*. Cambridge: Cambridge University Press.

Cagle, Julie A. B., Lippert, Robert L., and Moore, William T. (1996) 'Demutualization in the Property-Liability Insurance Industry', *Journal of Insurance Regulation* 14: 343–69.

Cannon, M. (1975) *Australia in the Victorian Age: Life in the Cities*. Melbourne: Thomas Nelson.

Carroll, Glenn R. (1984) 'Organizational Ecology', *Annual Review of Sociology* 10: 71–93.

Castillo, Santiago (ed.) (1994) *Solidaridad desde abajo. Trabajadores y Socorros Mutuos en la España Contemporánea*. Madrid: Unión General de Trabajadores y Confederación Nacional de Entidades de Previsión.

Castillo, Santiago and Ortiz de Orruño, J. M. (eds) (1997) *Estado, protesta y movimientos sociales*. Guipúzcoa: Universidad del País Vasco.

Castillo, Santiago and Ruzafa, R. (eds) (2009) *La previsión social en la Historia*. Madrid: Siglo XXI.

Chandler, Alfred D., Jr. (1994) *Scale and Scope: the Dynamics of Industrial Capitalism*. Cambridge, MA: Harvard University Press.

Chiyoda Mutual Life Insurance Company (1955) *The Fifty Year History of Chiyoda Mutual Life* (*Goju-nen-shi: Chiyoda Seimei Hoken Sogo-gaisha* in Japanese). Tokyo: Chiyoda Mutual Life Insurance Company.

Choi, B. P. (2010) 'The U.S. Property and Liability Industry: Firm Growth, Size, and Age', *Risk Management and Insurance Review* 13: 207–24.

Clark, Geoffrey (1999) *Betting on Lives: the Culture of Life Insurance in England 1695–1775*. Manchester: Manchester University Press.

Clayton, George and Osborn, W. T. (1965) *Insurance Company Investment: Principles and Policy*. London: George Allen and Unwin.

Cockerell, H. A. L. and Green, Edwin (1994) *The British Insurance Business, 1547–1970*. 2nd edition, Sheffield: Sheffield University Press.

Craig, R., Greenhill, B., Porter, J. H., and Slade, W. J. (1994) 'Some Aspects of the Business of Devon Shipping in the Nineteenth Century', in M. Duffy et al. (eds) *A New Maritime History of Devon, Vol. II: From the Late Eighteenth Century to the Present Day*. London: Conway Maritime Press, 99–107.

Crothers, A. Glenn (2004) 'Commercial Risk and Capital Formation in Early America: Virginia Merchants and the Rise of American Marine Insurance, 1750–1815', *Business History Review* 78: 607–33.

Cummins, J. D. and Venard, B. (2008) 'Insurance Market Dynamics: between Global Developments and Local Contingencies', *Risk Management and Insurance Review* 11: 295–326.

Cummins, J. D., Tennyson, S. and Weiss, M. A. (1999a) 'Consolidation and Efficiency in the US Life Insurance Industry', *Journal of Banking and Finance* 23: 325–57.

Cummins, J. D., Weiss M. A., and Zi, H. (1999b) 'Organizational Form and Efficiency: the Coexistence of Stock and Mutual Property-Liability Insurers', *Management Science* 45: 1254–69.

Cummins, J. D., Rubio-Misas, M., and Zi, H. (2004) 'The Effect of Organisational Structure on Efficiency: Evidence from the Spanish Insurance Industry', *Journal of Banking and Finance* 28: 3113–50.

Dai-ichi Mutual Life Insurance Company (1987) *The Eighty-Five Year History of Dai-ichi Life* (*Dai-ichiSeimeiHachijugo-nen-shi* in Japanese). Tokyo: Dai-ichi Mutual Life Insurance Company.

Dai-ichi Mutual Life Insurance Company (2004) *The Hundred Year History of Dai-ichi Life* (*Dai-ichiSeimeiHyaku-nen-shi* in Japanese). Tokyo: Dai-ichi Mutual Life Insurance Company.

Dalzell, Robert F. (1987) *Enterprising Elite: the Boston Associates and the World They Made.* New York: W. W. Norton.

Daston, L. J. (1987) 'The Domestication of Risk: Mathematical Probability and Insurance 1650–1830', in L. Krüger, L. J. Daston, and M. Heidelberger (eds) *The Probabilistic Revolution, Volume 1: Ideas in History.* Cambridge, MA: MIT Press, 237–60.

Davenport, T. R. H. and Saunders, C. (2000) *South Africa: a Modern History.* 5th edition, Craig Hall: Macmillan.

Davenport, T. R. H. and Saunders, C. S. (2002) *A Modern History of South Africa.* 9th edition, Johannesburg: Macmillan.

De Graaf, L. B. (1962) 'Negro Migration to Los Angeles, 1930 to 1950', unpublished PhD dissertation, University of California, Los Angeles.

De Gregorio y Villota, I. (1933) 'Nuestra mutualidad y el seguro obligatorio', *Boletin de la Agrupación de Propietarios de Fincas Rústicas de España* 16: 2.

De La Calle Velasco, Mª Dolores (2010) 'Mutualidades Laborales en el régimen de Franco', *Revista de la Historia de la Economía y de la Empresa* 4: 209–24.

De Mateo Avilés, E. (2000) *La sociedad de seguros contra incendios de edificios y los orígenes del servicio de Bomberos de Málaga durante el siglo XIX.* Málaga: Diputación de Málaga.

Del Angel, G. (2012) 'Mexico: a History of the Insurance Industry in Mexico', in Peter Borscheid and Niels-Viggo Haueter (eds) *World Insurance: the Evolution of a Global Risk Network.* Oxford: Oxford University Press, 599–619.

Dinsdale, W. A. (1954) *History of Accident Insurance in Great Britain.* London: Stone and Company.

Doe, Helen (2009) *From Coastal Sail to Global Shipping: the History of Steamship Mutual Underwriting Association, 1909 to 2009.* London: Steamship Insurance Management Services.

Doe, Helen (2013) 'Power, Authority and Communications: the Role of the Master and the Managing Owner in Nineteenth-Century British Merchant Shipping', *International Journal of Maritime History* 25: 1–24.

Doherty, N. A. and Dionne, G. (1993) 'Insurance with Undiversifiable Risk: Contract Structure and Organizational Form of Insurance Firms', *Journal of Risk and Uncertainty* 6: 187–203.

Dorwart, Reinhold A. (1958) 'The Earliest Fire Insurance Company in Berlin and Brandenburg, 1705–1711', *Business History Review* 32: 192–203.

Dowd, J. B., Albright, J., Raghunathan, T. E., Schoeni, R. F., LeClere, F., and Kaplan, G. A. (2011) 'Deeper and Wider: Income and Mortality in the USA over Three Decades', *International Journal of Epidemiology* 40: 183–8.

Drew, Bernard (1949) *The London Assurance: a Second Chronicle.* London: London Assurance.

Edvinsson R., Jacobson T., and Waldenström, D. (2010) *Exchange Rates, Prices, and Wages, 1277–2008.* Stockholm: Ekerlid.

Ehler, Hans-Jörg (2009) *Der Reichsverband der Privatversicherung: Eine Chronik der Ereignisse und Entwicklungen.* Karlsruhe: Verlag Versicherungswirtschaft.

Ehlers, A. (2002) *Die Geskiedenis van die Trustmaatskappye en Eksekuteurskamers van Boland Bank Beperk tot 1971*. Stellenbosch: University of Stellenbosch.

Englund, Karl (1982) *Försäkring och fusioner. Skandia, Skåne, Svea, Thule, Öresund 1855–1980*. Stockholm: Skandia.

Enskilt försäkringsväsen (1954) Hur det vuxit fram och hur det övervakas, beskrivet av Försäkringsinspektionen. Stockholm: Swedish Insurance Inspectorate.

Erhemjamts, O. and Leverty, J. T. (2010) 'The Demise of the Mutual Organisational Form: an Investigation of the Life Insurance Industry', *Journal of Money, Credit and Banking* 42: 1011–36.

Fama, E. F. and Jensen, M. C. (1983) 'Agency Problems and Residual Claims', *Journal of Law and Economics* 26: 327–49.

Faure, D. and Köll, E. (2012) 'China: the Indigenization of Insurance', in Peter Borscheid and Niels-Viggo Haueter (eds) *World Insurance: the Evolution of a Global Risk Network*. Oxford: Oxford University Press, 472–94.

Feldbæk, O., Løkke, A., and Leth Jeppessen, S. (2007) *Drømmen om tryghed: Tusind års dansk forsikring* (Copenhagen: Gads).

Feldman, Gerald D. (2001) *Allianz and the German Insurance Business 1933–1945*. Cambridge: Cambridge University Press.

Fernández Junquera, Manuela (1975) *La tributación del Seguro Privada*. Madrid: Ministerio de Hacienda, Instituto de Estudios Fiscales.

Fernández Pacheco, A. (1995) *25 años de Vida: Mapfre Vida 1970–1995*. Madrid: Mapfre Vida.

Fitzgerald, J. F. (1986) 'Demutualizing an Insurance Company: Determining and Distributing Policyholders' Shares', *Journal of Insurance Regulation* 4: 103–31.

Fitzgerald, J. F. (1990) 'Demutualization Case Studies: a 20-Year History', *Journal of Insurance Regulation* 9: 287–309.

Flamming, D. (2005) *Bound for Freedom: Black Los Angeles in Jim Crow America*. Berkeley and Los Angeles: University of California Press.

Folksams försäkringsutrednings betänkande (1962) *Folksam*. Stockholm: Folksam.

Frax, Esperanza and Matilla Quizà, María Jesús (2010) 'Los seguros negocios del franquismo. El proceso de bloqueo, expropiación y liquidación de las compañías de seguros con capital alemán', in Jerònia Pons Pons and Mª Angeles Pons Brías (eds) *Investigaciones Históricas sobre el Seguro Español*. Madrid: Fundación Mapfre, 227–58.

Freeman, John H. and Audia, Pino G. (2006) 'Community Ecology and the Sociology of Organizations', *Annual Review of Sociology* 32: 145–69.

Freeman, Mark, Pearson, Robin, and Taylor, James (2007) 'Technological Change and the Governance of Joint-Stock Enterprise in the Early Nineteenth Century: the Case of Coastal Shipping', *Business History* 49: 573–94.

García Ruiz, J. L. and Caruana, L. (2009) 'La internacionalización del seguro español en el siglo XX', *Revista de historia industrial* 41: 17–47.

Gesellschaft fuer Feuerversicherungsgeschichtliche Forschung e. v. (1913) *Das deutsche Feuerversicherungswesen*, 2 vols. Hanover: Rechts, Staats und Sozialwissenschaftlicher Verlag.

Gibrat, R. (1931) *Les Inegalites Economiques*. Paris: Recueil Sirey.

Giliomee, H. (2003) *The Afrikaners: Biography of a People*. Cape Town: Tafelberg.

Gloster, J. (1976) *North Carolina Mutual Life Insurance Company: Its Historical Development and Current Operations.* New York: Arno Press.

Go, Sabine (2009) *Marine Insurance in the Netherlands 1600–1870: a Comparative Institutional Approach.* Amsterdam: Aksant.

Gottlieb, D. (2007) 'Asymmetric Information in Late 19th Century Cooperative Insurance Societies', *Explorations in Economic History* 44: 270–92.

Graham, L. and Xie, X. (2007) 'The United States Insurance Market: Characteristics and Trends', in J. D. Cummins and B. Venard (eds) *Handbook of International Insurance: between Global Dynamics and Local Contingencies.* New York: Springer, 25–145.

Gray, A. C. (1977) *Life Insurance in Australia.* Melbourne: McCarron Bird.

Greene, M. R. and Johnson, R. E. (1980) 'Stocks vs Mutuals: Who Controls?', *Journal of Risk and Insurance* 47: 165–74.

Greenford, B. C., Mullins, M. M., Garvey J., Morris, L., and O'Meara, L. (2007) 'The Insurance Market in the Republic of Ireland', in J. D. Cummins and B. Venard (eds) *Handbook of International Insurance: between Global Dynamics and Local Contingencies.* New York: Springer, 553–95.

Grenholm, Å. (1955) *Försäkringsaktiebolaget Skandia 1855–1955.* Stockholm: Skandia.

Greve, Henrich R. and Rao, Hayagreeva (2012) 'Echoes of the Past: Organizational Foundings as Sources of an Institutional legacy of Mutualism', *American Journal of Sociology* 118: 635–75.

Greyling, L. and Verhoef, G. (2012) 'Savings and Economic Growth: a Historical Analysis of the Savings Behavior and Economic Performance in the Cape Colony, 1850–1909', unpublished paper, University of Johannesburg.

Grip, G. (1987) *Vill du frihet eller tvång? Svensk försäkringspolitik 1935–1945.* Uppsala: Uppsala University.

Grip, G. (1991) *Fondförsäkringsfrågan. Om livförsäkringar med anknytning till värdepappersfonder.* Stockholm: Folksam.

Grip, G. (1994) *Från stor livförsäkring till folkförsäkring: En skrift med anledning av Folksam Livs verksamhet 1914–1994.* Stockholm: Folksam.

Grip, G. (2009) *Folksam 1908–2008. Vol. 1, Försäkringsrörelsen.* Stockholm: Informationsförlaget.

Guillém Mesado, Juan Manuel (2010) 'La difícil mayoría de edad de las sociedades de seguro por acciones en la primera mitad del siglo XIX', in Jerònia Pons Pons and Mª Angeles Pons Brías (eds) *Investigaciones Históricas sobre el Seguro Español.* Madrid: Fundación Mapfre, 49–79.

Guinnane, Timothy W. and Streb, Jochen (2011) 'Moral Hazard in a Mutual-Health Insurance System: the German *Knappschaften*, 1867–1914', *Journal of Economic History* 71: 70–104.

Guinnane, Timothy W. and Streb, Jochen (2012) 'Incentives that Saved Lives: Government Regulation of Accident Insurance Associations in Germany 1884–1914', *Ruhr Economic Papers* 364, Ruhr-Universität Bochum.

Gunnarson, K., Kleverman, A., and Norrby, J. (1996) 'Svensk försäkring. Trender under efterkrigstiden', in B. Dufwa (ed.), *Vänbok till Erland Strömbäck.* Stockholm: Svenska Försäkringsföreningens Förlag, 157–78.

Hägg, P. G. T. (1998) *An Institutional Analysis of Insurance Regulation: the Case of Sweden.* Lund: Nationalekonomiska-institutionen.

Hamburger Feuerkasse (1976) *300 Jahre Hamburger Feuerkasse*. Karlsruhe: Verlag Versicherungswirtschaft e. V.

Hannan, Michael T. and Freeman, John (1977) 'The Population Ecology of Organizations', *American Journal of Sociology* 82: 929–64.

Hansmann, H. (1985) 'The Organisation of Insurance Companies: Mutual versus Stock', *Journal of Law, Economics and Organisation* 1: 125–52.

Hansmann, H. (1996) *The Ownership of Enterprise*. Cambridge, MA: Belknap Press of Harvard University Press.

Harrington, Scott E. and Niehaus, Gregory R. (2003) *Risk Management and Insurance*. 2nd edition, New York: McGraw-Hill.

Hart, Emma (2012) 'The Ambition for an All Brick City: Elites, Builders and the Growth of Eighteenth-Century Charleston, South Carolina', in Carole Shammas (ed.) *Investing in the Early Modern Built Environment: Europeans, Asians, Settlers and Indigenous Societies*. Leiden: Brill, 237–62.

Helmer, Georg (1925–6) *Die Geschichte der privaten Feuerversicherung in den Herzogtümern Schleswig und Holstein*. 2 vols, Berlin: Verband öffentlicher Feuerversicherungsanstalten.

Hernando de Larramendi, Ignacio (2000) *Así se hizo MAPFRE*. Madrid: Actas Editorial.

Hirao, Hachisaburo (2011, 2012) *The Diary of Hachisaburo Hirao*. Vols. 3–4 (2011), vols. 5–6 (2012). Kobe: Konan Gakuen (in Japanese).

Hirsch, H. M. (1962) 'Early Days of Insurance in South Africa,1826–1860', *African Insurance Record* September/October, 25–7: 39–43.

Henderson, A. B. (1990) *Atlanta Life Insurance Company: Guardian of Black Economic Dignity*. Tuscaloosa: University of Alabama Press.

Historisk Statistik för Sverige (1999) *Befolkningsutvecklingen under 250 år: historisk statistik för Sverige*. Stockholm: Statistiska Centralbyrån.

Hjärtström, P. (2005) (ed.) *Idéerna bakom länsförsäkringsgruppen: Från brandstodsbolag till finansiella varuhus*. Stockholm: Länsförsäkringar.

Horne, G. (1997) *Fire this Time: the Watts Uprising and the 1960s*. New York: Da Capo Press.

Houghton, D. H. (1976) *The South African Economy*. Cape Town: Oxford University Press.

Hussey, W. D. (1963) *The British Empire and the Commonwealth, 1500–1961*. Cambridge: Cambridge University Press.

Inagaki, Suesaburo (ed.) (1951) *A Memorandum of Kagami Kenkichi and His Reports and Proposals from London*. Tokyo: Tokio Marine Insurance Co (in Japanese).

Iwama, R. (1926) *Anecdotes of Kokko Life (KokkoSeimeiMukashiGatari* in Japanese). Tokyo: Kokko Mutual Life Insurance Company.

James, Harold (2013) 'Introduction: the Insuring Instinct', in Harold James et al. (eds) *The Value of Risk: Swiss Re and the History of Reinsurance*. Oxford: Oxford University Press, 1–22.

James, M. (1942) *Biography of a Business, 1792–1942: Insurance Company of North America*. Indianapolis, IN: Bobbs-Merrill.

Japan Business History Institute (1979) *Centenary History of Tokio Marine and Fire Insurance Company*. Tokyo: Tokio Marine and Fire Insurance Company, vol. 5 (in Japanese).

Japan Business History Institute (1996) *The Seventy-Five Year History of Mitsui Marine & Fire Insurance Company*. Tokyo: Mitsui Marine & Fire Insurance Company (in Japanese).

Jarvis, Rupert C. (1959) 'Fractional Shareholding in British Merchant Ships with Special Reference to the 64ths', *Mariners' Mirror* 45: 301–19.

Jeng, V. and Lai, G. C. (2005) 'Ownership Structure, Agency Costs, Specialization, and Efficiency: Analysis of Keiretsu and Independent Insurers in the Japanese Nonlife Insurance Industry', *Journal of Risk and Insurance* 72: 105–58.

Jeng, V., Lai, G. C., and McNamara, M. J. (2007) 'Efficiency and Demutualization: Evidence from the US Life Insurance Industry in the 1980s and 1990s', *Journal of Risk and Insurance* 74: 683–711.

Jennings, Edward (1843) *Hints on Sea-Risks: Containing Some Practical Suggestions for Diminishing Maritime Losses, Both of Life and Property: Addressed to Merchants, Ship-Owners and Mariners*. London: R. B. Bate.

Jennings, Edward (1844) *Practical Hints Addressed to Seamen for Preventing Accidents on Board Ship, and Especially for Guarding against Hurricanes, Collision, Fire etc.* Vol.1, London: R. B. Bate.

Johnson, Paul (2010) *Making the Market: Victorian Origins of Corporate Capitalism*. Cambridge: Cambridge University Press.

Jones, F. S. (1996) *The Great Imperial Banks: a Story of the Business of the Standard Bank and Barclays Bank, 1861–1961*. Pretoria: Unisa Press.

Jonung, Lars (1999) Med backspegeln som kompass: om stabiliseringspolitik som läroprocess, Ds (9). Stockholm.

Jüring, R. (1978) *Folksam: En berättelse om ett folkrörelseföretags roll i utvecklingen från ofärd till välfärd*. Stockholm: Folksam.

Jüring, R. (1983) *Det kooperativa alternativet i försäkring: Folksam 75 år 1908–1983*. Stockholm: Folksam.

Kader, H. A., Adams, M., Andersson, L. F., and Lindmark, M. (2010) 'The Determinants of Reinsurance in the Swedish Property Fire Insurance Market during the Interwar Years, 1919–39', *Business History* 52: 268–84.

Kamiya, Hisaaki (2012) 'The Marine Insurance Business in Japan in 1920s: the Background of Establishment of the Hull Insurers' Union', *Non-Life Insurance Review* 74: 31–67 (in Japanese).

Kantor, Shawn Everett and Fishback, Price V. (1996) 'Precautionary Saving, Insurance, and the Origins of Workers' Compensation', *Journal of Political Economy* 104: 419–42.

Keller, M. (1963) *The Life Insurance Enterprise, 1855–1910: a Study in the Limits of Corporate Power*. Cambridge, MA: Harvard University Press.

Keneley, M. J. (2002) 'The Origins of Formal Collusion in Australian Fire Insurance 1870–1920', *Australian Economic History Review* 42: 54–76.

Keneley M. J. (2005) 'Control of the Australian Life Insurance Industry: an Example of Regulatory Externalities within the Australian Financial Sector 1870–1945', *Australian Economic History Review* 45: 1–22.

Keneley, M. J. (2006) 'Mortgages and Bonds: the Asset Management Practices of Australian Life Insurers', *Accounting Business and Financial History* 16: 99–119.

Keneley, M. J. (2010) 'The Demise of the Mutual Life Insurer: an Analysis of the Impact of Regulatory Change on the Performance of Australian Life Insurers in the 1990s', *Accounting History* 15: 65–91.

Keneley, M. J. (2012) 'The Path to Project Darwin: the Evolution of the AMP's Organisational Structure', *Business History* 54: 342–62.

Keneley, M. and Verhoef, G. (2011) 'Pressures for Change in the Australian and South African Insurance Markets: a Comparison of Two Companies', *Competition and Change* 15: 136–54.

Kennedy, J. (1999) *Not by Chance: a History of the International Cooperative and Mutual Insurance Federation*. Manchester: Holyoake Books.

Kennedy, P. (2003) *A Guide to Econometrics*. 5th edition, Oxford: Blackwell.

Kenwood, A. G. and Lougheed, A. L. (1999) *The Growth of the International Economy, 1870–2000*. 4th edition, London: Routledge.

Kim, D. and Lee M. H. (2012) 'Korea: Insurance in a Tiger Market', in Peter Borscheid and Niels-Viggo Haueter (eds) *World Insurance: the Evolution of a Global Risk Network*. Oxford: Oxford University Press, 522–35.

Kingston, Christopher (2007) 'Marine Insurance in Britain and America, 1720–1844: a Comparative Institutional Analysis', *Journal of Economic History* 67: 379–409.

Kingston, Christopher (2011) 'Marine Insurance in Philadelphia during the Quasi-War with France, 1795–1801', *Journal of Economic History* 71: 162–84.

Kinoshita, N. (2010a) 'Minami California Ni Okeru Kokujin, Nikkei, Hispanic-Kei Kigyou Keiei No Shiteki Kohsatsu: Business to Jinsyu, Ethnicity, Nation, Local Community', unpublished PhD thesis, Hokkaido University.

Kinoshita, N. (2010b) 'Kokujin Seimei Hoken Gaisha No Hanbai Soshiki: Golden State Mutual No Jirei, 1925–1940', *Keieishigaku* 45: 57–74.

Klerk, G. J. de (1978) 'Versekeringswese: 'n Historiese oorsig en enkele bedryfsekonomie aspekte met spesiale verwysing na groepsversekering', unpublished D. Com thesis, University of Potchefstroom.

Knaggs, O. (1990) *Norwich Life, 1706–1990*. Cape Town: O. Knaggs and Associates.

Knights, D. and Willmott, H. (1993) '"It's a Very Foreign Discipline": the Genesis of Expenses Control in a Mutual Life Insurance Company', *British Journal of Management* 4: 1–18.

Kopper, Christopher (2012) 'Why Were Reinsurance Companies Always Organized as Joint Stock Companies—and Why Did They Hold Significant Equity of Insurance Companies?' Paper presented to the World Economic History Congress, Stellenbosch.

Kuno, Hideo (1970) 'The Account System of the Early Period of Mitsubishi', *Journal of the Department of Economics of Gakushuin University* 7: 83–98 (in Japanese).

Kwon, W. J. (2010) 'History of Insurance, Market Development, and Regulation in Seven Least Developed Countries in Asia', *Asia-Pacific Journal of Risk and Insurance* 5: 1–39.

Lai, Gene C., McNamara, Michael J., and Yu, Tong (2008) 'The Wealth Effect of Demutualization: Evidence from the U.S. Property-Liability and Life Insurance Industries', *Journal of Risk and Insurance* 75: 125–44.

Lamm-Tennant, Joan and Starks, Laura T. (1993) 'Stock versus Mutual Ownership Structures: the Risk Implications', *Journal of Business* 66: 29–46.

Larriñaga, Carlos and Lázaro, Carmen (1996) 'Los inicios del seguro privado en Guipúzcoa: de las sociedades de socorros mutuos a las primeras compañías (1842–1914)', *Espacio, Tiempo y Forma*, Serie V, Hª Contemporánea, 9: 43–66.

Larsson, M. (1991) 'Den reglerade marknaden: Svenskt försäkringsväsende 1850–1980', *SNS Occasional Paper* 23, Stockholm.

Larsson, M. (2011) *FPG 50 år i näringslivets tjänst*. Stockholm: Informationsförlaget.

Larsson, M. and Lönnborg, M. (2010) 'The History of Insurance Companies in Sweden: 1855–2005', in L. Caruana de las Cagigas (ed.) *Encuentro Internacional sobre la Historia del Seguro*. Madrid: Fundació Mapfre, 197–237.

Larsson, M., Lönnborg, M., and Svärd, S-E. (2005) *Den svenska försäkringsmodellens uppgång och fall*. Stockholm: Svenska Försäkringsföreningens Förlag.

Laux, Christian and Muermann, Alexander (2010) 'Financing Risk Transfer under Governance Problems: Mutual versus Stock Insurers', *Journal of Financial Intermediation* 19: 333–54.

Le Pichon, A. (ed.) (2006) *China, Trade and Empire: Jardine, Matheson & Co. and the Origins of British Rule in Hong Kong, 1827–1843*. Oxford: Oxford University Press.

Ledwith, F., Potter, E., Hayes, D., Jani, M. (1957) 'The History and Development of Protecting and Indemnity Clubs'. London: Chartered Insurance Institute, 8 January, unpublished typescript.

Lee, R. (2002) 'The Future of Securities Exchanges'. Working paper, Wharton Financial Institutions Centre, Wharton School.

Leonard, Adrian (2013) 'Contingent Commitment: the Development of English Marine Insurance in the Context of New Institutional Economics, 1577–1720', in D'Maris Coffman, Adrian Leonard, and Larry Neal (eds) *Questioning Credible Commitment: New Perspectives on the Rise of Financial Capitalism*. Cambridge: Cambridge University Press, 48–75.

Lille, A. (1882) *Försäkringsväsendet. Dess historiska utveckling och nationalekonomiska betydelse*. Helsingfors: Frenckell and Son.

Linge, G. J. R. (1979) *Industrial Awakening: a Geography of Australian Manufacturing*. Canberra: ANU Press.

Lönnborg, M. (1999) *Internationalisering av svenska försäkringsbolag: drivkrafter, organisering och utveckling 1855–1913*, PhD Dissertation, Uppsala Universitet.

McCusker, John J. (1991) 'The Early History of 'Lloyd's List', *Historical Research: Bulletin of the Institute of Historical Research* 64: 427–31.

McFall, L. and Dodsworth, F. (2009) 'Fabricating the Market: the Promotion of Life Insurance in the Long Nineteenth Century', *Journal of Historical Sociology* 22: 30–54.

Macintyre, A. C. (1898) *South African Red Book: a Record of Insurance, Banking and Commercial Affairs*. Cape Town: T Maskew Miller.

McLean, I. W. (2004) 'Australian Economic Growth in Historical Perspective', *Economic Record* 80: 330–45.

MacMinn, R. and Ren, Y. (2011) 'Mutual versus Stock Insurers: a Synthesis of the Theoretical and Empirical Research', *Journal of Insurance Issues* 34: 101–11.

McNamara, Michael and Rhee, S. Ghon (1992) 'Ownership Structure and Performance: the Demutualization of Life Insurers', *Journal of Risk and Insurance* 59: 221–38.

Macpherson, I. (1977) 'The Origins of Cooperative Insurance on the Canadian Prairies', *Business and Economic History*: 76–87.

Maestro, Manuel (1991) *Madrid, capital aseguradora de España, tomo III de historia del seguro español*. Madrid: INESE.

Mann, R. J. (1859) *The Colony of Natal*. London: Jarrold and Sons.

Mapfre (1983) *Cincuenta años: Mapfre hacia el future*. Madrid: Mapfre.

Martel, Y. B. and Rabetino, R. (2012) 'Argentina: the Changing Fortunes of the Argentinian Insurance Market', in Peter Borscheid and Niels-Viggo Haueter (eds) *World Insurance: the Evolution of a Global Risk Network*. Oxford: Oxford University Press, 620–44.

Martín Aceña, Pablo and Comín Comín, Francisco (1994) 'El grupo INI en perspectiva histórica: una aproximación cuantitativa (1941–1986)', in José Luis García Ruiz and Juan Hernández Andreu (eds) *Lecturas de historia empresarial*. Madrid: Civitas, 331–74.

Martínez Vara, Tomàs (2006) 'Salarios y Programas de Bienestar Industrial en la empresa ferroviaria MZA (1915–1935)', *Investigaciones de Historia Económica* 4: 101–38.

Matilla Quizà, María Jesús (2010) 'La formación de capital en la España del siglo XIX: las compañías de seguros', in Jerònia Pons Pons and Mª Angeles Pons Brías (eds) *Investigaciones Históricas sobre el Seguro Español*. Madrid: Fundación Mapfre, 17–48.

Matilla Quizà, M. J. and Frax Rosales, E. (1996) 'Los seguros en España: 1830–1934', *Revista de Historia Económica* 14: 183–203.

Mayers, David and Smith, Clifford W., Jr. (1981) 'Contractual Provisions, Organizational Structure and Conflict Control in Insurance Markets', *Journal of Business* 54: 407–34.

Mayers, David and Smith, Clifford W., Jr. (1986) 'Ownership Structure and Control: the Mutualisation of Stock Life Insurance Companies', *Journal of Financial Economics* 16: 73–98.

Mayers, David and Smith, Clifford W., Jr. (1988) 'Ownership Structure across Lines of Property-Casualty Insurance', *Journal of Law and Economics* 31: 351–78.

Mayers, David and Smith, Clifford W., Jr. (1992) 'Executive Compensation in the Life Insurance Industry', *Journal of Business* 65: 51–74.

Mayers, David and Smith, Clifford W., Jr. (2004) 'Incentives for Managing Accounting Information: Property-Liability Insurer Stock-Charter Conversions', *Journal of Risk and Insurance* 71: 2213–51.

Maza Zorrilla, E. (ed.) (2003) *Asociacionismo en la España contemporánea. Vertientes y análisis interdisciplinar*. Valladolid: Universidad de Valladolid.

Meiji Life Assurance Company (2004) *The 120 Years History of Meiji Life*. Tokyo: Meiji Life Assurance Company (in Japanese).

Miller, R. J. (1968) *Life Assurance in South Africa*. Johannesburg: Blue Crane Books.

Ministry of Commerce and Industry of Japan (1881–1932) *The Insurance Year Book* (annual publication). Tokyo: Association of Life Insurance Companies.

Mishima, Yasuo (1989) *Mitsubishi: Its Challenge and Strategy*, translated by Emiko Yamaguchi. London: JAI Press.

Mitchell, Brian R. (ed.) (2003a) *International Historical Statistics: Europe 1750–2000*. 5th edition, Basingstoke: Palgrave Macmillan.

Mitchell, Brian R. (ed.) (2003b) *International Historical Statistics: the Americas 1750–2000*. 5th edition, Basingstoke: Palgrave Macmillan.

Mitsubishi Syashi Publishing Group (1980) *Mitsubishi Syashi*, Vol. 22. Tokyo: University of Tokyo Press (in Japanese).

Mitsubishi Syashi Publishing Group (1981) *Mitsubishi Syashi*, Vol. 19. Tokyo: University of Tokyo Press (in Japanese).

Miura, H. (1929) 'The Initiative and Pioneers of Life Insurance Business in Japan', *Economic Review* (*Keizai-Ronso* in Japanese) 29: 36–55.

Mizushima, Kazuya (1977) 'Householder's Insurance in the Early Part of the Meiji Period', *Journal of KokuminKeizai* 136: 13–31.

Mizushima, Kazuya (1992) 'Historical Development of Mutualism', *Kokumin Keizai Zasshi*, Kobe University, 165: 1–18 (in Japanese).

Molinero, Carme (2005) *La captación de las masas. Política Social y propaganda en el régimen franquista*. Madrid: Cátedra.

Mori, S. (1929) 'The Rise of Modern Life Insurance Business in Japan: Part 1', *Journal of KokkaGakai* 43: 19–58.

Morris, Maxen O. (1956) 'Protection and Indemnity Insurance: a Brief Outline', *Journal of the Chartered Insurance Institute* 53: 237–57.

Müller, C. F. J. (1973) *Vyfhonderd Jaar Suid-Afrikaanse Geskiedenis*. Pretoria: Academica.

Müller, C. F. J. (1974) *Die Oorsprong van die Groot Trek*. Cape Town: Tafelberg Publishers.

Müller, C. F. J. (ed.) (1983) *500 Years of South African History*. 5th edition, Pretoria: Academica.

Murphy, Sharon Ann (2005) 'Securing Human Property: Slavery, Life Insurance, and Industrialization in the Upper South', *Journal of the Early Republic* 25: 615–52.

Murphy, Sharon Ann (2008) 'Selecting Risks in an Anonymous World: the Agency System for Life Insurance in Antebellum America', *Business History Review* 82: 1–30.

Murphy, Sharon Ann (2010) *Investing in Life: Insurance in Antebellum America*. Baltimore, MD: Johns Hopkins University Press.

Murray, Florence (1947) *The Negro Handbook 1946–1947*. New York: A. A. Wyn.

Nelson, Heather (2012) 'After the Frontier Settles: the Wawanesa Mutual Insurance Company and the Canadian Mutual Experience', paper presented to the International Workshop on Corporate Forms in Insurance, Kyoto Sangyo University, Kyoto.

Nelson, Richard R. and Winter, Sidney G. (1985) *An Evolutionary Theory of Economic Change*. Cambridge, MA: Belknap Press, Harvard University.

Nippon Life Insurance Company (1963) *Nippon Life: 70 Years History*. Tokyo: Nippon Life Mutual Insurance Company.

Nippon Life Insurance Company (1992a) *The Hundred Year History of Nippon Life: Volume 1* (*Nihon SeimeiHyaku-nen-shi: Jo-kan* in Japanese). Osaka: Nippon Life Insurance Company.

Nippon Life Insurance Company (1992b) *The Hundred Year History of Nippon Life: the Book of Materials* (*Nihon SeimeiHyaku-nen-shi: Shiryo-hen* in Japanese). Osaka: Nippon Life Insurance Company.

Nobbs, R. K. (1978) 'Ventures in Providence: the Development of Friendly Societies and Life Assurance in Nineteenth Century Australia', unpublished PhD thesis, Macquarie University.

North, Douglass C. (1954) 'Life Insurance and Investment Banking at the Time of the Armstrong Investigation of 1905–1906', *Journal of Economic History* 14: 226–46.

Oberholzner, Frank (2006) 'Ein Novum der Landwirtschaftlichen Risikovorsorge: Die Gründung der Bayerischen Landeshagelversicherungsanstalt 1884', in Andreas Dix and Ernst Langthaler (eds) *Grüne Revolutionen: Agrarsysteme und Umwelt im 19. und 20. Jahrhundert*. Jahrbuch für Geschichte des ländlichen Raumes. Innsbruck: Studien Verlag, 46–71.

O'Brien, C. and Fenn, P. (2012) 'Mutual Life Insurers: Origins and Performance in Pre-1900 Britain', *Business History* 54: 325–45.

Ogawa, I. (1987) 'Hostile Takeovers of Life Insurance Company by Osaka Life and Nippon Life's Correspondence', *Journal of Insurance Science* 516: 67–96.

Ohlmarks, Å. (1976) *De svenska landskapslagarna. I komplett översättning, med anmärkningar och förklaringar*. Stockholm: Stureförlaget.

Oldham, James (2004) *English Common Law in the Age of Mansfield*. Chapel Hill and London: University of North Carolina Press.

Oosenbrug, A. (2007) 'Insurance in the Netherlands: Market Structure and Recent Developments', in J. D. Cummins and B. Venard (eds) *Handbook of International Insurance: between Global Dynamics and Local Contingencies*. New York: Springer, 455–97.

Osterman, K. (1989) *Skadeförsäkring i EG: ett svenskt perspektiv*. Uppsala.

Packenham, T. (1992) *The Scramble for Africa 1876–1912*. New York: Weidenfeld and Nicholson.

Palmer, Sarah (1984) 'The Indemnity in the London Marine Insurance Market, 1824–50', in Oliver M. Westall (ed.) *The Historian and the Business of Insurance*. Manchester: Manchester University Press, 74–94.

Pearson, R. (2002) 'Mutuality Tested: the Rise and Fall of Mutual Fire Insurance Offices in Eighteenth-Century London', *Business History* 44: 1–28.

Pearson, Robin (2003a) 'Insurance: an Historical Overview', in J. Mokyr (ed.) *The Oxford Encyclopaedia of Economic History*. New York: Oxford University Press, vol. 3, 83–7.

Pearson, Robin (2004) *Insuring the Industrial Revolution: Fire Insurance in Great Britain, 1700–1850*. Aldershot: Ashgate.

Pearson, Robin (2006) 'Lloyd's of London', in John J. McCusker (ed.) *History of World Trade since 1450*, 2 vols. Farmington Hills, MI: Macmillan, vol. 2, 466–9.

Pearson, Robin (2010a) 'Introduction: Towards an International History of Insurance', in Robin Pearson (ed.) *The Development of International Insurance*. London: Pickering and Chatto, 1–23.

Pearson, Robin (2010b) 'Las compañías de seguros extranjeros en España antes de 1914', in Jerònia Pons Pons and María Ángeles Pons Brías (eds) *Investigaciones históricas sobre el Seguro español*. Madrid: Fundación Mapfre, Instituto de Ciencias del Seguro.

Pearson, Robin and Lönnborg, Mikael (2008) 'Regulatory Regime and Multinational Insurers before 1914', *Business History Review* 82: 59–86.

Pérez Castroviejo, Pedro (2010) 'La asistencia sanitaria de los trabajadores: beneficencia, mutualismo y previsión en Vizcaya, 1876–1936', *Revista de la Historia de la Economía y de la Empresa* 4: 127–52.

Platteau, J. P. (1997) 'Mutual Insurance as an Elusive Concept in Traditional Rural Communities', *Journal of Development Studies* 33: 764–96.

Pons Pons, Jerònia (1998) *El sector seguros en Baleares. Empresas y empresarios en los siglos XIX.* Palma de Mallorca: Ed. El Tall.

Pons Pons, Jerònia (2000) 'Biografía de Marcial Gómez Gil', in Eugenio Torres Villaneuva (ed.) *Los 100 empresarios españoles del Siglo XX.* Madrid: Editorial Lid.

Pons Pons, Jerònia (2006) 'El seguro de accidentes de trabajo en España', *Investigaciones de Historia Económica* 4: 77–100.

Pons Pons, Jerònia (2010) 'A History of Insurance Companies in Spain until 1936', in L. Caruana de las Cagigas (ed.) *Encuentro Internacional sobre la Historia del Seguro.* Madrid: Fundación Mapfre; Instituto de Ciencias del Seguro, 141–73.

Pons Pons, Jerònia (2011) 'La gestión patronal del seguro obligatorio de accidents de trabajo durante el franquismo (1940–1975)', *Revista de Historia Industrial* 45: 109–44.

Pons Pons, Jerònia (2012) 'Spain: International Influence on the Domestic Insurance Market', in Peter Borscheid and Niels-Viggo Haueter (eds) *World Insurance: the Evolution of a Global Risk Network.* Oxford: Oxford University Press, 189–212.

Pons Pons, Jerònia and Vilar Rodríguez, Margarita (2011) 'Friendly Societies, Commercial Insurance, and the State in Sickness Risk Coverage: the Case of Spain (1800–1944)', *International Review of Social History* 56: 71–101.

Pottier, S. W. and Sommer, D. W. (1997) 'Agency Theory and Life Insurer Ownership Structure', *Journal of Risk and Insurance* 64: 529–43.

Pretorius, F. (ed.) (2012) *Geskiedenis van Suid-Afrika: Van voortye tot vandag.* Cape Town: Tafelberg.

Pursell, G. (1964) 'The Development of Non-Life Insurance in Australia', unpublished PhD thesis, Australian National University.

Puth, R. C. (1976) *Supreme Life: the History of a Negro Life Insurance Company.* New York: Arno Press.

Ransom, Roger L. and Sutch, Richard (1987) 'Tontine Insurance and the Armstrong Investigation: a Case of Stifled Innovation, 1868–1905', *Journal of Economic History* 47: 379–90.

Raynes, Harold E. (1948) *A History of British Insurance.* London: Sir Isaac Pitman.

Rees, R. and Kessner, E. (1999) 'Regulation and Efficiency in European Insurance Markets', *Economic Policy* 14: 365–98.

Reina, Manuel (1999) *Compañías de seguros en España. El nacimiento del moderno sector asegurador en España, 1830–1910.* Madrid: Universidad Autónoma de Madrid.

Robinson, R., Gallagher, J., and Denny, A. (1961) *Africa and the Victorians: the Official Mind of Imperialism.* London: Macmillan.

Robson, L. L. (1969) *A Century of Life: the Story of the First One Hundred Years of the National Mutual Life.* Melbourne: NMLA.

Rodríguez Ocaña, Eduaro (1990) 'La asistencia médica colectiva en España hasta 1936', in J. A. Junco (ed.) *Historia de la Acción Social Pública en España.* Madrid: Ministerio de Trabajo y Seguridad Social, 321–60.

Rohrbach, Wolfgang (1988) 'Von den Anfängen bis zum Börsenkrach des Jahres 1873', in W. Rohrbach (ed.) *Versicherungsgeschichte Österreichs*, 3 vols. Vienna: A. Holzhausens Nfg, vol. 1, 46–432.

Rosen, Christine Meisner (1986) *The Limits of Power: Great Fires and the Process of City Growth in America*. Cambridge: Cambridge University Press.

Rosenhaft, Eve (2004) 'Secrecy and Publicity in the Emergence of Modern Business Culture: Pension Funds in Hamburg, 1760–1780', in A. Goldgar and R. I. Frost (eds) *Institutional Culture in Early Modern Society*. Leiden: Brill, 218–43.

Rubio-Misas, M. (2007) 'The Structure, Conduct and Performance of the Spanish Insurance Industry', in J. D. Cummins and B. Venard (eds) *Handbook of International Insurance: between Global Dynamics and Local Contingencies*. New York: Springer, 499–551.

Ruef, Martin (2000) 'The Emergence of Organisational Forms: a Community Ecology Approach', *American Journal of Sociology* 106: 658–71.

Ruwell, M. E. (1989) 'Eighteenth-Century Capitalists: the Formation of American Marine Insurance Companies', unpublished PhD thesis, University of Pennsylvania.

Sales de Bohigas, N. (1970) 'Sociedades de seguros contra las quintas (1865–1868)', in Clara E. Lida and Iris M. Zavala (eds) *La revolución de 1868. Historia, Pensamiento, Literatura*. New York: Edición las Américas, 109–25.

Saul, S. (2012) 'Maghreb: Naturalizing Insurance in Algeria, Morocco and Tunisia', in Peter Borscheid and Niels-Viggo Haueter (eds) *World Insurance: the Evolution of a Global Risk Network*. Oxford: Oxford University Press, 373–90.

Sawislak, Karen (1995) *Smoldering City: Chicagoans and the Great Fire, 1871–1874*. Chicago, IL: University of Chicago Press.

Sayers, R. S. (1952) *Banking in the British Commonwealth*. London: Clarendon Press.

Schweizerische Rückversicherungsgesellschaft (1964) *Die Versicherungsmärkte der Welt*. Zürich: Schweizerische Rückversicherungsgesellschaft.

Serifsoy, Baris (2008) 'Demutualization, Outsider Ownership, and Stock Exchange Performance: Empirical Evidence', *Economics of Governance* 9: 305–39.

Shibusawa, E. (1985) *The Analects of Confusius and Abacus*. Tokyo: Kokusho-Kankokai, reprinted (in Japanese).

Short, W. (1994) *Benjamin Short 1833–1912: a Migrant with a Mission*. Sydney: UNSW Press.

Sides, J. (2003) *L. A. City Limits: African American Los Angeles from the Great Depression to the Present*. Berkeley and Los Angeles: University of California Press.

Skogh, G. (1999) 'Risk-Sharing Institutions for Unpredictable Losses', *Journal of Institutional and Theoretical Economics* 155: 505–15.

Smith, Bruce D. and Stutzer, Michael J. (1990) 'Adverse Selection, Aggregate Uncertainty, and the Role of Mutual Insurance Contracts', *Journal of Business* 63: 493–510.

Smith, B. D. and Stutzer, M. (1995) 'A Theory of Mutual Formation and Moral Hazard with Evidence from the History of the Insurance Industry', *Review of Financial Studies* 8: 545–77.

Smith, R. J. (2006) *The Great Black Way: L.A. in the 1940s and the Lost African-American Renaissance*. New York: Public Affairs Books.

Söderberg, T. (1935) *Försäkringsväsendets historia i Sverige intill Karl Johanstiden*. Stockholm: Wesmanns skandinaviska försäkringsfond.

Solomon, V. E. (1983) 'Money and Banking', in F. L. Coleman (ed.) *Economic History of South Africa*. Pretoria: HAUM, 127–62.

Spooner, Frank C. (1983) *Risks at Sea: Amsterdam Insurance and Maritime Europe 1766–1780*. Cambridge: Cambridge University Press.

Spratt, W. (1968) 'Lessons Learned: British, American and Colonial Life Insurance in Australia', *Australasian Insurance and Banking Record* March: 132–4.

Spyrou, H. (1955) 'The Development of Insurance Business in the Union of South Africa', *South African Journal of Economics* 23: 325–40.

Stadlin, Christofer (2010) 'Actuarial Practice, Probabilistic Thinking and Actuarial Science in Private Casualty Insurance', in Robin Pearson (ed.) *The Development of International Insurance*. London: Pickering and Chatto, 37–62.

Stalson, J. Owen (1942) *Marketing Life Insurance: Its History in America*. Cambridge, MA: Harvard University Press.

Statens Offentliga Utredningar (1946) *Försäkringsutredningen. Förslag till lag om försäkringsrörelsen mm, Del II, Motiv*, vol. 34. Stockholm.

Statens Offentliga Utredningar (1949) *1945 års försäkringsutredning, I, Principbetänkande rörande försäkringsväsendet*, vol. 25. Stockholm: Allmänna Förlaget.

Statens Offentliga Utredningar (1991) *Försäkringsrörelse i förändring, delbetänkande av försäkringsutredningen*, vol. 89. Stockholm: Allmänna Förlaget.

Straus, André (2012) 'The Specificities of French Mutual Companies from the Second World War until Today', paper presented to the International Workshop on Corporate Forms in Insurance, Kyoto Sangyo University, Kyoto.

Stuart, M. S. (1969) *An Economic Detour: a History of Insurance in the Lives of American Negroes*. College Park, MD: McGrath Publishing Company.

Sturmey, S. G. (1962) *British Shipping and World Competition*. London: Athlone Press.

Sugiyama K. and Shimura, K. (1981) *The Hundred Year History of Meiji Life* (*Meiji SeimeiHyaku-nen-shi* in Japanese). Tokyo: Meiji Mutual Life Insurance Company.

Sun, Q., Suo, L., and Zheng, W. (2007) 'China's Insurance Industry: Developments and Prospects', in J. D. Cummins and B. Venard (eds) *Handbook of International Insurance: between Global Dynamics and Local Contingencies*. New York: Springer, 597–640.

Supple, Barry (1970) *The Royal Exchange Assurance*. Cambridge: Cambridge University Press.

Svenberg, S. (1997) (ed.) *Den lokala historien. 80 år av framgångsrikt samarbete: Jubileumsskrift för länsförsäkringsbolagens förening 1917–1997*. Stockholm: Länsförsäkringsgruppen.

Sylla, Richard and Wright, Robert E. (2013) 'Corporation Formation in the Ante-Bellum United States in Comparative Context', *Business History* 55: 653–69.

Symreng, J. (2000) 'Försäkringslagstiftningens och den statliga tillsynens utveckling', in *Svensk försäkrings framtid: Svenska Försäkringsföreningen 125 år*. Stockholm, 141–56.

Takatera, Sadao (1975) *The Study of the History of Depreciation in Meiji Era*. Tokyo: Mirai-sha (in Japanese).

Tebeau, Mark (2003) *Eating Smoke: Fire in Urban America, 1800–1950*. Baltimore, MD: Johns Hopkins University Press.

Teikoku Stock Life Insurance Company (1939) *The Fifty Year History of Teikoku Life* (*Teikoku Seimei Hoken Kabushiki-gaishaGoju-nen-shi* in Japanese). Tokyo: Teikoku Stock Life Insurance Company.

Thule (1900) *Lifförsäkrings-aktiebolaget Thule 1873–1898, festskrift vid bolagets tjugo-femårsjubileum*. Stockholm: Ivar Häggströms boktryckeri AB.

Tipton, Frank B. (2003) 'Government and the Economy in the Nineteenth Century', in Sheilagh Ogilvie and Richard Overy (eds) *Germany: a New Social and Economic History*. London: Arnold, vol. 3, 106–51.

Tokio Marine and Fire Insurance Company (1964) *The 80 Years History of Tokio Marine*. Tokyo: Tokio Marine and Fire Insurance Company (in Japanese).

Tortella Casares, Gabriel, Caruana de las Cagigas, Leonardo, and García Ruíz, José Luis (2009) *De mutua a Multinacional: Mapfre 1933–2008*. Madrid: Mapfre.

Trebilcock, Clive (1985, 1998) *Phoenix Assurance and the Development of British Insurance*. 2 vols, Cambridge: Cambridge University Press.

Van Selm, R. (1945) *History of the South African Mutual Life Assurance Society, 1845–1945*. Cape Town: SA Mutual Assurance Company.

Velarde, Juan, Guindos, A. De, and Lázaro, M. (1963) 'Aspectos estadísticos del seguro de accidentes de trabajo en España', *Revista de Trabajo* 4: 9–49.

Velarde Fuertes, Juan (1963) 'Problemas en torno al Mercado del seguro de accidentes de trabajo en España', *Revista de Trabajo* 3: 9–23.

Venard, B. (2007) 'The French Insurance Market: Background and Trends', in J. D. Cummins and B. Venard (eds) *Handbook of International Insurance: between Global Dynamics and Local Contingencies*. New York: Springer, 241–304.

Verhoef, G. (2006) 'From Friendly Societies to Compulsory Medical Aid Association: the History of Medical Aid Provision in South Africa's Public Sector', *Social Science History, Special Issue: the Persistence of the Health Insurance Dilemma* 30: 601–27.

Verhoef, G. (2007) 'Wie moet sorg? Gesondheidsbeleid en Mediese Fondse in Vergelykende Perspektief in Suid-Afrika en Gemenebeslande, 1900–1970', *Historia* 16: 19–51.

Verhoef, G. (2010) 'Life Offices to the Rescue! A History of Life Assurance in the South African Economy during the Twentieth Century', in R. Pearson (ed.) *The Development of International Insurance*. London: Pickering and Chatto, 145–66.

Verhoef, G. (2012) 'Mutuality and Regulation: the Transition from Mutual to Public in the South African Long-Term Insurance Industry', *Journal of Economic and Financial Sciences* 5: 567–90.

Vilar Rodríguez, Margarita and Pons Pons, Jerònia (2012) 'Economic Growth and Demand for Health Coverage in Spain: the Role of Friendly Societies (1870–1942)', in Bernard Harris (ed.) *Welfare and Old Age in Europe and North America: the Development of Social Insurance*. London: Pickering and Chatto, 65–88.

Vilar Rodríguez, Margarita and Pons Pons, Jerònia (2013) 'The Introduction of Sickness Insurance in Spain in the First Decades of the Franco Dictatorship (1939–1962)', *Social History of Medicine* 26: 267–87.

Viljoen, S. P. (1951) 'Die Britse Kolonies tot 1870', in A. J. H van der Walt, J. A. Wiid, and A. L Geyer (eds) *Geskiedenis van Suid-Afrika*. Cape Town: Nasionale Boekhandel, part 2, 182–211.

Viswanathan, K. S. and Cummins, J. D. (2003) 'Ownership Structure Changes in the Insurance Industry: an Analysis of Demutualization', *Journal of Risk and Insurance* 70: 401–37.

Vivian, R. W. (2001) *Morgan's History of the Insurance Movements of South Africa, 1899–1999*. Cape Town: Insurance Institute of South Africa.

Vivian, R. (2002) 'A History of the London and Lancashire Fire Insurance Company in South Africa', *South African Journal of Economic History* 17: 138–45.

Vivian, R. W. (2007) 'South African Insurance Markets', in J. D. Cummins and B. Venard (eds) *Handbook of International Insurance: between Global Dynamics and Local Contingencies*. New York: Springer, 679–741.

Walford, Cornelius (1878) *The Insurance Cyclopedia*. 6 volumes, London: Charles and Edwin Layton.

Walker, J. E. (1998) *The History of Black Business in America: Capitalism, Race, Entrepreneurship*. New York: Twayne Publishers.

Weare, W. B. (1973) *Black Business in the New South: a Social History of the North Carolina Mutual Life Insurance Company*. Urbana: University of Illinois Press.

Webb, A. C. M. (1992) *The Roots of the Tree: a Study in Early South African Banking: the Predecessors of the First National Bank, 1838–1926*. Johannesburg: First National Bank.

Webb, C. de B. and Brookes, E. H. (1967) *A History of Natal*. Pietermaritzburg: University of Natal Press.

Weems, R. E. (1996) *Black Business in the Black Metropolis: the Chicago Metropolitan Assurance Company, 1925–1985*. Bloomington: Indiana University Press.

Weems, R. E. (1998) *Desegregating the Dollar: African American Consumerism in the Twentieth Century*. New York: New York University Press.

Weems, R. E. (2009) *Business in Black and White: American Presidents and Black Entrepreneurs in the Twentieth Century*. New York: New York University Press.

Wermiel, Sara E. (2000) *The Fireproof Building: Technology and Public Safety in the Nineteenth-Century American City*. Baltimore, MD: Johns Hopkins University Press.

White, Gerald T. (1955) *A History of the Massachusetts Hospital Life Insurance Company*. Cambridge, MA: Harvard University Press.

Wickins, P. L. (1983) 'Land and Labour', in F. L. Coleman (ed.) *Economic History of South Africa*. Pretoria: HAUM, 1–36.

Wilkins, Mira (1970) *The Emergence of Multinational Enterprise: American Business Abroad from the Colonial Era to 1914*. Cambridge, MA: Harvard University Press.

Wilson, M. and Thompson, L. M. (1971) *The Oxford History of South Africa*. London: Oxford University Press, vol. 2.

Winegarden, C. R. and Murray, John E. (1998) 'The Contributions of Early Health Insurance Programs to Mortality Declines in Pre-World War I Europe: Evidence from Fixed-Effects Models', *Explorations in Economic History* 35: 431–46.

Worthington, A. and Higgs, H. (2006) 'Market Risk in Demutualized Self-Listed Stock Exchanges: an International Analysis of Selected Time-Varying Betas', *Global Economic Review* 35: 239–57.

Wright, Robert E. (2010) 'Insuring America: Market, Intermediated and Government Risk Management since 1790', in L. Caruana (ed.) *Encuentro Internacional sobre la Historia del Seguro*. Madrid: Mapfre Fundación, 239–98.

Wright, Robert E. and Kingston, Christopher (2012) 'Corporate Insurers in Antebellum America', *Business History Review* 86: 447–76.

Wright, Robert E. and Smith, George David (2004) *Mutually Beneficial: the Guardian and Life Insurance in America*. New York: New York University Press.

Yamori, N and Okada, T. (2007) 'The Japanese Insurance Market and Companies: Recent Trends', in J. D. Cummins and B. Venard (eds) *Handbook of International Insurance: between Global Dynamics and Local Contingencies*. New York: Springer, 147–204.

Yano, Tsuneta (1936) *Ichigonshu*. Tokyo: Kokuseisha (in Japanese).

Yano, Tsuneta Kinenkai (ed.) (1957) *A Biography of Yano Tsuneta*. Tokyo: privately published (in Japanese).

Yasuda Mutual Life Insurance Company (1961) *80 Years of Yasuda Life Insurance Company*. Tokyo: Yasuda Mutual Life Insurance Company (in Japanese).

Yasuda Mutual Life Insurance Company (1980) *The Centenary History of Yasuda Life* (*Yasuda SeimeiHyaku-nen-shi* in Japanese). Tokyo: Yasuda Mutual Life Insurance Company.

Yoneyama, Takau (2009) 'The Great Kanto Earthquake and the Response of Insurance Companies: a Historical Lesson on the Impact of a Major Disaster', *Hitotsubashi Journal of Commerce and Management* 43: 1, 11–26.

Yoneyama, Takau (2010) 'Policyholders in the Early Business of Japanese Life Assurance: a Demand-Side Study', in Robin Pearson (ed.) *The Development of International Insurance*. London: Pickering and Chatto, 103–15.

Yoneyama, Takau (2012) 'Japan: the Role of Insurance in the Rapid Modernization of Japan', in Peter Borscheid and Niels-Viggo Haueter (eds) *World Insurance: the Evolution of a Global Risk Network*. Oxford: Oxford University Press, 495–521.

Young, Peter (1995) *Mutuality: the Story of the UK P&I Club*. London; Thomas R. Miller and Co.

Young, Ruth C. (1988) 'Is Population Ecology a Useful Paradigm for the Study of Organisations?', *American Journal of Sociology* 94: 1–24.

Yui, T. and Tatsuki, M. (1982) *The Hundred Years of Historical Materials of Meiji Life* (*Meiji SeimeiHyaku-nen-shi Shiryo* in Japanese). Tokyo: Meiji Mutual Life Insurance Company.

Zanjani, G. (2007) 'Regulation, Capital, and the Evolution of Organisational Form in US Life Insurance', *American Economic Review* 97: 973–83.

Zelizer, Viviana A. (1983) *Morals and Markets: the Development of Life Insurance in the United States*. New Brunswick, NJ: Transaction Books.

Zwierlein, Cornel (2011) *Der gezähmte Prometheus. Feuer und Sicherheit zwischen Früher Neuzeit aund Moderne*. Göttingen: Vandenhoeck and Ruprecht.

Index

Drawings and Tables are given in italics.